סידור קורן אביב לימות החול • נוסח אשכנז

The Koren Aviv Weekday Siddur • Nusaḥ Ashkenaz

D15989⁴³

קוֹרֶן ירושלים

OU**PRESS**

קוֹרֶן ירושלים

THE MAGERMAN EDITION

סידור קורן אביב
לימות החול

THE KOREN AVIV WEEKDAY SIDDUR

DEVELOPED BY

Dr. Daniel Rose

AND

Ms. Debbie Stone

•

KOREN PUBLISHERS JERUSALEM

The Koren Aviv Weekday Siddur
First Hebrew/English Ashkenaz Edition, 2017
Combined American/Canadian Edition

Koren Publishers Jerusalem Ltd.
POB 4044, Jerusalem 91040, ISRAEL
POB 8531, New Milford, CT 06776, USA

www.korenpub.com

Koren Tanakh Font © 1962, 2017 Koren Publishers Jerusalem Ltd.
Koren Siddur Font and text design © 1981, 2017 Koren Publishers Jerusalem Ltd.
English translation © 2006, 2009, 2014 Jonathan Sacks

The English translation in this edition is based on the English translation
first published in Great Britain in 2006 in the Authorised Daily Prayer
Book of the United Hebrew Congregations of the Commonwealth: New Translation
and Commentary by Chief Rabbi Jonathan Sacks, (Fourth Edition, Compilation
© United Synagogue) by Collins, a division of HarperCollins Publishers, London.

Photograph Credits are listed in the Appendix "Guide to the Images" on p. 750.

Considerable research and expense have gone into the creation of this publication.
Unauthorized copying may be considered *geneivat da'at* and breach of copyright law.
No part of this publication (content or design, including use of the Koren fonts) may
be reproduced, stored in a retrieval system or transmitted in any form or by any means
electronic, mechanical, photocopying or otherwise, without the prior written permission of
the publisher, except in the case of brief quotations embedded in critical articles or reviews.

The creation of this Siddur was made possible with the generous support
of Torah Education in Israel.

Printed in the United States of America

Standard Size, Hardcover, ISBN 978 965 301 893 8

AT3AO1

וְשִׁנַּנְתָּם לְבָנֶיךָ

Dedicated to my wife,
Debra   צביה אהובה
and our children,
Elijah Matthew   מנחם מנדל
Zachary Noah   יצחק אבנר
Sydney Rachel   אלקה שיינה
Lexie Belle   רחל לאה

In celebration
of our joint and individual journeys
toward a better understanding of Torah
and our relationship to Hashem.

David Magerman

CONTENTS

PREFACE

It is with great excitement that we present to you the Magerman Edition of *The Koren Aviv Weekday Siddur*, an engaging and thoughtful siddur for the inquiring young person. This Siddur is part of the Magerman Series of appropriately designed siddurim for students from first to twelfth grade, and beyond. Each siddur has been created to inspire and develop connections to prayer and to God. These goals are achieved through encouraging personal reflection, spiritual and emotional connection, and cognitive learning.

It is always a privilege to collaborate on a project with those who share our commitment and enthusiasm for bringing out the beauty of *Tefilla*. We are grateful to Debra and David Magerman for their critical support and encouragement, and for enabling the creation of this and all the volumes in the series. On behalf of the students who will use this Siddur, we are forever in your debt.

We are fortunate to benefit from a world-class Educational Editorial Board assisting us in the building of this program. We would like to thank the Board's Chairman, Dr. Scott Goldberg of Yeshiva University; Rabbi Adam Englander of the Hillel Day School of Boca Raton; Rabbi Dr. Jay Goldmintz of the Azrieli Graduate School; Rabbi Boruch Sufrin of the Harkham Hillel Hebrew Academy of Beverly Hills; and Rabbi Benjy Levy of Sydney, Australia. Their broad knowledge and experience provided the framework to structure the program.

We wish to thank Rabbi Tzvi Hersh Weinreb for his foreword and support for this project. Special thanks go to Debbie Stone and NCSY/ OU Press for their partnership in this exciting endeavor. The small but highly professional team at Koren was led by Dr. Daniel Rose, Director of Educational Projects, and included Avishai Magence who managed

◂ the project

the project; Esther Be'er who designed and typeset the text; Rachel Meghnagi, our Language Editor; and Tani Bayer, our Art Director.

It is our sincere hope and prayer that this Siddur will provide a platform for the educational and spiritual growth of present and upcoming generations of committed Jews.

Matthew Miller, Publisher
Jerusalem, 5777 (2017)

FOREWORD

Prayer can be exciting, inspiring, educational, and comforting. It is an essential component of the religious life.

It is no wonder that this is is so. Prayer enables man to draw close to his Creator.

Scripture, Talmud, and sages throughout the centuries, have attested to the power of prayer.

The Psalmist has assured us that, "The LORD is near to all who call Him, to all who call upon Him in truth." (Psalms 145:18). Devout Jews recite this verse no less than three times a day.

The Talmud refers to prayer as a matter of the utmost importance; literally, "something which stands at the summit of the world" (*Berakhot* 6b).

The grandeur of prayer is exquisitely expressed in the words of those of our sages who were especially gifted with poetic genius. Thus, the "poet laureate of the Jewish People," Rabbi Yehuda HaLevi, writes:

"There are moments of the day that are designated for prayer. Those moments are the heart and the fruit of a person's day. Other times of day are but paths to those special moments. One is well-advised to anticipate the approach of these moments. It is during them that he is most in tune with his spirituality, and most removed from his animal nature" (*Kuzari* 3:5).

The Ba'al Shem Tov, with whom the Hasidic approach to prayer originated, put it this way:

"There are times when the love of God burns so powerfully within one's heart that the words of prayer seem to rush forth, without forethought. At such times, it is not you who speak; instead, it is *through* you that the words are spoken" (*Keter Shem Tov* 38b).

Closer to our own time, Rabbi Abraham Isaac Kook recorded these words in his diary:

◄ "Prayer

"Prayer is not adequate unless it is preceded by the realization that the soul is always praying. The soul ceaselessly yearns for its Lover. The never-ending prayer of the soul bursts forth at the moment that the ordinary person takes a prayer book into his hands." These words have been incorporated into the preface of Rabbi Kook's masterful commentary on the Siddur, Olat Re'iya.

All that has been said about the power of prayer and its beauty has not fallen upon deaf ears. Most of us often turn to God earnestly in prayer, certainly in times of crisis or great joy.

But there is room for improvement. The very passage in the Talmud, which classifies prayer as "something which stands at the summit of the world" bemoans the fact that prayer is often unappreciated, and sometimes even treated with contempt. Certainly, we all have occasionally taken prayer for granted, and our prayers are not always infused with sufficient devotion to enable them to "fly heavenwards."

Honest observers of the synagogue scene have long noted deficiencies in our conduct of prayer. Attempts have been made by teachers and preachers throughout the generations to address these deficiencies, and these attempts have never been perfectly successful.

The question arises, how can we tap into the reservoir of enthusiasm, hopefulness, and spiritual ardor that we know lies just beneath the surface of every synagogue participant? I have personally struggled with this question, as a parent, as a teacher, as a psychologist, and as a congregational rabbi.

I think I have an answer. It occurred to me long ago, but it crystalized when I first encountered the beautiful Siddur which you now hold in your hands.

The key to tapping into this reservoir lies in the hands of our youth. Is there a better place than in the hearts and minds of our young people to discover "reservoirs of enthusiasm, hopefulness, and spiritual ardor"? The typical adolescent has within him or her all the ingredients necessary for a rich, full, and sincere life of prayer: a sense of wonder, openness to the inner life, willingness to ask challenging questions, boundless optimism and idealistic goals, and so much more.

But reaching adolescents has always been difficult. The current

◄ generation

generation of adolescents has grown up in a rapidly and drastically changing society, making it even more difficult for adults to "speak their language."

Fortunately, a new generation of educators has also come to the fore in recent decades. These educators have found the words, images, concepts and ideas to reach the youngsters with whom they work. Our authors typify such educators. This Siddur is a demonstration of the pedagogical skill and impressive creativity of these master teachers.

Dr. Daniel Rose and Ms. Debbie Stone have, by virtue of their rich and diverse experiences in the field of Jewish education, come to know the problem thoroughly. They have learned from their own pedagogical experiments and from the creative approaches of others in their field.

As you can see for yourself, every page of the siddur is aesthetically sound, designed to please the eye, and frequently supplemented by colorful and stimulating images.

The student not only reads the prayers, but is encouraged to think for himself or herself. The exercises call for meditation and introspection, and unfailingly relate to the student's genuine personal concerns. Students are encouraged to ask questions, especially those questions which students often fear to ask.

I am proud to divulge to the reader that I have myself used this Siddur in my own *davening* and have found it stimulating and edifying, even for one whose adolescent years are but fading memories. I encourage its use in our schools, but advocate that it not be limited to formal educational settings, and not be restricted to any one age group. It can be gainfully integrated into seminars and study groups within a wide range of ages and levels of Jewish education.

I suspect that with this and similar efforts we will begin to witness a revolution in the prayer lives of our youth. I am confident that we will soon begin to see many more young people engaged in prayer, thoughtfully and with sincere devotion. Furthermore, I suspect that this book will have a positive effect upon the prayer lives of the "no longer young."

I close by resorting to the ultimate sourcebook on the subject of prayer, *Tehillim*, the book of Psalms. There we encounter a verse which contains an astonishingly apt metaphor for our Siddur and its goals:

◄ He satisfies

"He satisfies your old age with good things; your youth is renewed like the eagle's" (*Tehillim* 103:5).

May it be His will that this Siddur, written for the eagles, will not only enrich the prayer lives of the eagles, but will draw the rest of us closer to Him as well.

Rabbi Tzvi H. Weinreb

New York, 5777 (2017)

INTRODUCTION

The Koren Aviv Siddur

The Hebrew term for prayer – תפילה – is somewhat unclear in its etymo-logical meaning (word origin). Experts are divided as to what exactly the root of the word is. But what is clear is that the verb – להתפלל – is reflexive. That is, it is something we do to ourselves. Some believe the root of the term is פ-ל-ל which is to judge. This would imply that central to the act of praying in Judaism is the act of judging oneself. In the words of Rabbi J.B. Soloveitchik "We do not know the exact semantics of the term *tefilla*. Yet one thing is clear: the term is related to thinking, judging, discrimination."[1]

Where are these themes found in the Jewish concept of prayer? Standing before our Creator, we bare our soul and cry for the things we need. The things we acknowledge we are dependent on Him for. "Prayer tells the individual, as well as the community, what his, or its, genuine needs are, what he should, or should not, petition God about… Prayer enlightens man about his needs. It tells man the story of his hidden hopes and expectations." On some level, prayer is a vehicle for self-awakening, self-awareness and self-definition. In the language of the Rav, *tefilla* is "self-acquisition, self-discovery, self-objectification and self-redemption."[2]

Psychologists tell us that adolescence and the teenage years are the prime stage for identity formation and self-definition.[3] During this time young people assert their independence and autonomy from their parents and parent community, and begin the journey of formulating their own opinions and way of looking at and interacting with their world. So this

1. "Redemption, Prayer, Talmud Torah." *Tradition* 17:2 (Spring 1978).
2. Ibid.
3. For example E. Erikson, *Identity, Youth, and Crisis,* (1968) and J.E. Marcia, *Development and Validation of Egoidentity Status* (1966).

Siddur has been designed as a tool for young people to explore their relationship to their God, their people, their history, the values and religion of their people, and ultimately their own identity.

The vision of the Koren Aviv Siddur is built on these ideas – that teens are at the outset of an exciting journey of self-definition and identity building, and that *tefilla* can be a vehicle for the achievement of these same goals. This is reflected in the simple and elegant name we have chosen for the Siddur: אביב – *Aviv*, the Hebrew word for spring. Spring is the season where trees and flowers and vegetation awaken after the winter slumber and begin the journey to growth and maturation. And חודש אביב is how the Torah describes the time of the year when the Jewish People were born, with the exodus from Egypt (*Shemot* 13:4). Aviv is a fitting name for a siddur created as a companion to accompany Jewish teens on their own transition towards Jewish adulthood and mature relationship with God.

Imagine a magnificent synagogue, a majestic building with beautiful stained-glass windows, marble floors, an exquisitely designed *Aron Kodesh*. The ḥazan and the choir sing unique and sublime melodies in perfect pitch and harmony. You find yourself sitting in such a shul in awe, looking around mesmerized by the beauty and grandeur of it, and you watch it all and soak up the experience.

Imagine a second shul, a small and modest structure. Nothing memorable in its décor or furniture, just a simple shteibel, clean and comfortable but not special. The *ba'al tefilla* in this shul sings familiar tunes from his heart, and you feel something touch your heart, as your soul soars and joins in his song. In this shul you can't sit back passively watching and observing, listening to the *tefilla*. You feel a deep imperative to sing and express what is in your own soul, to join and connect to the people and the community found there, to become part of the melody itself.

Some books and commentaries are so beautiful and graceful you find enjoyment and inspiration from reading the words, allowing them to wash over you. The educational components in this Siddur are not like that. They require active participation, thoughtful responding to the ideas contained herein, connecting, self-introspection. This Siddur

◄ commentary

commentary is about joining in with the song of your people. Finding and expressing your own soul and its emotions, connecting to your community and your people, and contributing your own harmony to their melody.

With these ideas in mind several educational elements have been included in the Siddur, in order to place the user at the center of the *tefilla* experience, and facilitate the identity- and relationship-forming potential of *tefilla*.

TYPESETTING

As with all Koren siddurim, much thought and attention has been paid to the typesetting of the liturgical text. Not only in the beautiful aesthetic that has come to be expected from Koren publications, but in the pedagogic factors that have also been taken into account during the typesetting process. The Koren Aviv Siddur has been typeset in an intuitive way where each *tefilla* unit stands on its own, aiding the user in their *tefilla* experience and in their understanding of the *tefilla* text.

TRANSLATION AND RUBRICS

The translation found in the Koren Aviv Siddur, based on the translation by Rabbi Jonathan Sacks in the Koren Siddur has been adapted in a developmentally appropriate manner for the users of this Siddur. Explanatory rubrics have also been written in developmentally appropriate language.

EDUCATIONAL COMMENTARY

All four of the siddurim in the Koren Magerman Educational Siddur Series have reflection, connection, and learning at their core. We chose to use these three processes as the basis for the categories of our educational commentary, and added a pictorial commentary, to complete the four categories of commentary found in the Koren Aviv Siddur.

Each category uses color coding, and when appropriate, the text of the *tefilla* that the commentary is connected to will be highlighted in the same color. This increases the power and impact of the text of the commentary and helps the pray-er to connect it to the *tefilla*.

◄ The four

The four categories are:

- ‣ REFLECTION – Reflection and thought questions, sometimes preceded by a relevant and meaningful quote.
- ‣ CONNECTION – This section contains stories, narratives and quotes to help the pray-er to connect to the themes of the *tefilla* text.
- ‣ LEARNING – A *Biur Tefilla* section where historical, philosophical or halakhic explanation helps the pray-er to understand the full context and ritual norms of the *tefilla*.
- ‣ ... A THOUSAND WORDS – They say the power of a picture is worth a thousand words, and this is the most unique element of the Koren Aviv Siddur. A photographic commentary on the *tefilla* that creates connections between the *tefilla* and the world around us. Through photographs and images from our local and intimate world, as well as from the wider, more general world, different themes and ideas from the *tefillot* can be explored and connected to.

TORAH READING SUMMARIES

The first *aliya* of each of the weekday Torah readings is found with a short summary to help focus the pray-er during *Keriat HaTorah*.

GUIDE TO THE IMAGES – PHOTOGRAPH CREDITS AND SUMMARY

As an appendix, all photograph and image credits are found together with a short summary elucidation, in order to help the pray-er to find the full impact of the message of the image in the context of the text of the *tefilla*.

Acknowledgments

It is with deep gratitude that we would like to thank Matthew Miller and all at Koren Publishers for the opportunity to work on this wonderful project. Esther Be'er and Tani Bayer deserve specific thanks for the beautiful typesetting and aesthetic of the Siddur. Thanks also to Avishai Magence for his support and overseeing of the project and Aryeh Grossman for being a constant educational sounding board throughout the process.

Thank you to Rabbi Dovid Bashevkin of NCSY who has provided constant support, guidance and creativity at every stage of the creation

◄ of this Siddur.

of this Siddur. Thanks also to Rabbi Simon Posner, Eliyahu Krakowski, and Rabbi Menachem Genack at OU Press for their care and attention to all details. Thank you to Rachel First for her careful review. Thanks to Dayan Chanoch Ehrentreu, Rabbi Simcha Willig, and Rabbi David Block for contributing scholarly and analytical eyes, and for giving us a nuanced and mindful perspective.

Finally, special thanks go to Rabbi Dr. Jay Goldmintz, a world-renowned expert on *Tefilla* Education, a mentor, role model and friend to us both. Rabbi Goldmintz has had an inestimable impact on this project from its genesis in the Koren offices in early 2013, until his significant role with this Siddur. His influence can be found on every page of each of the siddurim in the Koren Magerman Educational Siddurim series.

Rabbi Sacks describes *tefilla* as a "profoundly transformative experience." It is our hope that this Siddur will be a catalyst for "self-acquisition and self-discovery," for personal growth and identity formation, and an aide to develop and nurture a relationship with God, through meaningful engagements with *tefilla*. From there, not only will the prayer-er be transformed for the better, but so, too, the whole world – "prayer changes the world because it changes us."[4]

Daniel Rose, Jerusalem, Israel
Debbie Stone, New York City, USA
5777 (2017)

---

4. "Understanding Jewish Prayer," Introduction to the Koren Sacks Siddur.

סידור אביב לימות החול

SIDDUR AVIV FOR WEEKDAYS

ימי חול
WEEKDAYS

Shaḥarit

ON WAKING

*On waking, our first thought should be that we are in the presence of God. Since
we are forbidden to speak God's name until we have washed our hands, the
following prayer is said, which, without mentioning God's name, acknowledges
His presence and gives thanks for a new day and for the gift of life.*

מוֹדָה I thank You, living and eternal King,
for giving me back my soul in mercy.
Great is Your faith in us.

Wash hands and say the following blessings.

בָּרוּךְ Blessed are You, Lᴏʀᴅ our God, King of the Universe,
who has made us holy through His commandments,
and has commanded us about washing hands.

CONNECTION

*Close your eyes and relax. What
do you have to be thankful for
today? Who do you need to be
thankful to for these things?*

*Think about all the people
who have helped and will help
you in some way today. From
your parents at home from the
moment you wake up, to the
bus driver, to the janitor at your*

... A THOUSAND WORDS

*school. How many people will help you in some way today? What will each one do for you?
How would your day be different without them in your life? Now choose one of them to
thank today, and choose two to thank tomorrow.*

Now take a moment to think about what you have to thank Hashem for.

Now say מוֹדֶה אֲנִי.

שחרית

השכמת הבוקר

On waking, our first thought should be that we are in the presence of God. Since we are forbidden to speak God's name until we have washed our hands, the following prayer is said, which, without mentioning God's name, acknowledges His presence and gives thanks for a new day and for the gift of life.

men מוֹדֶה /women מוֹדָה/ אֲנִי לְפָנֶיךָ מֶלֶךְ חַי וְקַיָּם

שֶׁהֶחֱזַרְתָּ בִּי נִשְׁמָתִי בְּחֶמְלָה

רַבָּה אֱמוּנָתֶךָ.

Wash hands and say the following blessings.

בָּרוּךְ אַתָּה יהוה אֱלֹהֵינוּ מֶלֶךְ הָעוֹלָם

אֲשֶׁר קִדְּשָׁנוּ בְּמִצְוֹתָיו וְצִוָּנוּ עַל נְטִילַת יָדָיִם.

REFLECTION

"The darkest hour is just before the dawn."

Yesterday is behind us. Today is a new beginning. What do you want to achieve today?

What experiences did you have yesterday that make you a new you today?

LEARNING

The halakha obligates us to wash our hands as soon as we wake up. Some identified this need with a "*ruaḥ ra'a*," a negative spirit, that was acquired during sleep, perhaps an ancient equivalent of a spiritual bacteria or perhaps simply an association with the seemingly lifeless state that comes with death. Others view it as a requirement to wash our hands whenever we pray, reminiscent of the Kohanim as they began their service in the *Beit HaMikdash*. Regardless, we view this as an opportunity for renewal, a way to begin one's day with a sense of higher purpose for our bodies and our souls.

According to some, there is also an obligation to wash hands before *tefilla*. If you said the blessing for washing after waking up, then do not repeat it again here. It is best to wash your hands with a cup, and the custom is to pour water from the cup onto the right hand and then the left, and then repeat, a total of three times.

בָּרוּךְ Blessed are You, LORD our God, King of the Universe,
who formed man with wisdom
and created in him many openings and cavities.
It is revealed and known before the throne of Your glory
that were one of them to be ruptured or blocked,
it would be impossible to survive and stand before You.
Blessed are You, LORD,
Healer of all flesh
who does miracles.

REFLECTION

*"We forget that we have
a holy body
no less than a holy spirit."*
(Rav Kook, *Orot HaTeḥiya* 33)

Is your body a highly
efficient scientific machine
or a miracle from God?
Can it be both?

Does your human body
help you to believe in God?

If your human body is a
gift from God, how would
that change the way you
treat your body?

CONNECTION

*"The human body contains 100 trillion cells.
Within each cell is a nucleus. Within each
nucleus is a double copy of the human genome. Each genome contains 3.1 billion letters
of genetic code, enough if transcribed to fill a
library of five thousand books. Each cell, in other
words, contains a blueprint of the entire body
of which it is a part. The cumulative force of these
scientific discoveries is nothing short of wondrous.
In ways undreamt of by our ancestors, we now
know to what extent the microcosm is a map
of the macrocosm. From a single cell, it may be
possible to reconstruct an entire organism."*
(Rabbi Jonathan Sacks,
Covenant & Conversation, Emor 5768)

LEARNING

This *berakha* is said after every
visit to the restroom, to thank
Hashem for the intricate wonders of the human body. It is

recommended to go to the restroom immediately after washing your hands in the morning, and then say both the *berakha* of *Netilat
Yadayim* and *Asher Yatzar.*

בָּרוּךְ אַתָּה יהוה אֱלֹהֵינוּ מֶלֶךְ הָעוֹלָם

אֲשֶׁר יָצַר אֶת הָאָדָם בְּחׇכְמָה

וּבָרָא בוֹ נְקָבִים נְקָבִים, חֲלוּלִים חֲלוּלִים.

גָּלוּי וְיָדוּעַ לִפְנֵי כִסֵּא כְבוֹדֶךָ

שֶׁאִם יִפָּתֵחַ אֶחָד מֵהֶם

אוֹ יִסָּתֵם אֶחָד מֵהֶם

אִי אֶפְשָׁר לְהִתְקַיֵּם וְלַעֲמֹד לְפָנֶיךָ.

בָּרוּךְ אַתָּה יהוה

רוֹפֵא כָל בָּשָׂר וּמַפְלִיא לַעֲשׂוֹת.

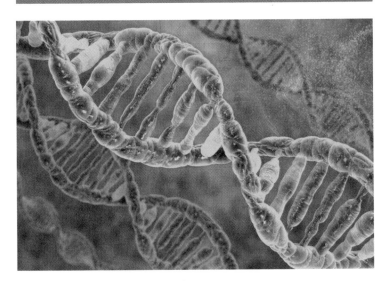

...A THOUSAND WORDS

אֱלֹהַי My God,
the soul You placed within me is pure.
You created it, You formed it, You breathed it into me,
and You guard it while it is within me.
One day You will take it from me,
and restore it to me in the time to come.
As long as the soul is within me, I will thank You,
LORD my God and God of my ancestors,
Master of all works, LORD of all souls.
Blessed are You, LORD, who restores souls to lifeless bodies.

TZITZIT

The following blessing is said before putting on tzitzit. Neither it nor the following prayer is said by those who wear a tallit. The blessing over the latter exempts the former.

בָּרוּךְ Blessed are You, LORD our God, King of the Universe,
who has made us holy through His commandments,
and has commanded us about the command of tzitzit.

After putting on tzitzit, say:

יְהִי רָצוֹן May it be Your will, LORD my God and God of my ancestors, that the commandment of the tzitzit be considered before You as if I had fulfilled it in all its specifics, details and intentions, as well as the 613 commandments dependent on it, Amen, Selah.

REFLECTION

וַיִּיצֶר יהוה אֱלֹהִים אֶת־הָאָדָם, עָפָר מִן־הָאֲדָמָה,
וַיִּפַּח בְּאַפָּיו, נִשְׁמַת חַיִּים; וַיְהִי הָאָדָם, לְנֶפֶשׁ חַיָּה.

"Then the LORD God formed man , dust of the ground; He breathed breath of life into his nostrils; and man became a living creature." (Bereshit 2:7)

What does having a soul mean to you?

Your body inherits genetics from your ancestors. Do you think your soul does too?

What is in your soul's DNA?

CONNECTION

One of the disciples of the Hasidic master Rebbe Bunam explained his greatness: "Remember what happened to Elisha? Elisha was a simple shepherd who spoke to his cattle, not to humans. Then one day he met the prophet Elijah and from then on he was another person: his soul had caught fire. Rebbe Bunam? You want to know about Rebbe Bunam? Simple. No matter how hardened, how icy your soul may be, at his touch it will burst into flames."

(Elie Wiesel, *Souls on Fire*)

אֱלֹהַי

נְשָׁמָה שֶׁנָּתַתָּ בִּי טְהוֹרָה הִיא.

אַתָּה בְרָאתָהּ, אַתָּה יְצַרְתָּהּ, אַתָּה נְפַחְתָּהּ בִּי
וְאַתָּה מְשַׁמְּרָהּ בְּקִרְבִּי, וְאַתָּה עָתִיד לִטְּלָהּ מִמֶּנִּי
וּלְהַחֲזִירָהּ בִּי לֶעָתִיד לָבוֹא.

כָּל זְמַן שֶׁהַנְּשָׁמָה בְקִרְבִּי, *men* / מוֹדֶה *women* / מוֹדָה/ אֲנִי לְפָנֶיךָ
יהוה אֱלֹהַי וֵאלֹהֵי אֲבוֹתַי, רִבּוֹן כָּל הַמַּעֲשִׂים, אֲדוֹן כָּל הַנְּשָׁמוֹת.
בָּרוּךְ אַתָּה יהוה, הַמַּחֲזִיר נְשָׁמוֹת לִפְגָרִים מֵתִים.

לְבִישַׁת צִיצִית

The following blessing is said before putting on a טלית קטן. *Neither it nor* יְהִי רָצוֹן *is
said by those who wear a* טלית. *The blessing over the latter exempts the former.*

בָּרוּךְ אַתָּה יהוה אֱלֹהֵינוּ מֶלֶךְ הָעוֹלָם
אֲשֶׁר קִדְּשָׁנוּ בְּמִצְוֹתָיו וְצִוָּנוּ עַל מִצְוַת צִיצִית.

After putting on the טלית קטן, *say:*

יְהִי רָצוֹן מִלְּפָנֶיךָ, יהוה אֱלֹהַי וֵאלֹהֵי אֲבוֹתַי, שֶׁתְּהֵא חֲשׁוּבָה מִצְוַת צִיצִית
לְפָנֶיךָ, כְּאִלּוּ קִיַּמְתִּיהָ בְּכָל פְּרָטֶיהָ וְדִקְדּוּקֶיהָ וְכַוָּנוֹתֶיהָ, וְתַרְיַ״ג מִצְוֹת הַתְּלוּיוֹת
בָּהּ, אָמֵן סֶלָה.

LEARNING

It is a mitzva from the Torah to wear tzitzit on any four-cornered garment. Since most garments today are not four cornered, the generally accepted custom is to wear a special *tallit katan* all day long and a *tallit gadol* during Shaḥarit. This *berakha* is for the *tallit katan* (the *berakha* for *tallit gadol* can be found on page 15). If you are going to put on a *tallit gadol* later then do not say this *berakha* when you put on a *tallit katan*. There are various traditions in how we tie the four strings to form the tzitzit. The majority Ashkenazi practice is Rashi's method, which doubles the four strings over to make eight, and has five knots, which added together with the numerical value of the word צִיצִית (600) totals 613. This is the number of mitzvot in the Torah, and according to Rashi hints at the intended purpose of the tzitzit as specified in the Torah – a sign to remind us of the 613 mitzvot in the Torah (*Bemidbar* 15:39–40).

BLESSINGS OVER THE TORAH

*In Judaism, study is greater even than prayer. So, before beginning to pray, we engage in a
brief act of study, after saying the blessings. The blessings are followed by brief selections
from Scripture, Mishna and Gemara, the three foundational texts of Judaism.*

בָּרוּךְ Blessed are You, LORD our God, King of the Universe,
who has made us holy through His commandments,
and has commanded us to be involved
in the study of the words of Torah.
Please, LORD our God, make the words of Your Torah
sweet in our mouths and in the mouths of Your people,
the house of Israel,
so that we, our descendants (and their descendants)
and the descendants of Your people, the house of Israel,
may all know Your name and study Your Torah for its own sake.
Blessed are You, LORD, who teaches Torah to His people Israel.

בָּרוּךְ Blessed are You, LORD our God, King of the Universe,
who has chosen us from all the peoples and given us His Torah.
Blessed are You, LORD, Giver of the Torah.

| LEARNING | ... A THOUSAND WORDS |

There is a mitzva in the Torah to learn Torah every day. Like most other mitzvot, we make a *berakha* before performing this mitzva. Since learning Torah is a mitzva that we are charged with fulfilling all day every day, we say the *berakhot* first thing in the morning for all the Torah we will learn that day.

While the word "Torah" often refers to the Five Books of Moses, it is commonly used in its widest sense, to include the rest of Tanakh, as well as the written formulations of the Oral Torah – the Talmud (Mishna and Gemara), and beyond.

In order to avoid an interruption between saying these *berakhot* and fulfilling the mitzva of *talmud Torah*, we immediately learn representative excerpts of these three foundational texts of Judaism – Tanakh, Mishna, with Gemara following shortly thereafter.

ברכות התורה

In Judaism, study is greater even than prayer. So, before beginning to pray, we engage in a brief act of study, after saying the blessings. The blessings are followed by brief selections from תנ"ך and משנה and גמרא, the three foundational texts of Judaism.

בָּרוּךְ אַתָּה יהוה אֱלֹהֵינוּ מֶלֶךְ הָעוֹלָם
אֲשֶׁר קִדְּשָׁנוּ בְּמִצְוֹתָיו וְצִוָּנוּ לַעֲסֹק בְּדִבְרֵי תוֹרָה.
וְהַעֲרֶב נָא יהוה אֱלֹהֵינוּ אֶת דִּבְרֵי תוֹרָתְךָ
בְּפִינוּ וּבְפִי עַמְּךָ בֵּית יִשְׂרָאֵל
וְנִהְיֶה אֲנַחְנוּ וְצֶאֱצָאֵינוּ (וְצֶאֱצָאֵי צֶאֱצָאֵינוּ)
וְצֶאֱצָאֵי עַמְּךָ בֵּית יִשְׂרָאֵל
כֻּלָּנוּ יוֹדְעֵי שְׁמֶךָ וְלוֹמְדֵי תוֹרָתְךָ לִשְׁמָהּ.
בָּרוּךְ אַתָּה יהוה, הַמְלַמֵּד תּוֹרָה לְעַמּוֹ יִשְׂרָאֵל.

בָּרוּךְ אַתָּה יהוה אֱלֹהֵינוּ מֶלֶךְ הָעוֹלָם
אֲשֶׁר בָּחַר בָּנוּ מִכָּל הָעַמִּים, וְנָתַן לָנוּ אֶת תּוֹרָתוֹ.
בָּרוּךְ אַתָּה יהוה, נוֹתֵן הַתּוֹרָה.

REFLECTION

"Rabbi Yishmael would say: One who studies Torah in order to teach will be given the opportunity to both study and to teach. One who studies in order to practice will be given the opportunity to study, to teach, to observe, and to practice." (Avot 4:5)

Why do you learn Torah?

How many generations do you think have been learning the same Torah you are going to learn today? How does that make you feel? Are you going to learn it exactly the same way or differently from them? How?

CONNECTION

The great Rabbi Akiva was 40 years old before he had studied any Torah. He was once standing by a well and noticed a rock with a hole carved in it. He asked his fellow shepherds: Who carved the hole in the rock? They replied to him that it had been formed by the steady dripping of water from the well over many, many years. Rabbi Akiva realized that if the soft water can chisel a hole in the hard rock, then words of Torah that are hard as iron can certainly make an impression on my heart of flesh and blood! He dedicated his life to learning Torah from then on.

(Avot DeRabbi Natan 6:2)

יְבָרֶכְךָ May the LORD bless you and protect you. *Num. 6*
May the LORD make His face shine on you and be generous to you.
May the LORD turn His face toward you and give you peace.

אֵלּוּ These are the things for which there is no fixed measure: *Mishna*
 the mitzvah of the corner of the field, first-fruits, *Pe'ah 1:1*
  appearing before the LORD [on festivals, with offerings],
 acts of kindness and the study of Torah.

אֵלּוּ These are the things whose fruits we eat in this world *Shabbat*
but whose full reward waits for us in the World to Come: *127a*
 honoring parents; acts of kindness;
 arriving early at the house of study morning and evening;
 hospitality to strangers; visiting the sick;
 helping the needy bride; attending to the dead;
 devotion in prayer;
 and bringing peace between people –
but the study of Torah is equal to them all.

---

against Ra'avad. In his defense the student expresses himself rashly, too outspoken in his critique of Ra'avad. Young boys are wont to speak in such a fashion. So I correct him and suggest more restrained tones. Another boy jumps up with a new idea. Rashba smiles gently. I try to analyze what the young boy meant. Another boy intervenes. Rabbeinu Tam is called upon to express his opinion, and suddenly a symposium of generations comes into existence. Young students debate earlier generations with an air of daring familiarity, and a crescendo of discussion ensues.

 We enjoy each other's company, speak one language, and pursue one goal. All are committed to a common vision, and all operate with the same halakhic categories. A mesora collegiality is achieved. It is a friendship, a comradeship of young and old, spanning antiquity, the Middle Ages, and modern times.

 This joining of the generations, this merger of identities will ultimately bring about the redemption of the Jewish People. It will fulfill the words of the last of the Hebrew prophets, Malakhi…

 After a two- or three-hour shiur, the rebbe emerges from the chamber young and rejuvenated. He has defeated age. The students look exhausted. In the mesora experience, years play no role. Hands, however parchment-dry and wrinkled, embrace warm and supple hands in a commonality, bridging the gap which separates the generations.

(Rabbi J.B. Soloveitchik, *Reflections of the Rav*, Vol. 2)

במדברו

יְבָרֶכְךָ יהוה וְיִשְׁמְרֶךָ:
יָאֵר יהוה פָּנָיו אֵלֶיךָ וִיחֻנֶּךָ:
יִשָּׂא יהוה פָּנָיו אֵלֶיךָ וְיָשֵׂם לְךָ שָׁלוֹם:

משנה,
פאה א: א

אֵלּוּ דְבָרִים שֶׁאֵין לָהֶם שִׁעוּר
הַפֵּאָה וְהַבִּכּוּרִים וְהָרֵאָיוֹן, וּגְמִילוּת חֲסָדִים וְתַלְמוּד תּוֹרָה.

שבת קכז.

אֵלּוּ דְבָרִים שֶׁאָדָם אוֹכֵל פֵּרוֹתֵיהֶם בָּעוֹלָם הַזֶּה
וְהַקֶּרֶן קַיֶּמֶת לוֹ לָעוֹלָם הַבָּא, וְאֵלּוּ הֵן
כִּבּוּד אָב וָאֵם, וּגְמִילוּת חֲסָדִים
וְהַשְׁכָּמַת בֵּית הַמִּדְרָשׁ שַׁחֲרִית וְעַרְבִית
וְהַכְנָסַת אוֹרְחִים, וּבִקּוּר חוֹלִים
וְהַכְנָסַת כַּלָּה, וּלְוָיַת הַמֵּת, וְעִיּוּן תְּפִלָּה
וַהֲבָאַת שָׁלוֹם בֵּין אָדָם לַחֲבֵרוֹ
וְתַלְמוּד תּוֹרָה כְּנֶגֶד כֻּלָּם.

CONNECTION

As I enter the classroom, I am filled with despair and pessimism. I always ask myself: Can there be a dialogue between an old teacher and young students, between a rebbe in his Indian summer and boys enjoying the spring of their lives? I start the shiur without knowing what the conclusion will be.

As I start the shiur, the door opens and another old man walks in and sits down. My students call me the Rav. He is older than the Rav. He is the grandfather of the Rav. His name is Rav Chaim of Brisk. Without his method of study, no shiur could be delivered nowadays. Then the door opens quietly again and another old man

comes in. He is older than Rav Chaim because he lived in the seventeenth century. His name is Rav Shabbetai HaKohen, the famous Shakh.... Then more visitors show up, some from the eleventh, twelfth, or thirteenth centuries. Some even lived in antiquity. Among them are Rabbi Akiva, Rashi, Rabbeinu Tam, Ra'avad, and Rashba. More and more keep on coming in.

What do I do? I introduce them to my pupils, and the dialogue commences. Maimonides states a halakha, and Ra'avad disagrees sharply. At times Ra'avad utilizes harsh language against Maimonides. A boy jumps up to defend Maimonides

TALLIT

*Some say the following paragraphs to prepare themselves
before putting on the tallit.*

בָּרְכִי נַפְשִׁי Bless the Lord, my soul. Lord, my God, You are very great, *Ps. 104* clothed in majesty and splendor, wrapped in a robe of light, spreading out the heavens like a tent.

Some say:
For the sake of the unification of the Holy One, blessed be He, and His Divine Presence, with fear and love, to unify the name *Yod-Heh* with *Vav-Heh* in perfect unity in the name of all Israel.

I am about to wrap myself in this tallit. So may my soul, my 248 limbs and 365 sinews be wrapped in the light of *hatzitzit* which amounts to 613 [commandments]. And just as I cover myself with a tallit in this world, so may I be worthy of rabbinical dress and a fine garment in the World to Come in the Garden of Eden. Through the commandment of tzitzit may my life's-breath, spirit, soul and prayer be saved from external obstacles, and may the tallit spread its wings over them like an eagle stirring up its nest, hovering over its young. May the *Deut. 32* commandment of tzitzit be considered before the Holy One, blessed be He, as if I had fulfilled it in all its specifics, details and intentions, as well as the 613 commandments dependent on it, Amen, Selah.

LEARNING

The mitzva in the Torah to wear tzitzit on any four-cornered garment is mentioned in the third paragraph of the Shema.

The generally accepted custom is to wear a special *tallit katan* all day long; some people, such as married men, wear a *tallit gadol* during Shaharit.

... A THOUSAND WORDS

In some communities (many Sephardic, and some Ashkenazic communities that follow the German custom) the custom is to wear a *tallit* from the age of Bar Mitzva (or even earlier). This *berakha* is for the *tallit gadol* (the *berakha* for *tallit katan* can be found on page 9). Those people who wear a *tallit gadol* do not say the *berakha* when putting on a *tallit katan*.

עֲטִיפַת טַלִּית

Some say the following paragraphs to prepare themselves before putting on the טַלִּית.

תהלים קד בָּרְכִי נַפְשִׁי אֶת־יהוה, יהוה אֱלֹהַי גָּדַלְתָּ מְּאֹד, הוֹד וְהָדָר לָבָשְׁתָּ: עֹטֶה־אוֹר כַּשַּׂלְמָה, נוֹטֶה שָׁמַיִם כַּיְרִיעָה:

Some say:

לְשֵׁם יִחוּד קֻדְשָׁא בְּרִיךְ הוּא וּשְׁכִינְתֵּהּ בִּדְחִילוּ וּרְחִימוּ, לְיַחֵד שֵׁם י״ה בּו״ה בְּיִחוּדָא שְׁלִים בְּשֵׁם כָּל יִשְׂרָאֵל.

הֲרֵינִי מִתְעַטֵּף בַּצִּיצִית. כֵּן תִּתְעַטֵּף נִשְׁמָתִי וְרַמַ״ח אֵבָרַי וּשְׁסַ״ה גִידַי בְּאוֹר הַצִּיצִית הָעוֹלָה תַרְי״ג. וּכְשֵׁם שֶׁאֲנִי מִתְכַּסֶּה בְּטַלִּית בָּעוֹלָם הַזֶּה, כָּךְ אֶזְכֶּה לַחֲלוּקָא דְרַבָּנָן וּלְטַלִּית נָאָה לָעוֹלָם הַבָּא בְּגַן עֵדֶן. וְעַל יְדֵי מִצְוַת צִיצִית תִּנָּצֵל נַפְשִׁי רוּחִי וְנִשְׁמָתִי וּתְפִלָּתִי מִן הַחִיצוֹנִים. וְהַטַּלִּית תִּפְרֹשׂ כְּנָפֶיהָ עֲלֵיהֶם וְתַצִּילֵם, דברים לב כְּנֶשֶׁר יָעִיר קִנּוֹ, עַל גּוֹזָלָיו יְרַחֵף: וּתְהֵא חֲשׁוּבָה מִצְוַת צִיצִית לִפְנֵי הַקָּדוֹשׁ בָּרוּךְ הוּא, כְּאִלּוּ קִיַּמְתִּיהָ בְּכָל פְּרָטֶיהָ וְדִקְדּוּקֶיהָ וְכַוָּנוֹתֶיהָ וְתַרְי״ג מִצְוֹת הַתְּלוּיוֹת בָּהּ, אָמֵן סֶלָה.

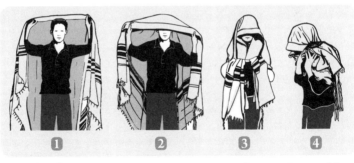

❶	❷	❸	❹
The tallit is held spread above one's head and the berakha is recited.	The tallit is placed upon one's head.	The tallit is rolled up upon one's shoulders.	The part of the tallit which has been rolled up is draped over one shoulder and held there for a short period.

Before wrapping oneself in the tallit, say:

בָּרוּךְ Blessed are You, LORD our God, King of the Universe, who has made us holy through His commandments, and has commanded us
to wrap ourselves in tzitzit.

*According to the Shela (R. Isaiah Horowitz), one should say
these verses after wrapping oneself in the tallit:*

מַה־יָּקָר How precious is Your loving-kindness, O God,   *Ps. 36*
and the children of men find refuge
under the shadow of Your wings.
They are filled with the rich plenty of Your House.
You give them drink from Your river of delights.
For with You is the fountain of life;
in Your light, we see light.
Continue Your loving-kindness to those who know You,
and Your righteousness to the upright in heart.

conviction. He waited for the waiter to walk in – but nothing happened! "I don't understand it! When the rich man tinkled his bell, all that food was served!" The next day he returned the bell. "The bell you sold me is useless. I got no response when I rang it."

"The obvious reason nothing happened," said the Dubno Maggid, "is because there is neither a waiter nor food prepared in the next room. The bell summons something that is there to be summoned. Much preparation is necessary before the bell can accomplish anything."

"In some ways many of us are like this man," continued the Dubno Maggid. "For example, the Torah tells us to look at our tzitzit so that we will be reminded to perform all of God's mitzvot. There are many people, though, who can look at a pair of tzitzit and not be reminded of anything. All they see are strings. Only if one studies and understands how the tzitzit represent the 613 mitzvot, and has studied what the 613 mitzvot are, can one appreciate what his viewing of the tzitzit should accomplish. Merely to look at them without any preparation is like tinkling a bell without having arranged for anyone to respond."

(Rabbi Paysach Krohn,
Around the Maggid's Table)

Before wrapping oneself in the טַלִית, *say:*

בָּרוּךְ אַתָּה יהוה אֱלֹהֵינוּ מֶלֶךְ הָעוֹלָם
אֲשֶׁר קִדְּשָׁנוּ בְּמִצְוֹתָיו
וְצִוָּנוּ לְהִתְעַטֵּף בַּצִּיצִית.

*According to the Shela (R. Isaiah Horowitz), one should say
these verses after wrapping oneself in the* טַלִית:

תהלים לו

מַה־יָּקָר חַסְדְּךָ אֱלֹהִים
וּבְנֵי אָדָם בְּצֵל כְּנָפֶיךָ יֶחֱסָיוּן:
יִרְוְיֻן מִדֶּשֶׁן בֵּיתֶךָ
וְנַחַל עֲדָנֶיךָ תַשְׁקֵם:
כִּי־עִמְּךָ מְקוֹר חַיִּים
בְּאוֹרְךָ נִרְאֶה־אוֹר:
מְשֹׁךְ חַסְדְּךָ לְיֹדְעֶיךָ
וְצִדְקָתְךָ לְיִשְׁרֵי־לֵב:

CONNECTION

A certain poor fellow, Rabbi Yona, was in-
vited to a meal at a wealthy man's house.
When all the diners were finished with their
portions, the rich man, who sat at the head
of the table, tinkled a bell. Almost at once,
waiters came in to remove the dishes and
bring in the next course. Rabbi Yona was
amazed. He had never seen anything like
that before.

After the second course was completed,
the host again tinkled the bell, and again

the waiters removed the plates and brought
in yet more food. Rabbi Yona was immense-
ly impressed. When the meal was finally
over, he went out to get such a bell for his
home as well.

He ran home excitedly to his wife.
"We're going to have unlimited food and
waiters. Wait until you see what I brought
home!" He immediately placed the bell on
the table and told his family to take their
regular seats. He then tinkled the bell with

TEFILLIN

Some say the following paragraphs to prepare themselves before putting on the tefillin.

For the sake of the unification of the Holy One, blessed be He, and His Divine Presence, with fear and love, to unify the name *Yod-Heh* with *Vav-Heh* in perfect unity in the name of all Israel.

By putting on the tefillin I hereby intend to fulfill the commandment of my Creator who commanded us to wear tefillin, as it is written in His Torah: "Bind them as a sign on your hand, and they shall be a sign on the center of your head." They contain these four sections of the Torah: one beginning with *Shema* [Deut. 6:4–9]; another with *Vehaya im shamo'a* [ibid. 11:13–21]; the third with *Kadesh Li* [Ex. 13:1–10]; and the fourth with *Vehaya ki yevi'akha* [ibid. 13:11–16]. These declare the uniqueness and unity of God, blessed be His name in the world. They also remind us of the miracles and wonders which He did for us when He brought us out of Egypt, and that He has the power and the dominion over the highest and the lowest to deal with them as He pleases. He commanded us to place one of the tefillin on the arm in memory of His "outstretched arm" (of redemption), setting it opposite the heart, to force the desires and thoughts of our heart to His service, blessed be His name. The other is to be on the head, opposite the brain, so that my mind, whose seat is in the brain, together with my other senses and abilities, may be forced to His service, blessed be His name. May the spiritual influence of the commandment of the tefillin be with me so that I may have a long life, a flow of holiness, and sacred thoughts, free from any suggestion of sin or wrongdoing. May the evil inclination neither tempt nor provoke us, but leave us to serve the LORD, as it is in our hearts to do.

Deut. 6

And may it be Your will, LORD our God and God of our ancestors, that the commandment of tefillin be considered before You as if I had fulfilled it in all its specifics, details and intentions, as well as the 613 commandments dependent on it, Amen, Selah.

The *tefillin shel yad* is placed on the arm that represents action, and the *tefillin shel rosh* is placed on the head that represents thought.

What are the differences between thought and action?

What thought are you going to have today that will lead you to action?

הנחת תפילין

Some say the following paragraphs to prepare themselves before putting on the תפילין.

לְשֵׁם יִחוּד קֻדְשָׁא בְּרִיךְ הוּא וּשְׁכִינְתֵּהּ בִּדְחִילוּ וּרְחִימוּ, לְיַחֵד שֵׁם י״ה
בְּו״ה בְּיִחוּדָא שְׁלִים בְּשֵׁם כָּל יִשְׂרָאֵל.

הִנְנִי מְכַוֵּן בַּהֲנָחַת תְּפִלִּין לְקַיֵּם מִצְוַת בּוֹרְאִי, שֶׁצִּוָּנוּ לְהָנִיחַ
תְּפִלִּין, כַּכָּתוּב בְּתוֹרָתוֹ: וּקְשַׁרְתָּם לְאוֹת עַל־יָדֶךָ, וְהָיוּ לְטֹטָפֹת בֵּין
עֵינֶיךָ: וְהֵן אַרְבַּע פָּרָשִׁיּוֹת אֵלּוּ, שְׁמַע, וְהָיָה אִם שָׁמֹעַ, קַדֶּשׁ לִי,
וְהָיָה כִּי יְבִאֲךָ, שֶׁיֵּשׁ בָּהֶם יִחוּדוֹ וְאַחְדוּתוֹ יִתְבָּרַךְ שְׁמוֹ בָּעוֹלָם,
וְשֶׁנִּזְכֹּר נִסִּים וְנִפְלָאוֹת שֶׁעָשָׂה עִמָּנוּ בְּהוֹצִיאוֹ אוֹתָנוּ מִמִּצְרָיִם,
וַאֲשֶׁר לוֹ הַכֹּחַ וְהַמֶּמְשָׁלָה בָּעֶלְיוֹנִים וּבַתַּחְתּוֹנִים לַעֲשׂוֹת בָּהֶם
כִּרְצוֹנוֹ. וְצִוָּנוּ לְהָנִיחַ עַל הַיָּד לְזִכָּרוֹן זְרוֹעַ הַנְּטוּיָה, וְשֶׁהִיא נֶגֶד
הַלֵּב, לְשַׁעְבֵּד בָּזֶה תַּאֲווֹת וּמַחְשְׁבוֹת לִבֵּנוּ לַעֲבוֹדָתוֹ יִתְבָּרַךְ
שְׁמוֹ. וְעַל הָרֹאשׁ נֶגֶד הַמֹּחַ, שֶׁהַנְּשָׁמָה שֶׁבְּמֹחִי עִם שְׁאָר חוּשַׁי
וְכֹחוֹתַי כֻּלָּם יִהְיוּ מְשֻׁעְבָּדִים לַעֲבוֹדָתוֹ, יִתְבָּרַךְ שְׁמוֹ. וּמִשֶּׁפַע
מִצְוַת תְּפִלִּין יִתְמַשֵּׁךְ עָלַי לִהְיוֹת לִי חַיִּים אֲרוּכִים וְשֶׁפַע קֹדֶשׁ
וּמַחְשָׁבוֹת קְדוֹשׁוֹת בְּלִי הִרְהוּר חֵטְא וְעָוֹן כְּלָל, וְשֶׁלֹּא יְפַתֵּנוּ וְלֹא
יִתְגָּרֶה בָּנוּ יֵצֶר הָרָע, וְיַנִּיחֵנוּ לַעֲבֹד אֶת יהוה כַּאֲשֶׁר עִם לְבָבֵנוּ.

וִיהִי רָצוֹן מִלְּפָנֶיךָ, יהוה אֱלֹהֵינוּ וֵאלֹהֵי אֲבוֹתֵינוּ, שֶׁתְּהֵא חֲשׁוּבָה מִצְוַת
הֲנָחַת תְּפִלִּין לִפְנֵי הַקָּדוֹשׁ בָּרוּךְ הוּא, כְּאִלּוּ קִיַּמְתִּיהָ בְּכָל פְּרָטֶיהָ וְדִקְדּוּקֶיהָ
וְכַוָּנוֹתֶיהָ וְתַרְיַ״ג מִצְוֹת הַתְּלוּיוֹת בָּהּ, אָמֵן סֶלָה.

דברים ו

"God so loved Israel that He surrounded them with mitzvot. Tefillin on the arm and head, tzitzit on their clothes, and a mezuza on their door." (Menaḥot 43b)

Are there any other mitzvot you can think of that "surround us"?

What does it feel like to you to be surrounded by mitzvot?

Stand and place the hand-tefillin on the biceps of the left arm (or right arm if you
are left-handed), angled toward the heart, and before tightening the strap, say:

בָּרוּךְ Blessed are You, LORD our God, King of the Universe,
who has made us holy through His commandments,
and has commanded us to put on tefillin.

Wrap the strap of the hand-tefillin seven times around the arm.
Place the head-tefillin above the hairline, centered between the eyes, and say quietly:

בָּרוּךְ Blessed are You, LORD our God, King of the Universe,
who has made us holy through His commandments,
and has commanded us about the commandment of tefillin.

Adjust the head-tefillin and say:

בָּרוּךְ Blessed be the name of His glorious kingdom for ever and all time.

Some say:

From Your wisdom, God most high, give me [wisdom], and from Your understanding, give me understanding. May You increase Your loving-kindness upon me, and
in Your might may my enemies and those who rise against me be subdued. Pour Your
goodly oil on the seven branches of the menora so that Your good flows down
upon Your creatures. You open Your hand, and satisfy every living thing with favor. *Ps. 145*

Wind the strap of the hand-tefillin three times around the middle finger, saying:

וְאֵרַשְׂתִּיךְ I will betroth you to Me for ever; I will betroth you to Me in *Hos. 2*
righteousness and justice, loving-kindness and compassion; I will betroth
you to Me in loyalty; and you shall know the LORD.

times. Without speaking, one places the
tefillin shel rosh on the head above the hairline, centered over the nose, and says the
blessing עַל מִצְוַת תְּפִלִּין. One then adjusts
the straps, so that the knot rests at the

base of the skull and the two straps hang
down the front of one's chest, and says:
בָּרוּךְ שֵׁם כְּבוֹד מַלְכוּתוֹ לְעוֹלָם וָעֶד. Finally,
one wraps the strap of the *tefillin shel yad*
around the fingers, while saying וְאֵרַשְׂתִּיךְ.

Stand and place the תפילין של יד *on the biceps of the left arm (or right arm if you are left-handed), angled toward the heart, and before tightening the strap, say:*

בָּרוּךְ אַתָּה יהוה אֱלֹהֵינוּ מֶלֶךְ הָעוֹלָם
אֲשֶׁר קִדְּשָׁנוּ בְּמִצְוֹתָיו, וְצִוָּנוּ לְהָנִיחַ תְּפִלִּין.

Wrap the strap of the תפילין של יד *seven times around the arm.*
Place the תפילין של ראש *above the hairline, centered between the eyes, and say quietly:*

בָּרוּךְ אַתָּה יהוה אֱלֹהֵינוּ מֶלֶךְ הָעוֹלָם
אֲשֶׁר קִדְּשָׁנוּ בְּמִצְוֹתָיו, וְצִוָּנוּ עַל מִצְוַת תְּפִלִּין.

Adjust the תפילין של ראש *and say:*

בָּרוּךְ שֵׁם כְּבוֹד מַלְכוּתוֹ לְעוֹלָם וָעֶד

Some say:

וּמֵחָכְמָתְךָ אֵל עֶלְיוֹן תַּאֲצִיל עָלַי, וּמִבִּינָתְךָ תְּבִינֵנִי, וּבְחַסְדְּךָ תַּגְדִּיל
עָלַי, וּבִגְבוּרָתְךָ תַּצְמִית אוֹיְבַי וְקָמַי. וְשֶׁמֶן הַטּוֹב תָּרִיק עַל שִׁבְעָה קְנֵי
הַמְּנוֹרָה, לְהַשְׁפִּיעַ טוּבְךָ לִבְרִיּוֹתֶיךָ. פּוֹתֵחַ אֶת־יָדֶךָ וּמַשְׂבִּיעַ לְכָל־חַי רָצוֹן: תהלים
קמה

Wind the strap of the תפילין של יד *three times around the middle finger, saying:*

וְאֵרַשְׂתִּיךְ לִי לְעוֹלָם, וְאֵרַשְׂתִּיךְ לִי בְּצֶדֶק וּבְמִשְׁפָּט וּבְחֶסֶד הושע ב
וּבְרַחֲמִים: וְאֵרַשְׂתִּיךְ לִי בֶּאֱמוּנָה, וְיָדַעַתְּ אֶת־יהוה:

LEARNING

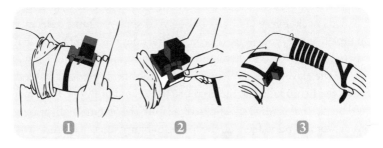

The *tefillin shel yad* is put on first, by placing the box on the biceps near the elbow joint, angled toward the heart, and saying

the blessing לְהָנִיחַ תְּפִלִּין. Then one tightens the strap around the muscle and wraps the strap around the forearm seven

After putting on the tefillin, say the following:

וַיְדַבֵּר The LORD spoke to Moses, saying, "Make holy to Me every *Ex. 13* firstborn male. The first offspring of every womb among the Israelites, whether man or beast, belongs to Me." Then Moses said to the people, "Remember this day on which you left Egypt, the slave-house, when the LORD brought you out of it with a mighty hand. No leaven shall be eaten. You are leaving on this day, in the month of Aviv. When the LORD brings you into the land of the Canaanites, Hittites, Amorites, Hivites and Jebusites, the land He swore to your ancestors to give you, a land flowing with milk and honey, you are to observe this service in this same month. For seven days you shall eat unleavened bread, and make the seventh day a festival to the LORD. Unleavened bread shall be eaten throughout the seven days. No leavened bread may be seen in your possession, and no leaven shall be seen anywhere within your borders. On that day you shall tell your son, 'This is because of what the LORD did for me when I left Egypt.' [These words] shall also be a sign on your hand, and a reminder above your forehead, so that the LORD's Torah may always be in your mouth, because with a mighty hand the LORD brought you out of Egypt. You shall therefore keep this law at its appointed time from year to year."

וְהָיָה After the LORD has brought you into the land of the Canaanites, as He swore to you and your ancestors, and He has given it to you, you shall set apart for the LORD the first offspring of every womb. All the firstborn males of your cattle belong to the LORD. Every firstling donkey you shall redeem with a lamb. If you do not redeem it, you must break its neck. Every firstborn among your sons you must redeem. If, in time to come, your son asks you, "What does this mean?" you shall say to him, "With a mighty hand the LORD brought us out of Egypt, out of the slave-house. When Pharaoh stubbornly refused to let us leave, the LORD killed all the firstborn in the land of Egypt, both man and beast. That is why I sacrifice to the LORD the first male offspring of every womb, and redeem all the firstborn of my sons." [These words] shall be a sign on your hand and as a sign above your forehead, that with a mighty hand the LORD brought us out of Egypt.

After putting on the תפילין, *say the following:*

שמות יג

וַיְדַבֵּר יהוה אֶל־מֹשֶׁה לֵּאמֹר: קַדֶּשׁ־לִי כָל־בְּכוֹר, פֶּטֶר כָּל־רֶחֶם
בִּבְנֵי יִשְׂרָאֵל, בָּאָדָם וּבַבְּהֵמָה, לִי הוּא: וַיֹּאמֶר מֹשֶׁה אֶל־הָעָם,
זָכוֹר אֶת־הַיּוֹם הַזֶּה, אֲשֶׁר יְצָאתֶם מִמִּצְרַיִם מִבֵּית עֲבָדִים, כִּי
בְּחֹזֶק יָד הוֹצִיא יהוה אֶתְכֶם מִזֶּה, וְלֹא יֵאָכֵל חָמֵץ: הַיּוֹם אַתֶּם
יֹצְאִים, בְּחֹדֶשׁ הָאָבִיב: וְהָיָה כִי־יְבִיאֲךָ יהוה אֶל־אֶרֶץ הַכְּנַעֲנִי
וְהַחִתִּי וְהָאֱמֹרִי וְהַחִוִּי וְהַיְבוּסִי, אֲשֶׁר נִשְׁבַּע לַאֲבֹתֶיךָ לָתֶת לָךְ,
אֶרֶץ זָבַת חָלָב וּדְבָשׁ, וְעָבַדְתָּ אֶת־הָעֲבֹדָה הַזֹּאת בַּחֹדֶשׁ הַזֶּה:
שִׁבְעַת יָמִים תֹּאכַל מַצֹּת, וּבַיּוֹם הַשְּׁבִיעִי חַג לַיהוה: מַצּוֹת יֵאָכֵל
אֵת שִׁבְעַת הַיָּמִים, וְלֹא־יֵרָאֶה לְךָ חָמֵץ וְלֹא־יֵרָאֶה לְךָ שְׂאֹר,
בְּכָל־גְּבֻלֶךָ: וְהִגַּדְתָּ לְבִנְךָ בַּיּוֹם הַהוּא לֵאמֹר, בַּעֲבוּר זֶה עָשָׂה
יהוה לִי בְּצֵאתִי מִמִּצְרָיִם: וְהָיָה לְךָ לְאוֹת עַל־יָדְךָ וּלְזִכָּרוֹן בֵּין
עֵינֶיךָ, לְמַעַן תִּהְיֶה תּוֹרַת יהוה בְּפִיךָ, כִּי בְּיָד חֲזָקָה הוֹצִאֲךָ יהוה
מִמִּצְרָיִם: וְשָׁמַרְתָּ אֶת־הַחֻקָּה הַזֹּאת לְמוֹעֲדָהּ, מִיָּמִים יָמִימָה:

וְהָיָה כִּי־יְבִאֲךָ יהוה אֶל־אֶרֶץ הַכְּנַעֲנִי כַּאֲשֶׁר נִשְׁבַּע לְךָ וְלַאֲבֹתֶיךָ,
וּנְתָנָהּ לָךְ: וְהַעֲבַרְתָּ כָל־פֶּטֶר־רֶחֶם לַיהוה, וְכָל־פֶּטֶר שֶׁגֶר בְּהֵמָה
אֲשֶׁר יִהְיֶה לְךָ הַזְּכָרִים, לַיהוה: וְכָל־פֶּטֶר חֲמֹר תִּפְדֶּה בְשֶׂה, וְאִם־
לֹא תִפְדֶּה וַעֲרַפְתּוֹ, וְכֹל בְּכוֹר אָדָם בְּבָנֶיךָ תִּפְדֶּה: וְהָיָה כִּי־יִשְׁאָלְךָ
בִנְךָ מָחָר, לֵאמֹר מַה־זֹּאת, וְאָמַרְתָּ אֵלָיו, בְּחֹזֶק יָד הוֹצִיאָנוּ יהוה
מִמִּצְרַיִם מִבֵּית עֲבָדִים: וַיְהִי כִּי־הִקְשָׁה פַרְעֹה לְשַׁלְּחֵנוּ, וַיַּהֲרֹג
יהוה כָּל־בְּכוֹר בְּאֶרֶץ מִצְרַיִם, מִבְּכֹר אָדָם וְעַד־בְּכוֹר בְּהֵמָה, עַל־
כֵּן אֲנִי זֹבֵחַ לַיהוה כָּל־פֶּטֶר רֶחֶם הַזְּכָרִים, וְכָל־בְּכוֹר בָּנַי אֶפְדֶּה:
וְהָיָה לְאוֹת עַל־יָדְכָה וּלְטוֹטָפֹת בֵּין עֵינֶיךָ, כִּי בְּחֹזֶק יָד הוֹצִיאָנוּ
יהוה מִמִּצְרָיִם:

PREPARATION FOR PRAYER

On entering the synagogue:

HOW GOODLY are your tents, Jacob
your dwelling places, Israel.
As for me, in Your great loving-kindness,
I will come into Your House.
I will bow down to Your holy Temple in awe of You.
Lord, I love the habitation of Your House,
the place where Your glory is present.

As for me, I will bow in worship;
I will bend the knee before the Lord my Maker.

As for me, may my prayer come to You, Lord,
at a time of favor.
God, in Your great loving-kindness,
answer me with Your faithful salvation.

Num. 24

Ps. 5

Ps. 26

Ps. 69

REFLECTION

What makes a
building a
Jewish building?

If you were
building a
"Jewish building"
what would it
look like?

Can you design
a building with
values?
How?

… A THOUSAND WORDS

הכנה לתפילה

On entering the בית כנסת:

במדבר כד

מַה־טֹּבוּ אֹהָלֶיךָ יַעֲקֹב

מִשְׁכְּנֹתֶיךָ יִשְׂרָאֵל:

תהלים ה

וַאֲנִי בְּרֹב חַסְדְּךָ אָבוֹא בֵיתֶךָ

אֶשְׁתַּחֲוֶה אֶל־הֵיכַל־קָדְשְׁךָ, בְּיִרְאָתֶךָ:

תהלים כו

יהוה אָהַבְתִּי מְעוֹן בֵּיתֶךָ

וּמְקוֹם מִשְׁכַּן כְּבוֹדֶךָ:

וַאֲנִי אֶשְׁתַּחֲוֶה

וְאֶכְרָעָה, אֶבְרְכָה לִפְנֵי יהוה עֹשִׂי.

תהלים סט

וַאֲנִי תְפִלָּתִי־לְךָ יהוה

עֵת רָצוֹן, אֱלֹהִים בְּרָב־חַסְדֶּךָ

עֲנֵנִי בֶּאֱמֶת יִשְׁעֶךָ:

LEARNING

This *tefilla* is known as "*Ma Tovu*" after the first and most famous of the verses from it. This verse (*Bemidbar* 24:5) is the climax of the story of the non-Jewish prophet Balaam, who, at the behest of Balak the king of Moab, attempted to curse the Children of Israel. Instead, however, these beautiful words of praise and blessing were uttered: "How goodly are your tents Jacob, your dwelling places, Israel." This *tefilla* is not really one single prayer but rather a collection of verses from Tanakh. They are all appropriately themed to inspire us and prepare us for entering the synagogue and begin our *tefilla*. They generally speak about Jewish buildings, including the *Beit HaMikdash*, and about worshiping Hashem.

LORD OF THE UNIVERSE,

who reigned before the birth of any thing –
When by His will all things were made
then was His name declared King.
And when all things shall cease to be
He alone will reign in awe.
He was, He is, and He shall be
glorious for evermore.
He is One, there is none else,
alone, unique, beyond compare;
Without beginning, without end,
His might, His rule are everywhere.
He is my God; my Redeemer lives.
He is the Rock on whom I rely –
My banner and my safe retreat,
my cup, my portion when I cry.
Into His hand my soul I place,
when I awake and when I sleep.
The LORD is with me, I shall not fear;
body and soul from harm will He keep.

CONNECTION

*"And you?" Rebbe Levi-Yitzhak of Berditchev
was asked. "What did you discover at the Great
Maggid's school?" – "I discovered that God exists, that He is of this world, of all worlds." – "But,
Rebbe, everybody knows that!" – "No," answered the illustrious Rebbe of Berditchev.
"They say it everywhere, but in Mezeritch they
know it."*

(Elie Wiesel, *Souls on Fire*)

... A THOUSAND WORDS

Do you think God exists or do you know He exists? How can you go from just
saying it to knowing it?

אֲדוֹן עוֹלָם

אֲשֶׁר מָלַךְ בְּטֶרֶם כָּל־יְצִיר נִבְרָא.

לְעֵת נַעֲשָׂה בְחֶפְצוֹ כֹּל אֲזַי מֶלֶךְ שְׁמוֹ נִקְרָא.

וְאַחֲרֵי כִּכְלוֹת הַכֹּל לְבַדּוֹ יִמְלֹךְ נוֹרָא.

וְהוּא הָיָה וְהוּא הֹוֶה וְהוּא יִהְיֶה בְּתִפְאָרָה.

וְהוּא אֶחָד וְאֵין שֵׁנִי לְהַמְשִׁיל לוֹ לְהַחְבִּירָה.

בְּלִי רֵאשִׁית בְּלִי תַכְלִית וְלוֹ הָעֹז וְהַמִּשְׂרָה.

וְהוּא אֵלִי וְחַי גּוֹאֲלִי וְצוּר חֶבְלִי בְּעֵת צָרָה.

וְהוּא נִסִּי וּמָנוֹס לִי מְנָת כּוֹסִי בְּיוֹם אֶקְרָא.

בְּיָדוֹ אַפְקִיד רוּחִי בְּעֵת אִישַׁן וְאָעִירָה.

וְעִם רוּחִי גְּוִיָּתִי יהוה לִי וְלֹא אִירָא.

LEARNING

Adon Olam is a poem written in the Middle Ages summarizing various statements of Jewish faith. These include:

- God is the creator of the universe.
- God is sovereign of the universe.
- God is eternal.
- God is one indivisible unity.
- God is infinite and limitless.
- God is a personal God active in one's individual life.

REFLECTION

Where can you see evidence that God created the world?

Where can you see evidence that God rules the world?

Where can you see evidence that God plays a role in your life?

GREAT

is the living God and praised.
>He exists, and His existence is beyond time.

He is One, and there is no unity like His.
>Unfathomable, His oneness is infinite.

He has neither bodily form nor substance;
>His holiness is beyond compare.

He preceded all that was created.
>He was first: there was no beginning to His beginning.

Behold He is Master of the Universe; and every creature
>shows His greatness and majesty.

The rich flow of His prophecy He gave
>to His treasured people in whom He gloried.

---

3. Belief in God's incorporeality
4. Belief in God's eternity
5. Belief that God alone should be the object of worship
6. Belief in revelation through God's prophets
7. Belief in the preeminence of Moses among the prophets
8. Belief that the Torah that we have today is the one dictated to Moses by God
9. Belief that the Torah given by Moses will not be replaced and that nothing may be added to or removed from it
10. Belief in God's awareness of all human actions and thoughts
11. Belief in the reward of good and punishment of evil
12. Belief in the coming of the Messiah
13. Belief in the resurrection of the dead

REFLECTION

What do you have to believe in to be a good Jew?

What is the source of your faith?

Now that we no longer have prophecy, where do you go to listen to God?

What do you think the world will look like during the messianic age? How would you like it to look?

יִגְדַּל

אֱלֹהִים חַי וְיִשְׁתַּבַּח
נִמְצָא וְאֵין עֵת אֶל מְצִיאוּתוֹ.

אֶחָד וְאֵין יָחִיד כְּיִחוּדוֹ
נֶעְלָם וְגַם אֵין סוֹף לְאַחְדוּתוֹ.

אֵין לוֹ דְּמוּת הַגּוּף וְאֵינוֹ גוּף
לֹא נַעֲרֹךְ אֵלָיו קְדֻשָּׁתוֹ.

קַדְמוֹן לְכָל דָּבָר אֲשֶׁר נִבְרָא
רִאשׁוֹן וְאֵין רֵאשִׁית לְרֵאשִׁיתוֹ.

הִנּוֹ אֲדוֹן עוֹלָם
וְכָל נוֹצָר יוֹרֶה גְדֻלָּתוֹ וּמַלְכוּתוֹ.

שֶׁפַע נְבוּאָתוֹ נְתָנוֹ
אֶל־אַנְשֵׁי סְגֻלָּתוֹ וְתִפְאַרְתּוֹ.

LEARNING

Yigdal, believed to be written by Rabbi Yehuda ben Daniel in the fourteenth century, is a poem based on Rambam's Thirteen Principles of Faith. Rambam (Maimonides) is perhaps the most famous Jewish philosopher/halakhist of medieval times. Born in Spain in 1135, he fled Muslim persecution in Spain and settled in Egypt where he became physician to the sultan, making him the most prominent doctor in the land. He died in 1204 and was buried in Tiberias, where his grave can still be visited today.

While some of Rambam's formulations have generated controversy, his enumeration of the 13 core principles of the Jewish faith has nevertheless been widely accepted. These are:

1. Belief in the existence of God
2. Belief in God's unity and indivisibility into elements

Never in Israel has there arisen another like Moses,
    a prophet who beheld God's image.

God gave His people a Torah of truth
    by the hand of His prophet, most faithful of His House.

God will not alter or change His law
    for any other, for eternity.

He sees and knows our secret thoughts;
    as soon as something is begun, He foresees its end.

He rewards people with loving-kindness according to their deeds;
    He punishes the wicked according to his wickedness.

At the end of days He will send our Messiah
    to redeem those who await His final salvation.

God will revive the dead in His great loving-kindness.
    Blessed for evermore is His glorious name!

Akiva], "How do you know this?" and he replied, "This is the law given to Moses at Sinai"; and his strength returned.
    (Menaḥot 29b)

We believe in the truth of Moses' prophecy. But Moses himself believed in the truth of Rabbi Akiva and his interpretation of the Torah. Judaism is all about the transmission of tradition.

... A THOUSAND WORDS

לֹא קָם בְּיִשְׂרָאֵל כְּמֹשֶׁה
עוֹד נָבִיא וּמַבִּיט אֶת תְּמוּנָתוֹ.

תּוֹרַת אֱמֶת נָתַן לְעַמּוֹ אֵל
עַל יַד נְבִיאוֹ נֶאֱמַן בֵּיתוֹ.

לֹא יַחֲלִיף הָאֵל וְלֹא יָמִיר דָּתוֹ
לְעוֹלָמִים לְזוּלָתוֹ.

צוֹפֶה וְיוֹדֵעַ סְתָרֵינוּ
מַבִּיט לְסוֹף דָּבָר בְּקַדְמָתוֹ.

גּוֹמֵל לְאִישׁ חֶסֶד כְּמִפְעָלוֹ
נוֹתֵן לְרָשָׁע רָע כְּרִשְׁעָתוֹ.

יִשְׁלַח לְקֵץ יָמִין מְשִׁיחֵנוּ
לִפְדּוֹת מְחַכֵּי קֵץ יְשׁוּעָתוֹ.

מֵתִים יְחַיֶּה אֵל בְּרֹב חַסְדּוֹ
בָּרוּךְ עֲדֵי עַד שֵׁם תְּהִלָּתוֹ.

CONNECTION

When Moses reached heaven he found the Holy One, blessed be He, fixing tiny crowns to the letters of the Sefer Torah. Moses asked God, "LORD of the Universe, what compels You to do this?" God replied, "There will one day be a man, at the end of many generations, Akiva ben Yosef will be his name, who will deduce heaps and heaps of laws from every tiny point [of every crown of every letter]." "LORD of the Universe," Moses said, "let me see this man." God replied, "Turn around." Moses went and sat eight rows back [and listened to the discussion in the beit midrash of Rabbi Akiva]. But he was not able to follow and became faint because of it. Until they came to discuss a certain subject and the students asked [Rabbi

MORNING BLESSINGS

The following blessings are said aloud by the Leader, but each individual should say them quietly as well. It is our custom to say them standing.

בָּרוּךְ Blessed are You, LORD our God,
King of the Universe,
who gives the heart understanding
to distinguish day from night.

Blessed are You, LORD our God,
King of the Universe,
who has not made me a gentile.

Blessed are You, LORD our God,
King of the Universe,
who has not made me a slave.

CONNECTION

Have you ever wondered why God designed it that humans need sleep? Why did He create us to require a sleep mode?

We've all had one of those days: you oversleep because your alarm clock fails to wake you. As you stumble out of bed, you stub your toe. You hobble to the bathroom to find it occupied by your sister, who seems to have no concept of time. You finally make it downstairs to discover there is no milk left for your cereal, it is raining, and now you've missed the bus. In school it just gets worse: in the rush this morning you forgot your homework, your teacher yells at you and it's only 9 a.m.! On a day when everything seems to go wrong and everything just seems miserable, how are you going to feel better?

Often, just the simple magic of a good night's sleep will help. Sleep mode, shutting everything off, somehow makes us feel better when we wake up the next morning. The creation of night and sleep and the ability to separate between each day is a gift; every day can offer us a fresh start.

LEARNING

טוֹב לְהֹדוֹת לַיהוה, וּלְזַמֵּר לְשִׁמְךָ
עֶלְיוֹן. לְהַגִּיד בַּבֹּקֶר חַסְדֶּךָ,
וֶאֱמוּנָתְךָ בַּלֵּילוֹת

"It is good to give thanks to the LORD, and to sing to Your name, Most High, to relate Your kindness in the morning, and Your faithfulness in the evening."
(Tehillim 92:2)

Rashi explains that the day represents good times, light, clarity – we can clearly see God's kindness and it is easy to be thankful. Night represents hard times, darkness, when we cannot see God. It is during these times that we need to trust and have faith that all will be good eventually.

ברכות השחר

The following blessings are said aloud by the שליח ציבור, but each individual should say them quietly as well. It is our custom to say them standing.

בָּרוּךְ אַתָּה יהוה אֱלֹהֵינוּ מֶלֶךְ הָעוֹלָם
אֲשֶׁר נָתַן לַשֶּׂכְוִי בִינָה
לְהַבְחִין בֵּין יוֹם וּבֵין לַיְלָה.

בָּרוּךְ אַתָּה יהוה אֱלֹהֵינוּ מֶלֶךְ הָעוֹלָם
שֶׁלֹּא עָשַׂנִי גּוֹי.

בָּרוּךְ אַתָּה יהוה אֱלֹהֵינוּ מֶלֶךְ הָעוֹלָם
שֶׁלֹּא עָשַׂנִי עָבֶד.

REFLECTION

"It is a common experience that a problem difficult at night is resolved in the morning after the committee of sleep has worked on it."
(John Steinbeck)

Have you ever lost a night's sleep? How did it make you feel?

Why do people say "It will feel better in the morning"?

Notice the blessings that are written in the negative. What situations are you grateful not to be in?

... A THOUSAND WORDS

Blessed are You, LORD our God,
King of the Universe,
men: who has not made me a woman.
women: who has made me according to His will.

Blessed are You, LORD our God,
King of the Universe,
who gives sight to the blind.

Blessed are You, LORD our God,
King of the Universe,
who clothes the naked.

A group of American schoolchildren was asked to list what they thought were the present "Seven Wonders of the World." Though there were some disagreements, the following received the most votes: Egypt's Great Pyramids, the Taj Mahal, the Grand Canyon, the Panama Canal, the Empire State Building, St. Peter's Basilica, and the Great Wall of China.

While gathering the votes, the teacher noted that one student had not finished her paper yet. So she asked the girl if she was having trouble with her list. The little girl replied, "Yes, a little. I couldn't quite make up my mind because there are so many." The teacher said, "Well, tell us what you have, and maybe we can help." The girl hesitated, then read, "I think the 'Seven Wonders of the World' are:

> To see
> To hear
> To touch
> To taste
> To feel
> To laugh
> To love."

The room was so quiet you could hear a pin drop. The things we overlook as simple and ordinary and that we take for granted are truly wondrous. A gentle reminder – that the most precious things in life cannot be built by hand or bought by man.

בָּרוּךְ אַתָּה יהוה אֱלֹהֵינוּ מֶלֶךְ הָעוֹלָם
men שֶׁלֹּא עָשַׂנִי אִשָּׁה.
women שֶׁעָשַׂנִי כִּרְצוֹנוֹ.

בָּרוּךְ אַתָּה יהוה אֱלֹהֵינוּ מֶלֶךְ הָעוֹלָם
פּוֹקֵחַ עִוְרִים.

בָּרוּךְ אַתָּה יהוה אֱלֹהֵינוּ מֶלֶךְ הָעוֹלָם
מַלְבִּישׁ עֲרֻמִּים.

... A THOUSAND WORDS

REFLECTION

What is the most
beautiful thing you
have ever seen?

In what areas of your
life would you like to ask
God for more clarity?

Clothes show people
who we are: what
do your clothes say
about you?

LEARNING

וַיִּפְקַח אֱלֹהִים אֶת עֵינֶיהָ וַתֵּרֶא בְּאֵר מָיִם

"And God opened her eyes and she saw a well of water."
(Bereshit 21:19)

Seforno explains that Hagar was not blind; rather God widened Hagar's perspective
and gave her the ability to "see" that which she could not previously see. God allowed
her to recognize where she was and what she needed to see.

Blessed are You, LORD our God,
King of the Universe,
who sets captives free.

Blessed are You, LORD our God,
King of the Universe,
who raises those bowed down.

... A THOUSAND WORDS

This is the bowing stage of development, where we bend ourselves in an attempt to destroy the problematic elements within us.

However, teaches Rav Kook, subjugation and self-negation are only preparatory stages of development. "The goal is to shine with the light of God, with an abundance of strength and joy. Then, all of the powers of the soul straighten up and endure with much courage and an elevated and lofty life force." First we bow, but then we straighten up.

בָּרוּךְ אַתָּה יהוה אֱלֹהֵינוּ מֶלֶךְ הָעוֹלָם
מַתִּיר אֲסוּרִים.

בָּרוּךְ אַתָּה יהוה אֱלֹהֵינוּ מֶלֶךְ הָעוֹלָם
זוֹקֵף כְּפוּפִים.

CONNECTION

A little boy once found a cocoon of a butterfly. One day a small opening appeared. He sat and watched for hours as the butterfly struggled to squeeze itself out through the tiny hole. Then it stopped, as if it could go no further. The little boy decided to help the poor butterfly. He took a tiny pair of scissors and snipped off the remaining bit of the cocoon. The butterfly emerged easily but it had a swollen body and shriveled wings. The boy waited, expecting that any minute the wings would expand to support the butterfly. Nothing happened. The butterfly spent the rest of its life dragging its swollen body around; it was never able to fly.

In his haste and kindness to help the butterfly, the little boy failed to understand that the struggle that the butterfly had to go through to push through the small hole in the cocoon was nature's way of forcing the extra fluid from its body and strengthening its wings.

Only by struggling through the hole would the butterfly be ready for flight.

Sometimes struggles are exactly what we need in our lives. If we did not struggle, we would not have the strength to fly.

REFLECTION

Have you ever felt unable to move physically or emotionally?

How do you want God to support you?

Do you have any areas in your life that make you feel trapped?

LEARNING

Rav Kook (*Siddur Olat Re'iya*, vol. 1): Bowing and straightening up are a metaphor for two stages of personal development. People begin with all sorts of negative forces they need to weed out, suppress, and destroy. This is difficult work that demands a lot of subjugation – of one's ego, and of negative inner forces in general.

Blessed are You, LORD our God,
> King of the Universe,
> who spreads the earth above the waters.

Blessed are You, LORD our God,
> King of the Universe,
> who has provided me with all I need.

Blessed are You, LORD our God,
> King of the Universe,
> who makes firm the steps of man.

CONNECTION

One night I dreamed a dream.
> *As I was walking along the beach with the LORD.*
> *Across the dark sky flashed scenes from my life.*
> *For each scene, I noticed two sets of footprints in the sand,*
> *One belonging to me and one to the LORD.*
> *After the last scene of my life flashed before me,*
> *I looked back at the footprints in the sand.*
> *I noticed that at many times along the path of my life,*
> *especially at the very lowest and saddest times,*
> *there was only one set of footprints.*
> *This really troubled me,*
> *so I asked the LORD about it.*
> *"LORD, You said once I decided to follow You,*
> *You'd walk with me all the way.*
> *But I noticed that during the saddest and most troublesome times of my life,*
> *there was only one set of footprints.*
> *I don't understand why, when I needed You the most, You would leave me."*
> *He whispered,*
> *"My precious child, I love you and will never leave you.*
> *Never, ever, during your trials and testings.*
> *When you saw only one set of footprints,*
> *It was then that I carried you."*

בָּרוּךְ אַתָּה יהוה אֱלֹהֵינוּ מֶלֶךְ הָעוֹלָם
רוֹקַע הָאָרֶץ עַל הַמָּיִם.

בָּרוּךְ אַתָּה יהוה אֱלֹהֵינוּ מֶלֶךְ הָעוֹלָם
שֶׁעָשָׂה לִי כָּל צָרְכִּי.

בָּרוּךְ אַתָּה יהוה אֱלֹהֵינוּ מֶלֶךְ הָעוֹלָם
הַמֵּכִין מִצְעֲדֵי גָבֶר.

REFLECTION

Have you ever seen a flood or witnessed water overflowing its boundaries? What boundaries do you have in your life that you are careful not to cross?

What is lacking in your life and what do you need to ask God for?

How is God guiding your steps? What path are you going to choose today?

... A THOUSAND WORDS

LEARNING

Gemara *Bava Batra* 17a explains that three people lived as if they were in the World to Come. This is proven by the use of the word כָּל in describing them. The word כָּל is all-encompassing, it includes all things. Avraham, Yitzḥak, and Yaakov were all blessed with the perception that they possessed all they could possibly need. This perception and appreciation allows a person to live in a state of tranquil bliss, as if already in *Olam HaBa*. Are you able to look at your life and see how much you have rather than how much you are lacking?

Blessed are You, LORD our God,
King of the Universe,
who binds Israel with strength.

Blessed are You, LORD our God,
King of the Universe,
who crowns Israel with glory.

Blessed are You, LORD our God,
King of the Universe,
who gives strength to the tired.

LEARNING

"The *tefillin* serve as a sign of dignity. The word *'tife-ret'* (used in reference to the *tefillin*) indicates that it is an item that elevates us from our natural state into a Godly dignity. All items described with the word *'tiferet'* serve a similar purpose; the garments of the Kohen in the Temple, the Temple itself, and *tefillin*. The sages say that the *tefillin* are the glory of the Jewish People because wearing them shows that we are with Hashem and inheritors of His Torah." (*HaKtav VeHaKabbala Shemot* 13:14)

REFLECTION

Are you tired today? What makes you most tired?

Aside from lack of sleep, what else makes you tired? Why?

Can you think of ways to help yourself be really awake today?

CONNECTION

In 1992 Derek Redmond was favored to win a medal in the Olympic 400-meter sprint. After a lightning start, about 150 meters in, Redmond felt a searing pain; in agony he fell to the ground with a torn hamstring. Not willing to give up, determined to finish the race, he continued, half running, half hopping along the track, tears of agony and exertion pouring down his face.

Breaking through security, a man came to Derek's side. It was his father. "You don't have to do this," he told him. "Yes, I do," Derek cried. "Well then, we are going to finish this together."

Arm in arm, leaning heavily on his father, Derek limped, sobbing, along the track. Together, father and son continued. Just before the finish line, Derek's father let him go to complete his race, receiving a standing ovation from a crowd of over 65,000.

בָּרוּךְ אַתָּה יהוה אֱלֹהֵינוּ מֶלֶךְ הָעוֹלָם
אוֹזֵר יִשְׂרָאֵל בִּגְבוּרָה.

בָּרוּךְ אַתָּה יהוה אֱלֹהֵינוּ מֶלֶךְ הָעוֹלָם
עוֹטֵר יִשְׂרָאֵל בְּתִפְאָרָה.

בָּרוּךְ אַתָּה יהוה אֱלֹהֵינוּ מֶלֶךְ הָעוֹלָם
הַנּוֹתֵן לַיָּעֵף כֹּחַ.

... A THOUSAND WORDS

REFLECTION

"Who is strong? He who conquers
his evil inclination."
(Pirkei Avot 4:1)

What is your greatest strength?

When have you shown
strength? When have the
Jewish People shown strength?
What do the Jewish People
need strength for?

How do you behave with
dignity?

How can the Jewish People
show dignity and glory?

CONNECTION

The Jewish People's strength is a unique strength. It is a strength that is manifest not through the conquering of others, by overpowering them or destroying them; rather, it is a strength that comes from the ability of man to conquer himself. This is a strength of the divine soul, the ability of man to conquer his physicality and his base desires, which is thousands of times greater than the strength to take over a city.

This is the strength that girds the Jewish People, the foundation of pure morality and the pinnacle of man that raises him above the animals.

(Rav Kook, *Olat Re'iya*)

בָּרוּךְ Blessed are You, LORD our God, King of the Universe,
who removes sleep from my eyes and slumber from my eyelids.
And may it be Your will, LORD our God
and God of our ancestors, to accustom us to Your Torah,
and make us attached to Your commandments.
Lead us not into error,
sin, wrongdoing, temptation or disgrace.
Do not let the evil instinct dominate us.
Keep us far from a bad person and a bad friend.
Help us attach ourselves to the good instinct and to good deeds
and bend our instincts to be subservient to You.
Give us, this day and every day, grace, loving-kindness
and compassion in Your eyes
and in the eyes of all who see us,
and act with loving-kindness toward us.
Blessed are You, LORD,
who acts with loving-kindness toward His people Israel.

יְהִי רָצוֹן May it be Your will, LORD my God and God of my ancestors,
to save me today and every day, from the arrogant and from arrogance itself,   *Berakhot*
from a bad person, a bad friend, a bad neighbor,   *16b*
a bad mishap, a destructive enemy,
a harsh trial and a harsh opponent,
whether or not he is a son of the covenant.

LEARNING

"A person should get up like a lion in the morning to serve his Creator."
(Shulhan Arukh 1:1)

The *Mishna Berura* expands: if your *yetzer hara* entices you to stay in bed you must strengthen yourself against it and not listen. You must say, "If I were needed to serve a human king, how enthusiastic and excited would I be to get up early to prepare for this service? How much more so for the King of kings – God Himself."

בָּרוּךְ אַתָּה יהוה אֱלֹהֵינוּ מֶלֶךְ הָעוֹלָם

הַמַּעֲבִיר שֵׁנָה מֵעֵינַי וּתְנוּמָה מֵעַפְעַפָּי.

וִיהִי רָצוֹן מִלְּפָנֶיךָ יהוה אֱלֹהֵינוּ וֵאלֹהֵי אֲבוֹתֵינוּ

שֶׁתַּרְגִּילֵנוּ בְּתוֹרָתֶךָ

וְדַבְּקֵנוּ בְּמִצְוֹתֶיךָ

וְאַל תְּבִיאֵנוּ לֹא לִידֵי חֵטְא

וְלֹא לִידֵי עֲבֵרָה וְעָוֹן

וְלֹא לִידֵי נִסָּיוֹן וְלֹא לִידֵי בִזָּיוֹן

וְאַל תַּשְׁלֶט בָּנוּ יֵצֶר הָרָע

וְהַרְחִיקֵנוּ מֵאָדָם רָע וּמֵחָבֵר רָע

וְדַבְּקֵנוּ בְּיֵצֶר הַטּוֹב וּבְמַעֲשִׂים טוֹבִים

וְכֹף אֶת יִצְרֵנוּ לְהִשְׁתַּעְבֶּד לָךְ

וּתְנֵנוּ הַיּוֹם וּבְכָל יוֹם לְחֵן וּלְחֶסֶד וּלְרַחֲמִים

בְּעֵינֶיךָ, וּבְעֵינֵי כָל רוֹאֵינוּ

וְתִגְמְלֵנוּ חֲסָדִים טוֹבִים.

בָּרוּךְ אַתָּה יהוה

גּוֹמֵל חֲסָדִים טוֹבִים לְעַמּוֹ יִשְׂרָאֵל.

ברכות טז:

יְהִי רָצוֹן מִלְּפָנֶיךָ יהוה אֱלֹהַי וֵאלֹהֵי אֲבוֹתַי

שֶׁתַּצִּילֵנִי הַיּוֹם וּבְכָל יוֹם מֵעַזֵּי פָנִים וּמֵעַזּוּת פָּנִים

מֵאָדָם רָע, וּמֵחָבֵר רָע, וּמִשָּׁכֵן רָע

וּמִפֶּגַע רָע, וּמִשָּׂטָן הַמַּשְׁחִית

מִדִּין קָשֶׁה, וּמִבַּעַל דִּין קָשֶׁה

בֵּין שֶׁהוּא בֶן בְּרִית וּבֵין שֶׁאֵינוֹ בֶן בְּרִית.

THE BINDING OF ISAAC

*On the basis of Jewish mystical tradition, some have the custom of
saying daily the biblical passage describing the Binding of Isaac,
the trial of faith in which Abraham demonstrated
his love of God above all other loves.*

Our God and God of our ancestors, remember us with a favorable memory,
and recall us with a remembrance of salvation and compassion from the
highest of high heavens. Remember, LORD our God, on our behalf, the love
of the ancients, Abraham, Isaac and Yisrael Your servants; the covenant, the
loving-kindness, and the oath You swore to Abraham our father on Mount
Moriah, and the Binding, when he bound Isaac his son on the altar, as is
written in Your Torah:

It happened after these things that God tested Abraham. He *Gen. 22*
said to him, "Abraham!" "Here I am," he replied. He said,
"Take your son, your only son, Isaac, whom you love, and go
to the land of Moriah and offer him there as a burnt-offering
on one of the mountains which I shall say to you." Early the
next morning Abraham rose and saddled his donkey and
took his two lads with him, and Isaac his son, and he cut
wood for the burnt-offering, and he set out for the place of
which God had told him. On the third day Abraham looked
up and saw the place from afar. Abraham said to his lads,
"Stay here with the donkey while I and the boy go on ahead.
We will worship and we will return to you." Abraham took
the wood for the burnt-offering and placed it on Isaac his
son, and he took in his hand the fire and the knife, and the
two of them went together. Isaac said to Abraham his father,
"Father?" and he said "Here I am, my son." And he said, "Here
are the fire and the wood, but where is the sheep for the
burnt-offering?" Abraham said, "God will see to the sheep
for the burnt-offering, my son." And the two of them went
together. They came to the place God had told him about,

פרשת העקדה

On the basis of Jewish mystical tradition, some have the custom of
saying daily the biblical passage describing the Binding of Isaac,
the trial of faith in which Abraham demonstrated
his love of God above all other loves.

אֱלֹהֵינוּ וֵאלֹהֵי אֲבוֹתֵינוּ, זָכְרֵנוּ בְּזִכְרוֹן טוֹב לְפָנֶיךָ, וּפָקְדֵנוּ בִּפְקֻדַּת יְשׁוּעָה
וְרַחֲמִים מִשְּׁמֵי שְׁמֵי קֶדֶם, וּזְכָר לָנוּ יהוה אֱלֹהֵינוּ, אַהֲבַת הַקַּדְמוֹנִים אַבְרָהָם
יִצְחָק וְיִשְׂרָאֵל עֲבָדֶיךָ, אֶת הַבְּרִית וְאֶת הַחֶסֶד וְאֶת הַשְּׁבוּעָה שֶׁנִּשְׁבַּעְתָּ
לְאַבְרָהָם אָבִינוּ בְּהַר הַמּוֹרִיָּה, וְאֶת הָעֲקֵדָה שֶׁעָקַד אֶת יִצְחָק בְּנוֹ עַל גַּבֵּי
הַמִּזְבֵּחַ, כַּכָּתוּב בְּתוֹרָתֶךָ:

בראשית כב

וַיְהִי אַחַר הַדְּבָרִים הָאֵלֶּה, וְהָאֱלֹהִים נִסָּה אֶת־אַבְרָהָם,
וַיֹּאמֶר אֵלָיו אַבְרָהָם, וַיֹּאמֶר הִנֵּנִי: וַיֹּאמֶר קַח־נָא אֶת־בִּנְךָ
אֶת־יְחִידְךָ אֲשֶׁר־אָהַבְתָּ, אֶת־יִצְחָק, וְלֶךְ־לְךָ אֶל־אֶרֶץ
הַמֹּרִיָּה, וְהַעֲלֵהוּ שָׁם לְעֹלָה עַל אַחַד הֶהָרִים אֲשֶׁר אֹמַר
אֵלֶיךָ: וַיַּשְׁכֵּם אַבְרָהָם בַּבֹּקֶר, וַיַּחֲבֹשׁ אֶת־חֲמֹרוֹ, וַיִּקַּח אֶת־
שְׁנֵי נְעָרָיו אִתּוֹ וְאֵת יִצְחָק בְּנוֹ, וַיְבַקַּע עֲצֵי עֹלָה, וַיָּקָם וַיֵּלֶךְ
אֶל־הַמָּקוֹם אֲשֶׁר־אָמַר־לוֹ הָאֱלֹהִים: בַּיּוֹם הַשְּׁלִישִׁי וַיִּשָּׂא
אַבְרָהָם אֶת־עֵינָיו וַיַּרְא אֶת־הַמָּקוֹם מֵרָחֹק: וַיֹּאמֶר אַבְרָהָם
אֶל־נְעָרָיו, שְׁבוּ־לָכֶם פֹּה עִם־הַחֲמוֹר, וַאֲנִי וְהַנַּעַר נֵלְכָה עַד־
כֹּה, וְנִשְׁתַּחֲוֶה וְנָשׁוּבָה אֲלֵיכֶם: וַיִּקַּח אַבְרָהָם אֶת־עֲצֵי הָעֹלָה
וַיָּשֶׂם עַל־יִצְחָק בְּנוֹ, וַיִּקַּח בְּיָדוֹ אֶת־הָאֵשׁ וְאֶת־הַמַּאֲכֶלֶת,
וַיֵּלְכוּ שְׁנֵיהֶם יַחְדָּו: וַיֹּאמֶר יִצְחָק אֶל־אַבְרָהָם אָבִיו, וַיֹּאמֶר
אָבִי, וַיֹּאמֶר הִנֶּנִּי בְנִי, וַיֹּאמֶר, הִנֵּה הָאֵשׁ וְהָעֵצִים, וְאַיֵּה
הַשֶּׂה לְעֹלָה: וַיֹּאמֶר אַבְרָהָם, אֱלֹהִים יִרְאֶה־לּוֹ הַשֶּׂה לְעֹלָה,
בְּנִי, וַיֵּלְכוּ שְׁנֵיהֶם יַחְדָּו: וַיָּבֹאוּ אֶל־הַמָּקוֹם אֲשֶׁר אָמַר־לוֹ

and Abraham built there an altar and arranged the wood and bound Isaac his son and laid him on the altar on top of the wood. He reached out his hand and took the knife to slay his son. Then an angel of the LORD called out to him from heaven, "Abraham! Abraham!" He said, "Here I am." He said, "Do not reach out your hand against the boy; do not do anything to him, for now I know that you fear God, because you have not held back your son, your only son, from Me." Abraham looked up and there he saw a ram caught in a thicket by its horns, and Abraham went and took the ram and offered it as a burnt-offering instead of his son. Abraham called that place "The LORD will see," as is said to this day, "On the mountain of the LORD He will be seen." The angel of the LORD called to Abraham a second time from heaven, and said, "By Myself I swear, declares the LORD, that because you have done this and have not held back your son, your only son, I will greatly bless you and greatly multiply your descendants, as the stars of heaven and the sand of the seashore, and your descendants shall take possession of the gates of their enemies. Through your descendants, all the nations of the earth will be blessed, because you have listened to My voice." Then Abraham returned to his lads, and they rose and went together to Beersheba, and Abraham stayed in Beersheba.

Master of the Universe, just as Abraham our father suppressed his compassion to do Your will wholeheartedly, so may Your compassion suppress Your anger from us and may Your compassion prevail over Your other attributes. Deal with us, LORD our God, with the attributes of loving-kindness and compassion, and in Your great goodness may Your anger be turned away from Your people, Your city, Your land and Your inheritance. Fulfill in us, LORD our God, the promise You made in Your Torah through the hand of Moses Your servant, as it is said: "I will remember My covenant with Jacob, *Lev. 26* and also My covenant with Isaac, and also My covenant with Abraham I will remember, and the land I will remember."

הָאֱלֹהִים, וַיִּבֶן שָׁם אַבְרָהָם אֶת־הַמִּזְבֵּחַ וַיַּעֲרֹךְ אֶת־הָעֵצִים,
וַיַּעֲקֹד אֶת־יִצְחָק בְּנוֹ, וַיָּשֶׂם אֹתוֹ עַל־הַמִּזְבֵּחַ מִמַּעַל לָעֵצִים:
וַיִּשְׁלַח אַבְרָהָם אֶת־יָדוֹ, וַיִּקַּח אֶת־הַמַּאֲכֶלֶת, לִשְׁחֹט אֶת־
בְּנוֹ: וַיִּקְרָא אֵלָיו מַלְאַךְ יהוה מִן־הַשָּׁמַיִם, וַיֹּאמֶר אַבְרָהָם
אַבְרָהָם, וַיֹּאמֶר הִנֵּנִי: וַיֹּאמֶר אַל־תִּשְׁלַח יָדְךָ אֶל־הַנַּעַר,
וְאַל־תַּעַשׂ לוֹ מְאוּמָה, כִּי עַתָּה יָדַעְתִּי כִּי־יְרֵא אֱלֹהִים אַתָּה,
וְלֹא חָשַׂכְתָּ אֶת־בִּנְךָ אֶת־יְחִידְךָ מִמֶּנִּי: וַיִּשָּׂא אַבְרָהָם אֶת־
עֵינָיו, וַיַּרְא וְהִנֵּה־אַיִל, אַחַר נֶאֱחַז בַּסְּבַךְ בְּקַרְנָיו, וַיֵּלֶךְ
אַבְרָהָם וַיִּקַּח אֶת־הָאַיִל, וַיַּעֲלֵהוּ לְעֹלָה תַּחַת בְּנוֹ: וַיִּקְרָא
אַבְרָהָם שֵׁם־הַמָּקוֹם הַהוּא יהוה יִרְאֶה, אֲשֶׁר יֵאָמֵר הַיּוֹם
בְּהַר יהוה יֵרָאֶה: וַיִּקְרָא מַלְאַךְ יהוה אֶל־אַבְרָהָם שֵׁנִית
מִן־הַשָּׁמַיִם: וַיֹּאמֶר, בִּי נִשְׁבַּעְתִּי נְאֻם־יהוה, כִּי יַעַן אֲשֶׁר
עָשִׂיתָ אֶת־הַדָּבָר הַזֶּה, וְלֹא חָשַׂכְתָּ אֶת־בִּנְךָ אֶת־יְחִידֶךָ:
כִּי־בָרֵךְ אֲבָרֶכְךָ, וְהַרְבָּה אַרְבֶּה אֶת־זַרְעֲךָ כְּכוֹכְבֵי הַשָּׁמַיִם,
וְכַחוֹל אֲשֶׁר עַל־שְׂפַת הַיָּם, וְיִרַשׁ זַרְעֲךָ אֵת שַׁעַר אֹיְבָיו:
וְהִתְבָּרְכוּ בְזַרְעֲךָ כֹּל גּוֹיֵי הָאָרֶץ, עֵקֶב אֲשֶׁר שָׁמַעְתָּ בְּקֹלִי:
וַיָּשָׁב אַבְרָהָם אֶל־נְעָרָיו, וַיָּקֻמוּ וַיֵּלְכוּ יַחְדָּו אֶל־בְּאֵר שָׁבַע,
וַיֵּשֶׁב אַבְרָהָם בִּבְאֵר שָׁבַע:

רִבּוֹנוֹ שֶׁל עוֹלָם, כְּמוֹ שֶׁכָּבַשׁ אַבְרָהָם אָבִינוּ אֶת רַחֲמָיו לַעֲשׂוֹת רְצוֹנְךָ
בְּלֵבָב שָׁלֵם, כֵּן יִכְבְּשׁוּ רַחֲמֶיךָ אֶת כַּעַסְךָ מֵעָלֵינוּ וְיִגֹּלּוּ רַחֲמֶיךָ עַל מִדּוֹתֶיךָ.
וְתִתְנַהֵג עִמָּנוּ יהוה אֱלֹהֵינוּ בְּמִדַּת הַחֶסֶד וּבְמִדַּת הָרַחֲמִים, וּבְטוּבְךָ הַגָּדוֹל
יָשׁוּב חֲרוֹן אַפְּךָ מֵעַמְּךָ וּמֵעִירְךָ וּמֵאַרְצְךָ וּמִנַּחֲלָתֶךָ. וְקַיֶּם לָנוּ יהוה אֱלֹהֵינוּ
אֶת הַדָּבָר שֶׁהִבְטַחְתָּנוּ בְּתוֹרָתֶךָ עַל יְדֵי מֹשֶׁה עַבְדֶּךָ, כָּאָמוּר: וְזָכַרְתִּי ויקרא כו
אֶת־בְּרִיתִי יַעֲקוֹב וְאַף אֶת־בְּרִיתִי יִצְחָק, וְאַף אֶת־בְּרִיתִי אַבְרָהָם אֶזְכֹּר,
וְהָאָרֶץ אֶזְכֹּר:

ACCEPTING THE SOVEREIGNTY OF HEAVEN

לְעוֹלָם A person should always be God-fearing, privately and publicly,
acknowledging the truth and speaking it in his heart.
He should rise early and say:

Tanna DeVei Eliyahu, ch. 21

> Master of all worlds,
> not because of our righteousness
> do we lay our pleas before You,
> but because of Your great compassion.

Dan. 9

What are we? What are our lives?
What is our loving-kindness?
What is our righteousness?
What is our salvation?
What is our strength? What is our might?
What shall we say before You,
LORD our God and God of our ancestors?
Are not all the mighty like nothing before You,
the men of renown as if they had never been,
the wise as if they know nothing,
and the understanding as if they lack intelligence?
For their many works are in vain,
and the days of their lives like a fleeting breath before You.
The pre-eminence of man over the animals is nothing,
for all is but a fleeting breath.

Eccl. 3

אֲבָל Yet we are Your people, the children of Your covenant,
the children of Abraham, Your beloved,
to whom You made a promise on Mount Moriah;
the offspring of Isaac his only one who was bound on the altar;
the congregation of Jacob Your firstborn son
whom – because of the love with which You loved him
and the joy with which You rejoiced in him –
You called Yisrael and Yeshurun.

קבלת עול מלכות שמים

תנא דבי
אליהו,
פרק כא

לְעוֹלָם יְהֵא אָדָם יְרֵא שָׁמַיִם בְּסֵתֶר וּבְגָלוּי
וּמוֹדֶה עַל הָאֱמֶת, וְדוֹבֵר אֱמֶת בִּלְבָבוֹ
וְיַשְׁכֵּם וְיֹאמַר

רִבּוֹן כָּל הָעוֹלָמִים

דניאל ט לֹא עַל־צִדְקוֹתֵינוּ אֲנַחְנוּ מַפִּילִים תַּחֲנוּנֵינוּ לְפָנֶיךָ
כִּי עַל־רַחֲמֶיךָ הָרַבִּים:

מָה אָנוּ, מֶה חַיֵּינוּ

מֶה חַסְדֵּנוּ, מַה צִּדְקוֹתֵינוּ

מַה יְשׁוּעָתֵנוּ, מַה כֹּחֵנוּ, מַה גְּבוּרָתֵנוּ

מַה נֹּאמַר לְפָנֶיךָ, יהוה אֱלֹהֵינוּ וֵאלֹהֵי אֲבוֹתֵינוּ

הֲלֹא כָל הַגִּבּוֹרִים כְּאַיִן לְפָנֶיךָ

וְאַנְשֵׁי הַשֵּׁם כְּלֹא הָיוּ

וַחֲכָמִים כִּבְלִי מַדָּע, וּנְבוֹנִים כִּבְלִי הַשְׂכֵּל

כִּי רֹב מַעֲשֵׂיהֶם תֹּהוּ, וִימֵי חַיֵּיהֶם הֶבֶל לְפָנֶיךָ

וּמוֹתַר הָאָדָם מִן־הַבְּהֵמָה אָיִן

קהלת ג כִּי הַכֹּל הָבֶל:

אֲבָל אֲנַחְנוּ עַמְּךָ בְּנֵי בְרִיתֶךָ

בְּנֵי אַבְרָהָם אֹהַבְךָ שֶׁנִּשְׁבַּעְתָּ לּוֹ בְּהַר הַמּוֹרִיָּה

זֶרַע יִצְחָק יְחִידוֹ שֶׁנֶּעֱקַד עַל גַּבֵּי הַמִּזְבֵּחַ

עֲדַת יַעֲקֹב בִּנְךָ בְּכוֹרֶךָ

שֶׁמֵּאַהֲבָתְךָ שֶׁאָהַבְתָּ אוֹתוֹ, וּמִשִּׂמְחָתְךָ שֶׁשָּׂמַחְתָּ בּוֹ

קָרָאתָ אֶת שְׁמוֹ יִשְׂרָאֵל וִישֻׁרוּן.

לְפִיכָךְ Therefore it is our duty
to thank You, and to praise, glorify, bless, sanctify
and give praise and thanks to Your name.
Happy are we, how good is our portion,
how lovely our fate, how beautiful our heritage.

▸ Happy are we who, early and late,
evening and morning,
say twice each day –

Listen, Israel: the LORD is our God, the LORD is One.   *Deut. 6*

Quietly: Blessed be the name of His glorious kingdom for ever and all time.

*Some congregations say the entire first paragraph of the Shema (below) at this point.
If there is a concern that the Shema will not be recited within the
prescribed time, then all three paragraphs should be said.*

Love the LORD your God with all your heart, with all your soul, and with all your
might. These words which I command you today shall be on your heart. Teach them
repeatedly to your children, speaking of them when you sit at home and when you
travel on the way, when you lie down and when you rise. Bind them as a sign on your
hand, and they shall be a sign between your eyes. Write them on the doorposts of
your house and gates.

אַתָּה הוּא It was You who existed
before the world was created,
it is You now that the world has been created.
It is You in this world
and You in the World to Come.
▸ Sanctify Your name
through those who sanctify Your name,
and sanctify Your name
throughout Your world.
By Your salvation may our pride be exalted;
raise high our pride.
Blessed are You, LORD,
who sanctifies His name among the multitudes.

לְפִיכָךְ אֲנַחְנוּ חַיָּבִים
לְהוֹדוֹת לְךָ וּלְשַׁבֵּחֲךָ וּלְפָאֶרְךָ
וּלְבָרֵךְ וּלְקַדֵּשׁ וְלָתֵת שֶׁבַח וְהוֹדָיָה לִשְׁמֶךָ.
אַשְׁרֵינוּ, מַה טּוֹב חֶלְקֵנוּ
וּמַה נָּעִים גּוֹרָלֵנוּ, וּמַה יָּפָה יְרֻשָּׁתֵנוּ.

‹ אַשְׁרֵינוּ, שֶׁאֲנַחְנוּ מַשְׁכִּימִים וּמַעֲרִיבִים עֶרֶב וָבְקֶר
וְאוֹמְרִים פַּעֲמַיִם בְּכָל יוֹם

דברים ו

שְׁמַע יִשְׂרָאֵל, יהוה אֱלֹהֵינוּ, יהוה אֶחָד:

Quietly בָּרוּךְ שֵׁם כְּבוֹד מַלְכוּתוֹ לְעוֹלָם וָעֶד.

Some congregations say the entire first paragraph of the שמע (below) at this point.
If there is a concern that the שמע will not be recited within the
prescribed time, then all three paragraphs should be said.

וְאָהַבְתָּ אֵת יהוה אֱלֹהֶיךָ, בְּכָל־לְבָבְךָ, וּבְכָל־נַפְשְׁךָ, וּבְכָל־מְאֹדֶךָ: וְהָיוּ הַדְּבָרִים
הָאֵלֶּה, אֲשֶׁר אָנֹכִי מְצַוְּךָ הַיּוֹם, עַל־לְבָבֶךָ: וְשִׁנַּנְתָּם לְבָנֶיךָ, וְדִבַּרְתָּ בָּם, בְּשִׁבְתְּךָ
בְּבֵיתֶךָ, וּבְלֶכְתְּךָ בַדֶּרֶךְ, וּבְשָׁכְבְּךָ וּבְקוּמֶךָ: וּקְשַׁרְתָּם לְאוֹת עַל־יָדֶךָ וְהָיוּ לְטֹטָפֹת
בֵּין עֵינֶיךָ: וּכְתַבְתָּם עַל־מְזֻזוֹת בֵּיתֶךָ וּבִשְׁעָרֶיךָ:

אַתָּה הוּא עַד שֶׁלֹּא נִבְרָא הָעוֹלָם
אַתָּה הוּא מִשֶּׁנִּבְרָא הָעוֹלָם.
אַתָּה הוּא בָּעוֹלָם הַזֶּה
וְאַתָּה הוּא לָעוֹלָם הַבָּא.
‹ קַדֵּשׁ אֶת שִׁמְךָ עַל מַקְדִּישֵׁי שְׁמֶךָ
וְקַדֵּשׁ אֶת שִׁמְךָ בְּעוֹלָמֶךָ
וּבִישׁוּעָתְךָ תָּרוּם וְתַגְבִּיהַּ קַרְנֵנוּ.
בָּרוּךְ אַתָּה יהוה, הַמְקַדֵּשׁ אֶת שְׁמוֹ בָּרַבִּים.

אַתָּה הוּא You are the LORD our God
in heaven and on earth,
and in the highest heaven of heavens.
Truly, You are the first
and You are the last,
and besides You there is no god.
Gather those who hope in You
from the four quarters of the earth.
May all mankind recognize and know
that You alone are God
over all the kingdoms on earth.

You made the heavens and the earth,
the sea and all they contain.
Who among all the works of Your hands,
above and below,
can tell You what to do?

Heavenly Father,
deal kindly with us
for the sake of Your great name
by which we are called,
and fulfill for us,
LORD our God,
that which is written:

> "At that time I will bring you home,   *Zeph. 3*
> and at that time I will gather you,
> for I will give you renown and praise
> among all the peoples of the earth
> when I bring back your exiles
> before your eyes,
> says the LORD."

אַתָּה הוּא יהוה אֱלֹהֵינוּ
בַּשָּׁמַיִם וּבָאָרֶץ
וּבִשְׁמֵי הַשָּׁמַיִם הָעֶלְיוֹנִים.
אֱמֶת, אַתָּה הוּא רִאשׁוֹן
וְאַתָּה הוּא אַחֲרוֹן
וּמִבַּלְעָדֶיךָ אֵין אֱלֹהִים.
קַבֵּץ קוֹיֶךָ מֵאַרְבַּע כַּנְפוֹת הָאָרֶץ.
יַכִּירוּ וְיֵדְעוּ כָּל בָּאֵי עוֹלָם
כִּי אַתָּה הוּא הָאֱלֹהִים לְבַדְּךָ לְכֹל מַמְלְכוֹת הָאָרֶץ.

אַתָּה עָשִׂיתָ אֶת הַשָּׁמַיִם וְאֶת הָאָרֶץ
אֶת הַיָּם וְאֶת כָּל אֲשֶׁר בָּם
וּמִי בְּכָל מַעֲשֵׂי יָדֶיךָ בָּעֶלְיוֹנִים אוֹ בַתַּחְתּוֹנִים
שֶׁיֹּאמַר לְךָ מַה תַּעֲשֶׂה.

אָבִינוּ שֶׁבַּשָּׁמַיִם
עֲשֵׂה עִמָּנוּ חֶסֶד
בַּעֲבוּר שִׁמְךָ הַגָּדוֹל שֶׁנִּקְרָא עָלֵינוּ
וְקַיֵּם לָנוּ יהוה אֱלֹהֵינוּ
מַה שֶּׁכָּתוּב:

צפניה ג

בָּעֵת הַהִיא אָבִיא אֶתְכֶם, וּבָעֵת קַבְּצִי אֶתְכֶם
כִּי־אֶתֵּן אֶתְכֶם לְשֵׁם וְלִתְהִלָּה בְּכֹל עַמֵּי הָאָרֶץ
בְּשׁוּבִי אֶת־שְׁבוּתֵיכֶם לְעֵינֵיכֶם
אָמַר יהוה:

OFFERINGS

The sages held that, in the absence of the Temple, studying the laws of sacrifices is the equivalent of offering them. Hence the following texts. There are different customs as to how many passages are to be said, and one should follow the custom of one's congregation. The minimum requirement is to say the verses relating to The Daily Sacrifice on the next page.

THE BASIN

The LORD spoke to Moses, saying: Make a bronze basin, with *Ex. 30* its bronze stand for washing, and place it between the Tent of Meeting and the altar, and put water in it. From it, Aaron and his sons are to wash their hands and feet. When they enter the Tent of Meeting, they shall wash with water so that they will not die; likewise when they approach the altar to minister, presenting a fire-offering to the LORD. They must wash their hands and feet so that they will not die. This shall be an everlasting ordinance for Aaron and his descendants throughout their generations.

TAKING OF THE ASHES

The LORD spoke to Moses, saying: Instruct Aaron and his sons, *Lev. 6* saying, This is the law of the burnt-offering. The burnt-offering shall remain on the altar hearth throughout the night until morning, and the altar fire shall be kept burning on it. The priest shall then put on his linen garments, and linen breeches next to his body, and shall remove the ashes of the burnt-offering that the fire has consumed on the altar and place them beside the altar. Then he shall take off these clothes and put on others, and carry the ashes outside the camp to a clean place. The fire on the altar must be kept burning; it must not go out. Each morning the priest shall burn wood on it, and prepare on it the burnt-offering and burn the fat of the peace-offerings. A perpetual fire must be kept burning on the altar; it must not go out.

May it be Your will, LORD our God and God of our ancestors, that You have compassion on us and pardon us all our sins, grant atonement for all our iniquities and forgive all our transgressions. May You rebuild the Temple swiftly in our days so that we may offer You the continual-offering that it may atone for us as You have prescribed for us in Your Torah through Moses Your servant, from the mouthpiece of Your glory, as it is said:

סדר הקרבנות

חז״ל held that, in the absence of the Temple, studying the laws of sacrifices is the equivalent of offering them. Hence the following texts. There are different customs as to how many passages are to be said, and one should follow the custom of one's congregation. The minimum requirement is to say the verses relating to the קרבן תמיד on the next page.

פרשת הכיור

וַיְדַבֵּר יהוה אֶל־מֹשֶׁה לֵּאמֹר: וְעָשִׂיתָ כִּיּוֹר נְחֹשֶׁת וְכַנּוֹ נְחֹשֶׁת לְרָחְצָה, שמות ל
וְנָתַתָּ אֹתוֹ בֵּין־אֹהֶל מוֹעֵד וּבֵין הַמִּזְבֵּחַ, וְנָתַתָּ שָׁמָּה מָיִם: וְרָחֲצוּ אַהֲרֹן
וּבָנָיו מִמֶּנּוּ אֶת־יְדֵיהֶם וְאֶת־רַגְלֵיהֶם: בְּבֹאָם אֶל־אֹהֶל מוֹעֵד יִרְחֲצוּ־
מַיִם, וְלֹא יָמֻתוּ, אוֹ בְגִשְׁתָּם אֶל־הַמִּזְבֵּחַ לְשָׁרֵת, לְהַקְטִיר אִשֶּׁה לַיהוה:
וְרָחֲצוּ יְדֵיהֶם וְרַגְלֵיהֶם וְלֹא יָמֻתוּ, וְהָיְתָה לָהֶם חָק־עוֹלָם, לוֹ וּלְזַרְעוֹ
לְדֹרֹתָם:

פרשת תרומת הדשן

וַיְדַבֵּר יהוה אֶל־מֹשֶׁה לֵּאמֹר: צַו אֶת־אַהֲרֹן וְאֶת־בָּנָיו לֵאמֹר, זֹאת ויקרא
תּוֹרַת הָעֹלָה, הִוא הָעֹלָה עַל מוֹקְדָה עַל־הַמִּזְבֵּחַ כָּל־הַלַּיְלָה עַד־
הַבֹּקֶר, וְאֵשׁ הַמִּזְבֵּחַ תּוּקַד בּוֹ: וְלָבַשׁ הַכֹּהֵן מִדּוֹ בַד, וּמִכְנְסֵי־בַד יִלְבַּשׁ
עַל־בְּשָׂרוֹ, וְהֵרִים אֶת־הַדֶּשֶׁן אֲשֶׁר תֹּאכַל הָאֵשׁ אֶת־הָעֹלָה, עַל־
הַמִּזְבֵּחַ, וְשָׂמוֹ אֵצֶל הַמִּזְבֵּחַ: וּפָשַׁט אֶת־בְּגָדָיו, וְלָבַשׁ בְּגָדִים אֲחֵרִים,
וְהוֹצִיא אֶת־הַדֶּשֶׁן אֶל־מִחוּץ לַמַּחֲנֶה, אֶל־מָקוֹם טָהוֹר: וְהָאֵשׁ עַל־
הַמִּזְבֵּחַ תּוּקַד־בּוֹ, לֹא תִכְבֶּה, וּבִעֵר עָלֶיהָ הַכֹּהֵן עֵצִים בַּבֹּקֶר בַּבֹּקֶר,
וְעָרַךְ עָלֶיהָ הָעֹלָה, וְהִקְטִיר עָלֶיהָ חֶלְבֵי הַשְּׁלָמִים: אֵשׁ, תָּמִיד תּוּקַד
עַל־הַמִּזְבֵּחַ, לֹא תִכְבֶּה:

יְהִי רָצוֹן מִלְּפָנֶיךָ יהוה אֱלֹהֵינוּ וֵאלֹהֵי אֲבוֹתֵינוּ, שֶׁתְּרַחֵם עָלֵינוּ, וְתִמְחָל לָנוּ עַל כָּל
חַטֹּאתֵינוּ וּתְכַפֵּר לָנוּ עַל כָּל עֲוֹנוֹתֵינוּ וְתִסְלַח לָנוּ עַל כָּל פְּשָׁעֵינוּ, וְתִבְנֶה בֵּית הַמִּקְדָּשׁ
בִּמְהֵרָה בְיָמֵינוּ, וְנַקְרִיב לְפָנֶיךָ קָרְבַּן הַתָּמִיד שֶׁיְּכַפֵּר בַּעֲדֵנוּ, כְּמוֹ שֶׁכָּתַבְתָּ עָלֵינוּ בְּתוֹרָתֶךָ
עַל יְדֵי מֹשֶׁה עַבְדֶּךָ מִפִּי כְבוֹדֶךָ, כָּאָמוּר

THE DAILY SACRIFICE

וַיְדַבֵּר The LORD said to Moses, "Command the Israelites and *Num. 28*
tell them: 'Be careful to offer to Me at the appointed time
My food-offering consumed by fire, as an aroma pleasing to
Me.' Tell them: 'This is the fire-offering you shall offer to the
LORD – two lambs a year old without blemish, as a regular
burnt-offering each day. Prepare one lamb in the morning and
the other toward evening, together with a meal-offering of a
tenth of an ephah of fine flour mixed with a quarter of a hin of
oil from pressed olives. This is the regular burnt-offering instituted at Mount Sinai as a pleasing aroma, a fire-offering made
to the LORD. Its libation is to be a quarter of a hin [of wine]
with each lamb, poured in the Sanctuary as a libation of strong
drink to the LORD. Prepare the second lamb in the afternoon,
along with the same meal-offering and libation as in the morning. This is a fire-offering, an aroma pleasing to the LORD.'"

| CONNECTION | ... A THOUSAND WORDS |

*The Gemara (Sota 49a)
recalls that when the
Greek army besieged
Jerusalem, the Koha-
nim would lower a
purse full of money
over the walls, and the
Greeks, in return, sent
over two lambs for the*
korban tamid *sacri-
fices. One day an evil
elderly man saw this
and said to the Greeks, "As long as the Jews continue to offer the* korban tamid *sacrifice,
you will never defeat them!" The next day, as usual, the Kohanim lowered a bag full of
money over the wall in anticipation of a lamb for their* korban. *In return, instead of a lamb,
the Greeks sent a pig. From that day on, the* korban tamid *could no longer be brought and
soon thereafter the Temple was destroyed.*

פרשת קרבן התמיד

וַיְדַבֵּר יהוה אֶל־מֹשֶׁה לֵּאמֹר: צַו אֶת־בְּנֵי יִשְׂרָאֵל וְאָמַרְתָּ אֲלֵהֶם, אֶת־קָרְבָּנִי לַחְמִי לְאִשַּׁי, רֵיחַ נִיחֹחִי, תִּשְׁמְרוּ לְהַקְרִיב לִי בְּמוֹעֲדוֹ: וְאָמַרְתָּ לָהֶם, זֶה הָאִשֶּׁה אֲשֶׁר תַּקְרִיבוּ לַיהוה, כְּבָשִׂים בְּנֵי־שָׁנָה תְמִימִם שְׁנַיִם לַיּוֹם, עֹלָה תָמִיד: אֶת־הַכֶּבֶשׂ אֶחָד תַּעֲשֶׂה בַבֹּקֶר, וְאֵת הַכֶּבֶשׂ הַשֵּׁנִי תַּעֲשֶׂה בֵּין הָעַרְבָּיִם: וַעֲשִׂירִית הָאֵיפָה סֹלֶת לְמִנְחָה, בְּלוּלָה בְּשֶׁמֶן כָּתִית רְבִיעִת הַהִין: עֹלַת תָּמִיד, הָעֲשֻׂיָה בְּהַר סִינַי, לְרֵיחַ נִיחֹחַ אִשֶּׁה לַיהוה: וְנִסְכּוֹ רְבִיעִת הַהִין לַכֶּבֶשׂ הָאֶחָד, בַּקֹּדֶשׁ הַסֵּךְ נֶסֶךְ שֵׁכָר לַיהוה: וְאֵת הַכֶּבֶשׂ הַשֵּׁנִי תַּעֲשֶׂה בֵּין הָעַרְבָּיִם, כְּמִנְחַת הַבֹּקֶר וּכְנִסְכּוֹ תַּעֲשֶׂה, אִשֶּׁה רֵיחַ נִיחֹחַ לַיהוה:

במדבר כח

What are you
committed to
doing every
single day?

What is the
value of doing
the same thing
every day?

Are there areas
in your relation-
ship with God
in which you
could be more
consistent?

"Other religions and belief systems focus almost entirely on
spiritual peaks – on those exceptional bursts of upliftment,
enlightenment, and elevation, on the once-a-year celebration.
We, too, have our celebrations, our pinnacles and peaks, but
these are not the essence of our spiritual growth. Judaism
focuses particularly on the everyday, the common, regular,
mundane activities which comprise the bulk of our lives....
From the very beginning of the Tabernacle's function and
every day thereafter, a new foundation is laid – a foundation
consisting of the most regular, the most plain, daily sacrifice. In order to build any building, to create any framework,
one needs to focus not on the one-time opening ceremony,
but rather on the daily routine, the ordinary, gray, unnoticed
things which form the framework's basis. It is these things
which define the context and matrix in which all actions, all
thoughts and all other development take place." (Rav Aharon
Lichtenstein, The Daily Sacrifice – "A Great Principle of the Torah")

וְשָׁחַט He shall slaughter it at the north side of the altar before *Lev. 1* the LORD, and Aaron's sons the priests shall sprinkle its blood against the altar on all sides.

May it be Your will, LORD our God and God of our ancestors, that this recitation be considered accepted and favored before You as if we had offered the daily sacrifice at its appointed time and place, according to its laws.

It is You, LORD our God, to whom our ancestors offered fragrant incense when the Temple stood, as You commanded them through Moses Your prophet, as is written in Your Torah:

THE INCENSE

The LORD said to Moses: Take fragrant spices – balsam, onycha, galba- *Ex. 30* num and pure frankincense, all in equal amounts – and make a fragrant blend of incense, the work of a perfumer, well mixed, pure and holy. Grind it very finely and place it in front of the [Ark of] Testimony in the Tent of Meeting, where I will meet with you. It shall be most holy to you.

And it is said:

Aaron shall burn fragrant incense on the altar every morning when he cleans the lamps. He shall burn incense again when he lights the lamps toward evening so that there will be incense before the LORD at all times, throughout your generations.

The rabbis taught: How was the incense prepared? It weighed 368 manehs, 365 cor- *Keritot 6a* responding to the number of days in a solar year, a maneh for each day, half to be offered in the morning and half in the afternoon, and three additional manehs from which the High Priest took two handfuls on Yom Kippur. These were put back into the mortar on the day before Yom Kippur and ground again very thoroughly so as to be extremely fine. The incense contained eleven kinds of spices: balsam, onycha, galbanum and frankincense, each weighing seventy manehs; myrrh, cassia, spikenard and saffron, each weighing sixteen manehs; twelve manehs of costus, three of aromatic bark; nine of cinnamon; nine kabs of Carsina lye; three seahs and three kabs of Cyprus wine. If Cyprus wine was not available, old white wine might be used. A quarter of a kab of Sodom salt, and a minute amount of a smoke-raising herb. Rabbi Nathan the Babylonian says: also a minute amount of Jordan amber. If one added honey to the mixture, he rendered it unfit for sacred use. If he omitted any one of its ingredients, he is guilty of a capital offence.

Rabban Simeon ben Gamliel says: "Balsam" refers to the sap that drips from the balsam tree. The Carsina lye was used for bleaching the onycha to improve it. The Cyprus wine was used to soak the onycha in it to make it pungent. Though urine is suitable for this purpose, it is not brought into the Temple out of respect.

וְשָׁחַט אֹתוֹ עַל יֶרֶךְ הַמִּזְבֵּחַ צָפֹנָה לִפְנֵי יְהוָה, וְזָרְקוּ בְּנֵי אַהֲרֹן ויקרא א
הַכֹּהֲנִים אֶת־דָּמוֹ עַל־הַמִּזְבֵּחַ, סָבִיב:

יְהִי רָצוֹן מִלְּפָנֶיךָ, יְהוָה אֱלֹהֵינוּ וֵאלֹהֵי אֲבוֹתֵינוּ, שֶׁתְּהֵא אֲמִירָה זוֹ חֲשׁוּבָה וּמְקֻבֶּלֶת
וּמְרֻצָּה לְפָנֶיךָ, כְּאִלּוּ הִקְרַבְנוּ קָרְבַּן הַתָּמִיד בְּמוֹעֲדוֹ וּבִמְקוֹמוֹ וּכְהִלְכָתוֹ.

אַתָּה הוּא יְהוָה אֱלֹהֵינוּ שֶׁהִקְטִירוּ אֲבוֹתֵינוּ לְפָנֶיךָ אֶת קְטֹרֶת הַסַּמִּים בִּזְמַן שֶׁבֵּית
הַמִּקְדָּשׁ הָיָה קַיָּם, כַּאֲשֶׁר צִוִּיתָ אוֹתָם עַל יְדֵי מֹשֶׁה נְבִיאֶךָ, כַּכָּתוּב בְּתוֹרָתֶךָ:

פרשת הקטורת

וַיֹּאמֶר יְהוָה אֶל־מֹשֶׁה, קַח־לְךָ סַמִּים נָטָף וּשְׁחֵלֶת וְחֶלְבְּנָה, סַמִּים וּלְבֹנָה שמות ל
זַכָּה, בַּד בְּבַד יִהְיֶה: וְעָשִׂיתָ אֹתָהּ קְטֹרֶת, רֹקַח מַעֲשֵׂה רוֹקֵחַ, מְמֻלָּח, טָהוֹר
קֹדֶשׁ: וְשָׁחַקְתָּ מִמֶּנָּה הָדֵק, וְנָתַתָּה מִמֶּנָּה לִפְנֵי הָעֵדֻת בְּאֹהֶל מוֹעֵד אֲשֶׁר
אִוָּעֵד לְךָ שָׁמָּה, קֹדֶשׁ קָדָשִׁים תִּהְיֶה לָכֶם:

וְנֶאֱמַר

וְהִקְטִיר עָלָיו אַהֲרֹן קְטֹרֶת סַמִּים, בַּבֹּקֶר בַּבֹּקֶר בְּהֵיטִיבוֹ אֶת־הַנֵּרֹת
יַקְטִירֶנָּה: וּבְהַעֲלֹת אַהֲרֹן אֶת־הַנֵּרֹת בֵּין הָעַרְבַּיִם יַקְטִירֶנָּה, קְטֹרֶת תָּמִיד
לִפְנֵי יְהוָה לְדֹרֹתֵיכֶם:

תָּנוּ רַבָּנָן: פִּטּוּם הַקְּטֹרֶת כֵּיצַד, שְׁלֹשׁ מֵאוֹת וְשִׁשִּׁים וּשְׁמוֹנָה מָנִים הָיוּ בָהּ. שְׁלֹשׁ כריתות ו
מֵאוֹת וְשִׁשִּׁים וַחֲמִשָּׁה כְּמִנְיַן יְמוֹת הַחַמָּה, מָנֶה לְכָל יוֹם, פְּרַס בְּשַׁחֲרִית וּפְרַס
בֵּין הָעַרְבַּיִם, וּשְׁלֹשָׁה מָנִים יְתֵרִים שֶׁמֵּהֶם מַכְנִיס כֹּהֵן גָּדוֹל מְלֹא חָפְנָיו בְּיוֹם
הַכִּפּוּרִים, וּמַחֲזִירָן לְמַכְתֶּשֶׁת בְּעֶרֶב יוֹם הַכִּפּוּרִים וְשׁוֹחֵק יָפֶה יָפֶה, כְּדֵי שֶׁתְּהֵא
דַקָּה מִן הַדַּקָּה. וְאֶחָד עָשָׂר סַמָּנִים הָיוּ בָהּ, וְאֵלּוּ הֵן: הַצֳּרִי, וְהַצִּפֹּרֶן, וְהַחֶלְבְּנָה,
וְהַלְּבוֹנָה מִשְׁקָל שִׁבְעִים שִׁבְעִים מָנֶה, מוֹר, וּקְצִיעָה, שִׁבֹּלֶת נֵרְדְּ, וְכַרְכֹּם מִשְׁקָל
שִׁשָּׁה עָשָׂר שִׁשָּׁה עָשָׂר מָנֶה, הַקֹּשְׁטְ שְׁנֵים עָשָׂר, קִלּוּפָה שְׁלֹשָׁה, קִנָּמוֹן תִּשְׁעָה,
בֹּרִית כַּרְשִׁינָה תִּשְׁעָה קַבִּין, יֵין קַפְרִיסִין סְאִין תְּלָת וְקַבִּין תְּלָתָא, וְאִם לֹא מָצָא
יֵין קַפְרִיסִין, מֵבִיא חֲמַר חִוַּרְיָן עַתִּיק. מֶלַח סְדוֹמִית רֹבַע, מַעֲלֶה עָשָׁן כָּל שֶׁהוּא.
רַבִּי נָתָן הַבַּבְלִי אוֹמֵר: אַף כִּפַּת הַיַּרְדֵּן כָּל שֶׁהוּא, וְאִם נָתַן בָּהּ דְּבַשׁ פְּסָלָהּ, וְאִם
חִסֵּר אֶחָד מִכָּל סַמָּנֶיהָ, חַיָּב מִיתָה.

רַבָּן שִׁמְעוֹן בֶּן גַּמְלִיאֵל אוֹמֵר: הַצֳּרִי אֵינוֹ אֶלָּא שְׂרָף הַנּוֹטֵף מֵעֲצֵי הַקְּטָף. בֹּרִית
כַּרְשִׁינָה שֶׁשָּׁפִין בָּהּ אֶת הַצִּפֹּרֶן כְּדֵי שֶׁתְּהֵא נָאָה, יֵין קַפְרִיסִין שֶׁשּׁוֹרִין בּוֹ אֶת
הַצִּפֹּרֶן כְּדֵי שֶׁתְּהֵא עַזָּה, וַהֲלֹא מֵי רַגְלַיִם יָפִין לָהּ, אֶלָּא שֶׁאֵין מַכְנִיסִין מֵי רַגְלַיִם
בַּמִּקְדָּשׁ מִפְּנֵי הַכָּבוֹד.

It was taught, Rabbi Nathan says: While it was being ground, another would say, "Grind well, well grind," because the [rhythmic] sound is good for spices. If it was mixed in half-quantities, it is fit for use, but we have not heard whether this applies to a third or a quarter. Rabbi Judah said: The general rule is that if it was made in the correct proportions, it is fit for use even if made in half-quantity, but if he omitted any one of its ingredients, he is guilty of a capital offense.

It was taught, Bar Kappara says: Once every sixty or seventy years, the accumulated surpluses amounted to half the yearly quantity. Bar Kappara also taught: If a minute quantity of honey had been mixed into the incense, no one could have resisted the scent. Why did they not put honey into it? Because the Torah says, "For you are not to burn any leaven or honey in a fire-offering made to the LORD." *JT Yoma 4:5* *Lev. 2*

The following three verses are each said three times:

The LORD of multitudes is with us; the God of Jacob is our stronghold, Selah. *Ps. 46*

LORD of multitudes, happy is the one who trusts in You. *Ps. 84*

LORD, save! May the King answer us on the day we call. *Ps. 20*

You are my hiding place; You will protect me from distress and surround me with songs of salvation, Selah. Then the offering of Judah and Jerusalem will be pleasing to the LORD as in the days of old and as in former years. *Ps. 32* *Mal. 3*

THE ORDER OF THE PRIESTLY FUNCTIONS

Abaye related the order of the daily priestly functions in the name of tradition and in accordance with Abba Shaul: The large pile [of wood] comes before the second pile for the incense; the second pile for the incense precedes the laying in order of the two logs of wood; the laying in order of the two logs of wood comes before the removing of ashes from the inner altar; the removing of ashes from the inner altar precedes the cleaning of the five lamps; the cleaning of the five lamps comes before the blood of the daily offering; the blood of the daily offering precedes the cleaning of the [other] two lamps; the cleaning of the two lamps comes before the incense-offering; the incense-offering precedes the burning of the limbs; the burning of the limbs comes before the meal-offering; the meal-offering precedes the pancakes; the pancakes come before the wine-libations; the wine-libations precede the additional offerings; the additional offerings come before the [frankincense] censers; the censers precede the daily afternoon offering; as it is said, "On it he shall arrange burnt-offerings, and on it he shall burn the fat of the peace-offerings" – "on it" [the daily offering] all the offerings were completed. *Yoma 33a* *Lev. 6*

Please, by the power of Your great right hand, set the captive nation free. Accept Your people's prayer. Strengthen us, purify us, You who are feared. Please, Mighty One, guard like the pupil of the eye those who seek Your unity. Bless them, cleanse them, have compassion on them, give them Your righteousness always. Mighty One, Holy One, in Your great goodness guide Your congregation. Only One, elevated One, turn to Your people, who declare Your holiness. Accept our plea and listen to our cry, You who know all secret thoughts.

Blessed be the name of His glorious kingdom for ever and all time.

תַּנְיָא, רַבִּי נָתָן אוֹמֵר: כְּשֶׁהוּא שׁוֹחֵק אוֹמֵר, הָדֵק הֵיטֵב הֵיטֵב הָדֵק, מִפְּנֵי שֶׁהַקּוֹל יָפֶה לַבְּשָׂמִים. פִּטְּמָהּ לַחֲצָאִין כְּשֵׁרָה, לִשְׁלִישׁ וְלִרְבִיעַ לֹא שָׁמֵעְנוּ. אָמַר רַבִּי יְהוּדָה: זֶה הַכְּלָל, אִם כְּמִדָּתָהּ כְּשֵׁרָה לַחֲצָאִין, וְאִם חִסַּר אֶחָד מִכָּל סַמְּמָנֶיהָ חַיָּב מִיתָה.

ירושלמי
יומא ד,
הלכה ה

ויקרא ב

תַּנְיָא, בַּר קַפָּרָא אוֹמֵר: אַחַת לְשִׁשִּׁים אוֹ לְשִׁבְעִים שָׁנָה הָיְתָה בָאָה שֶׁל שִׁירַיִם לַחֲצָאִין. וְעוֹד תָּנֵי בַּר קַפָּרָא: אִלּוּ הָיָה נוֹתֵן בָּהּ קוֹרְטוֹב שֶׁל דְּבַשׁ אֵין אָדָם יָכוֹל לַעֲמֹד מִפְּנֵי רֵיחָהּ, וְלָמָּה אֵין מְעָרְבִין בָּהּ דְּבַשׁ, מִפְּנֵי שֶׁהַתּוֹרָה אָמְרָה: כִּי כָל־שְׂאֹר וְכָל־דְּבַשׁ לֹא־תַקְטִירוּ מִמֶּנּוּ אִשֶּׁה לַיהוה:

The following three verses are each said three times:

תהלים מו

תהלים פד

תהלים כ

יהוה צְבָאוֹת עִמָּנוּ, מִשְׂגָּב לָנוּ אֱלֹהֵי יַעֲקֹב סֶלָה:

יהוה צְבָאוֹת, אַשְׁרֵי אָדָם בֹּטֵחַ בָּךְ:

יהוה הוֹשִׁיעָה, הַמֶּלֶךְ יַעֲנֵנוּ בְיוֹם־קָרְאֵנוּ:

תהלים לב

מלאכי ג

אַתָּה סֵתֶר לִי, מִצַּר תִּצְּרֵנִי, רָנֵּי פַלֵּט תְּסוֹבְבֵנִי סֶלָה:

וְעָרְבָה לַיהוה מִנְחַת יְהוּדָה וִירוּשָׁלָ͏ִם, כִּימֵי עוֹלָם וּכְשָׁנִים קַדְמֹנִיּוֹת:

סדר המערכה

יומא לג

אַבַּיֵי הֲוָה מְסַדֵּר סֵדֶר הַמַּעֲרָכָה מִשְּׁמָא דִגְמָרָא, וְאַלִּבָּא דְאַבָּא שָׁאוּל: מַעֲרָכָה גְדוֹלָה קוֹדֶמֶת לְמַעֲרָכָה שְׁנִיָּה שֶׁל קְטֹרֶת, וּמַעֲרָכָה שְׁנִיָּה שֶׁל קְטֹרֶת קוֹדֶמֶת לְסִדּוּר שְׁנֵי גִזְרֵי עֵצִים, וְסִדּוּר שְׁנֵי גִזְרֵי עֵצִים קוֹדֵם לְדִשּׁוּן מִזְבֵּחַ הַפְּנִימִי, וְדִשּׁוּן מִזְבֵּחַ הַפְּנִימִי קוֹדֵם לַהֲטָבַת חָמֵשׁ נֵרוֹת, וַהֲטָבַת חָמֵשׁ נֵרוֹת קוֹדֶמֶת לְדַם הַתָּמִיד, וְדַם הַתָּמִיד קוֹדֵם לַהֲטָבַת שְׁתֵּי נֵרוֹת, וַהֲטָבַת שְׁתֵּי נֵרוֹת קוֹדֶמֶת לִקְטֹרֶת, וּקְטֹרֶת קוֹדֶמֶת לְאֵבָרִים, וְאֵבָרִים לְמִנְחָה, וּמִנְחָה לַחֲבִתִּין, וַחֲבִתִּין לִנְסָכִין, וּנְסָכִין לְמוּסָפִין, וּמוּסָפִין לְבָזִיכִין, וּבָזִיכִין קוֹדְמִין לְתָמִיד שֶׁל בֵּין הָעַרְבָּיִם. שֶׁנֶּאֱמַר: וְעָרַךְ עָלֶיהָ הָעֹלָה, וְהִקְטִיר עָלֶיהָ חֶלְבֵי הַשְּׁלָמִים: עָלֶיהָ הַשְׁלֵם כָּל הַקָּרְבָּנוֹת כֻּלָּם.

ויקרא ו

אָנָּא, בְּכֹחַ גְּדֻלַּת יְמִינְךָ, תַּתִּיר צְרוּרָה.
קַבֵּל רִנַּת עַמְּךָ, שַׂגְּבֵנוּ, טַהֲרֵנוּ, נוֹרָא.
נָא גִבּוֹר, דּוֹרְשֵׁי יִחוּדְךָ כְּבָבַת שָׁמְרֵם.
בָּרְכֵם, טַהֲרֵם, רַחֲמֵם, צִדְקָתְךָ תָּמִיד גָּמְלֵם.
חֲסִין קָדוֹשׁ, בְּרֹב טוּבְךָ נַהֵל עֲדָתֶךָ.
יָחִיד גֵּאֶה, לְעַמְּךָ פְּנֵה, זוֹכְרֵי קְדֻשָּׁתֶךָ.
שַׁוְעָתֵנוּ קַבֵּל וּשְׁמַע צַעֲקָתֵנוּ, יוֹדֵעַ תַּעֲלוּמוֹת.
בָּרוּךְ שֵׁם כְּבוֹד מַלְכוּתוֹ לְעוֹלָם וָעֶד.

Master of the Universe, You have commanded us to offer the daily sacrifice at its appointed time with the priests at their service, the Levites on their platform, and the Israelites at their post. Now, because of our sins, the Temple is destroyed and the daily sacrifice discontinued, and we have no priest at his service, no Levite on his platform, no Israelite at his post. But You said: "We will offer in place of bullocks [the prayer of] our lips." Therefore may it be Your will, Lord our God and God of our ancestors, that the prayer of our lips be considered, accepted and favored before You as if we had offered the daily sacrifice at its appointed time and place, according to its laws.

Hos. 14

On Rosh Ḥodesh:

וּבְרָאשֵׁי חָדְשֵׁיכֶם On your new moons, present as a burnt-offering to the Lord, two young bulls, one ram, and seven yearling lambs without blemish. There shall be a meal-offering of three-tenths of an ephah of fine flour mixed with oil for each bull, two-tenths of an ephah of fine flour mixed with oil for the ram, and one-tenth of an ephah of fine flour mixed with oil for each lamb. This is the burnt-offering – a fire-offering of pleasing aroma to the Lord. Their libations shall be: half a hin of wine for each bull, a third of a hin for the ram, and a quarter of a hin for each lamb. This is the monthly burnt-offering to be made at each new moon throughout the year. One male goat should be offered as a sin-offering to God, in addition to the regular daily burnt-offering and its libation.

Num. 28

LAWS OF OFFERINGS, MISHNA ZEVAḤIM

אֵיזֶהוּ מְקוֹמָן What is the location for sacrifices? The holiest offerings were slaughtered on the north side. The bull and he-goat of Yom Kippur were slaughtered on the north side. Their blood was received in a sacred vessel on the north side, and had to be sprinkled between the poles [of the Ark], toward the veil [screening the Holy of Holies], and on the golden altar. [The omission of] one of these sprinklings invalidated [the atonement ceremony]. The leftover blood was to be poured onto the western base of the outer altar. If this was not done, however, the omission did not invalidate [the ceremony].

Zevaḥim Ch. 5

The bulls and he-goats that were completely burnt were slaughtered on the north side, their blood was received in a sacred vessel on the north side, and had to be sprinkled toward the veil and on the golden altar. [The omission of] one of these sprinklings invalidated [the ceremony]. The leftover blood was to be poured onto the western base of the outer altar. If this was not done, however, the omission did not invalidate [the ceremony]. All these offerings were burnt where the altar ashes were deposited.

The communal and individual sin-offerings – these are the communal sin-offerings: the he-goats offered on Rosh Ḥodesh and Festivals were slaughtered on the north side, their blood was received in a sacred vessel on the north side, and required four sprinklings, one on each of the four corners of the altar. How was this done? The

רִבּוֹן הָעוֹלָמִים, אַתָּה צִוִּיתָנוּ לְהַקְרִיב קָרְבַּן הַתָּמִיד בְּמוֹעֲדוֹ וְלִהְיוֹת כֹּהֲנִים בַּעֲבוֹדָתָם וּלְוִיִּים בְּדוּכָנָם וְיִשְׂרָאֵל בְּמַעֲמָדָם, וְעַתָּה בַּעֲוֹנוֹתֵינוּ חָרַב בֵּית הַמִּקְדָּשׁ וּבָטַל הַתָּמִיד וְאֵין לָנוּ לֹא כֹהֵן בַּעֲבוֹדָתוֹ וְלֹא לֵוִי בְּדוּכָנוֹ וְלֹא יִשְׂרָאֵל בְּמַעֲמָדוֹ, וְאַתָּה אָמַרְתָּ: וּנְשַׁלְּמָה פָרִים שְׂפָתֵינוּ: לָכֵן יְהִי רָצוֹן מִלְּפָנֶיךָ יהוה אֱלֹהֵינוּ וֵאלֹהֵי הוֹשֵׁעַ יד אֲבוֹתֵינוּ, שֶׁיְּהֵא שִׂיחַ שִׂפְתוֹתֵינוּ חָשׁוּב וּמְקֻבָּל וּמְרֻצֶּה לְפָנֶיךָ, כְּאִלּוּ הִקְרַבְנוּ קָרְבַּן הַתָּמִיד בְּמוֹעֲדוֹ וּבִמְקוֹמוֹ וּכְהִלְכָתוֹ.

וּבְרָאשֵׁי חָדְשֵׁיכֶם תַּקְרִיבוּ עֹלָה לַיהוה, פָּרִים בְּנֵי־בָקָר שְׁנַיִם, בַּמִּדְבָּר כח בְּרֹאשׁ חוֹדֶשׁ: וְאַיִל אֶחָד, כְּבָשִׂים בְּנֵי־שָׁנָה שִׁבְעָה, תְּמִימִם: וּשְׁלֹשָׁה עֶשְׂרֹנִים סֹלֶת מִנְחָה בְּלוּלָה בַשֶּׁמֶן לַפָּר הָאֶחָד, וּשְׁנֵי עֶשְׂרֹנִים סֹלֶת מִנְחָה בְּלוּלָה בַשֶּׁמֶן לָאַיִל הָאֶחָד: וְעִשָּׂרֹן עִשָּׂרוֹן סֹלֶת מִנְחָה בְּלוּלָה בַשֶּׁמֶן לַכֶּבֶשׂ הָאֶחָד, עֹלָה רֵיחַ נִיחֹחַ, אִשֶּׁה לַיהוה: וְנִסְכֵּיהֶם, חֲצִי הַהִין יִהְיֶה לַפָּר, וּשְׁלִישִׁת הַהִין לָאַיִל, וּרְבִיעִת הַהִין לַכֶּבֶשׂ יָיִן, זֹאת עֹלַת חֹדֶשׁ בְּחָדְשׁוֹ לְחָדְשֵׁי הַשָּׁנָה: וּשְׂעִיר עִזִּים אֶחָד לְחַטָּאת לַיהוה, עַל־עֹלַת הַתָּמִיד יֵעָשֶׂה, וְנִסְכּוֹ:

דיני זבחים

אֵיזֶהוּ מְקוֹמָן שֶׁל זְבָחִים. קָדְשֵׁי קָדָשִׁים שְׁחִיטָתָן בַּצָּפוֹן. פָּר וְשָׂעִיר שֶׁל זְבָחִים פֶּרֶק ה יוֹם הַכִּפּוּרִים, שְׁחִיטָתָן בַּצָּפוֹן, וְקִבּוּל דָּמָן בִּכְלִי שָׁרֵת בַּצָּפוֹן, וְדָמָן טָעוּן הַזָּיָה עַל בֵּין הַבַּדִּים, וְעַל הַפָּרֹכֶת, וְעַל מִזְבַּח הַזָּהָב. מַתָּנָה אַחַת מֵהֶן מְעַכֶּבֶת. שְׁיָרֵי הַדָּם הָיָה שׁוֹפֵךְ עַל יְסוֹד מַעֲרָבִי שֶׁל מִזְבֵּחַ הַחִיצוֹן, אִם לֹא נָתַן לֹא עִכֵּב.

פָּרִים הַנִּשְׂרָפִים וּשְׂעִירִים הַנִּשְׂרָפִים, שְׁחִיטָתָן בַּצָּפוֹן, וְקִבּוּל דָּמָן בִּכְלִי שָׁרֵת בַּצָּפוֹן, וְדָמָן טָעוּן הַזָּיָה עַל הַפָּרֹכֶת וְעַל מִזְבַּח הַזָּהָב. מַתָּנָה אַחַת מֵהֶן מְעַכֶּבֶת. שְׁיָרֵי הַדָּם הָיָה שׁוֹפֵךְ עַל יְסוֹד מַעֲרָבִי שֶׁל מִזְבֵּחַ הַחִיצוֹן, אִם לֹא נָתַן לֹא עִכֵּב. אֵלּוּ וָאֵלּוּ נִשְׂרָפִין בְּבֵית הַדָּשֶׁן.

חַטֹּאת הַצִּבּוּר וְהַיָּחִיד. אֵלּוּ הֵן חַטֹּאת הַצִּבּוּר: שְׂעִירֵי רָאשֵׁי חֳדָשִׁים וְשֶׁל מוֹעֲדוֹת. שְׁחִיטָתָן בַּצָּפוֹן, וְקִבּוּל דָּמָן בִּכְלִי שָׁרֵת בַּצָּפוֹן, וְדָמָן טָעוּן אַרְבַּע

priest ascended the ramp and turned [right] onto the surrounding ledge. He came to the southeast corner, then went to the northeast, then to the northwest, then to the southwest. The leftover blood he poured onto the southern base. [The meat of these offerings], prepared in any manner, was eaten within the [courtyard] curtains, by males of the priest-hood, on that day and the following night, until midnight.

The burnt-offering was among the holiest of sacrifices. It was slaughtered on the north side, its blood was received in a sacred vessel on the north side, and required two sprinklings [at opposite corners of the altar], making four in all. The offering had to be flayed, dismembered and wholly consumed by fire.

The communal peace-offerings and the guilt-offerings – these are the guilt-offerings: the guilt-offering for robbery; the guilt-offering for profane use of a sacred object; the guilt-offering [for violating] a betrothed maidservant; the guilt-offering of a Nazirite [who had become defiled by a corpse]; the guilt-offering of a leper [at his cleansing]; and the guilt-offering in case of doubt. All these were slaughtered on the north side, their blood was received in a sacred vessel on the north side, and required two sprinklings [at opposite corners of the altar], making four in all. [The meat of these offerings], prepared in any manner, was eaten within the [courtyard] curtains, by males of the priesthood, on that day and the following night, until midnight.

The thanksgiving-offering and the ram of a Nazirite were offerings of lesser holiness. They could be slaughtered anywhere in the Temple court, and their blood required two sprinklings [at opposite corners of the altar], making four in all. The meat of these offerings, prepared in any manner, was eaten anywhere within the city [Jerusalem], by anyone during that day and the following night until midnight. This also applied to the portion of these sacrifices [given to the priests], except that the priests' portion was only to be eaten by the priests, their wives, children and servants.

Peace-offerings were [also] of lesser holiness. They could be slaughtered anywhere in the Temple court, and their blood required two sprinklings [at opposite corners of the altar], making four in all. The meat of these offerings, prepared in any manner, was eaten anywhere within the city [Jerusalem], by anyone, for two days and one night. This also applied to the portion of these sacrifices [given to the priests], except that the priests' portion was only to be eaten by the priests, their wives, children and servants.

The firstborn and tithe of cattle and the Pesaḥ lamb were sacrifices of lesser holiness. They could be slaughtered anywhere in the Temple court, and their blood required only one sprinkling, which had to be done at the base of the altar. They differed in their consumption: the firstborn was eaten only by priests, while the tithe could be eaten by anyone. Both could be eaten anywhere within the city, prepared in any manner, during two days and one night. The Pesaḥ lamb had to be eaten that night until midnight. It could only be eaten by those who had been numbered for it, and eaten only roasted.

מַתָּנוֹת עַל אַרְבַּע קְרָנוֹת. כֵּיצַד, עָלָה בַכֶּבֶשׁ, וּפָנָה לַסּוֹבֵב, וּבָא לוֹ לְקֶרֶן דְּרוֹמִית מִזְרָחִית, מִזְרָחִית צְפוֹנִית, צְפוֹנִית מַעֲרָבִית, מַעֲרָבִית דְּרוֹמִית. שְׁיָרֵי הַדָּם הָיָה שׁוֹפֵךְ עַל יְסוֹד דְּרוֹמִי. וְנֶאֱכָלִין לִפְנִים מִן הַקְּלָעִים, לְזִכְרֵי כְהֻנָּה, בְּכָל מַאֲכָל, לְיוֹם וָלַיְלָה עַד חֲצוֹת.

הָעוֹלָה קֹדֶשׁ קָדָשִׁים. שְׁחִיטָתָהּ בַּצָּפוֹן, וְקִבּוּל דָּמָהּ בִּכְלִי שָׁרֵת בַּצָּפוֹן, וְדָמָהּ טָעוּן שְׁתֵּי מַתָּנוֹת שֶׁהֵן אַרְבַּע, וּטְעוּנָה הֶפְשֵׁט וְנִתּוּחַ, וְכָלִיל לָאִשִּׁים.

זִבְחֵי שַׁלְמֵי צִבּוּר וַאֲשָׁמוֹת. אֵלּוּ הֵן אֲשָׁמוֹת: אֲשַׁם גְּזֵלוֹת, אֲשַׁם מְעִילוֹת, אֲשַׁם שִׁפְחָה חֲרוּפָה, אֲשַׁם נָזִיר, אֲשַׁם מְצֹרָע, אָשָׁם תָּלוּי. שְׁחִיטָתָן בַּצָּפוֹן, וְקִבּוּל דָּמָן בִּכְלִי שָׁרֵת בַּצָּפוֹן, וְדָמָן טָעוּן שְׁתֵּי מַתָּנוֹת שֶׁהֵן אַרְבַּע. וְנֶאֱכָלִין לִפְנִים מִן הַקְּלָעִים, לְזִכְרֵי כְהֻנָּה, בְּכָל מַאֲכָל, לְיוֹם וָלַיְלָה עַד חֲצוֹת.

הַתּוֹדָה וְאֵיל נָזִיר קָדָשִׁים קַלִּים. שְׁחִיטָתָן בְּכָל מָקוֹם בָּעֲזָרָה, וְדָמָן טָעוּן שְׁתֵּי מַתָּנוֹת שֶׁהֵן אַרְבַּע, וְנֶאֱכָלִין בְּכָל הָעִיר, לְכָל אָדָם, בְּכָל מַאֲכָל, לְיוֹם וָלַיְלָה עַד חֲצוֹת. הַמּוּרָם מֵהֶם כַּיּוֹצֵא בָהֶם, אֶלָּא שֶׁהַמּוּרָם נֶאֱכָל לַכֹּהֲנִים, לִנְשֵׁיהֶם, וְלִבְנֵיהֶם וּלְעַבְדֵּיהֶם.

שְׁלָמִים קָדָשִׁים קַלִּים. שְׁחִיטָתָן בְּכָל מָקוֹם בָּעֲזָרָה, וְדָמָן טָעוּן שְׁתֵּי מַתָּנוֹת שֶׁהֵן אַרְבַּע, וְנֶאֱכָלִין בְּכָל הָעִיר, לְכָל אָדָם, בְּכָל מַאֲכָל, לִשְׁנֵי יָמִים וְלַיְלָה אֶחָד. הַמּוּרָם מֵהֶם כַּיּוֹצֵא בָהֶם, אֶלָּא שֶׁהַמּוּרָם נֶאֱכָל לַכֹּהֲנִים, לִנְשֵׁיהֶם, וְלִבְנֵיהֶם וּלְעַבְדֵּיהֶם.

הַבְּכוֹר וְהַמַּעֲשֵׂר וְהַפֶּסַח קָדָשִׁים קַלִּים. שְׁחִיטָתָן בְּכָל מָקוֹם בָּעֲזָרָה, וְדָמָן טָעוּן מַתָּנָה אֶחָת, וּבִלְבַד שֶׁיִּתֵּן כְּנֶגֶד הַיְסוֹד. שִׁנָּה בַּאֲכִילָתָן, הַבְּכוֹר נֶאֱכָל לַכֹּהֲנִים וְהַמַּעֲשֵׂר לְכָל אָדָם, וְנֶאֱכָלִין בְּכָל הָעִיר, בְּכָל מַאֲכָל, לִשְׁנֵי יָמִים וְלַיְלָה אֶחָד. הַפֶּסַח אֵינוֹ נֶאֱכָל אֶלָּא בַלַּיְלָה, וְאֵינוֹ נֶאֱכָל אֶלָּא עַד חֲצוֹת, וְאֵינוֹ נֶאֱכָל אֶלָּא לִמְנוּיָיו, וְאֵינוֹ נֶאֱכָל אֶלָּא צָלִי.

THE INTERPRETIVE PRINCIPLES OF RABBI YISHMAEL

רַבִּי יִשְׁמָעֵאל Rabbi Yishmael says:

The Torah is expounded by thirteen principles:

1. An inference from a lenient law to a strict one, and vice versa.

2. An inference drawn from identical words in two passages.

3. A general principle derived from one text or two related texts.

4. A general law followed by specific examples
   [where the law applies exclusively to those examples].

5. A specific example followed by a general law
   [where the law applies to everything implied in the general statement].

6. A general law followed by specific examples and concluding with a general law:
   here you may infer only cases similar to the examples.

7. When a general statement requires clarification by a specific example,
   or a specific example requires clarification by a general statement
   [then rules 4 and 5 do not apply].

8. When a particular case, already included in the general statement,
   is expressly mentioned to teach something new, that special provision
   applies to all other cases included in the general statement.

9. When a particular case, though included in the general statement,
   is expressly mentioned with a provision similar to the general law,
   such a case is singled out to lessen the severity of the law, not to increase it.

10. When a particular case, though included in the general statement,
    is explicitly mentioned with a provision differing from the general law,
    it is singled out to lessen in some respects,
    and in others to increase, the severity of the law.

11. When a particular case, though included in the general statement,
    is explicitly mentioned with a new provision,
    the terms of the general statement no longer apply to it,
    unless Scripture indicates explicitly that they do apply.

12. A matter elucidated from its context, or from the following passage.

▸ 13. Also, when two passages [seem to] contradict each other,
     [they are to be elucidated by] a third passage that reconciles them.

May it be Your will, LORD our God and God of our ancestors, that the Temple be speedily rebuilt in our days, and grant us our share in Your Torah. And may we serve You there in reverence, as in the days of old and as in former years.

ברייתא דרבי ישמעאל

רַבִּי יִשְׁמָעֵאל אוֹמֵר: בִּשְׁלֹשׁ עֶשְׂרֵה מִדּוֹת הַתּוֹרָה נִדְרֶשֶׁת

א מִקַּל וָחֹמֶר

ב וּמִגְּזֵרָה שָׁוָה

ג מִבִּנְיַן אָב מִכָּתוּב אֶחָד, וּמִבִּנְיַן אָב מִשְּׁנֵי כְתוּבִים

ד מִכְּלָל וּפְרָט

ה מִפְּרָט וּכְלָל

ו כְּלָל וּפְרָט וּכְלָל, אִי אַתָּה דָן אֶלָּא כְּעֵין הַפְּרָט

ז מִכְּלָל שֶׁהוּא צָרִיךְ לִפְרָט, וּמִפְּרָט שֶׁהוּא צָרִיךְ לִכְלָל

ח כָּל דָּבָר שֶׁהָיָה בִּכְלָל, וְיָצָא מִן הַכְּלָל לְלַמֵּד
לֹא לְלַמֵּד עַל עַצְמוֹ יָצָא
אֶלָּא לְלַמֵּד עַל הַכְּלָל כֻּלּוֹ יָצָא

ט כָּל דָּבָר שֶׁהָיָה בִּכְלָל, וְיָצָא לִטְעוֹן טְעַן אֶחָד שֶׁהוּא כְעִנְיָנוֹ
יָצָא לְהָקֵל וְלֹא לְהַחֲמִיר

י כָּל דָּבָר שֶׁהָיָה בִּכְלָל, וְיָצָא לִטְעוֹן טְעַן אַחֵר שֶׁלֹּא כְעִנְיָנוֹ
יָצָא לְהָקֵל וּלְהַחֲמִיר

יא כָּל דָּבָר שֶׁהָיָה בִּכְלָל, וְיָצָא לִדּוֹן בַּדָּבָר הֶחָדָשׁ
אִי אַתָּה יָכוֹל לְהַחֲזִירוֹ לִכְלָלוֹ
עַד שֶׁיַּחֲזִירֶנּוּ הַכָּתוּב לִכְלָלוֹ בְּפֵרוּשׁ

יב דָּבָר הַלָּמֵד מֵעִנְיָנוֹ, וְדָבָר הַלָּמֵד מִסּוֹפוֹ

◄ יג וְכֵן שְׁנֵי כְתוּבִים הַמַּכְחִישִׁים זֶה אֶת זֶה
עַד שֶׁיָּבוֹא הַכָּתוּב הַשְּׁלִישִׁי וְיַכְרִיעַ בֵּינֵיהֶם.

יְהִי רָצוֹן מִלְּפָנֶיךָ, יהוה אֱלֹהֵינוּ וֵאלֹהֵי אֲבוֹתֵינוּ, שֶׁיִּבָּנֶה בֵּית הַמִּקְדָּשׁ
בִּמְהֵרָה בְיָמֵינוּ, וְתֵן חֶלְקֵנוּ בְּתוֹרָתֶךָ, וְשָׁם נַעֲבָדְךָ בְּיִרְאָה כִּימֵי עוֹלָם
וּכְשָׁנִים קַדְמוֹנִיּוֹת.

THE RABBIS' KADDISH

The following prayer, said by mourners, requires the presence of a minyan.
A transliteration can be found on page 748.

Mourner: **יִתְגַּדַּל** Magnified and sanctified
may His great name be,
in the world He created by His will.
May He establish His kingdom in your lifetime
and in your days,
and in the lifetime of all the house of Israel,
swiftly and soon –
and say: Amen.

All: May His great name be blessed for ever and all time.

Mourner: Blessed and praised, glorified and great,
raised and honored, uplifted and praised
be the name of the Holy One,
blessed be He,
beyond any blessing,
song, praise and consolation
uttered in the world –
and say: Amen.

LEARNING

Kaddish marks the end of a section of the service. This Kaddish marks the end of *Birkhot HaShaḥar* and *Korbanot*. There are four versions of the Kaddish prayer: the Rabbis' Kaddish, the Mourner's Kaddish, the Full Kaddish, and the Half Kaddish.

The Rabbis' Kaddish (*Kaddish De-Rabbanan*), which honors Torah scholars, is recited by mourners after Torah study. The *Birkhot HaShaḥar* section of Shaḥarit, which concludes with *Korbanot*, contains verses from Tanakh and studies from Talmudic passages and is therefore followed by the recitation of *Kaddish DeRabbanan*.

Kaddish is written mostly in Aramaic, the everyday language of the Jews of Talmudic times.

קדיש דרבנן

The following prayer, said by mourners, requires the presence of a מנין.
A transliteration can be found on page 748.

אבל: יִתְגַּדַּל וְיִתְקַדַּשׁ שְׁמֵהּ רַבָּא (קהל: אָמֵן)
בְּעָלְמָא דִּי בְרָא כִרְעוּתֵהּ
וְיַמְלִיךְ מַלְכוּתֵהּ
בְּחַיֵּיכוֹן וּבְיוֹמֵיכוֹן וּבְחַיֵּי דְּכָל בֵּית יִשְׂרָאֵל
בַּעֲגָלָא וּבִזְמַן קָרִיב
וְאִמְרוּ אָמֵן. (קהל: אָמֵן)

קהל
ואבל: יְהֵא שְׁמֵהּ רַבָּא מְבָרַךְ לְעָלַם וּלְעָלְמֵי עָלְמַיָּא.

אבל: יִתְבָּרַךְ וְיִשְׁתַּבַּח וְיִתְפָּאַר וְיִתְרוֹמַם וְיִתְנַשֵּׂא
וְיִתְהַדָּר וְיִתְעַלֶּה וְיִתְהַלָּל
שְׁמֵהּ דְּקֻדְשָׁא בְּרִיךְ הוּא (קהל: בְּרִיךְ הוּא)
לְעֵלָּא מִן כָּל בִּרְכָתָא
/ בעשרת ימי תשובה: לְעֵלָּא לְעֵלָּא מִכָּל בִּרְכָתָא/
וְשִׁירָתָא, תֻּשְׁבְּחָתָא וְנֶחֱמָתָא
דַּאֲמִירָן בְּעָלְמָא
וְאִמְרוּ אָמֵן. (קהל: אָמֵן)

REFLECTION

"The parent brings the child into the life of this world,
whereas the teacher, who teaches him wisdom,
brings him into the life of the World to Come."

(Bava Metzia 33a)

Take a minute to think
about which teachers most
impacted your life.

How do you honor them?

To Israel, to the teachers, their disciples
and their disciples' disciples,
and to all who engage in the study of Torah,
in this (*in Israel add:* holy) place or elsewhere,
may there come to them and you great peace,
grace, kindness and compassion,
long life, abundant sustenance and deliverance,
from their Father in Heaven –
and say: Amen.

May there be great peace from heaven,
and (good) life for us and all Israel –
and say: Amen.

Bow, take three steps back, as if taking leave of the Divine Presence,
then bow, first left, then right, then center, while saying:

May He who makes peace in His high places,
in His compassion make peace
for us and all Israel –
and say: Amen.

On Hoshana Raba, and in many communities
on Yom HaAtzma'ut and Yom Yerushalayim,
continue Shaharit on page 450.

spiritual father, I was tearing my
clothes for him… Rabbi Auerbach
remains an example to me. I think
about him often, missing him as a
scholar educator, and mainly, as a
person. Even now, years after his
death, his spirit remains close to my
heart, and his absence has left a
void that cannot be filled."
(Rabbi Yisrael Meir Lau,
Out of the Depths)

… A THOUSAND WORDS

עַל יִשְׂרָאֵל וְעַל רַבָּנָן וְעַל תַּלְמִידֵיהוֹן

וְעַל כָּל תַּלְמִידֵי תַלְמִידֵיהוֹן

וְעַל כָּל מָאן דְּעָסְקִין בְּאוֹרַיְתָא

דִּי בְאַתְרָא (בארץ ישראל: קַדִּישָׁא) הָדֵין, וְדִי בְּכָל אֲתַר וַאֲתַר

יְהֵא לְהוֹן וּלְכוֹן שְׁלָמָא רַבָּא

חִנָּא וְחִסְדָּא, וְרַחֲמֵי

וְחַיֵּי אֲרִיכֵי, וּמְזוֹנֵי רְוִיחֵי

וּפֻרְקָנָא מִן קֳדָם אֲבוּהוֹן דִּי בִשְׁמַיָּא

וְאִמְרוּ אָמֵן. (קהל: אָמֵן)

יְהֵא שְׁלָמָא רַבָּא מִן שְׁמַיָּא

וְחַיִּים (טוֹבִים) עָלֵינוּ וְעַל כָּל יִשְׂרָאֵל

וְאִמְרוּ אָמֵן. (קהל: אָמֵן)

Bow, take three steps back, as if taking leave of the Divine Presence,
then bow, first left, then right, then center, while saying:

עֹשֶׂה שָׁלוֹם/ בעשרת ימי תשובה: הַשָּׁלוֹם/ בִּמְרוֹמָיו

הוּא יַעֲשֶׂה בְרַחֲמָיו שָׁלוֹם, עָלֵינוּ וְעַל כָּל יִשְׂרָאֵל

וְאִמְרוּ אָמֵן. (קהל: אָמֵן)

On הושענא רבה, *and in many communities*
on יום ירושלים *and* יום העצמאות, *continue* שחרית *on page 451.*

CONNECTION

"When Rabbi Shlomo Zalman [Auerbach] died, I followed the tradition of tearing my clothing, as a son would do for his father. He was the only person for whom I have ever done so. Someone saw me and, noticing my torn suit, asked in a worried voice what had happened. I answered that I had not had the opportunity to tear my clothing for my biological father. Because Rabbi Shlomo Zalman was my

A PSALM BEFORE VERSES OF PRAISE

מִזְמוֹר שִׁיר A psalm of David. A song for the dedication of the House. *Ps. 30* I will elevate You, LORD, for You have lifted me up, and not let my enemies rejoice over me. LORD, my God, I cried to You for help and You healed me. LORD, You lifted my soul from the grave; You spared me from going down to the pit. Sing to the LORD, you His devoted ones, and give thanks to His holy name. For His anger is for a moment, but His favor for a lifetime. At night there may be weeping, but in the morning there is joy. When I felt secure, I said, "I shall never be shaken." LORD, when You favored me, You made me stand firm as a mountain, but when You hid Your face, I was terrified. To You, LORD, I called; I pleaded with my LORD: "What gain would there be if I died and went down to the grave? Can dust thank You? Can it declare Your truth? Hear, LORD, and be generous to me; LORD, be my help." ‣ You have turned my sorrow into dancing. You have removed my sackcloth and clothed me with joy, so that my soul may sing to You and not be silent. LORD my God, for ever will I thank You.

LEARNING

A theme of this *perek* is the contrast between negativity and positivity. The author explores the depths of despair and heights of joy and the thin line between them. The chapter teaches us that turning to God is how we can transcend from despair to hope. When we are able to turn to God in our hardest times and recognize His power to help, the door to hope opens. It is critical that we understand and internalize this idea before we begin the first section of *tefilla: Pesukei DeZimra*. The chapter shows us the power of *tefilla*. When we turn to God, the contrast between pain and hope becomes powerfully real for us. This is a chapter of hope, transition, and inspiration.

CONNECTION

Ordeal leads to transcendence. In the paradox of facing crisis with a lion's strength and yet inwardly knowing that only Hashem manifests here, we reveal Him openly. What is possible and what is impossible is not our concern. The Alter of Kelm used to say, "Ask not if a thing is possible, ask only if it is necessary." Our concern is to rise to that partnership with the Divine which invites Him, as it were, to reach down to us.

(Rabbi Akiva Tatz, *Living Inspired*)

מזמור לפני פסוקי דזמרה

מִזְמוֹר שִׁיר־חֲנֻכַּת הַבַּיִת לְדָוִד: אֲרוֹמִמְךָ יהוה כִּי דִלִּיתָנִי, תהלים ל
וְלֹא־שִׂמַּחְתָּ אֹיְבַי לִי: יהוה אֱלֹהָי, שִׁוַּעְתִּי אֵלֶיךָ וַתִּרְפָּאֵנִי:
יהוה, הֶעֱלִיתָ מִן־שְׁאוֹל נַפְשִׁי, חִיִּיתַנִי מִיָּרְדִי־בוֹר: זַמְּרוּ לַיהוה
חֲסִידָיו, וְהוֹדוּ לְזֵכֶר קָדְשׁוֹ: כִּי רֶגַע בְּאַפּוֹ, חַיִּים בִּרְצוֹנוֹ, בָּעֶרֶב
יָלִין בֶּכִי וְלַבֹּקֶר רִנָּה: וַאֲנִי אָמַרְתִּי בְשַׁלְוִי, בַּל־אֶמּוֹט לְעוֹלָם:
יהוה, בִּרְצוֹנְךָ הֶעֱמַדְתָּה לְהַרְרִי עֹז, הִסְתַּרְתָּ פָנֶיךָ הָיִיתִי נִבְהָל:
אֵלֶיךָ יהוה אֶקְרָא, וְאֶל־אֲדֹנָי אֶתְחַנָּן: מַה־בֶּצַע בְּדָמִי, בְּרִדְתִּי
אֶל שָׁחַת, הֲיוֹדְךָ עָפָר, הֲיַגִּיד אֲמִתֶּךָ: שְׁמַע־יהוה וְחָנֵּנִי, יהוה
הֱיֵה־עֹזֵר לִי: ◂ הָפַכְתָּ מִסְפְּדִי לְמָחוֹל לִי, פִּתַּחְתָּ שַׂקִּי, וַתְּאַזְּרֵנִי
שִׂמְחָה: לְמַעַן יְזַמֶּרְךָ כָבוֹד וְלֹא יִדֹּם, יהוה אֱלֹהָי, לְעוֹלָם אוֹדֶךָּ:

REFLECTION

Can you think of a time when your pain transitioned into a time of joy?

How can you ask God to help you? How does asking for help provide hope?

MOURNER'S KADDISH

The following prayer, said by mourners, requires the presence of a minyan.
A transliteration can be found on page 749.

Mourner: יִתְגַּדַּל Magnified and sanctified may His great name be,
in the world He created by His will.
May He establish His kingdom
in your lifetime and in your days,
and in the lifetime of all the house of Israel,
swiftly and soon – and say: Amen.

All: May His great name be blessed for ever and all time.

Mourner: Blessed and praised, glorified and great,
raised and honored, uplifted and praised
be the name of the Holy One,
blessed be He,
beyond any blessing,
song, praise and consolation
uttered in the world – and say: Amen.

May there be great peace from heaven,
and life for us and all Israel – and say: Amen.

Bow, take three steps back, as if taking leave of the Divine Presence,
then bow, first left, then right, then center, while saying:
May He who makes peace in His high places,
make peace for us and all Israel – and say: Amen.

REFLECTION	... A THOUSAND WORDS

How can you carry someone else's
memory?

How can you show that you accept
God's judgment?

Do you know anyone saying this
Kaddish? What do you think they are
thinking about?

קדיש יתום

The following prayer, said by mourners, requires the presence of a מִנְיָן.
A transliteration can be found on page 749.

אבל: יִתְגַּדַּל וְיִתְקַדַּשׁ שְׁמֵהּ רַבָּא (קהל: אָמֵן)
בְּעָלְמָא דִּי בְרָא כִרְעוּתֵהּ, וְיַמְלִיךְ מַלְכוּתֵהּ
בְּחַיֵּיכוֹן וּבְיוֹמֵיכוֹן וּבְחַיֵּי דְכָל בֵּית יִשְׂרָאֵל
בַּעֲגָלָא וּבִזְמַן קָרִיב, וְאִמְרוּ אָמֵן. (קהל: אָמֵן)

קהל ואבל: יְהֵא שְׁמֵהּ רַבָּא מְבָרַךְ לְעָלַם וּלְעָלְמֵי עָלְמַיָּא.

אבל: יִתְבָּרַךְ וְיִשְׁתַּבַּח וְיִתְפָּאַר
וְיִתְרוֹמַם וְיִתְנַשֵּׂא וְיִתְהַדָּר וְיִתְעַלֶּה וְיִתְהַלָּל
שְׁמֵהּ דְּקֻדְשָׁא בְּרִיךְ הוּא (קהל: בְּרִיךְ הוּא)
לְעֵלָּא מִן כָּל בִּרְכָתָא /בעשרת ימי תשובה: לְעֵלָּא לְעֵלָּא מִכָּל בִּרְכָתָא/
וְשִׁירָתָא, תֻּשְׁבְּחָתָא וְנֶחֱמָתָא
דַּאֲמִירָן בְּעָלְמָא, וְאִמְרוּ אָמֵן. (קהל: אָמֵן)

יְהֵא שְׁלָמָא רַבָּא מִן שְׁמַיָּא
וְחַיִּים, עָלֵינוּ וְעַל כָּל יִשְׂרָאֵל, וְאִמְרוּ אָמֵן. (קהל: אָמֵן)

Bow, take three steps back, as if taking leave of the Divine Presence,
then bow, first left, then right, then center, while saying:

עֹשֶׂה שָׁלוֹם/ בעשרת ימי תשובה: הַשָּׁלוֹם/ בִּמְרוֹמָיו
הוּא יַעֲשֶׂה שָׁלוֹם עָלֵינוּ וְעַל כָּל יִשְׂרָאֵל, וְאִמְרוּ אָמֵן. (קהל: אָמֵן)

LEARNING

The custom of reciting Kaddish as an atonement for the soul of a departed family member is first recorded in the thirteenth century by Rabbi Yitzḥak ben Moshe of Vienna in his *Or Zarua*. Rabbi Ḥayyim ben Bezalel (*Sefer HaḤayyim*) explains that when a child's parent has been taken from him and despite his pain and mourning, the child is able to stand up and pronounce God's greatness in public, the departed soul receives atonement. The child, in overcoming his anguish and publicly praising God, becomes a credit to the departed parent and for this reason the soul derives benefit and merit.

PESUKEI DEZIMRA

The introductory blessing to the Pesukei DeZimra (Verses of Praise) is said standing. There is a custom to hold the two front tzitziot of the tallit until the end of the blessing at "songs of praise" (on page 78) after which they are kissed and released. From the beginning of this prayer to the end of the Amida, conversation is forbidden.

Some say:

I hereby prepare my mouth to thank, praise and laud my Creator, for the sake of the unification of the Holy One, blessed be He, and His Divine Presence, through that which is hidden and concealed, in the name of all Israel.

BLESSED IS HE WHO SPOKE

and the world came into being, **blessed is He.**

> Blessed is He who creates the universe.
> Blessed is He who speaks and acts.
> Blessed is He who decrees and fulfills.
> Blessed is He who shows compassion to the earth.
> Blessed is He who shows compassion to all creatures.
> Blessed is He who gives a good reward
> to those who fear Him.
> Blessed is He who lives for ever and exists to eternity.
> Blessed is He who redeems and saves.
> Blessed is His name.

Pesukei DeZimra is a stand-alone section of the *tefilla* service and is bracketed by two *berakhot* – *Yishtabaḥ* at the end and *Barukh SheAmar* at the beginning. *Barukh SheAmar* can be divided into two parts. The first contains ten praises of God, each beginning with the word "*Barukh.*" They attest to the way He created the world and remains involved in it on a constant basis, and correspond to the ten times the word "*vayomer*" is found in the first chapter of *Bereshit* as God creates the world with words and speech. The second section is a statement of intent and serves as an introduction to *Pesukei DeZimra* – we will now use the words of David HaMelekh from *Tehillim* to praise Hashem.

REFLECTION

"By ten acts of speech the world was created."

(*Avot* 5:1)

How can speech create worlds?

When did you last use words for the power of good?

When did you last use words for the power of bad?

פסוקי דזמרה

The introductory blessing to the פסוקי דזמרה *is said standing. There is a custom to hold the two front* ציציות *of the* טלית *until the end of the blessing at* בְּתִשְׁבָּחוֹת *(on page 79) after which they are kissed and released. From the beginning of this prayer to the end of the* עמידה, *conversation is forbidden.*

Some say:

הֲרֵינִי מְזַמֵּן אֶת פִּי לְהוֹדוֹת וּלְהַלֵּל וּלְשַׁבֵּחַ אֶת בּוֹרְאִי, לְשֵׁם יִחוּד קֻדְשָׁא בְּרִיךְ הוּא וּשְׁכִינְתֵּהּ, עַל יְדֵי הַהוּא טָמִיר וְנֶעְלָם בְּשֵׁם כָּל יִשְׂרָאֵל.

בָּרוּךְ שֶׁאָמַר

וְהָיָה הָעוֹלָם, בָּרוּךְ הוּא.

בָּרוּךְ עוֹשֶׂה בְרֵאשִׁית

בָּרוּךְ אוֹמֵר וְעוֹשֶׂה

בָּרוּךְ גּוֹזֵר וּמְקַיֵּם

בָּרוּךְ מְרַחֵם עַל הָאָרֶץ

בָּרוּךְ מְרַחֵם עַל הַבְּרִיּוֹת

בָּרוּךְ מְשַׁלֵּם שָׂכָר טוֹב לִירֵאָיו

בָּרוּךְ חַי לָעַד וְקַיָּם לָנֶצַח

בָּרוּךְ פּוֹדֶה וּמַצִּיל

בָּרוּךְ שְׁמוֹ

LEARNING

Have you ever needed to psyche yourself up before an important event or performance? To get your mind in the right zone? *Pesukei DeZimra* is designed to do just that. Through the reciting of verses from Tanakh that describe God's magnificent universe and the way He created it, and His majestic role in history,

Pesukei DeZimra aims to inspire us and lift us to a place where we are ready to stand before Hashem and open our souls to Him. Like an athlete who listens to music before entering the arena, we say "verses of song" before we enter the ultimate arena and stand before Hashem.

Blessed are You, LORD our God, King of the Universe,
God, compassionate Father,
celebrated by the mouth of His people,
praised and glorified by the tongue of His devoted ones
and those who serve Him.
With the songs of Your servant David
we will praise You, O LORD our God.
With praises and psalms
we will magnify and praise You, glorify You,
Speak Your name and declare Your kingship,
our King, our God, ▸ the only One, Giver of life to the worlds,
the King whose great name is praised
and glorified to all eternity.
Blessed are You, LORD,
the King celebrated with songs of praise.

"Four score and seven years ago our fathers brought forth on this continent a new nation, conceived in liberty, and dedicated to the proposition that all men are created equal. Now we are engaged in a great civil war, testing whether that nation, or any nation so conceived and so dedicated, can long endure. We are met on a great battlefield of that war. We have come to dedicate a portion of that field, as a final resting place for those who here gave their lives that that nation might live.... The brave men, living and dead, who struggled here, have consecrated it, far above our poor power to add or detract. The world will little note, nor long remember what we say here, but it can never forget what they did here. "

(Abraham Lincoln,
The Gettysburg Address)

"I have a dream that one day this nation will rise up and live out the true meaning of its creed: 'We hold these truths to be self-evident, that all men are created equal.'

I have a dream that one day on the red hills of Georgia, the sons of former slaves and the sons of former slave owners will be able to sit down together at the table of brotherhood.

I have a dream that one day even the state of Mississippi, a state sweltering with the heat of injustice, sweltering with the heat of oppression, will be transformed into an oasis of freedom and justice.

I have a dream that my four little children will one day live in a nation where they will not be judged by the color of their skin but by the content of their character."

(Martin Luther King,
delivered August 28, 1963, at the
Lincoln Memorial, Washington D.C.)

בָּרוּךְ אַתָּה יהוה אֱלֹהֵינוּ מֶלֶךְ הָעוֹלָם
הָאֵל הָאָב הָרַחֲמָן הַמְהֻלָּל בְּפִי עַמּוֹ
מְשֻׁבָּח וּמְפֹאָר בִּלְשׁוֹן חֲסִידָיו וַעֲבָדָיו
וּבְשִׁירֵי דָוִד עַבְדֶּךָ נְהַלֶּלְךָ יהוה אֱלֹהֵינוּ.
בִּשְׁבָחוֹת וּבִזְמִירוֹת, נְגַדֶּלְךָ וּנְשַׁבֵּחֲךָ וּנְפָאֶרְךָ
וְנַזְכִּיר שִׁמְךָ וְנַמְלִיכְךָ מַלְכֵּנוּ אֱלֹהֵינוּ, ◦ יָחִיד חֵי הָעוֹלָמִים
מֶלֶךְ, מְשֻׁבָּח וּמְפֹאָר עֲדֵי עַד שְׁמוֹ הַגָּדוֹל
בָּרוּךְ אַתָּה יהוה, מֶלֶךְ מְהֻלָּל בַּתִּשְׁבָּחוֹת.

| REFLECTION | ... A THOUSAND WORDS |

"[Music's] language is a language which the soul alone understands, but which the soul can never translate."
(Arnold Bennett)

When do you listen to music? Why?

When do you sing? Why?

CONNECTION

SPEECHES THAT CHANGED THE WORLD

"Even though large tracts of Europe and many old and famous States have fallen or may fall into the grip of the Gestapo and all the odious apparatus of Nazi rule, we shall not flag or fail. We shall go on to the end, we shall fight in France, we shall fight on the seas and oceans, we shall fight with growing confidence and growing strength in the air, we shall defend our Island, whatever the cost may be, we shall fight on the beaches, we shall fight on the landing grounds, we shall fight in the fields and in the streets, we shall fight in the hills; we shall never surrender."

(Winston Churchill, Address to the House of Commons, June 4, 1940)

הוֹדוּ לַיהוה Thank the Lord, call on His name, make His acts known *1 Chr. 16* among the peoples. Sing to Him, make music to Him, tell of all His wonders. Glory in His holy name; let the hearts of those who seek the Lord rejoice. Search out the Lord and His strength; seek His presence at all times. Remember the wonders He has done, His miracles, and the judgments He pronounced. Descendants of Yisrael His servant, sons of Jacob His chosen ones: He is the Lord our God. His judgments are throughout the earth. Remember His covenant for ever, the word He commanded for a thousand genera- tions. He made it with Abraham, vowed it to Isaac, and confirmed it to Jacob as a law and to Israel as an everlasting covenant, saying, "To you I will give the land of Canaan as your heritage." You were then small in number, few, strangers there, wandering from nation to nation, from one kingdom to another, but He let no man oppress them, and for their sake He rebuked kings: "Do not touch My anointed ones, and do My prophets no harm." Sing to the Lord, all the earth; tell of His salvation daily. Declare His glory among the nations, His marvels among all the peoples. For great is the Lord and greatly to be praised; He is awesome beyond all heavenly powers. ▸ For all the gods of the peoples are mere idols; it was the Lord who made the heavens.

CONNECTION

"There is an inner connection between music and the spirit...

Words are the language of the mind. Music is the language of the soul.

So when we seek to express or evoke emotion we turn to melody. Deborah sang after Israel's victory over the forces of Siserah. Hannah sang when she had a child. When Saul was depressed, David would play for him and his spirit would be restored. David himself was known as the 'sweet singer of Israel.' Elisha called for a harpist to play so that the prophetic spirit could rest upon him. The Levites sang in the Temple. Every day, in Judaism, we preface our morning prayers with Pesukei DeZimra, the 'Verses of Song' with their magnificent crescendo, Psalm 150, in which instruments and the human voice combine to sing God's praises."

(Rabbi Jonathan Sacks, *Covenant & Conversation*, Beshalaḥ, 5772)

דברי
הימים
א, טז

הוֹדוּ לַיהוה קִרְאוּ בִשְׁמוֹ, הוֹדִיעוּ בָעַמִּים עֲלִילֹתָיו: שִׁירוּ לוֹ,
זַמְּרוּ־לוֹ, שִׂיחוּ בְּכָל־נִפְלְאֹתָיו: הִתְהַלְלוּ בְּשֵׁם קָדְשׁוֹ, יִשְׂמַח לֵב
מְבַקְשֵׁי יהוה: דִּרְשׁוּ יהוה וְעֻזּוֹ, בַּקְּשׁוּ פָנָיו תָּמִיד: זִכְרוּ נִפְלְאֹתָיו
אֲשֶׁר עָשָׂה, מֹפְתָיו וּמִשְׁפְּטֵי־פִיהוּ: זֶרַע יִשְׂרָאֵל עַבְדּוֹ, בְּנֵי יַעֲקֹב
בְּחִירָיו: הוּא יהוה אֱלֹהֵינוּ בְּכָל־הָאָרֶץ מִשְׁפָּטָיו: זִכְרוּ לְעוֹלָם
בְּרִיתוֹ, דָּבָר צִוָּה לְאֶלֶף דּוֹר: אֲשֶׁר כָּרַת אֶת־אַבְרָהָם, וּשְׁבוּעָתוֹ
לְיִצְחָק: וַיַּעֲמִידֶהָ לְיַעֲקֹב לְחֹק, לְיִשְׂרָאֵל בְּרִית עוֹלָם: לֵאמֹר,
לְךָ אֶתֵּן אֶרֶץ־כְּנָעַן, חֶבֶל נַחֲלַתְכֶם: בִּהְיוֹתְכֶם מְתֵי מִסְפָּר,
כִּמְעַט וְגָרִים בָּהּ: וַיִּתְהַלְּכוּ מִגּוֹי אֶל־גּוֹי, וּמִמַּמְלָכָה אֶל־עַם
אַחֵר: לֹא־הִנִּיחַ לְאִישׁ לְעָשְׁקָם, וַיּוֹכַח עֲלֵיהֶם מְלָכִים: אַל־
תִּגְּעוּ בִמְשִׁיחָי, וּבִנְבִיאַי אַל־תָּרֵעוּ: שִׁירוּ לַיהוה כָּל־הָאָרֶץ,
בַּשְּׂרוּ מִיּוֹם־אֶל־יוֹם יְשׁוּעָתוֹ: סַפְּרוּ בַגּוֹיִם אֶת־כְּבוֹדוֹ, בְּכָל־
הָעַמִּים נִפְלְאֹתָיו: כִּי גָדוֹל יהוה וּמְהֻלָּל מְאֹד, וְנוֹרָא הוּא עַל־
כָּל־אֱלֹהִים: ‹ כִּי כָּל־אֱלֹהֵי הָעַמִּים אֱלִילִים, וַיהוה שָׁמַיִם עָשָׂה:

REFLECTION

What miracles
in Jewish history
inspire you?

Have you
or anyone in your family
lived through any miracles
in Jewish history?

Ask your parents
and grandparents
this question
next time
you see them.

... A THOUSAND WORDS

Before Him are majesty and splendor; there is strength and beauty in His holy place. Give to the LORD, families of the peoples, give to the LORD honor and might. Give to the LORD the glory due to His name; bring an offering and come before Him; bow down to the LORD in the splendor of holiness. Tremble before Him, all the earth; the world stands firm, it will not be shaken. Let the heavens rejoice and the earth be glad; let them declare among the nations, "The LORD is King." Let the sea roar, and all that is in it; let the fields be jubilant, and all they contain. Then the trees of the forest will sing for joy before the LORD, for He is coming to judge the earth. Thank the LORD for He is good; His loving-kindness is for ever. Say: "Save us, God of our salvation; gather us and rescue us from the nations, to acknowledge Your holy name and glory in Your praise. Blessed is the LORD, God of Israel, from this world to eternity." And let all the people say "Amen" and "Praise the LORD."

▸ Elevate the LORD our God and bow before His footstool: He *Ps. 99* is holy. Elevate the LORD our God and bow at His holy mountain; for holy is the LORD our God.

... A THOUSAND WORDS

הוֹד וְהָדָר לְפָנָיו, עֹז וְחֶדְוָה בִּמְקֹמוֹ: הָבוּ לַיהוה מִשְׁפְּחוֹת עַמִּים, הָבוּ לַיהוה כָּבוֹד וָעֹז: הָבוּ לַיהוה כְּבוֹד שְׁמוֹ, שְׂאוּ מִנְחָה וּבֹאוּ לְפָנָיו, הִשְׁתַּחֲווּ לַיהוה בְּהַדְרַת־קֹדֶשׁ: חִילוּ מִלְּפָנָיו כָּל־הָאָרֶץ, אַף־תִּכּוֹן תֵּבֵל בַּל־תִּמּוֹט: יִשְׂמְחוּ הַשָּׁמַיִם וְתָגֵל הָאָרֶץ, וְיֹאמְרוּ בַגּוֹיִם יהוה מָלָךְ: יִרְעַם הַיָּם וּמְלֹאוֹ, יַעֲלֹץ הַשָּׂדֶה וְכָל־אֲשֶׁר־בּוֹ: אָז יְרַנְּנוּ עֲצֵי הַיָּעַר, מִלִּפְנֵי יהוה, כִּי־בָא לִשְׁפּוֹט אֶת־הָאָרֶץ: הוֹדוּ לַיהוה כִּי טוֹב, כִּי לְעוֹלָם חַסְדּוֹ: וְאִמְרוּ, הוֹשִׁיעֵנוּ אֱלֹהֵי יִשְׁעֵנוּ, וְקַבְּצֵנוּ וְהַצִּילֵנוּ מִן־הַגּוֹיִם, לְהֹדוֹת לְשֵׁם קָדְשֶׁךָ, לְהִשְׁתַּבֵּחַ בִּתְהִלָּתֶךָ: בָּרוּךְ יהוה אֱלֹהֵי יִשְׂרָאֵל מִן־הָעוֹלָם וְעַד־הָעֹלָם, וַיֹּאמְרוּ כָל־הָעָם אָמֵן, וְהַלֵּל לַיהוה:

‹ רוֹמְמוּ יהוה אֱלֹהֵינוּ וְהִשְׁתַּחֲווּ לַהֲדֹם רַגְלָיו, קָדוֹשׁ הוּא: תהלים צט רוֹמְמוּ יהוה אֱלֹהֵינוּ וְהִשְׁתַּחֲווּ לְהַר קָדְשׁוֹ, כִּי־קָדוֹשׁ יהוה אֱלֹהֵינוּ:

| CONNECTION | REFLECTION |

There's music in the sighing of a reed;
There's music in the gushing of a rill;
There's music in all things,
    if men had ears:

Their earth is but an echo
    of the spheres.

(Lord Byron)

"Earth laughs in flowers."
(Ralph Waldo Emerson)

Close your eyes. Can you hear
nature? What is it saying?
Is it praising God?

Have you ever seen
a natural phenomenon
that took your breath away?
What was it?

Think of it now as you say
this tefilla.

He is compassionate. He forgives wrongdoing and does not *Ps. 78*
destroy. Repeatedly He suppresses His anger, not rousing His
full fury. You, LORD: do not withhold Your compassion from me. *Ps. 40*
May Your loving-kindness and truth always guard me. Remember, *Ps. 25*
LORD, Your acts of compassion and love, for they have existed for
ever. Ascribe power to God, whose majesty is over Israel and whose *Ps. 68*
might is in the skies. You are awesome, God, in Your holy places.
It is the God of Israel who gives might and strength to the people,
may God be blessed. God of retribution, LORD, God of retribu- *Ps. 94*
tion, appear. Arise, Judge of the earth, to repay the arrogant their
just deserts. Salvation belongs to the LORD; may Your blessing rest *Ps. 3*
upon Your people, Selah! ▸ The LORD of multitudes is with us, the *Ps. 46*
God of Jacob is our stronghold, Selah! LORD of multitudes, happy *Ps. 84*
is the one who trusts in You. LORD, save! May the King answer us *Ps. 20*
on the day we call.

Save Your people and bless Your heritage; tend them and carry *Ps. 28*
them for ever. Our soul longs for the LORD; He is our Help and *Ps. 33*
Shield. For in Him our hearts rejoice, for in His holy name we have
trusted. May Your loving-kindness, LORD, be upon us, as we have
put our hope in You. Show us, LORD, Your loving-kindness and *Ps. 85*
give us Your salvation. Arise, help us and redeem us for the sake of *Ps. 44*
Your love. I am the LORD your God who brought you up from the *Ps. 81*
land of Egypt: open your mouth wide and I will fill it. Happy is the *Ps. 144*
people for whom this is so; happy is the people whose God is the
LORD. ▸ As for me, I trust in Your loving-kindness; my heart rejoices *Ps. 13*
in Your salvation. I will sing to the LORD for He has been good to me.

CONNECTION

Close your eyes. Consider for a moment whom you trust most in the world. Perhaps your best friend? Your sibling? Your parents? Think about how it feels to place your life in their hands. Do you trust them with your life? Does that feel safe or does that make you feel vulnerable? Now take a moment to think about your relationship with God. Do you feel vulnerable or safe in the knowledge that your life is in His hands? How does it feel to know that your every waking moment is dependent on Him and His kindness?

תהלים עח וְהוּא רַחוּם, יְכַפֵּר עָוֹן וְלֹא־יַשְׁחִית, וְהִרְבָּה לְהָשִׁיב אַפּוֹ,

תהלים מ וְלֹא־יָעִיר כָּל־חֲמָתוֹ: אַתָּה יהוה לֹא־תִכְלָא רַחֲמֶיךָ מִמֶּנִּי, חַסְדְּךָ

תהלים כה וַאֲמִתְּךָ תָּמִיד יִצְּרוּנִי: זְכֹר־רַחֲמֶיךָ יהוה וַחֲסָדֶיךָ, כִּי מֵעוֹלָם

תהלים סח הֵמָּה: תְּנוּ עֹז לֵאלֹהִים, עַל־יִשְׂרָאֵל גַּאֲוָתוֹ, וְעֻזּוֹ בַּשְּׁחָקִים:

נוֹרָא אֱלֹהִים מִמִּקְדָּשֶׁיךָ, אֵל יִשְׂרָאֵל הוּא נֹתֵן עֹז וְתַעֲצֻמוֹת

תהלים צד לָעָם, בָּרוּךְ אֱלֹהִים: אֵל־נְקָמוֹת יהוה, אֵל נְקָמוֹת הוֹפִיעַ: הִנָּשֵׂא

תהלים ג שֹׁפֵט הָאָרֶץ, הָשֵׁב גְּמוּל עַל־גֵּאִים: לַיהוה הַיְשׁוּעָה, עַל־עַמְּךָ

תהלים מו בִרְכָתֶךָ סֶּלָה: ‹ יהוה צְבָאוֹת עִמָּנוּ, מִשְׂגָּב לָנוּ אֱלֹהֵי יַעֲקֹב

תהלים פד
תהלים כ סֶלָה: יהוה צְבָאוֹת, אַשְׁרֵי אָדָם בֹּטֵחַ בָּךְ: יהוה הוֹשִׁיעָה, הַמֶּלֶךְ

יַעֲנֵנוּ בְיוֹם־קָרְאֵנוּ:

תהלים כח הוֹשִׁיעָה אֶת־עַמֶּךָ, וּבָרֵךְ אֶת־נַחֲלָתֶךָ, וּרְעֵם וְנַשְּׂאֵם עַד־

תהלים לג הָעוֹלָם: נַפְשֵׁנוּ חִכְּתָה לַיהוה, עֶזְרֵנוּ וּמָגִנֵּנוּ הוּא: כִּי־בוֹ יִשְׂמַח

לִבֵּנוּ, כִּי בְשֵׁם קָדְשׁוֹ בָטָחְנוּ: יְהִי־חַסְדְּךָ יהוה עָלֵינוּ, כַּאֲשֶׁר

תהלים פה
תהלים מד יִחַלְנוּ לָךְ: הַרְאֵנוּ יהוה חַסְדֶּךָ, וְיֶשְׁעֲךָ תִּתֶּן־לָנוּ: קוּמָה עֶזְרָתָה

תהלים פא לָנוּ, וּפְדֵנוּ לְמַעַן חַסְדֶּךָ: אָנֹכִי יהוה אֱלֹהֶיךָ הַמַּעַלְךָ מֵאֶרֶץ

תהלים קמד מִצְרָיִם, הַרְחֶב־פִּיךָ וַאֲמַלְאֵהוּ: אַשְׁרֵי הָעָם שֶׁכָּכָה לּוֹ, אַשְׁרֵי

תהלים יג הָעָם שֶׁיהוה אֱלֹהָיו: ‹ וַאֲנִי בְּחַסְדְּךָ בָטַחְתִּי, יָגֵל לִבִּי בִּישׁוּעָתֶךָ,

אָשִׁירָה לַיהוה, כִּי גָמַל עָלָי:

REFLECTION

... A THOUSAND WORDS

Do you have faith
in God?
Why?

Do you think God
has faith in us?

The following psalm recalls the thanksgiving-offering in Temple times.
It is not said on Erev Pesaḥ, on Ḥol HaMo'ed Pesaḥ, or Erev Yom Kippur
since no thanksgiving-offerings were brought on these days.
To emphasize its sacrificial nature, the custom is to say it standing.

מִזְמוֹר A psalm of thanksgiving. Shout joyously to the Lord, *Ps. 100*
all the earth. Serve the Lord with joy. Come before Him
with celebration. Know that the Lord is God. He made us
and we are His. We are His people and the flock He tends.
Enter His gates with thanksgiving, His courts with praise.
Thank Him and bless His name. ‣ For the Lord is good,
His loving-kindness is everlasting, and His truthfulness is
for every generation.

CONNECTION

During a time when Jews had a curfew and were barred
from the streets of Russia at night, a holy Hasid of the
Rebbe of Karlin risked his life to be close to his rebbe
and braved the streets in order to bathe in the light and
warmth of the rebbe's service of Hashem. Grasping his
tiny book of Tehillim *in his hand the Hasid ran wildly*
through the streets of Karlin in order to reach the home
of the rebbe, until his path was blocked by a Russian
policeman. He was grabbed and dragged to jail, and
his book of Tehillim *was confiscated. Weeping silently*
in his cell, the Hasid said to himself, "They have taken
away my opportunity to be close to my rebbe tonight,
and snatched my Tehillim, *but they can't stop me from*
being a Jew." And with that he jumped to his feet with
joy and tears in his eyes, and he began to dance a jubi-
lant dance. The prison guard stared at him with disbelief
and amusement in equal measure as he gave way to
hysterical laughing at the bizarre sight of the dancing Jew. With that he opened the cell
and sent the Jew on his way, shouting after him, "There is no room in this jail for mentally
imbalanced people!" As the Hasid arrived at the rebbe's house he was greeted with a warm
knowing smile and the words, "If one is truly happy to be a Jew and part of the Jewish People,
then one can be rescued from anything!"

REFLECTION

"מִצְוָה גְדוֹלָה
לִהְיוֹת בְּשִׂמְחָה"
"It is a great mitzva
to always be happy."
(Rabbi Naḥman
of Breslov)

**What makes you
happy?**

**Does believing
in God make you
feel happy?**

**How can we
serve Hashem
with happiness?**

The following psalm recalls the קרבן תודה in Temple times.
It is not said on חול המועד פסח ,ערב פסח or ערב יום כיפור,
since no קרבנות תודה were brought on these days.
To emphasize its sacrificial nature, the custom is to say it standing.

תהילים ק

מִזְמוֹר לְתוֹדָה, הָרִיעוּ לַיהוה כָּל־הָאָרֶץ: עִבְדוּ אֶת־
יהוה בְּשִׂמְחָה, בֹּאוּ לְפָנָיו בִּרְנָנָה: דְּעוּ כִּי־יהוה הוּא
אֱלֹהִים, הוּא עָשָׂנוּ וְלוֹ אֲנַחְנוּ, עַמּוֹ וְצֹאן מַרְעִיתוֹ: בֹּאוּ
שְׁעָרָיו בְּתוֹדָה, חֲצֵרֹתָיו בִּתְהִלָּה, הוֹדוּ לוֹ, בָּרְכוּ שְׁמוֹ:
‹ כִּי־טוֹב יהוה, לְעוֹלָם חַסְדּוֹ, וְעַד־דֹּר וָדֹר אֱמוּנָתוֹ:

... A THOUSAND WORDS

LEARNING

This Psalm of Thanksgiving was said in the *Beit HaMikdash* when the *korban toda* (thanksgiving offering) was brought. This happened when a person survived life-threatening ordeal such as a hazardous journey, an illness, or being subjected to captivity. We include this chapter from *Tehillim* here to further proclaim our mood of thanksgiving as we consider Hashem's role in the world.

יְהִי כְבוֹד May the Lord's glory be for ever; may the Lord rejoice *Ps. 104* in His works. May the Lord's name be blessed, now and for ever. *Ps. 113* From the rising of the sun to its setting, may the Lord's name be praised. The Lord is high above all nations; His glory is above the heavens. Lord, Your name is for ever. Your reputation, Lord, is for *Ps. 135* all generations. The Lord has established His throne in heaven; *Ps. 103* His kingdom rules all. Let the heavens rejoice and the earth be *1 Chr. 16* glad. Let them say among the nations, "The Lord is King." The Lord is King, the Lord was King, the Lord will be King for ever and all time. The Lord is King for ever and all time; nations will *Ps. 10* perish from His land. The Lord foils the plans of nations; He *Ps. 33* frustrates the intentions of peoples. Many are the intentions in a *Prov. 19* person's mind, but the Lord's plan prevails. The Lord's plan shall *Ps. 33* stand for ever, His mind's intent for all generations. For He spoke and it was; He commanded and it stood firm. For the Lord has *Ps. 132* chosen Zion; He desired it for His dwelling. For the Lord has *Ps. 135* chosen Jacob as His own, Israel as His special treasure. For the *Ps. 94* Lord will not abandon His people; nor will He abandon His heritage. ▸ He is compassionate. He forgives wrongdoing and does *Ps. 78* not destroy. Repeatedly He suppresses His anger, not rousing His full fury. Lord, save! May the King answer us on the day we call. *Ps. 20*

... A THOUSAND WORDS

יְהִי כְבוֹד יהוה לְעוֹלָם, יִשְׂמַח יהוה בְּמַעֲשָׂיו: יְהִי שֵׁם יהוה מְבֹרָךְ, **תהלים קד**
תהלים קג
מֵעַתָּה וְעַד־עוֹלָם: מִמִּזְרַח־שֶׁמֶשׁ עַד־מְבוֹאוֹ, מְהֻלָּל שֵׁם יהוה:

רָם עַל־כָּל־גּוֹיִם יהוה, עַל הַשָּׁמַיִם כְּבוֹדוֹ: יהוה שִׁמְךָ לְעוֹלָם, **תהלים קלה**

יהוה זִכְרְךָ לְדֹר־וָדֹר: יהוה בַּשָּׁמַיִם הֵכִין כִּסְאוֹ, וּמַלְכוּתוֹ בַּכֹּל **תהלים קג**

מָשָׁלָה: יִשְׂמְחוּ הַשָּׁמַיִם וְתָגֵל הָאָרֶץ, וְיֹאמְרוּ בַגּוֹיִם יהוה מָלָךְ: **דברי הימים**
א' טז

יהוה מֶלֶךְ, יהוה מָלָךְ, יהוה יִמְלֹךְ לְעוֹלָם וָעֶד. יהוה מֶלֶךְ עוֹלָם **תהלים י**

וָעֶד, אָבְדוּ גוֹיִם מֵאַרְצוֹ: יהוה הֵפִיר עֲצַת־גּוֹיִם, הֵנִיא מַחְשְׁבוֹת **תהלים לג**

עַמִּים: רַבּוֹת מַחֲשָׁבוֹת בְּלֶב־אִישׁ, וַעֲצַת יהוה הִיא תָקוּם: **משלי יט**

עֲצַת יהוה לְעוֹלָם תַּעֲמֹד, מַחְשְׁבוֹת לִבּוֹ לְדֹר וָדֹר: כִּי הוּא אָמַר **תהלים לג**

וַיֶּהִי, הוּא־צִוָּה וַיַּעֲמֹד: כִּי־בָחַר יהוה בְּצִיּוֹן, אִוָּהּ לְמוֹשָׁב לוֹ: **תהלים קלב**

כִּי־יַעֲקֹב בָּחַר לוֹ יָהּ, יִשְׂרָאֵל לִסְגֻלָּתוֹ: כִּי לֹא־יִטֹּשׁ יהוה עַמּוֹ, **תהלים קלה**
תהלים צד

וְנַחֲלָתוֹ לֹא יַעֲזֹב: ‹ וְהוּא רַחוּם, יְכַפֵּר עָוֹן וְלֹא־יַשְׁחִית, וְהִרְבָּה **תהלים עח**

לְהָשִׁיב אַפּוֹ, וְלֹא־יָעִיר כָּל־חֲמָתוֹ: יהוה הוֹשִׁיעָה, הַמֶּלֶךְ יַעֲנֵנוּ **תהלים כ**

בְיוֹם־קָרְאֵנוּ:

| REFLECTION | CONNECTION |

וַיְבִאֵנוּ אֶל־הַמָּקוֹם הַזֶּה, וַיִּתֶּן־לָנוּ
אֶת־הָאָרֶץ הַזֹּאת, אֶרֶץ זָבַת חָלָב וּדְבָשׁ.

*"He brought us to this place and
gave us this land, a land flowing
with milk and honey."*

(Devarim 26:9)

What is special about
Eretz Yisrael?

Why do you think God chose it
for our homeland?

Do we need a homeland at all?
Why?

Does it matter where this is?

*"I will insist that the Hebrews have done more to
civilize men than any other nation. If I were an
atheist, and believed in blind eternal fate, I should
still believe that fate had ordained the Jews to be
the most essential instrument for civilizing the
nations. If I were an atheist of the other sect, who
believe or pretend to believe that all is ordered
by chance, I should believe that chance had ordered the Jews to preserve and propagate to all
mankind the doctrine of a supreme, intelligent,
wise, almighty sovereign of the universe, which
I believe to be the great essential principle of all
morality, and consequently of all civilization."*

(President John Adams, 1809)

The line beginning with "You open Your hand" should be said with special concentration, representing as it does the key idea of this psalm, and of Pesukei DeZimra as a whole, that God is the creator and sustainer of all. Some have the custom to touch the hand-tefillin at °, and the head-tefillin at °°.

אַשְׁרֵי Happy are those who live in Your House;   *Ps. 84*
    they shall continue to praise You, Selah!

Happy are the people for whom this is so;   *Ps. 144*
    happy are the people whose God is the LORD.

A song of praise by David.   *Ps. 145*
    I will elevate You, my God, the King,
        and bless Your name for ever and all time.
    Every day I will bless You,
        and praise Your name for ever and all time.
    Great is the LORD and greatly to be praised;
        His greatness is unfathomable.
    One generation will praise Your works to the next,
        and tell of Your mighty deeds.
    On the glorious splendor of Your majesty I will meditate,
        and on the acts of Your wonders.
    They shall talk of the power of Your awesome deeds,
        and I will tell of Your greatness.
    They shall recite the record of Your great goodness,
        and sing with joy of Your righteousness.
    The LORD is generous and compassionate,
        slow to anger and great in loving-kindness.
    The LORD is good to all,
        and His compassion extends to all His works.
    All Your works shall thank You, LORD,
        and Your devoted ones shall bless You.
    They shall talk of the glory of Your kingship,
        and speak of Your might.

---

we have available to us. In truth, the entire *alef-beit* is not represented here. Can you see which letter is missing? This is because it would represent "*nefila*" and refer to the fall of man. Instead we choose to focus on the opposite when the very next verse refers to God supporting and carrying those that fall.

The line beginning with פּוֹתֵחַ אֶת יָדֶךָ should be said with special concentration, representing as it does the key idea of this psalm, and of פסוקי דזמרה as a whole, that God is the creator and sustainer of all. Some have the custom to touch the תפילין של יד at °, and the תפילין של ראש at °°.

תהלים פד

אַשְׁרֵי יוֹשְׁבֵי בֵיתֶךָ, עוֹד יְהַלְלוּךָ סֶּלָה:
אַשְׁרֵי הָעָם שֶׁכָּכָה לּוֹ, אַשְׁרֵי הָעָם שֶׁיהוה אֱלֹהָיו:

תהלים קמד

תְּהִלָּה לְדָוִד

תהלים קמה

אֲרוֹמִמְךָ אֱלוֹהַי הַמֶּלֶךְ, וַאֲבָרְכָה שִׁמְךָ לְעוֹלָם וָעֶד:
בְּכָל־יוֹם אֲבָרְכֶךָּ, וַאֲהַלְלָה שִׁמְךָ לְעוֹלָם וָעֶד:
גָּדוֹל יהוה וּמְהֻלָּל מְאֹד, וְלִגְדֻלָּתוֹ אֵין חֵקֶר:
דּוֹר לְדוֹר יְשַׁבַּח מַעֲשֶׂיךָ, וּגְבוּרֹתֶיךָ יַגִּידוּ:
הֲדַר כְּבוֹד הוֹדֶךָ, וְדִבְרֵי נִפְלְאֹתֶיךָ אָשִׂיחָה:
וֶעֱזוּז נוֹרְאֹתֶיךָ יֹאמֵרוּ, וּגְדוּלָּתְךָ אֲסַפְּרֶנָּה:
זֵכֶר רַב־טוּבְךָ יַבִּיעוּ, וְצִדְקָתְךָ יְרַנֵּנוּ:
חַנּוּן וְרַחוּם יהוה, אֶרֶךְ אַפַּיִם וּגְדָל־חָסֶד:
טוֹב־יהוה לַכֹּל, וְרַחֲמָיו עַל־כָּל־מַעֲשָׂיו:
יוֹדוּךָ יהוה כָּל־מַעֲשֶׂיךָ, וַחֲסִידֶיךָ יְבָרְכוּכָה:
כְּבוֹד מַלְכוּתְךָ יֹאמֵרוּ, וּגְבוּרָתְךָ יְדַבֵּרוּ:

LEARNING

This is the first of three times that we say *Ashrei* in our daily *tefillot*. We first say *Ashrei* here as the centerpiece of *Pesukei DeZimra*, and then repeat it toward the end of Shaḥarit, and then again as a "mini-*Pesukei DeZimra*" at the beginning of Minḥa. The Talmud states (*Berakhot* 4b) that whoever says *Ashrei* three times every day is guaranteed a place in the World to Come. Maybe this is because

Ashrei describes a perfect world, and ideal state in which all the world is in harmony.

This chapter of *Tehillim* is written with an *alef-beit* acrostic. This is a classic literary technique, and has some obvious advantages such as ease of memorization, and the simple beauty of the *alef-beit* format. However, there is also a deeper message here: we praise Hashem with every sound, every letter and every form of speech that

To make known to mankind His mighty deeds
and the glorious majesty of His kingship.
Your kingdom is an everlasting kingdom,
and Your reign is for all generations.
The LORD supports all who fall,
and raises all who are bowed down.
All raise their eyes to You in hope,
and You give them their food in due season.
°You open Your hand, °°and satisfy every living thing with favor.
The LORD is righteous in all His ways, and kind in all He does.
The LORD is close to all who call on Him,
to all who call on Him in truth.
He fulfills the will of those who fear Him;
He hears their cry and saves them.
The LORD guards all who love Him,
but all the wicked He will destroy.
‣ My mouth shall speak the praise of the LORD,
and all creatures shall bless His holy name for ever and all time.
We will bless the LORD now and for ever. Halleluya!

Ps. 115

REFLECTION

Can you think
of something
amazing about
the world
beginning with
every letter of
the alphabet?

Do you feel close to
Hashem right now?

How do you think
you could get closer?

CONNECTION

Joseph Gitler made aliya from New Jersey in the year 2000. In 2002, he read a report from Israel's National Insurance Institute that told a bleak story of Israel's poor and unemployed. This together with witnessing himself tremendous food wastage in Israel – from social events, restaurants, and stores, and from unharvested farm fields – inspired him to found Leket in 2003 – Israel's largest national food bank and food-rescue. With the help of thousands of volunteers each year, Leket salvages 115 tons of food every week that would otherwise be destroyed. It delivers this excess food to hundreds of thousands of needy Israelis through its partnership with non-profit agencies throughout the country. Joseph Gitler saw a desperate need in Israel that went unaddressed and stood up and took responsibility, to help the poor of Israel.

לְהוֹדִיעַ לִבְנֵי הָאָדָם גְּבוּרֹתָיו, וּכְבוֹד הֲדַר מַלְכוּתוֹ:

מַלְכוּתְךָ מַלְכוּת כָּל־עֹלָמִים, וּמֶמְשַׁלְתְּךָ בְּכָל־דּוֹר וָדֹר:

סוֹמֵךְ יהוה לְכָל־הַנֹּפְלִים, וְזוֹקֵף לְכָל־הַכְּפוּפִים:

עֵינֵי־כֹל אֵלֶיךָ יְשַׂבֵּרוּ, וְאַתָּה נוֹתֵן־לָהֶם אֶת־אָכְלָם בְּעִתּוֹ:

°פּוֹתֵחַ אֶת־יָדֶךָ, °°וּמַשְׂבִּיעַ לְכָל־חַי רָצוֹן:

צַדִּיק יהוה בְּכָל־דְּרָכָיו, וְחָסִיד בְּכָל־מַעֲשָׂיו:

קָרוֹב יהוה לְכָל־קֹרְאָיו, לְכֹל אֲשֶׁר יִקְרָאֻהוּ בֶאֱמֶת:

רְצוֹן־יְרֵאָיו יַעֲשֶׂה, וְאֶת־שַׁוְעָתָם יִשְׁמַע, וְיוֹשִׁיעֵם:

שׁוֹמֵר יהוה אֶת־כָּל־אֹהֲבָיו, וְאֵת כָּל־הָרְשָׁעִים יַשְׁמִיד:

‹ תְּהִלַּת יהוה יְדַבֶּר פִּי, וִיבָרֵךְ כָּל־בָּשָׂר שֵׁם קָדְשׁוֹ לְעוֹלָם וָעֶד:

וַאֲנַחְנוּ נְבָרֵךְ יָהּ מֵעַתָּה וְעַד־עוֹלָם, הַלְלוּיָהּ:

תהלים קטו

... A THOUSAND WORDS

הַלְלוּיָהּ Halleluya! Praise the LORD, my soul. I will praise the *Ps. 146* LORD all my life; I will sing to my God as long as I live. Put not your trust in princes, or in mortal man who cannot save. His breath expires, he returns to the earth; on that day his plans come to an end. Happy is he whose help is the God of Jacob, whose hope is in the LORD his God who made heaven and earth, the sea and all they contain; He who keeps faith for ever. He secures justice for the oppressed. He gives food to the hungry. The LORD sets captives free. The LORD gives sight to the blind. The LORD raises those bowed down. The LORD loves the righteous. The LORD protects the stranger. He gives courage to the orphan and widow. He defeats the way of the wicked. ► The LORD shall reign for ever. He is your God, Zion, for all generations. Halleluya!

REFLECTION	CONNECTION

Who
is weak
in your society?

How
does God
protect them?

How
do you
protect them?

Not like the brazen giant of Greek fame,
With conquering limbs astride from land to land;
Here at our sea-washed, sunset gates shall stand
A mighty woman with a torch, whose flame
Is the imprisoned lightning, and her name
Mother of Exiles. From her beacon-hand
Glows world-wide welcome; her mild eyes command
The air-bridged harbor that twin cities frame.

"Keep, ancient lands, your storied pomp!" cries she
With silent lips. "Give me your tired, your poor,
Your huddled masses yearning to breathe free,
The wretched refuse of your teeming shore.
Send these, the homeless, tempest-tost to me,
I lift my lamp beside the golden door!"

(Emma Lazarus, *The New Colossus*, engraved inside the pedestal of the Statue of Liberty)

תהילים קמו

הַלְלוּיָהּ, הַלְלִי נַפְשִׁי אֶת־יהוה: אֲהַלְלָה יהוה בְּחַיָּי, אֲזַמְּרָה לֵאלֹהַי בְּעוֹדִי: אַל־תִּבְטְחוּ בִנְדִיבִים, בְּבֶן־אָדָם שֶׁאֵין לוֹ תְשׁוּעָה: תֵּצֵא רוּחוֹ, יָשֻׁב לְאַדְמָתוֹ, בַּיּוֹם הַהוּא אָבְדוּ עֶשְׁתֹּנֹתָיו: אַשְׁרֵי שֶׁאֵל יַעֲקֹב בְּעֶזְרוֹ, שִׂבְרוֹ עַל־יהוה אֱלֹהָיו: עֹשֶׂה שָׁמַיִם וָאָרֶץ, אֶת־הַיָּם וְאֶת־כָּל־אֲשֶׁר־בָּם, הַשֹּׁמֵר אֱמֶת לְעוֹלָם: עֹשֶׂה מִשְׁפָּט לַעֲשׁוּקִים, נֹתֵן לֶחֶם לָרְעֵבִים, יהוה מַתִּיר אֲסוּרִים: יהוה פֹּקֵחַ עִוְרִים, יהוה זֹקֵף כְּפוּפִים, יהוה אֹהֵב צַדִּיקִים: יהוה שֹׁמֵר אֶת־גֵּרִים, יָתוֹם וְאַלְמָנָה יְעוֹדֵד, וְדֶרֶךְ רְשָׁעִים יְעַוֵּת: ‹ יִמְלֹךְ יהוה לְעוֹלָם, אֱלֹהַיִךְ צִיּוֹן לְדֹר וָדֹר, הַלְלוּיָהּ:

... A THOUSAND WORDS

הַלְלוּיָהּ Halleluya! How good it is to sing songs to our God; how *Ps. 147* pleasant and fitting to praise Him. The LORD rebuilds Jerusalem. He gathers the scattered exiles of Israel. He heals the brokenhearted and binds up their wounds. He counts the number of the stars, calling each by name. Great is our LORD and mighty in power; His understanding has no limit. The LORD gives courage to the humble, but casts the wicked to the ground. Sing to the LORD in thanks; make music to our God on the harp. He covers the sky with clouds. He provides the earth with rain and makes grass grow on the hills. He gives food to the cattle and to the ravens when they cry. He does not take delight in the strength of horses nor pleasure in the fleetness of man. The LORD takes pleasure in those who fear Him, who put their hope in His loving care. Praise the LORD, Jerusalem; sing to your God, Zion, for He has strengthened the bars of your gates and blessed your children in your midst. He has brought peace to your borders, and satisfied you with the finest wheat. He sends His commandment to earth; swiftly runs His word. He spreads snow like fleece, sprinkles frost like ashes, scatters hail like crumbs. Who can stand His cold? He sends His word and melts them; He makes the wind blow and the waters flow. ▸ He has declared His words to Jacob, His statutes and laws to Israel. He has done this for no other nation; such laws they do not know. Halleluya!

REFLECTION	... A THOUSAND WORDS

"A change in the weather is sufficient to recreate the world and ourselves."
(Marcel Proust)

Have you ever felt God in the weather? When?

Look outside. Can you find God in the weather today?

Think about it now as you say this *tefilla*.

תהלים קמז

הַלְלוּיָהּ, כִּי־טוֹב זַמְּרָה אֱלֹהֵינוּ, כִּי־נָעִים נָאוָה תְהִלָּה: בּוֹנֵה יְרוּשָׁלַ͏ִם יהוה, נִדְחֵי יִשְׂרָאֵל יְכַנֵּס: הָרוֹפֵא לִשְׁבוּרֵי לֵב, וּמְחַבֵּשׁ לְעַצְּבוֹתָם: מוֹנֶה מִסְפָּר לַכּוֹכָבִים, לְכֻלָּם שֵׁמוֹת יִקְרָא: גָּדוֹל אֲדוֹנֵינוּ וְרַב־כֹּחַ, לִתְבוּנָתוֹ אֵין מִסְפָּר: מְעוֹדֵד עֲנָוִים יהוה, מַשְׁפִּיל רְשָׁעִים עֲדֵי־אָרֶץ: עֱנוּ לַיהוה בְּתוֹדָה, זַמְּרוּ לֵאלֹהֵינוּ בְכִנּוֹר: הַמְכַסֶּה שָׁמַיִם בְּעָבִים, הַמֵּכִין לָאָרֶץ מָטָר, הַמַּצְמִיחַ הָרִים חָצִיר: נוֹתֵן לִבְהֵמָה לַחְמָהּ, לִבְנֵי עֹרֵב אֲשֶׁר יִקְרָאוּ: לֹא בִגְבוּרַת הַסּוּס יֶחְפָּץ, לֹא־בְשׁוֹקֵי הָאִישׁ יִרְצֶה: רוֹצֶה יהוה אֶת־ יְרֵאָיו, אֶת־הַמְיַחֲלִים לְחַסְדּוֹ: שַׁבְּחִי יְרוּשָׁלַ͏ִם אֶת־יהוה, הַלְלִי אֱלֹהַיִךְ צִיּוֹן: כִּי־חִזַּק בְּרִיחֵי שְׁעָרָיִךְ, בֵּרַךְ בָּנַיִךְ בְּקִרְבֵּךְ: הַשָּׂם־ גְּבוּלֵךְ שָׁלוֹם, חֵלֶב חִטִּים יַשְׂבִּיעֵךְ: הַשֹּׁלֵחַ אִמְרָתוֹ אָרֶץ, עַד־ מְהֵרָה יָרוּץ דְּבָרוֹ: הַנֹּתֵן שֶׁלֶג כַּצָּמֶר, כְּפוֹר כָּאֵפֶר יְפַזֵּר: מַשְׁלִיךְ קַרְחוֹ כְפִתִּים, לִפְנֵי קָרָתוֹ מִי יַעֲמֹד: יִשְׁלַח דְּבָרוֹ וְיַמְסֵם, יַשֵּׁב רוּחוֹ יִזְּלוּ־מָיִם: ◄ מַגִּיד דְּבָרָו לְיַעֲקֹב, חֻקָּיו וּמִשְׁפָּטָיו לְיִשְׂרָאֵל: לֹא עָשָׂה כֵן לְכָל־גּוֹי, וּמִשְׁפָּטִים בַּל־יְדָעוּם, הַלְלוּיָהּ:

CONNECTION

"Once it happened that it didn't rain for almost the whole of winter in Eretz Yisrael. The people were desperate and so they sent for Ḥoni to whom they knew Hashem would listen. Ḥoni drew a circle with a stick in the dirt and cried out to Hashem: 'Hashem, have mercy on Your children and let it rain. I won't leave this circle until You do!' At once a few drops of rain began to fall but nothing more than a drizzle. Ḥoni cried out to Hashem again: 'I didn't pray to You for rain like this. Your children need real rain that will fill their wells and reservoirs.' Immediately torrents of rain began to pour, threatening to flood the towns and villages. Once again Ḥoni cried to Hashem: 'I didn't pray to You, Hashem, for rain like this. This rain will destroy the world! Your children need rain of love and kindness.' Finally the rains calmed to a normal level, the wind began to blow and the clouds dispersed and the sun shone, and the people were saved. They ran out into the fields and gathered mushrooms and truffles."

(Ta'anit 23a)

הַלְלוּיָהּ Halleluya! Praise the LORD from the heavens, praise Him *Ps. 148* in the heights. Praise Him, all His angels; praise Him, all His multitudes. Praise Him, sun and moon; praise Him, all shining stars. Praise Him, highest heavens and the waters above the heavens. Let them praise the name of the LORD, for He commanded and they were created. He established them for ever and all time, issuing a decree that will never change. Praise the LORD from the earth: sea monsters and all the deep seas; fire and hail, snow and mist, storm winds that obey His word; mountains and all hills, fruit trees and all cedars; wild animals and all cattle, creeping things and winged birds; kings of the earth and all nations, princes and all judges on earth; youths and maidens, old and young. ‣ Let them praise the name of the LORD, for His name alone is sublime; His majesty is above earth and heaven. He has raised the pride of His people, for the glory of all His devoted ones, the children of Israel, the people close to Him. Halleluya!

... A THOUSAND WORDS

תהלים קמח

הַלְלוּיָהּ, הַלְלוּ אֶת־יהוה מִן־הַשָּׁמַיִם, הַלְלְוּהוּ בַּמְּרוֹמִים: הַלְלְוּהוּ כָל־מַלְאָכָיו, הַלְלְוּהוּ כָּל־צְבָאָו: הַלְלְוּהוּ שֶׁמֶשׁ וְיָרֵחַ, הַלְלְוּהוּ כָּל־כְּוֹכְבֵי אוֹר: הַלְלְוּהוּ שְׁמֵי הַשָּׁמָיִם, וְהַמַּיִם אֲשֶׁר מֵעַל הַשָּׁמָיִם: יְהַלְלוּ אֶת־שֵׁם יהוה, כִּי הוּא צִוָּה וְנִבְרָאוּ: וַיַּעֲמִידֵם לָעַד לְעוֹלָם, חָק־נָתַן וְלֹא יַעֲבוֹר: הַלְלוּ אֶת־יהוה מִן־הָאָרֶץ, תַּנִּינִים וְכָל־תְּהֹמוֹת: אֵשׁ וּבָרָד שֶׁלֶג וְקִיטוֹר, רוּחַ סְעָרָה עֹשָׂה דְבָרוֹ: הֶהָרִים וְכָל־גְּבָעוֹת, עֵץ פְּרִי וְכָל־אֲרָזִים: הַחַיָּה וְכָל־בְּהֵמָה, רֶמֶשׂ וְצִפּוֹר כָּנָף: מַלְכֵי־אֶרֶץ וְכָל־לְאֻמִּים, שָׂרִים וְכָל־שֹׁפְטֵי אָרֶץ: בַּחוּרִים וְגַם־בְּתוּלוֹת, זְקֵנִים עִם־נְעָרִים: ‹ יְהַלְלוּ אֶת־שֵׁם יהוה, כִּי־נִשְׂגָּב שְׁמוֹ לְבַדּוֹ, הוֹדוֹ עַל־אֶרֶץ וְשָׁמָיִם: וַיָּרֶם קֶרֶן לְעַמּוֹ, תְּהִלָּה לְכָל־חֲסִידָיו, לִבְנֵי יִשְׂרָאֵל עַם קְרֹבוֹ, הַלְלוּיָהּ:

REFLECTION

Can you find a way to praise God in a large way (like the vastness of the cosmos) and a tiny way (like the beauty of each blade of grass)?

Imagine the amazing things that nature has witnessed over time – what would it highlight?

What part are you playing in the orchestra of creation? What is your unique contribution?

CONNECTION

"The best remedy for those who are afraid, lonely, or unhappy is to go outside, somewhere where they can be quite alone with the heavens, nature, and God. Because only then does one feel that all is as it should be and that God wishes to see people happy, amidst the simple beauty of nature. As long as this exists, and it certainly always will, I know that then there will always be comfort for every sorrow, whatever the circumstances may be. And I firmly believe that nature brings solace in all troubles."

(Anne Frank, *The Diary of a Young Girl*)

הַלְלוּיָהּ Halleluya! Sing to the LORD a new song, His praise in the *Ps. 149*
assembly of the devoted. Let Israel rejoice in its Maker; let the children of Zion rejoice in their King. Let them praise His name with
dancing; sing praises to Him with drum and harp. For the LORD
delights in His people; He adorns the humble with salvation. Let
the devoted celebrate in glory; let them sing for joy on their beds.
Let high praises of God be in their throats, and a two-edged sword
in their hand: to impose retribution on the nations, punishment
on the peoples, ▸ binding their kings with chains, their nobles with
iron shackles, carrying out the judgment written against them. This
is the glory of all His devoted ones. Halleluya!

REFLECTION

*"A generation in which
the Temple is not built is
considered as if it was one
in which it was destroyed."*

(Yerushalmi, *Yoma* 1:1)

What would you like to see in the time of the
final *geula*? What can you do to help perfect
the world?

How are you contributing to the rebuilding
of the Temple?

... A THOUSAND WORDS

תהלים קמט

הַלְלוּיָה, שִׁירוּ לַיהוה שִׁיר חָדָשׁ, תְּהִלָּתוֹ בִּקְהַל חֲסִידִים: יִשְׂמַח יִשְׂרָאֵל בְּעֹשָׂיו, בְּנֵי־צִיּוֹן יָגִילוּ בְמַלְכָּם: יְהַלְלוּ שְׁמוֹ בְמָחוֹל, בְּתֹף וְכִנּוֹר יְזַמְּרוּ־לוֹ: כִּי־רוֹצֶה יהוה בְּעַמּוֹ, יְפָאֵר עֲנָוִים בִּישׁוּעָה: יַעְלְזוּ חֲסִידִים בְּכָבוֹד, יְרַנְּנוּ עַל־מִשְׁכְּבוֹתָם: רוֹמְמוֹת אֵל בִּגְרוֹנָם, וְחֶרֶב פִּיפִיּוֹת בְּיָדָם: לַעֲשׂוֹת נְקָמָה בַּגּוֹיִם, תּוֹכֵחוֹת בַּלְאֻמִּים: ◀ לֶאְסֹר מַלְכֵיהֶם בְּזִקִּים, וְנִכְבְּדֵיהֶם בְּכַבְלֵי בַרְזֶל: לַעֲשׂוֹת בָּהֶם מִשְׁפָּט כָּתוּב, הָדָר הוּא לְכָל־חֲסִידָיו, הַלְלוּיָה:

CONNECTION

Several years after the destruction of the Holy Temple, Rabban Gamliel, Rabbi Eliezer ben Azarya, Rabbi Yehoshua, and Rabbi Akiva were going up to Jerusalem. When they reached Mount Scopus, the site of the Temple came into view, and they tore their garments in mourning. When they reached the Temple Mount, they saw a fox dart out from the spot where the Holy of Holies had stood in the Holy Temple. The rabbis began to weep, but Rabbi Akiva laughed. They said to him: "Akiva, you never cease to amaze us. We are crying, and you laugh!" But Rabbi Akiva said, "And you, why are you crying?"

The rabbis responded: "What? Shall we not weep? The place about which Scripture states (Bemidbar 1:51), 'And the stranger who draws close shall die,' has become a den of foxes! Indeed, this is a fulfillment of the verse, 'For Mount Zion which lies desolate, foxes prowl over it' (Eikha 5:18)."

Rabbi Akiva answered them: "This is exactly why I laugh. For just as we have seen the prophecies of Jerusalem's destruction have come to pass, so too, know that the prophecies of her future consolation shall also be fulfilled. I laughed because I remembered the verses (Zekharya 8:4–5), 'Old men and old women will once again sit in the streets of Jerusalem, each with his staff in his hand because of advanced age; and the city will be filled with boys and girls playing in its streets.' The Holy One, blessed be He, has declared that just as the first prophecies have been fulfilled, so shall the latter. I am joyous that the first have already come to pass, for the latter shall be fulfilled in the future."

Said the rabbis, "You have comforted us, Akiva, you have comforted us. May you be comforted by the footsteps of the Messiah."

(Adapted from Midrash Raba Eikha, 5)

הַלְלוּיָהּ Halleluya! Praise God in His holy place; Ps. 150
  praise Him in the heavens of His power.
  Praise Him for His mighty deeds;
  praise Him for His immense greatness.
  Praise Him with blasts of the shofar;
  praise Him with the harp and lyre.
  Praise Him with drum and dance;
  praise Him with strings and flute.
  Praise Him with clashing cymbals;
  praise Him with resounding cymbals.
  ▸ Let all that breathes praise the LORD. Halleluya!
  Let all that breathes praise the LORD. Halleluya!

"And David was dancing with full might before the LORD, and David was wearing a linen ephod."
(Shmuel Beit 6:14)

How can you use your mind, heart, hands, and mouth to praise God?

Have you ever felt music speak to you in ways that words could not?

Can you think of other ways to connect to God other than prayer?

תהלים קנ

הַלְלוּיָהּ, הַלְלוּ־אֵל בְּקָדְשׁוֹ

הַלְלוּהוּ בִּרְקִיעַ עֻזּוֹ:

הַלְלוּהוּ בִגְבוּרֹתָיו

הַלְלוּהוּ כְּרֹב גֻּדְלוֹ:

הַלְלוּהוּ בְּתֵקַע שׁוֹפָר

הַלְלוּהוּ בְּנֵבֶל וְכִנּוֹר:

הַלְלוּהוּ בְּתֹף וּמָחוֹל

הַלְלוּהוּ בְּמִנִּים וְעֻגָב:

הַלְלוּהוּ בְצִלְצְלֵי־שָׁמַע

הַלְלוּהוּ בְּצִלְצְלֵי תְרוּעָה:

‹ כֹּל הַנְּשָׁמָה תְּהַלֵּל יָהּ, הַלְלוּיָהּ:

כֹּל הַנְּשָׁמָה תְּהַלֵּל יָהּ, הַלְלוּיָהּ:

CONNECTION

The Rabbi of Karlin was asked the following question: "Why do Hasidim dance so much?"

The rabbi smiled and answered, "Ah, you see, when a person dances, his feet are a few of inches off the ground. This means that while a person is dancing, he is a few inches closer to heaven."

LEARNING

The *Yalkut Shimoni* Midrash *Tehillim* 889 says that when King David finished writing *Sefer Tehillim*, he felt proud and said to God, "Is there any other creature You created in Your world that can recite song and praise more than I do?" At that moment a frog said to King David, "David, don't be so proud, I sing songs and praise more than you do. Not only that, but for every song that I sing, three thousand parables can be derived from it."

בָּרוּךְ Blessed be the LORD for ever.   *Ps. 89*
        Amen and Amen.
   Blessed from Zion be the LORD   *Ps. 135*
      who is present in Jerusalem. Halleluya!
   Blessed be the LORD, God of Israel,   *Ps. 72*
      who alone does wonders.
 ‣ Blessed be His glorious name for ever,
      and may all the earth be filled with His glory.
      Amen and Amen.

---

be more important than reciting an entire blessing to Hashem?

Imagine an official of the king, who praises the king warmly in front of a large gathering. If people ignore the official's words, it is incredibly disrespectful to the king. It is an indication that no one really agrees with his praise. On the other hand, if the gathering breaks out into hearty applause, this confirms the praise and proves that the king is worthy of honor.

...A THOUSAND WORDS

תהלים פט

בָּרוּךְ יהוה לְעוֹלָם
אָמֵן וְאָמֵן:

תהלים קלה

בָּרוּךְ יהוה מִצִּיּוֹן
שֹׁכֵן יְרוּשָׁלָםִ, הַלְלוּיָהּ:

תהלים עב

בָּרוּךְ יהוה אֱלֹהִים אֱלֹהֵי יִשְׂרָאֵל
עֹשֵׂה נִפְלָאוֹת לְבַדּוֹ:
‹ וּבָרוּךְ שֵׁם כְּבוֹדוֹ לְעוֹלָם
וְיִמָּלֵא כְבוֹדוֹ אֶת־כָּל־הָאָרֶץ
אָמֵן וְאָמֵן:

REFLECTION	CONNECTION
How do you show you agree with something?	In the sefer "Mofet HaDor," the biography of Rebbe Yechezkel Levenstein, it is said that he once saw a grandchild of Rebbe Yisrael Salanter crying.
Can you think of ways to emphasize something you really believe in when you're talking to someone?	He asked the boy of five years old, "Why are you crying, sweet one?" The child said, "Because I want to eat." "Why don't you eat?" Reb Yechezkel asked him. "Because I need first to recite a blessing," the child answered.
What things have you said that you can imagine God saying "Amen" to you?	"Do you not know the blessing to be recited over this food?" Rebbe Yechezkel asked. "Yes, I know it," the child responded, "but there is no one to answer 'Amen' after my blessing. How can I say it?"

LEARNING

The Gemara tells us – "Answering Amen is greater than reciting a blessing" (Berakhot 53b). At first, this may seem surprising. How can saying one short, simple word

Stand until after "Bless the Lord" on page 120.

וַיְבָרֶךְ David blessed the Lord in front of the entire assembly. David *1 Chr. 29* said, "Blessed are You, Lord, God of our father Yisrael, for ever and ever. Yours, Lord, are the greatness and the power, the glory, majesty and splendor, for everything in heaven and earth is Yours. Yours, Lord, is the kingdom; You are great as Head over all. Both riches and honor are in Your gift and You reign over all things. In Your hand are strength and might. It is in Your power to make great and give strength to all. Therefore, our God, we thank You and praise Your glorious name." You alone are the Lord. *Neh. 9*

| REFLECTION | ...A THOUSAND WORDS |

"Tzedaka and acts of kindness are the equivalent of all the mitzvot of the Torah." (Yerushalmi, Pe'ah 1:1)

How do you dedicate your money toward God?

How will you be generous today?

Do you make God proud in how you use your money?

Stand until after בָּרְכוּ *on page 121.*

דברי
הימים א,
כט

וַיְבָרֶךְ דָּוִיד אֶת־יהוה לְעֵינֵי כָּל־הַקָּהָל, וַיֹּאמֶר דָּוִיד, בָּרוּךְ אַתָּה יהוה, אֱלֹהֵי יִשְׂרָאֵל אָבִינוּ, מֵעוֹלָם וְעַד־עוֹלָם: לְךָ יהוה הַגְּדֻלָּה וְהַגְּבוּרָה וְהַתִּפְאֶרֶת וְהַנֵּצַח וְהַהוֹד, כִּי־כֹל בַּשָּׁמַיִם וּבָאָרֶץ, לְךָ יהוה הַמַּמְלָכָה וְהַמִּתְנַשֵּׂא לְכֹל לְרֹאשׁ: וְהָעֹשֶׁר וְהַכָּבוֹד מִלְּפָנֶיךָ, וְאַתָּה מוֹשֵׁל בַּכֹּל, וּבְיָדְךָ כֹּחַ וּגְבוּרָה, וּבְיָדְךָ לְגַדֵּל וּלְחַזֵּק לַכֹּל: וְעַתָּה אֱלֹהֵינוּ מוֹדִים אֲנַחְנוּ לָךְ, וּמְהַלְלִים לְשֵׁם תִּפְאַרְתֶּךָ: אַתָּה־הוּא יהוה לְבַדֶּךָ, אַתָּ עָשִׂיתָ

נחמיה ט

| CONNECTION | LEARNING |

There was once a boy called Tommy. He was actually known as "Tommy Doesn't Give" because despite that fact that Tommy was a sweet, polite, and charming young man, he lived with his motto "Tommy doesn't give." Tommy never gave anything to anyone. One day, Tommy went swimming and found himself caught in a whirlpool. He struggled to stay afloat and waved for the attention of a lifeguard. The lifeguard approached on a small boat. "Tommy," he yelled, "give me your hand."

Tommy, struggling to keep his head above the waves, shouted back, "Tommy doesn't give!" The lifeguard exasperatedly tried again, but each time his plea was answered with Tommy's staunch refusal to cooperate.

Finally the lifeguard cried, "OK Tommy, take my hand." Automatically Tommy reached out and took the lifeguard's hand to safety.

Sometimes, we lose sight of the fact that giving is actually the most important way of receiving.

This verse was recited by King David when he had amassed all of his wealth and was dedicating it to build the *Beit HaMikdash*. The Talmud (*Gittin* 7b) says: "Even a poor person who receives *tzedaka* must give from what he or she receives." This is telling us that an individual's sense of *kavod*, his or her self-dignity, is expressed through giving. Freeing a person from the responsibility of giving is actually taking away a privilege. It is therefore a widely accepted custom to give some *tzedaka* at this point in the *tefilla*.

You made the heavens, even the highest heavens, and all their multitudes, the earth and all that is on it, the seas and all they contain. You give life to them all, and the multitudes of heaven worship You. ▸ You are the LORD God who chose Abram and brought him out of Ur of the Chaldees, changing his name to Abraham. You found his heart faithful toward You, ◂ and You made a covenant with him to give to his descendants the land of the Canaanites, Hittites, Amorites, Perizzites, Jebusites and Girgashites. You fulfilled Your promise for You are righteous. You saw the suffering of our ancestors in Egypt. You heard their cry at the Sea of Reeds. You sent signs and wonders against Pharaoh, all his servants and all the people of his land, because You knew how arrogantly the Egyptians treated them. You created for Yourself reputation that remains to this day. ▸ You divided the sea before them, so that they passed through the sea on dry land, but You cast their pursuers into the depths, like a stone into mighty waters.

...A THOUSAND WORDS **REFLECTION**

How are you
connected
to your
ancestors?

What is the
greatest thing
God has done
for you?

How do your
memories
affect you?

אֶת־הַשָּׁמַיִם, שְׁמֵי הַשָּׁמַיִם וְכָל־צְבָאָם, הָאָרֶץ וְכָל־אֲשֶׁר עָלֶיהָ,
הַיַּמִּים וְכָל־אֲשֶׁר בָּהֶם, וְאַתָּה מְחַיֶּה אֶת־כֻּלָּם, וּצְבָא הַשָּׁמַיִם לְךָ
מִשְׁתַּחֲוִים: ◄ אַתָּה הוּא יהוה הָאֱלֹהִים אֲשֶׁר בָּחַרְתָּ בְּאַבְרָם,
וְהוֹצֵאתוֹ מֵאוּר כַּשְׂדִּים, וְשַׂמְתָּ שְּׁמוֹ אַבְרָהָם: וּמָצֵאתָ אֶת־
לְבָבוֹ נֶאֱמָן לְפָנֶיךָ, ◄ וְכָרוֹת עִמּוֹ הַבְּרִית לָתֵת אֶת־אֶרֶץ הַכְּנַעֲנִי
הַחִתִּי הָאֱמֹרִי וְהַפְּרִזִּי וְהַיְבוּסִי וְהַגִּרְגָּשִׁי, לָתֵת לְזַרְעוֹ, וַתָּקֶם
אֶת־דְּבָרֶיךָ, כִּי צַדִּיק אָתָּה: וַתֵּרֶא אֶת־עֳנִי אֲבֹתֵינוּ בְּמִצְרָיִם,
וְאֶת־זַעֲקָתָם שָׁמַעְתָּ עַל־יַם־סוּף: וַתִּתֵּן אֹתֹת וּמֹפְתִים בְּפַרְעֹה
וּבְכָל־עֲבָדָיו וּבְכָל־עַם אַרְצוֹ, כִּי יָדַעְתָּ כִּי הֵזִידוּ עֲלֵיהֶם, וַתַּעַשׂ־
לְךָ שֵׁם כְּהַיּוֹם הַזֶּה: ◄ וְהַיָּם בָּקַעְתָּ לִפְנֵיהֶם, וַיַּעַבְרוּ בְתוֹךְ־הַיָּם
בַּיַּבָּשָׁה, וְאֶת־רֹדְפֵיהֶם הִשְׁלַכְתָּ בִמְצוֹלֹת כְּמוֹ־אֶבֶן, בְּמַיִם עַזִּים:

CONNECTION

"There is a profound difference between history and memory. History is his story – an event that happened sometime else to someone else. Memory is my story – something that happened to me and is part of who I am. History is information. Memory, by contrast, is part of identity. I can study the history of other peoples, cultures and civilizations. They deepen my knowledge and broaden my horizons. But they do not make a claim on me. They are the past as past. Memory is the past as present, as it lives on in me. Without memory there can be no identity."

(The Jonathan Sacks Haggada)

LEARNING

This section of prayers originated at a time when the Temple was still in ruins and the Jewish nation was returning from captivity in Babylon. It was important to re-inspire the nation with a renewed consciousness of its origin and destiny and to persuade it to make sacrifices for the fulfillment of its mission. (Rabbi S.R. Hirsch)

וַיּוֹשַׁע That day the Lᴏʀᴅ saved Israel from the hands of the   *Ex. 14*
Egyptians, **and Israel saw the Egyptians lying dead on the seashore.**
‣ When Israel saw the great power the Lᴏʀᴅ had displayed against
the Egyptians, the people feared the Lᴏʀᴅ, and believed in the
Lᴏʀᴅ and in His servant, Moses.

LEARNING

"And the people feared God and they believed in Him." By seeing with their own eyes and witnessing the hand of God, the Jewish People internalized their faith. This group of people who left Egypt was the beginning of the Jewish nation. Their faith became deeply rooted in the nature of the nation and its traditions and therefore all subsequent generations can tap into this faith and loyalty forever. (Rabbi Avigdor Miller)

CONNECTION

A young man once came to Rabbi Akiva. The student seemed troubled and asked to be taught about the nature of faith. The rabbi brought the student over to a sprout in the ground and said, "Pull it up." The student bent over and did so without any trouble. The two of them walked over to a sapling. The sage pointed and said to the student, "All right, now pull that one up." The sapling took more effort but the student was able to do it. Rabbi Akiva took the student to a shrub. The same command was given, and this time the student used all his strength to pull the shrub out of the ground. Finally, Rabbi

Akiva took the young man to a fully grown tree. "Now," the rabbi said, "uproot it." The young student put both his hands around the tree and pulled as hard as he could, but the tree would not move.

Rabbi Akiva spoke to the student: "That is how it is with faith. If the roots of our faith are deep, if our religious views are mature and developed, our faith cannot be uprooted even by someone trying very hard to do so. Always remember that the strength of your faith first depends on the strength of its roots."

שמות יד

וַיּוֹשַׁע יהוה בַּיּוֹם הַהוּא אֶת־יִשְׂרָאֵל מִיַּד מִצְרָיִם, **וַיַּרְא יִשְׂרָאֵל** אֶת־מִצְרַיִם מֵת עַל־שְׂפַת הַיָּם: ◂ וַיַּרְא יִשְׂרָאֵל אֶת־הַיָּד הַגְּדֹלָה אֲשֶׁר עָשָׂה יהוה בְּמִצְרַיִם, וַיִּירְאוּ הָעָם אֶת־יהוה, וַיַּאֲמִינוּ בַּיהוה וּבְמֹשֶׁה עַבְדּוֹ:

Do you feel a deep sense of faith? How can you deepen it? How did you develop your faith in the first place?

How do you show faith as an individual?

How can the Jewish People show faith as a nation?

אָז יָשִׁיר־מֹשֶׁה Then Moses and the Israelites sang this song to the *Ex. 15*
LORD, saying:
> I will sing to the LORD, for He has triumphed gloriously;
> horse and rider He has hurled into the sea.
The LORD is my strength and song; He has become my salvation.
> This is my God, and I will beautify Him,
> my father's God, and I will elevate Him.
The LORD is a Master of war; LORD is His name.
Pharaoh's chariots and army He cast into the sea;
> the best of his officers drowned in the Sea of Reeds.
The deep waters covered them;
> they went down to the depths like a stone.
Your right hand, LORD, is majestic in power.
> Your right hand, LORD, shatters the enemy.
In the greatness of Your majesty, You overthrew those who rose
> against You.
> You sent out Your fury; it consumed them like straw.
By the blast of Your nostrils the waters piled up.
> The surging waters stood straight like a wall;
> the deeps congealed in the heart of the sea.
The enemy said, "I will pursue. I will overtake. I will divide the spoil.
> My desire shall have its fill of them.
> I will draw my sword. My hand will destroy them."
You blew with Your wind; the sea covered them.
> They sank in the mighty waters like lead.
Who is like You, LORD, among the mighty?
> Who is like You – majestic in holiness, awesome in glory,
> working wonders?

REFLECTION

"In Israel, in order to be a realist you must believe in miracles."
(David Ben-Gurion)

Have you ever experienced a miracle?
Would seeing a miracle change how you understand God?
Have you ever had a moment of seeing God's hand?

שמות טו

אָז יָשִׁיר־מֹשֶׁה וּבְנֵי יִשְׂרָאֵל אֶת־הַשִּׁירָה הַזֹּאת לַיהוה, וַיֹּאמְרוּ
לֵאמֹר, אָשִׁירָה לַיהוה כִּי־גָאֹה גָּאָה, סוּס
וְרֹכְבוֹ רָמָה בַיָּם: עָזִּי וְזִמְרָת יָהּ וַיְהִי־לִי
לִישׁוּעָה, ‌זֶה אֵלִי וְאַנְוֵהוּ,‌ אֱלֹהֵי
אָבִי וַאֲרֹמְמֶנְהוּ: יהוה אִישׁ מִלְחָמָה, יהוה
שְׁמוֹ: מַרְכְּבֹת פַּרְעֹה וְחֵילוֹ יָרָה בַיָּם, וּמִבְחַר
שָׁלִשָׁיו טֻבְּעוּ בְיַם־סוּף: תְּהֹמֹת יְכַסְיֻמוּ, יָרְדוּ בִמְצוֹלֹת כְּמוֹ־
אָבֶן: יְמִינְךָ יהוה נֶאְדָּרִי בַּכֹּחַ, יְמִינְךָ
יהוה תִּרְעַץ אוֹיֵב: וּבְרֹב גְּאוֹנְךָ תַּהֲרֹס
קָמֶיךָ, תְּשַׁלַּח חֲרֹנְךָ יֹאכְלֵמוֹ כַּקַּשׁ: וּבְרוּחַ
אַפֶּיךָ נֶעֶרְמוּ מַיִם, נִצְּבוּ כְמוֹ־נֵד
נֹזְלִים, קָפְאוּ תְהֹמֹת בְּלֶב־יָם: אָמַר
אוֹיֵב אֶרְדֹּף, אַשִּׂיג, אֲחַלֵּק שָׁלָל, תִּמְלָאֵמוֹ
נַפְשִׁי, אָרִיק חַרְבִּי תּוֹרִישֵׁמוֹ יָדִי: נָשַׁפְתָּ
בְרוּחֲךָ כִּסָּמוֹ יָם, צָלְלוּ כַּעוֹפֶרֶת בְּמַיִם
אַדִּירִים: מִי־כָמֹכָה בָּאֵלִם יהוה, מִי
כָּמֹכָה נֶאְדָּר בַּקֹּדֶשׁ, נוֹרָא תְהִלֹּת עֹשֵׂה

LEARNING

The Gemara (*Pesaḥim* 118a and *Sota* 2a) teaches that "finding a marriage partner and making a living are as difficult as splitting the sea."

How do we understand that the splitting of the sea was difficult for God? Is anything difficult for God?

Perhaps a solution is that in all these challenges – making a living, finding a soulmate, and the splitting of the sea – there are clear instances where God plays such an open role in supporting us that His natural hiddenness is revealed. God is supposed to be hidden, so that we have space to choose to believe. It is not that His actions are difficult for Him, but it is difficult that His power is so clearly revealed, which leaves us little room to doubt His role.

You stretched out Your right hand, the earth swallowed them.
In Your loving-kindness, You led the people You redeemed.
    In Your strength, You guided them to Your holy abode.
Nations heard and trembled;
    terror gripped Philistia's inhabitants.
The chiefs of Edom were dismayed,
    Moab's leaders were seized with trembling,
    the people of Canaan melted away.
Fear and dread fell upon them.
    By the power of Your arm, they were still as stone –
    until Your people crossed, LORD,
    until the people You acquired crossed over.
You will bring them and plant them
    on the mountain of Your heritage –
    the place, LORD, You made for Your presence,
    the Sanctuary, LORD, Your hands established.
    The LORD will reign for ever and all time.

The LORD will reign for ever and all time.
The LORD's kingship is established for ever and to all eternity.

When Pharaoh's horses, chariots and riders went into the sea,
    the LORD brought the waters of the sea back over them,
    but the Israelites walked on dry land through the sea.

> ‣ For kingship is the LORD's   *Ps. 22*
>   and He rules over the nations.
>   Saviors shall go up to Mount Zion   *Ob. 1*
>   to judge Mount Esau,
>   and the LORD's shall be the kingdom.
>
>   Then the LORD shall be King over all the earth;   *Zech. 14*
>   on that day the LORD shall be One and His name One,
>
>   (as it is written in Your Torah, saying:
>   Listen, Israel: the LORD is our God, the LORD is One.)   *Deut. 6*

נָחִיתָ נָטִיתָ יְמִינְךָ תִּבְלָעֵמוֹ אָרֶץ: פֶּלֶא:

בְּחַסְדְּךָ עַם־זוּ גָּאָלְתָּ, נֵהַלְתָּ בְעָזְּךָ אֶל־נְוֵה

חִיל שָׁמְעוּ עַמִּים יִרְגָּזוּן, קָדְשֶׁךָ:

אָחַז יֹשְׁבֵי פְּלָשֶׁת: אָז נִבְהֲלוּ אַלּוּפֵי

נָמֹגוּ אֵילֵי מוֹאָב יֹאחֲזֵמוֹ רָעַד, אֱדוֹם

כֹּל יֹשְׁבֵי כְנָעַן: תִּפֹּל עֲלֵיהֶם אֵימָתָה

עַד־ בִּגְדֹל זְרוֹעֲךָ יִדְּמוּ כָּאָבֶן, וָפַחַד,

עַד־יַעֲבֹר עַם־זוּ יַעֲבֹר עַמְּךָ יהוה,

מָכוֹן תְּבִאֵמוֹ וְתִטָּעֵמוֹ בְּהַר נַחֲלָתְךָ, קָנִיתָ:

מִקְּדָשׁ אֲדֹנָי כּוֹנְנוּ לְשִׁבְתְּךָ פָּעַלְתָּ יהוה,

יָדֶיךָ: יהוה יִמְלֹךְ לְעֹלָם וָעֶד:

יהוה יִמְלֹךְ לְעֹלָם וָעֶד.

יהוה מַלְכוּתֵהּ קָאֵם לְעָלַם וּלְעָלְמֵי עָלְמַיָּא.

כִּי

בָּא סוּס פַּרְעֹה בְּרִכְבּוֹ וּבְפָרָשָׁיו בַּיָּם, וַיָּשֶׁב יהוה עֲלֵהֶם אֶת־מֵי

הַיָּם, וּבְנֵי יִשְׂרָאֵל הָלְכוּ בַיַּבָּשָׁה בְּתוֹךְ הַיָּם:

תהלים כב

‣ כִּי לַיהוה הַמְּלוּכָה וּמֹשֵׁל בַּגּוֹיִם:

עובדיה א

וְעָלוּ מוֹשִׁעִים בְּהַר צִיּוֹן לִשְׁפֹּט אֶת־הַר עֵשָׂו
וְהָיְתָה לַיהוה הַמְּלוּכָה:

זכריה יד

וְהָיָה יהוה לְמֶלֶךְ עַל־כָּל־הָאָרֶץ
בַּיּוֹם הַהוּא יִהְיֶה יהוה אֶחָד וּשְׁמוֹ אֶחָד:

דברים ו

(וּבְתוֹרָתְךָ כָּתוּב לֵאמֹר, שְׁמַע יִשְׂרָאֵל, יהוה אֱלֹהֵינוּ יהוה אֶחָד:)

יִשְׁתַּבַּח May Your name be praised
for ever, our King,
the great and holy God,
King in heaven and on earth.
For to You, LORD our God and God of our ancestors,
it is right to offer
song and praise, hymn and psalm,
strength and dominion,
eternity, greatness and power,
song of praise and glory,
holiness and kingship,
▸ blessings and thanks, from now and for ever.
Blessed are You, LORD,
God and King, great in praises,
God of thanksgivings,
Master of wonders,
who delights in hymns of song,
King, God, Giver of life to the worlds.

REFLECTION

What do
you want to
praise God for
today?

Can you think
of fifteen blessings
God has
given you?

Can you think
of fifteen things
God would
praise
you for?

LEARNING

There are fifteen expressions of praise in *Yishtabaḥ*. The number fifteen is a very significant number in Judaism – Tu BiShvat, Sukkot, Pesaḥ, and Tu B'av all fall on the fifteenth of their respective Hebrew months. Beyond the calendrical concentration, the number fifteen features prominently in the Pesaḥ Seder: the fifteen stages of the Seder, the fifteen events described in the song *Dayeinu* which culminate in the building of the *Beit HaMikdash*. The fifteen steps of the Seder are modeled on the fifteen steps leading up to the courtyard of the *Beit HaMikdash* where the *Levi'im* would sing the fifteen psalms beginning *Shir HaMa'alot*. In the siddur *Avodat Yisrael* in the name of the Shela we find a parallel drawn to the fifteen words of *Birkat Kohanim* (the priestly blessing). God blesses us with fifteen, so, we too, bless Him with fifteen.

יִשְׁתַּבַּח

שִׁמְךָ לָעַד, מַלְכֵּנוּ
הָאֵל הַמֶּלֶךְ הַגָּדוֹל וְהַקָּדוֹשׁ בַּשָּׁמַיִם וּבָאָרֶץ
כִּי לְךָ נָאֶה, יהוה אֱלֹהֵינוּ וֵאלֹהֵי אֲבוֹתֵינוּ
שִׁיר וּשְׁבָחָה, הַלֵּל וְזִמְרָה
עֹז וּמֶמְשָׁלָה, נֶצַח, גְּדֻלָּה וּגְבוּרָה
תְּהִלָּה וְתִפְאֶרֶת, קְדֻשָּׁה וּמַלְכוּת
‹ בְּרָכוֹת וְהוֹדָאוֹת, מֵעַתָּה וְעַד עוֹלָם.
בָּרוּךְ אַתָּה יהוה
אֵל מֶלֶךְ גָּדוֹל בַּתִּשְׁבָּחוֹת
אֵל הַהוֹדָאוֹת, אֲדוֹן הַנִּפְלָאוֹת
הַבּוֹחֵר בְּשִׁירֵי זִמְרָה, מֶלֶךְ, אֵל, חֵי הָעוֹלָמִים.

CONNECTION

...A THOUSAND WORDS

The Rebbe of Kotzk explained the following about Yishtabaḥ: The prayer states that God "chooses musical songs." The Hebrew word for "songs" – shirim – shares a root with the word shirayim – meaning "remains." God chooses not "songs" but what remains after that song is over. If the song is true, it does not fade; if the feeling is genuine, it will leave a resonance. These "remains" are not necessarily something intellectual or even emotional; they are merely an impression of something that had been. And the indication of whether the experience left such an impression is whether some change has been wrought in the individual. If the answer is yes, that is all the proof that is needed to show that this was indeed a genuine experience.

(Rabbi Adin Steinsaltz)

Between Rosh HaShana and Yom Kippur, and on Hoshana Raba,
many congregations open the Ark and say this psalm responsively, verse by verse.

שִׁיר הַמַּעֲלוֹת A song of ascents. From the depths I have called to You, LORD. *Ps. 130*
LORD, hear my voice; let Your ears be attentive to my plea. If You, LORD,
should keep account of sins, O LORD, who could stand? But with You there
is forgiveness, that You may be held in awe. I wait for the LORD, my soul waits,
and in His word I put my hope. My soul waits for the LORD more than watchmen wait for the morning, more than watchmen wait for the morning. Israel,
put your hope in the LORD, for with the LORD there is loving-kindness, and
great is His power to redeem. It is He who will redeem Israel from all their sins.

HALF KADDISH

Leader: יִתְגַּדַּל Magnified and sanctified may His great name be,
in the world He created by His will.
May He establish His kingdom
in your lifetime and in your days,
and in the lifetime of all the house of Israel,
swiftly and soon – and say: Amen.

All: May His great name be blessed for ever and all time.

Leader: Blessed and praised, glorified and great,
raised and honored, uplifted and praised
be the name of the Holy One, blessed be He,
beyond any blessing, song, praise and consolation
uttered in the world – and say: Amen.

This is what is meant in *Tehillim* 130 by the double expres-
sion of 'listen' and 'hearken.' When a Jew prays and he is
answered, his subsequent prayers are even stronger and
he is stimulated to greater passion. But now we have not
been answered, and the situation has become even more
grievous. We have sunk from one depth to another, as
King David said: 'Out of the depths I called upon You.' That
is, I called not just from one depth, but from two depths.
Though I called upon You when I fell into the first crisis, not
only was I not answered and rescued, but I plunged even
deeper into crisis – depth within depth. Nevertheless, I
take strength and call upon You again."

REFLECTION

When were you
saddest or most
angry or upset
in your life?

What do you
want to ask
forgiveness for?

What do you need
God's help with?

During the הושענא רבה, *and on* עשרת ימי תשובה,
many congregations open the ארון קודש *and say this psalm responsively, verse by verse.*

תהלים קל

שִׁיר הַמַּעֲלוֹת, מִמַּעֲמַקִּים קְרָאתִיךָ יהוה: אֲדֹנָי שִׁמְעָה בְקוֹלִי, תִּהְיֶינָה אָזְנֶיךָ קַשֻּׁבוֹת לְקוֹל תַּחֲנוּנָי: אִם־עֲוֹנוֹת תִּשְׁמָר־יָהּ, אֲדֹנָי מִי יַעֲמֹד: כִּי־עִמְּךָ הַסְּלִיחָה, לְמַעַן תִּוָּרֵא: קִוִּיתִי יהוה קִוְּתָה נַפְשִׁי, וְלִדְבָרוֹ הוֹחָלְתִּי: נַפְשִׁי לַאדֹנָי, מִשֹּׁמְרִים לַבֹּקֶר, שֹׁמְרִים לַבֹּקֶר: יַחֵל יִשְׂרָאֵל אֶל יהוה, כִּי־עִם־יהוה הַחֶסֶד, וְהַרְבֵּה עִמּוֹ פְדוּת: וְהוּא יִפְדֶּה אֶת־יִשְׂרָאֵל, מִכֹּל עֲוֹנוֹתָיו:

חצי קדיש

ש״ץ יִתְגַּדַּל וְיִתְקַדַּשׁ שְׁמֵהּ רַבָּא (קהל: אָמֵן)
בְּעָלְמָא דִּי בְרָא כִרְעוּתֵהּ, וְיַמְלִיךְ מַלְכוּתֵהּ
בְּחַיֵּיכוֹן וּבְיוֹמֵיכוֹן וּבְחַיֵּי דְכָל בֵּית יִשְׂרָאֵל
בַּעֲגָלָא וּבִזְמַן קָרִיב, וְאִמְרוּ אָמֵן. (קהל: אָמֵן)

קהל
 וש״ץ יְהֵא שְׁמֵהּ רַבָּא מְבָרַךְ לְעָלַם וּלְעָלְמֵי עָלְמַיָּא.

ש״ץ יִתְבָּרַךְ וְיִשְׁתַּבַּח וְיִתְפָּאַר וְיִתְרוֹמַם וְיִתְנַשֵּׂא
וְיִתְהַדָּר וְיִתְעַלֶּה וְיִתְהַלָּל
שְׁמֵהּ דְּקֻדְשָׁא בְּרִיךְ הוּא (קהל: בְּרִיךְ הוּא)
לְעֵלָּא מִן כָּל בִּרְכָתָא / בעשרת ימי תשובה: לְעֵלָּא לְעֵלָּא מִכָּל בִּרְכָתָא/
וְשִׁירָתָא, תֻּשְׁבְּחָתָא וְנֶחֱמָתָא
דַּאֲמִירָן בְּעָלְמָא, וְאִמְרוּ אָמֵן. (קהל: אָמֵן)

LEARNING

The *Eish Kodesh* (Rabbi Kalonymous Kalmish Shapira, also known as the Piaseczner Rebbe), was living through the horrors of the Warsaw Ghetto. Writing before *Shabbat Shuva* in 1942, he comments as follows on this chapter of *Tehillim*: "When we pray out loud, the sound arouses greater intention. And with greater intention there is also a stronger voice. But alas, what can we do when they do not allow us to cry out or gather together to pray? Only secretly can we approach Hashem, but nonetheless our prayers are from the depths of our heart.

BLESSINGS OF THE SHEMA

The following blessing and response are said only in the presence of a minyan.
They represent a formal summons to the congregation to engage in an act of collective prayer.

The Leader says the following, bowing at "Bless," standing straight at "the LORD."
The congregation, followed by the Leader, responds, bowing at "Bless,"
standing straight at "the LORD."

Leader: 🔲 BLESS

🔲 the LORD, the blessed One.

Congregation: 🔲 Bless 🔲 the LORD, the blessed One,
for ever and all time.

Leader: 🔲 Bless 🔲 the LORD, the blessed One,
for ever and all time.

The custom is to sit from this point until the Amida, since the primary
emotion of this section of the prayers is love rather than awe.
Conversation is forbidden until after the Amida.

בָּרוּךְ Blessed are You, LORD our God, King of the Universe,
who forms light and creates darkness, makes peace and creates all. *Is. 45*

REFLECTION

"Unless we believe that God renews creation every day, our prayers grow habitual and tedious."
(Ba'al Shem Tov)

What can you do with your new day?

What will you do with your new day?
What specific blessings has God brought you today?

What goodness can you find in the darkness?

... A THOUSAND WORDS

קריאת שמע וברכותיה

The following blessing and response are said only in the presence of a מנין.
They represent a formal summons to the קהל *to engage in an act of collective prayer.*
The שליח ציבור *says the following, bowing at* בָּרְכוּ, *standing straight at* 'ה. *The* קהל,
followed by the שליח ציבור, *responds, bowing at* בָּרוּךְ, *standing straight at* 'ה.

ש״ץ: **בָּרְכוּ**

אֶת יהוה הַמְבֹרָךְ.

קהל: **בָּרוּךְ** יהוה הַמְבֹרָךְ לְעוֹלָם וָעֶד.

ש״ץ: **בָּרוּךְ** יהוה הַמְבֹרָךְ לְעוֹלָם וָעֶד.

The custom is to sit from this point until the עמידה, *since the primary
emotion of this section of the prayers is love rather than awe.
Conversation is forbidden until after the* עמידה.

בָּרוּךְ אַתָּה יהוה אֱלֹהֵינוּ מֶלֶךְ הָעוֹלָם

ישעיה מה

יוֹצֵר אוֹר וּבוֹרֵא חֹשֶׁךְ, עֹשֶׂה שָׁלוֹם וּבוֹרֵא אֶת הַכֹּל.

CONNECTION

Our masters taught: When Adam, on the day of his creation, saw the sun sinking in the sky before him, he said, "Woe is me! Because I acted offensively, the world is darkening for me and is about to return to darkness and desolation – indeed, this is the death that Heaven has decreed for me." So he sat down to fast and to weep throughout the night, while Eve wept beside him. But when the dawn began slowly rising like a column, he said, "Such is the way of nature," and then proceeded to offer up a bull.

Adam thought that the end of the day meant the end of the world. When the sun came up he realized that he would be able to begin again, and so he offered a sacrifice to express his profound gratitude. How do you feel at the beginning of a new day?

(Avoda Zara 8a)

הַמֵּאִיר In compassion He gives light to the earth and its inhabitants,
and in His goodness continually renews the work of creation,
day after day.

How numerous are Your works, LORD;   Ps. 104
You made them all in wisdom;
the earth is full of Your creations.
He is the King great alone since the beginning of time –
praised, glorified and elevated since the world began.
Eternal God,
    in Your great compassion, have compassion on us,
    LORD of our strength, Rock of our refuge,
    Shield of our salvation, You are our stronghold.

CONNECTION

Avram didn't grow up in a home that knew about God. Avram had to go out and find God on his own. As a boy, he looked up at the vast sky and wondered, "Who created this magnificent world? Who created the stars and the sky and the earth on which we walk? Who created me?" At first he was certain it was the sun. "The sun must be the creator of all; it is so powerful, it shines light on the world and heats all living things." So Avram spent the day praying to the sun. However, in the evening as the sun set, slowly disappearing in the west as the moon rose in the east, Avram said, "Forgive me, Moon, I was mistaken. You must be the creator of the heavens and the earth. Those beautiful shining stars must be your crown." Little Avram stayed up all night praying to the moon. In the morning, the moon sank in the west and the sun rose in the east once again. Avram realized: "Neither the sun nor the moon could have created the world, neither is powerful enough, there must be an even greater power, God, who created the sun, moon, and stars and everything else." So Avram began to pray to God, the Master of creation.

(Midrash HaGadol, Bereshit 11:28)

LEARNING

Rav Tzaddok explains the words "the earth is full of Your creations" that the world is not simply filled with God's possessions, but rather the world is filled with that which a person can acquire to bring God into his own world. How can you use the world to access God? What inspires you to seek out God?

הַמֵּאִיר לָאָרֶץ וְלַדָּרִים עָלֶיהָ בְּרַחֲמִים
וּבְטוּבוֹ מְחַדֵּשׁ בְּכָל יוֹם תָּמִיד מַעֲשֵׂה בְרֵאשִׁית.

תהלים קד

מָה־רַבּוּ מַעֲשֶׂיךָ יהוה
כֻּלָּם בְּחָכְמָה עָשִׂיתָ
מָלְאָה הָאָרֶץ קִנְיָנֶךָ:
הַמֶּלֶךְ הַמְרוֹמָם לְבַדּוֹ מֵאָז
הַמְשֻׁבָּח וְהַמְפֹאָר וְהַמִּתְנַשֵּׂא מִימוֹת עוֹלָם.
אֱלֹהֵי עוֹלָם
בְּרַחֲמֶיךָ הָרַבִּים רַחֵם עָלֵינוּ
אֲדוֹן עֻזֵּנוּ
צוּר מִשְׂגַּבֵּנוּ
מָגֵן יִשְׁעֵנוּ
מִשְׂגָּב בַּעֲדֵנוּ.

REFLECTION

Have you ever looked at creation and seen the beauty of God's work? How did it make you feel?

When you look up at the multitude of stars what do you think about?

... A THOUSAND WORDS

The blessed God, great in knowledge,
prepared and made the rays of the sun.
He who is good formed glory for His name,
surrounding His power with radiant stars.
The leaders of His multitudes, the holy ones,
elevate the Almighty,
constantly declaring God's glory and holiness.
Be blessed, Lord our God,
for the magnificence of Your handiwork
and for the radiant lights You have made.
May they glorify You, Selah!

REFLECTION

What do you want to ask God about the world?

How many words can you think of to describe God?

...A THOUSAND WORDS

אֵל בָּרוּךְ גְּדוֹל דֵּעָה
הֵכִין וּפָעַל זָהֳרֵי חַמָּה
טוֹב יָצַר כָּבוֹד לִשְׁמוֹ
מְאוֹרוֹת נָתַן סְבִיבוֹת עֻזּוֹ
פִּנּוֹת צְבָאָיו קְדוֹשִׁים, רוֹמְמֵי שַׁדַּי
תָּמִיד מְסַפְּרִים כְּבוֹד אֵל וּקְדֻשָּׁתוֹ.
תִּתְבָּרַךְ יהוה אֱלֹהֵינוּ
עַל שֶׁבַח מַעֲשֵׂה יָדֶיךָ.
וְעַל מְאוֹרֵי אוֹר שֶׁעָשִׂיתָ
יְפָאֲרוּךָ סֶּלָה.

CONNECTION

There was a simple shepherd boy who was passing by a synagogue and heard people inside praying. He came inside to join them. The only problem was they were all praying from prayer books. The shepherd, however, did not know how to read, though he did know how to say the letters of the Hebrew alphabet. Not knowing what else to do, he stood in the back of the synagogue and yelled out "Alef! Beit! Gimmel!" until he finished the entire alphabet.

Two of the worshipers were so offended that they went over to the shepherd boy and were about to escort him outside, when the rabbi told them: "Stop! That boy's shouting was more precious than any other prayers said here today! His prayer went straight up to Heaven!"

LEARNING

בְּרֵאשִׁית בָּרָא אֱלֹהִים
אֵת הַשָּׁמַיִם וְאֵת הָאָרֶץ

"In the beginning God created the heavens and the earth."
(Bereshit 1:1)

A kabbalistic reading of this passage is, "*Bereshit bara Elokim ET [alef-tav]*" signifying the entire *alef-beit*. The Hebrew letters, *alef, beit, gimmel...* they are living things. They are the building blocks of creation. Like oxygen and hydrogen, God formed the world through combinations of the Hebrew letters. God used the primal forces contained in these letters as the instruments of all further creation.

תִּתְבָּרֵךְ May You be blessed,
our Rock, King and Redeemer, Creator of holy beings.
May Your name be praised for ever,
our King, Creator of the ministering angels,
all of whom stand in the universe's heights,
declaring together, in awe, aloud,
the words of the living God, the eternal King.
They are all beloved, all pure, all mighty,
and all perform in awe and fear the will of their Maker.

▸ All open their mouths in holiness and purity,
with song and psalm,

> and bless, praise, glorify,
> fear, sanctify and declare the sovereignty of – ◂

... A THOUSAND WORDS

תִּתְבָּרַךְ

צוּרֵנוּ מַלְכֵּנוּ וְגוֹאֲלֵנוּ, בּוֹרֵא קְדוֹשִׁים

יִשְׁתַּבַּח שִׁמְךָ לָעַד

מַלְכֵּנוּ, יוֹצֵר מְשָׁרְתִים

וַאֲשֶׁר מְשָׁרְתָיו כֻּלָּם עוֹמְדִים בְּרוּם עוֹלָם

וּמַשְׁמִיעִים בְּיִרְאָה יַחַד בְּקוֹל

דִּבְרֵי אֱלֹהִים חַיִּים וּמֶלֶךְ עוֹלָם.

כֻּלָּם אֲהוּבִים, כֻּלָּם בְּרוּרִים, כֻּלָּם גִּבּוֹרִים

וְכֻלָּם עוֹשִׂים בְּאֵימָה וּבְיִרְאָה רְצוֹן קוֹנָם

◂ וְכֻלָּם פּוֹתְחִים אֶת פִּיהֶם בִּקְדֻשָּׁה וּבְטָהֳרָה

בְּשִׁירָה וּבְזִמְרָה

וּמְבָרְכִים וּמְשַׁבְּחִים וּמְפָאֲרִים

◂ וּמַעֲרִיצִים וּמַקְדִּישִׁים וּמַמְלִיכִים

LEARNING

Why do we want to be like angels? Typically we embrace humanity with its unique ability for creativity and ingenuity. What is it about angels that we are trying to emulate? The Maharal of Prague, in his commentary on *Bereshit* 18:2, says that the essence of what it means to be an angel is to act on someone else's behalf. This is the underlying angelic value we aspire to; the selflessness that angels embody.

REFLECTION

How can you be angelic today?

What does it mean to be angelic? Are angels the only beings that can achieve selflessness?

What selfless thing will you do today?

CONNECTION

Today, I watched a teenage boy help an elderly woman with a cane onto the city bus I was riding. He was so careful with her, assisting her every step of the way. The woman had the biggest smile on her face. They both sat directly across from me, and just as I was about to compliment her on having a wonderful grandson, the boy looked at her and said, "My name is Jonathan. What's your name, ma'am?"

The name of the great, mighty and awesome God and King,
holy is He.
▸ All accept on themselves, one from another,
the yoke of the kingdom of heaven,
giving permission to one another
to sanctify the One who formed them, in peaceful spirit,
pure speech and sweet melody.
All, as one, declare His holiness,
saying in awe:

> *All say aloud:* Holy, holy, holy is the LORD of multitudes; *Is. 6*
> the whole world is filled with His glory.

▸ Then the Ophanim and the Holy Ḥayyot, with a roar of noise,
raise themselves toward the Seraphim and,
facing them, give praise, saying:

> *All say aloud:* Blessed is the LORD's glory from His place. *Ezek. 3*

... A THOUSAND WORDS

REFLECTION

What does holiness
mean to you?

Are there places
where you feel
more close to God?

What does it mean
that God has a place?

CONNECTION

"O LORD, where shall I find You?
All-hidden and exalted is Your place;
And where shall I not find You?
Full of Your glory is the infinite space."

(Rabbi Yehuda HaLevi)

אֶת שֵׁם הָאֵל הַמֶּלֶךְ הַגָּדוֹל, הַגִּבּוֹר וְהַנּוֹרָא
קָדוֹשׁ הוּא.

◂ וְכֻלָּם מְקַבְּלִים עֲלֵיהֶם עֹל מַלְכוּת שָׁמַיִם זֶה מִזֶּה

וְנוֹתְנִים רְשׁוּת זֶה לָזֶה

לְהַקְדִּישׁ לְיוֹצְרָם בְּנַחַת רוּחַ

בְּשָׂפָה בְרוּרָה וּבִנְעִימָה

קְדֻשָּׁה כֻּלָּם כְּאֶחָד

עוֹנִים וְאוֹמְרִים בְּיִרְאָה

ישעיה ו

All say aloud קָדוֹשׁ, קָדוֹשׁ, קָדוֹשׁ יהוה צְבָאוֹת

מְלֹא כָל־הָאָרֶץ כְּבוֹדוֹ:

◂ וְהָאוֹפַנִּים וְחַיּוֹת הַקֹּדֶשׁ

בְּרַעַשׁ גָּדוֹל מִתְנַשְּׂאִים לְעֻמַּת שְׂרָפִים

לְעֻמָּתָם מְשַׁבְּחִים וְאוֹמְרִים

יחזקאל ג

All say aloud בָּרוּךְ כְּבוֹד־יהוה מִמְּקוֹמוֹ:

LEARNING

The first time God speaks to Moshe is at the burning bush in the desert. This encounter, according to the sages, took place at Mount Horeb or Mount Sinai, the place where the Torah would be given to the Jewish People.

> The Lord saw that he turned to see, and God called to him from within the bush, and He said: "Moses, Moses," and he said: "Here I am!"

He said: "Do not approach here; remove your shoes from your feet, as the place upon which you are standing is sacred ground." (*Shemot* 3:4–5)

There are some places that are more conducive to holiness, and God is more easily accessible there. The place where Moshe first encounters God was a considered and planned location. It was a place where the largest mass revelation of God in the world would take place, Mount Sinai – a place imbued with holiness.

לְאֵל To the blessed God they offer melodies.
To the King, living and eternal God,
they say psalms and declare praises.

For it is He alone
who does mighty deeds
and creates new things,
who is Master of battles,
and sows righteousness,
who makes salvation grow
and creates cures,
who is feared in praises,
Lord of wonders,
who in His goodness, continually renews the work of creation,
day after day, as it is said:

"[Praise] Him who made the great lights,   Ps. 136
for His love endures for ever."

▸ May You make a new light shine over Zion,
and may we all soon be worthy of its light.
Blessed are You, Lord, who forms the radiant lights.

CONNECTION

In 1997, Mr. Rogers, an icon of American children's entertainment and education, walked on stage to accept the Emmy Lifetime Achievement Award. In front of all the soap-opera stars he made his small bow and said into the microphone, "All of us have special ones who have loved us into being. Would you just take, along with me, ten seconds to think of the people who have helped you become who you are.... Ten seconds of silence." And then he lifted his wrist, and looked at the audience, and looked at his watch, and said softly, "I'll watch the time." There was, at first, a small whoop from the crowd, a giddy, strangled hiccup of laughter, as people realized that he wasn't kidding, that Mr. Rogers was an authority figure who actually expected them to do what he asked... and so they did. One second, two seconds, three seconds... and now the jaws clenched, and the chests heaved, and the mascara ran, and the tears fell upon the bejeweled gathering like rain leaking down a crystal chandelier, and Mr. Rogers finally looked up from his watch and said, "May God be with you."

לָאֵל בָּרוּךְ נְעִימוֹת יִתֵּנוּ, לְמֶלֶךְ אֵל חַי וְקַיָּם

זְמִירוֹת יֹאמֵרוּ וְתִשְׁבָּחוֹת יַשְׁמִיעוּ

כִּי הוּא לְבַדּוֹ

פּוֹעֵל גְּבוּרוֹת, עוֹשֶׂה חֲדָשׁוֹת

בַּעַל מִלְחָמוֹת, זוֹרֵעַ צְדָקוֹת

מַצְמִיחַ יְשׁוּעוֹת, בּוֹרֵא רְפוּאוֹת

נוֹרָא תְהִלּוֹת, אֲדוֹן הַנִּפְלָאוֹת

הַמְחַדֵּשׁ בְּטוּבוֹ בְּכָל יוֹם תָּמִיד מַעֲשֵׂה בְרֵאשִׁית

כָּאָמוּר

תהלים קלו

לְעֹשֵׂה אוֹרִים גְּדֹלִים, כִּי לְעוֹלָם חַסְדּוֹ:

‹ אוֹר חָדָשׁ עַל צִיּוֹן תָּאִיר וְנִזְכֶּה כֻלָּנוּ מְהֵרָה לְאוֹרוֹ.

בָּרוּךְ אַתָּה יהוה, יוֹצֵר הַמְּאוֹרוֹת.

REFLECTION

What is the best compliment you have ever received?

What is the best compliment you have ever given?

How do you find the appropriate accolades to praise God?

Has someone ever taken your compliment badly?

LEARNING

Silence is the greatest form of praising God. "To You silence is praise" (Tehillim 65:2). As the Gemara (Berakhot 33b) relates: A man came in front of Rabbi Ḥanina and praised God using every possible adjective he could think of. When he finished, the rabbi asked him, "Have you no praises left for your Master?! Why did you say so many? We may say the first three that you said 'great, mighty, and awesome' only because Moshe said them; but otherwise, it's like a mortal king who had millions of gold coins, and someone was praising him for having silver! What an insult!"

This is why we stop. To make sure we are focusing on the right things. The particular language of the tefilla is worded very carefully when it comes to praising God. Look at the words chosen to praise God. Why do you think these are the compliments we use to praise God?

אַהֲבָה You have loved us with great love, Lᴏʀᴅ our God,
and with immense compassion have You had compassion on us.
Our Father, our King,
for the sake of our ancestors who trusted in You,
and to whom You taught the laws of life,
be generous also to us and teach us.
Our Father, compassionate Father, ever compassionate,
have compassion on us.
Instill in our hearts the desire to understand and discern,
to listen, learn and teach, to observe, perform and fulfill
all the teachings of Your Torah in love.
Enlighten our eyes in Your Torah
and let our hearts cling to Your commandments.
Unite our hearts to love and fear Your name,
so that we may never be ashamed.
And because we have trusted in Your holy, great and feared name,
may we be glad and rejoice in Your salvation.

At this point, gather the four tzitziot of the tallit, holding them in the left hand.
Bring us back in peace from the four quarters of the earth
and lead us upright to our land.
▸ For You are a God who performs acts of salvation,
and You chose us from all peoples and tongues,
bringing us close to Your great name for ever in truth,
that we may thank You and declare Your oneness in love.
Blessed are You, Lᴏʀᴅ, who chooses His people Israel in love.

---

studies Torah, his mind meets and communicates with the mind of God. This compares well to a mother and her child looking at a family album together. The mother is like God, the child is like the Jew. Their perspectives of the album are certainly different, but a deep bond is nonetheless created.

(Rabbi Adin Steinsaltz)

REFLECTION

Who teaches you Torah?

Do you feel more connected to your Judaism or to God when you learn Torah?

How has the Torah impacted the Jewish People?

What is your favorite Torah teaching?

אַהֲבָה רַבָּה אֲהַבְתָּנוּ, יהוה אֱלֹהֵינוּ
חֶמְלָה גְדוֹלָה וִיתֵרָה חָמַלְתָּ עָלֵינוּ.
אָבִינוּ מַלְכֵּנוּ, בַּעֲבוּר אֲבוֹתֵינוּ שֶׁבָּטְחוּ בְךָ
וַתְּלַמְּדֵם חֻקֵּי חַיִּים, כֵּן תְּחָנֵּנוּ וּתְלַמְּדֵנוּ.
אָבִינוּ, הָאָב הָרַחֲמָן, הַמְרַחֵם
רַחֵם עָלֵינוּ
וְתֵן בְּלִבֵּנוּ לְהָבִין וּלְהַשְׂכִּיל
לִשְׁמֹעַ, לִלְמֹד וּלְלַמֵּד, לִשְׁמֹר וְלַעֲשׂוֹת, וּלְקַיֵּם
אֶת כָּל דִּבְרֵי תַלְמוּד תּוֹרָתֶךָ בְּאַהֲבָה.
וְהָאֵר עֵינֵינוּ בְּתוֹרָתֶךָ, וְדַבֵּק לִבֵּנוּ בְּמִצְוֹתֶיךָ
וְיַחֵד לְבָבֵנוּ לְאַהֲבָה וּלְיִרְאָה אֶת שְׁמֶךָ
וְלֹא נֵבוֹשׁ לְעוֹלָם וָעֶד.
כִּי בְשֵׁם קָדְשְׁךָ הַגָּדוֹל וְהַנּוֹרָא בָּטָחְנוּ
נָגִילָה וְנִשְׂמְחָה בִּישׁוּעָתֶךָ.

At this point, gather the four ציצית of the טלית, holding them in the left hand.

וַהֲבִיאֵנוּ לְשָׁלוֹם מֵאַרְבַּע כַּנְפוֹת הָאָרֶץ
וְתוֹלִיכֵנוּ קוֹמְמִיּוּת לְאַרְצֵנוּ.
◂ כִּי אֵל פּוֹעֵל יְשׁוּעוֹת אָתָּה, וּבָנוּ בָחַרְתָּ מִכָּל עַם וְלָשׁוֹן
וְקֵרַבְתָּנוּ לְשִׁמְךָ הַגָּדוֹל סֶלָה, בֶּאֱמֶת
לְהוֹדוֹת לְךָ וּלְיַחֶדְךָ בְּאַהֲבָה.
בָּרוּךְ אַתָּה יהוה, הַבּוֹחֵר בְּעַמּוֹ יִשְׂרָאֵל בְּאַהֲבָה.

CONNECTION

Why would God want us to study? You might say, it is a way to commune with Him. Perhaps, the study of Torah is best defined as a meeting of minds. When a Jew

*The Shema must be said with intense concentration. In the first paragraph one
should accept, with love, the sovereignty of God; in the second, the mitzvot as
the will of God. The end of the third paragraph constitutes fulfillment of the
mitzva to remember, morning and evening, the exodus from Egypt.*

When not praying with a minyan, say:

God, faithful King!

The following verse should be said aloud, while covering the eyes with the right hand:

Listen, Israel: the LORD is our God, the LORD is One.

Deut. 6

Quietly: Blessed be the name of His glorious kingdom for ever and all time.

Touch the hand-tefillin at ° and the head-tefillin at °°.

וְאָהַבְתָּ Love the LORD your God with all your heart, with all
your soul, and with all your might. These words which I command you today shall be on your heart. Teach them repeatedly
to your children, speaking of them when you sit at home and
when you travel on the way, when you lie down and when you
rise. °Bind them as a sign on your hand, and °°they shall be a sign
between your eyes. Write them on the doorposts of your house
and gates.

Deut. 6

LEARNING

Despite many people believing the
Shema is the most important prayer, it
is in fact not a prayer at all, but a declaration of Jewish belief. That is why we
call it *Keriat Shema* ("the reading of the
Shema") instead of *Tefillat Shema*. Much
like a national anthem, we say it as much
for ourselves as for anyone else.

The first paragraph focuses on our
accepting God as the ultimate Ruler in
our lives. The second paragraph focuses

on our acceptance of the responsibility
to do mitzvot, and the reward and punishment that comes with that responsibility. The third paragraph focuses on the
daily mitzva to recall the exodus from
Egypt – a basic tenet of Jewish faith. The
thematic progression between the three
paragraphs goes from God as King of the
universe, to the Jewish People's unique
relationship with God, to God's role in
Jewish history.

The שמע must be said with intense concentration. In the first paragraph one should accept, with love, the sovereignty of God; in the second, the מצוות as the will of God. The end of the third paragraph constitutes fulfillment of the מצוה to remember, morning and evening, the exodus from Egypt.

When not praying with a מנין, say:

אֵל מֶלֶךְ נֶאֱמָן

The following verse should be said aloud, while covering the eyes with the right hand:

דברים ו

שְׁמַע יִשְׂרָאֵל, יְהוָה אֱלֹהֵינוּ, יְהוָה ׀ אֶחָד:

Quietly בָּרוּךְ שֵׁם כְּבוֹד מַלְכוּתוֹ לְעוֹלָם וָעֶד.

Touch the תפילין של יד *at* ° *and the* תפילין של ראש *at* °°.

דברים ו

וְאָהַבְתָּ אֵת יְהוָה אֱלֹהֶיךָ, בְּכָל־לְבָבְךָ וּבְכָל־נַפְשְׁךָ וּבְכָל־
מְאֹדֶךָ: וְהָיוּ הַדְּבָרִים הָאֵלֶּה, אֲשֶׁר אָנֹכִי מְצַוְּךָ הַיּוֹם, עַל־לְבָבֶךָ:
וְשִׁנַּנְתָּם לְבָנֶיךָ וְדִבַּרְתָּ בָּם, בְּשִׁבְתְּךָ בְּבֵיתֶךָ וּבְלֶכְתְּךָ בַדֶּרֶךְ,
וּבְשָׁכְבְּךָ וּבְקוּמֶךָ: °וּקְשַׁרְתָּם לְאוֹת עַל־יָדֶךָ °°וְהָיוּ לְטֹטָפֹת
בֵּין עֵינֶיךָ: וּכְתַבְתָּם עַל־מְזֻזוֹת בֵּיתֶךָ וּבִשְׁעָרֶיךָ:

CONNECTION	...A THOUSAND WORDS

It once happened on the battlefield between two warring nations, that Jew faced Jew in mortal combat. As one of the Jewish soldiers ran for cover into a foxhole, the other called out, "Surrender, or I'll shoot." The hiding soldier, quivering in fear, closed his eyes, and crying, recited the familiar words from his child-hood: "Shema Yisrael, Hashem Elokeinu, Hashem Eḥad." As the

other soldier heard these words, he responded with surprise and emotion, "Barukh shem kevod malkhuto le'olam va'ed." As he laid down his gun he extended a hand to his former enemy, and they embraced as brothers.

Touch the hand-tefillin at ° and the head-tefillin at °°.

וְהָיָה If you indeed follow My commandments with which I charge *Deut. 11*
you today, to love the LORD your God and worship Him with all
your heart and with all your soul, I will give rain in your land in its
season, the early and late rain; and you shall gather in your grain,
wine and oil. I will give grass in your field for your cattle, and you
shall eat and be satisfied. Be careful lest your heart be tempted
and you go astray and worship other gods, bowing down to them.
Then the LORD's anger will flare against you and He will close
the heavens so that there will be no rain. The land will not yield
its crops, and you will perish swiftly from the good land that the
LORD is giving you. Therefore, set these, My words, on your heart
and soul. °Bind them as a sign on your hand, °°and they shall be a
sign between your eyes. Teach them to your children, speaking of
them when you sit at home and when you travel on the way, when
you lie down and when you rise. Write them on the doorposts of
your house and gates, so that you and your children may live long
in the land that the LORD swore to your ancestors to give them, for
as long as the heavens are above the earth.

REFLECTION

*"Run to do even a minor
mitzva, and flee from sin,
for one mitzva leads to
another, and one sin leads to
another – for the reward of
a mitzva is another mitzva,
and the punishment of a sin
is another sin." (Avot 4:2)*

What is more important,
believing in Hashem
or keeping mitzvot?

What extra mitzva
will you do today?

... A THOUSAND WORDS

Touch the תפילין של יד at °° and the תפילין של ראש at °.

דברים יא

וְהָיָ֗ה אִם־שָׁמֹ֤עַ תִּשְׁמְעוּ֙ אֶל־מִצְוֺתַ֔י אֲשֶׁ֧ר אָנֹכִ֛י מְצַוֶּ֥ה אֶתְכֶ֖ם הַיּ֑וֹם, לְאַהֲבָ֞ה אֶת־יהו֤ה אֱלֹֽהֵיכֶם֙ וּלְעָבְד֔וֹ, בְּכָל־לְבַבְכֶ֖ם וּבְכָל־נַפְשְׁכֶֽם: וְנָתַתִּ֧י מְטַֽר־אַרְצְכֶ֛ם בְּעִתּ֖וֹ, יוֹרֶ֣ה וּמַלְק֑וֹשׁ, וְאָסַפְתָּ֣ דְגָנֶ֔ךָ וְתִֽירֹשְׁךָ֖ וְיִצְהָרֶֽךָ: וְנָתַתִּ֛י עֵ֥שֶׂב בְּשָׂדְךָ֖ לִבְהֶמְתֶּ֑ךָ, וְאָכַלְתָּ֖ וְשָׂבָֽעְתָּ: הִשָּֽׁמְר֣וּ לָכֶ֔ם פֶּ֥ן יִפְתֶּ֖ה לְבַבְכֶ֑ם, וְסַרְתֶּ֗ם וַעֲבַדְתֶּם֙ אֱלֹהִ֣ים אֲחֵרִ֔ים וְהִשְׁתַּחֲוִיתֶ֖ם לָהֶֽם: וְחָרָ֨ה אַף־יהו֜ה בָּכֶ֗ם וְעָצַ֤ר אֶת־הַשָּׁמַ֨יִם֙ וְלֹֽא־יִהְיֶ֣ה מָטָ֔ר, וְהָ֣אֲדָמָ֔ה לֹ֥א תִתֵּ֖ן אֶת־יְבוּלָ֑הּ, וַאֲבַדְתֶּ֣ם מְהֵרָ֗ה מֵעַל֙ הָאָ֣רֶץ הַטֹּבָ֔ה אֲשֶׁ֥ר יהו֖ה נֹתֵ֥ן לָכֶֽם: וְשַׂמְתֶּם֙ אֶת־דְּבָרַ֣י אֵ֔לֶּה עַל־לְבַבְכֶ֖ם וְעַֽל־נַפְשְׁכֶ֑ם, °וּקְשַׁרְתֶּ֨ם אֹתָ֤ם לְאוֹת֙ עַל־יֶדְכֶ֔ם, °°וְהָי֥וּ לְטֽוֹטָפֹ֖ת בֵּ֥ין עֵינֵיכֶֽם: וְלִמַּדְתֶּ֥ם אֹתָ֛ם אֶת־בְּנֵיכֶ֖ם לְדַבֵּ֣ר בָּ֑ם, בְּשִׁבְתְּךָ֤ בְּבֵיתֶ֨ךָ֙ וּבְלֶכְתְּךָ֣ בַדֶּ֔רֶךְ, וּֽבְשָׁכְבְּךָ֖ וּבְקוּמֶֽךָ: וּכְתַבְתָּ֛ם עַל־מְזוּז֥וֹת בֵּיתֶ֖ךָ וּבִשְׁעָרֶֽיךָ: לְמַ֨עַן יִרְבּ֤וּ יְמֵיכֶם֙ וִימֵ֣י בְנֵיכֶ֔ם עַ֚ל הָֽאֲדָמָ֔ה אֲשֶׁ֨ר נִשְׁבַּ֧ע יהו֛ה לַאֲבֹֽתֵיכֶ֖ם לָתֵ֣ת לָהֶ֑ם, כִּימֵ֥י הַשָּׁמַ֖יִם עַל־הָאָֽרֶץ:

LEARNING

The major philosophical theme of the second paragraph of the *Shema* is reward and punishment for keeping and transgressing mitzvot. This is the eleventh of Rambam's Thirteen Principles of Jewish Faith: "I believe with perfect faith that the Creator, blessed be His name, rewards those who keep His commandments and punishes those who transgress them."

CONNECTION

"To defend a land, you need an army. But to defend freedom, you need education. You need families and schools to ensure that your ideals are passed on to the next generation and never lost, or despaired of, or obscured. The citadels of liberty are houses of study. Its heroes are teachers, its passion is education and the life of the mind. Moses realized that a people achieves immortality not by building temples or mausoleums, but by engraving their values on the hearts of their children, and they on theirs, and so on until the end of time."

(Rabbi Jonathan Sacks, *A Letter in the Scroll*)

Hold the tzitziot in the right hand also (some transfer to the right hand), kissing them at °.

וַיֹּאמֶר The LORD spoke to Moses, saying: Speak to the Israelites *Num. 15* and tell them to make °tzitzit on the corners of their garments for all generations. They shall attach to the °tzitzit at each corner a thread of blue. This shall be your °tzitzit, and you shall see it and remember all of the LORD's commandments and keep them, not straying after your heart and after your eyes, following your own sinful desires. Thus you will be reminded to keep all My commandments, and be holy to your God. I am the LORD your God, who brought you out of the land of Egypt to be your God. I am the LORD your God.

°True –

The Leader repeats:

▸ The LORD your God is true –

REFLECTION

לֹא תַטֶּה מִשְׁפַּט גֵּר יָתוֹם וְלֹא תַחֲבֹל בֶּגֶד
אַלְמָנָה: וְזָכַרְתָּ כִּי עֶבֶד הָיִיתָ בְּמִצְרַיִם
וַיִּפְדְּךָ יהוה אֱלֹהֶיךָ מִשָּׁם עַל־כֵּן אָנֹכִי
מְצַוְּךָ לַעֲשׂוֹת אֶת־הַדָּבָר הַזֶּה:
(דברים כד יז-יח)

"You shall not pervert the judgment of a stranger, or an orphan; you shall not take a widow's garment as a pledge. And you shall remember that you were a slave in Egypt, and the LORD your God redeemed you from there; therefore, I command you to do this thing."
(Devarim 24:17–18)

Why do you think the history of the Jewish People begins with slavery in Egypt?

Why do you think there is a mitzva to remember the exodus every day?

LEARNING

If you are wearing tzitzit then at the beginning of the third paragraph of the *Shema* you should transfer them to your right hand. Some have the custom to kiss the tzitzit every time the word צִיצִת is mentioned (three times) and then again at the word אֱמֶת at the end of the paragraph. This is to demonstrate our love for this mitzva. The tzitzit should also be passed before the eyes and stared at, at the mention of the words וּרְאִיתֶם אֹתוֹ – "and you shall see it." This reflects the emphasis on the visual aspect of this mitzva – i.e., the tzitzit are a visual reminder of all the other mitzvot. (The numerical value of the word צִיצִת comes to 600. If you add the number of strings [8] and knots [5] to 600 you arrive at 613, the number of mitzvot found in the Torah.)

Hold the ציצית in the right hand also (some transfer to the right hand), kissing them at °.

במדבר טו

וַיֹּאמֶר יְהוֹה אֶל־מֹשֶׁה לֵּאמֹר: דַּבֵּר אֶל־בְּנֵי יִשְׂרָאֵל וְאָמַרְתָּ אֲלֵהֶם, וְעָשׂוּ לָהֶם °צִיצִת עַל־כַּנְפֵי בִגְדֵיהֶם לְדֹרֹתָם, וְנָתְנוּ °עַל־צִיצִת הַכָּנָף פְּתִיל תְּכֵלֶת: וְהָיָה לָכֶם °לְצִיצִת, וּרְאִיתֶם אֹתוֹ וּזְכַרְתֶּם אֶת־כָּל־מִצְוֹת יְהוֹה וַעֲשִׂיתֶם אֹתָם, וְלֹא תָתוּרוּ אַחֲרֵי לְבַבְכֶם וְאַחֲרֵי עֵינֵיכֶם, אֲשֶׁר־אַתֶּם זֹנִים אַחֲרֵיהֶם: לְמַעַן תִּזְכְּרוּ וַעֲשִׂיתֶם אֶת־כָּל־מִצְוֹתָי, וִהְיִיתֶם קְדֹשִׁים לֵאלֹהֵיכֶם: אֲנִי יְהוָה אֱלֹהֵיכֶם, אֲשֶׁר הוֹצֵאתִי אֶתְכֶם מֵאֶרֶץ מִצְרַיִם, לִהְיוֹת לָכֶם לֵאלֹהִים, אֲנִי יְהוָה אֱלֹהֵיכֶם:

°אֱמֶת

The שליח ציבור repeats:

‹ יְהוֹה אֱלֹהֵיכֶם אֱמֶת

CONNECTION

...A THOUSAND WORDS

Three hundred years ago a ship called the Mayflower set sail to the New World. This was a great event in the history of England. Yet I wonder if there is one Englishman who knows at what time the ship set sail? Do the English know how many people embarked on this voyage? What quality of bread did they eat? Yet more than 3,300 years ago, before the Mayflower set sail, the Jews left Egypt. Every Jew in the world, even in America or Soviet Russia, knows on exactly what date they

left – the fifteenth of the month of Nisan. Everyone knows what kind of bread they ate. Even today the Jews worldwide eat matza on the fifteenth of Nisan. They retell the story of the exodus and all the troubles Jews have endured since being exiled. They conclude this evening with two statements: This year slaves. Next year, free men. This year here. Next year in Jerusalem, in Zion, in Eretz Yisrael. That is the nature of the Jews.

(David Ben-Gurion)

וְיַצִּיב And firm, established and enduring, right, faithful,
beloved, cherished, delightful, pleasant,
awesome, mighty, perfect, accepted, good and beautiful
is this faith for us for ever.

True is the eternal God, our King,
Rock of Jacob, Shield of our salvation.
He exists and His name exists through all generations.
His throne is established,
His kingship and trustworthiness endure for ever.

At °, kiss the tzitziot and release them.

His words live and persist, faithful and desirable
°for ever and all time.

‣ So they were for our ancestors, so they are for us,
and so they will be for our children and all our generations
and for all future generations
of the seed of Israel, Your servants. ◂

"It once happened that Ḥoni the Circle Drawer was walking along the way and he saw an old man planting a young fruit tree. Ḥoni asked the man how long it would take until the tree would produce fruit. 'Seventy years,' the old man answered him. 'Do you really think you will be alive for another seventy years so you can enjoy the fruit from this tree?' Ḥoni asked the man with wonder. The man replied, 'Just as I was born into a world with fully grown fruit trees that were planted by my ancestors, so I plant a tree for my children.'"

(Ta'anit 23a)

...A THOUSAND WORDS

REFLECTION

"On three things does the world stand – on truth, justice, and peace."
(Avot 1:18)

What are you sure is absolutely true in your world?

Who is loyal to you?
Who are you loyal to?
Who is God loyal to?

וְיַצִּיב, וְנָכוֹן וְקַיָּם, וְיָשָׁר וְנֶאֱמָן

וְאָהוּב וְחָבִיב, וְנֶחְמָד וְנָעִים

וְנוֹרָא וְאַדִּיר, וּמְתֻקָּן וּמְקֻבָּל

וְטוֹב וְיָפֶה

הַדָּבָר הַזֶּה עָלֵינוּ לְעוֹלָם וָעֶד.

אֱמֶת אֱלֹהֵי עוֹלָם מַלְכֵּנוּ

צוּר יַעֲקֹב מָגֵן יִשְׁעֵנוּ

לְדוֹר וָדוֹר הוּא קַיָּם וּשְׁמוֹ קַיָּם

וְכִסְאוֹ נָכוֹן

וּמַלְכוּתוֹ וֶאֱמוּנָתוֹ לָעַד קַיֶּמֶת.

At °, kiss the ציציות *and release them.*

וּדְבָרָיו חָיִים וְקַיָּמִים, נֶאֱמָנִים וְנֶחְמָדִים

°לָעַד וּלְעוֹלְמֵי עוֹלָמִים

◂ עַל אֲבוֹתֵינוּ וְעָלֵינוּ

עַל בָּנֵינוּ וְעַל דּוֹרוֹתֵינוּ

וְעַל כָּל דּוֹרוֹת זֶרַע יִשְׂרָאֵל עֲבָדֶיךָ. ◂

LEARNING

The siddur is most likely the first book of Jewish philosophy that any Jew finds in his hands. On its pages are numerous examples of deep principles of Jewish faith and theology, sometimes expressed directly and sometimes only implied. This *tefilla*, commencing with a burst of descriptive terms, proclaims the absolute and everlasting truth of God's message to us that is embodied in the *Shema*, and expresses our faith in God's redemption of the Jewish People. Stressing the importance of these concepts, the Gemara tells us, "Whoever has not recited *Emet Ve-yatziv* in *Shaḥarit* and *Emet Ve-emuna* in *Arvit* has not fulfilled his obligation" (*Berakhot* 12a). Rashi comments that *Emet Ve-yatziv* acknowledges God's past redemption of the Jews from Egypt, and *Emet Ve-emuna*, recited in *Ma'ariv*, confirms our faith in God's redemption of the Jews in the future.

For the early
and the later generations
this faith has proved good and enduring for ever –

True   and faithful, an irrevocable law.

True   You are the LORD: our God and God of our ancestors,
   ‣ our King and King of our ancestors,
      our Redeemer and Redeemer of our ancestors,
      our Maker, Rock of our salvation,
      our Deliverer and Rescuer:
      this has ever been Your name.
      There is no God but You.

REFLECTION

*"If I have seen further,
it is by standing on
the shoulders of
giants."*
(Sir Isaac Newton)

**What knowledge
have your
ancestors passed
along to you
about God?**

**How do you
imagine God?**

**Think about
your ancestors,
and about their
relationship
to God.
How does it
compare
to yours?**

CONNECTION

*There once was a severe drought, and the people of the town
had no water to drink. The rabbi called everyone together to
pray for rain. The people gathered in the center of the town and
cried out with emotion and sincerity to ask Hashem to send
the rains they so desperately needed. Among the crowd was a
small girl and her father. She tugged on her father's hand and
asked him, "Abba, if we have all come to pray to Hashem for rain,
then why has nobody brought an umbrella?"*

LEARNING

Rambam wrote the thirteen things every Jew must believe
in a list that is known as his Thirteen Principles of Faith. The
first one is:

I believe with perfect faith that the Creator, blessed
be His name, is the Creator and Guide of everything that
has been created; He alone has made, does make, and will
make all things.

The twelfth one is:

I believe with perfect faith in the coming of the Messiah;
and even though he may be delayed, nonetheless, I wait
every day for his coming.

עַל הָרִאשׁוֹנִים
וְעַל הָאַחֲרוֹנִים
דָּבָר טוֹב וְקַיָּם לְעוֹלָם וָעֶד

אֱמֶת וֶאֱמוּנָה, חֹק וְלֹא יַעֲבֹר.

אֱמֶת שָׁאַתָּה הוּא יהוה אֱלֹהֵינוּ וֵאלֹהֵי אֲבוֹתֵינוּ
‹ מַלְכֵּנוּ מֶלֶךְ אֲבוֹתֵינוּ
גּוֹאֲלֵנוּ גּוֹאֵל אֲבוֹתֵינוּ
יוֹצְרֵנוּ צוּר יְשׁוּעָתֵנוּ
פּוֹדֵנוּ וּמַצִּילֵנוּ מֵעוֹלָם שְׁמֶךָ
אֵין אֱלֹהִים זוּלָתֶךָ.

...A THOUSAND WORDS

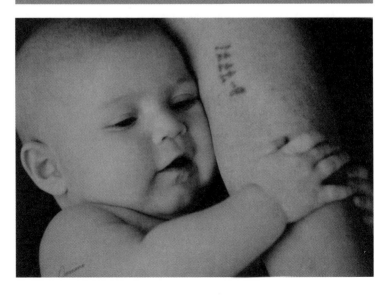

עֶזְרַת You have always been the help of our ancestors,
Shield and Savior of their children after them
in every generation.
Your presence is in the heights of the universe,
and Your judgments and righteousness
reach to the ends of the earth.
Happy is the one who obeys Your commandments
and takes to heart Your teaching and Your word.

True You are the Master of Your people
and a mighty King who pleads their cause.

True You are the first and You are the last.
Besides You, we have no king, redeemer or savior.
From Egypt You redeemed us, LORD our God,
and from the slave-house You saved us.
All their firstborn You killed,
but Your firstborn You redeemed.
You split the Sea of Reeds and drowned the arrogant.
You brought Your beloved ones across.
The water covered their enemies, not one of them was left.   *Ps. 106*

| REFLECTION | ... A THOUSAND WORDS |

"[My] faith [in God] has been persistently reinforced by Jewish History.... 'These are His awesome effects, for were it not for awe of God, how could one nation survive among the nations?' (Yoma, 69b) ... Our singular history has provided much reinforcement."
(Rabbi Aharon Lichtenstein)

What is your favorite period of Jewish history? Why? What role do you think God played then?

Does your understanding of Jewish history help your belief in God or hinder it?

עֶזְרַת אֲבוֹתֵינוּ אַתָּה הוּא מֵעוֹלָם
מָגֵן וּמוֹשִׁיעַ לִבְנֵיהֶם אַחֲרֵיהֶם בְּכָל דּוֹר וָדוֹר.
בְּרוּם עוֹלָם מוֹשָׁבֶךָ
וּמִשְׁפָּטֶיךָ וְצִדְקָתְךָ עַד אַפְסֵי אָרֶץ.
אַשְׁרֵי אִישׁ שֶׁיִּשְׁמַע לְמִצְוֹתֶיךָ
וְתוֹרָתְךָ וּדְבָרְךָ יָשִׂים עַל לִבּוֹ.

אֱמֶת אַתָּה הוּא אָדוֹן לְעַמֶּךָ
וּמֶלֶךְ גִּבּוֹר לָרִיב רִיבָם.

אֱמֶת אַתָּה הוּא רִאשׁוֹן וְאַתָּה הוּא אַחֲרוֹן
וּמִבַּלְעָדֶיךָ אֵין לָנוּ מֶלֶךְ גּוֹאֵל וּמוֹשִׁיעַ.
מִמִּצְרַיִם גְּאַלְתָּנוּ, יהוה אֱלֹהֵינוּ
וּמִבֵּית עֲבָדִים פְּדִיתָנוּ
כָּל בְּכוֹרֵיהֶם הָרָגְתָּ, וּבְכוֹרְךָ גָּאָלְתָּ
וְיַם סוּף בָּקַעְתָּ, וְזֵדִים טִבַּעְתָּ, וִידִידִים הֶעֱבַרְתָּ
וַיְכַסּוּ מַיִם צָרֵיהֶם, אֶחָד מֵהֶם לֹא נוֹתָר:

תהלים קו

CONNECTION

"First the knock of the Beloved was heard in the political arena. No one can deny that from the standpoint of international relations, the establishment of the State of Israel, in a political sense, was an almost supernatural occurrence. *Both Russia and the Western countries jointly supported the idea of the establishment of the State. This was perhaps the only proposal where East and West were united.* I am inclined to believe that the United Nations organization was created specifically for this purpose – in order to carry out the mission which divine providence had set for it…

"Second, the knocking of the Beloved could be heard on the battlefield. The small Israeli defense forces defeated the mighty armies of the Arab countries. *The miracle of 'the many in the hands of the few' took place before our very eyes…*"

(Rabbi J.B. Soloveitchik, *Kol Dodi Dofek*)

For this, the beloved ones praised and great God,
the cherished ones sang psalms, songs and praises,
blessings and thanksgivings to the King,
the living and enduring God.
High and elevated, great and awesome,
He humbles the arrogant and raises the lowly,
freeing captives and redeeming those in need, helping the poor
and answering His people when they cry out to Him.

Stand in preparation for the Amida. Take three steps back before beginning the Amida.

▸ Praises to God Most High, the Blessed One who is blessed.
Moses and the children of Israel
recited to You a song with great joy,
and they all exclaimed:

"Who is like You, LORD, among the mighty?   *Ex. 15*
Who is like You, majestic in holiness,
awesome in praises, doing wonders?"

▸ With a new song, the redeemed people praised
Your name at the seashore.
Together they all gave thanks, proclaimed Your kingship,
and declared:

"The LORD shall reign for ever and ever."   *Ex. 15*

CONNECTION

"[The Ba'al Shem Tov] explained to them that abstract erudition is not the sole vessel of truth or the sole path leading to saintliness. And that saintliness is not the only link between man and the eternity he carries inside him. Song is more precious than words, *intention more important than formulas. And since it is given to every man to acquire all the powers, why despair? Why give up the fight? One tear, one prayer can change the course of events; one fragment of melody can contain all the joy in the world, and by letting it go free, influence fate. And no elite has a monopoly on song or tears; God listens to the shepherd playing his flute as readily as He listens to the saint renouncing his earthly attachments. The prisoner's craving equals the wise man's: the one, like the other, has a bearing on the essence of man."*

(Elie Wiesel, *Souls on Fire*)

עַל זֹאת שִׁבְּחוּ אֲהוּבִים, וְרוֹמְמוּ אֵל
וְנָתְנוּ יְדִידִים זְמִירוֹת, שִׁירוֹת וְתִשְׁבָּחוֹת
בְּרָכוֹת וְהוֹדָאוֹת לְמֶלֶךְ אֵל חַי וְקַיָּם
רָם וְנִשָּׂא, גָּדוֹל וְנוֹרָא
מַשְׁפִּיל גֵּאִים וּמַגְבִּיהַּ שְׁפָלִים
מוֹצִיא אֲסִירִים, וּפוֹדֶה עֲנָוִים וְעוֹזֵר דַּלִּים
וְעוֹנֶה לְעַמּוֹ בְּעֵת שַׁוְּעָם אֵלָיו.

Stand in preparation for the עמידה. Take three steps back before beginning the עמידה.

‹ תְּהִלּוֹת לְאֵל עֶלְיוֹן, בָּרוּךְ הוּא וּמְבֹרָךְ
מֹשֶׁה וּבְנֵי יִשְׂרָאֵל, לְךָ עָנוּ שִׁירָה בְּשִׂמְחָה רַבָּה
וְאָמְרוּ כֻלָּם

שמות טו

מִי־כָמֹכָה בָּאֵלִם, יהוה
מִי כָּמֹכָה נֶאְדָּר בַּקֹּדֶשׁ, נוֹרָא תְהִלֹּת, עֹשֵׂה פֶלֶא:

‹ שִׁירָה חֲדָשָׁה שִׁבְּחוּ גְאוּלִים
לְשִׁמְךָ עַל שְׂפַת הַיָּם
יַחַד כֻּלָּם הוֹדוּ וְהִמְלִיכוּ
וְאָמְרוּ

שמות טו

יהוה יִמְלֹךְ לְעֹלָם וָעֶד:

REFLECTION

Can you think of a time in modern history when God has answered His people when they have cried out to Him?

For what in Jewish history do you want to show gratitude to God?

... A THOUSAND WORDS

Congregants should end the following blessing together with the Leader so as to be able to move directly from the words "redeemed Israel" to the Amida, without the interruption of saying Amen.

▸ **צוּר יִשְׂרָאֵל** Rock of Israel! Arise to the help of Israel.
Deliver, as You promised, Judah and Israel.

Our Redeemer, the Lᴏʀᴅ of multitudes is His name,   Is. 47
the Holy One of Israel.

Blessed are You, Lᴏʀᴅ, who redeemed Israel.

LEARNING

INTRODUCTION TO *AMIDA*

The *Amida* prayer is the central prayer of the *tefilla* service, to which everything up until this point has been building up. The *Amida* encompasses within it all the elements of prayer. Originally composed by the Men of the Great Assembly, the *Amida* consisted of eighteen blessings, hence its other name, *Shemoneh Esreh* (Eighteen). Later, in Talmudic times, a nineteenth prayer was added (the thirteenth *berakha* according to our number – Against Informers).

The *Amida* has its own internal logical structure. The first three *berakhot* are blessings of praise (*shevaḥ*), followed by thirteen requests (*bakashot*), and then the *Amida* concludes with three blessings of thanks (*hoda'a*). Within the thirteen (originally twelve) *berakhot* of requests, the first six focus on personal needs, and the remaining six (now seven) focus on our national needs.

We derive many of the laws for how to conduct ourselves when saying the *Amida* prayer from a woman called Ḥana. Ḥana was married for many years and despite her many prayers, she was unable to have children. One Rosh HaShana,

Ḥana prayed at the *Mishkan*. So powerful and devout were her prayers that she was granted a child. Not just any child, but the next leader of the Jewish People; the future prophet Shmuel. Ḥana prayed silently; only her lips moved, audible only to herself. We therefore pray in quiet devotion just as Ḥana did, standing and supplicating God for our deepest desires.

Before we begin our *Amida* prayer, we take a few moments to focus and take stock. Facing Jerusalem, we take three steps back and remove all foreign and distracting thoughts from our minds. We then slowly take three steps forward and in doing so, we show our readiness to approach the Master of the Universe.

Take a moment to disconnect from everything; as you take your three steps back, focus your mind, think about what you are about to do. Remember that as you approach God, you are seizing a special opportunity to stand before Him in a personal audience and speak directly to Him. If the conversation seems difficult to start, remember that **אֲדֹנָי, שְׂפָתַי תִּפְתָּח** is the prayer to be able to pray.

The קהל *should end the following blessing together with the* שליח ציבור
so as to be able to move directly from the words גָּאַל יִשְׂרָאֵל *to*
the עמידה, *without the interruption of saying* אמן.

צוּר יִשְׂרָאֵל, קוּמָה בְּעֶזְרַת יִשְׂרָאֵל
וּפְדֵה כִנְאֻמֶךָ יְהוּדָה וְיִשְׂרָאֵל.
גֹּאֲלֵנוּ יהוה צְבָאוֹת שְׁמוֹ, קְדוֹשׁ יִשְׂרָאֵל:
בָּרוּךְ אַתָּה יהוה, גָּאַל יִשְׂרָאֵל.

ישעיה מו

REFLECTION

אָבִינוּ שֶׁבַּשָּׁמַיִם, צוּר יִשְׂרָאֵל וְגוֹאֲלוֹ,
בָּרֵךְ אֶת מְדִינַת יִשְׂרָאֵל,
רֵאשִׁית צְמִיחַת גְּאֻלָּתֵנוּ.

"Heavenly Father, Israel's Rock and
Redeemer, bless the State of Israel,
the first flowering of our redemption."

Close your eyes. Think about when
the Mashiaḥ comes. What will the
world look like? How will it be
different from your world today?

What can you do today to make your
world closer to the Messianic one?

CONNECTION

It is said that Napoleon, passing a synagogue
on Tisha B'Av, was struck by the sounds of la-
ment coming from the building. "What," he
asked one of his officers, "are the Jews crying
for?" "For Jerusalem," came the reply. "How long
ago did they lose Jerusalem?" "More than seven-
teen hundred years ago." Napoleon was silent
for a moment and then said, "A people that can
remember Jerusalem for so long will one day
have it restored to them." So it has come to pass
in our time.

LEARNING

The halakha forbids any interruption between the conclusion of
the *berakha* גָּאַל יִשְׂרָאֵל and the
beginning of the *Amida*. This includes any kind of speech, and
according to some even the response "Amen" to that *berakha*.
Many people have the custom to
be careful to complete the *berakha* at the same time as the leader
so there is no opportunity to say
Amen.

A possible reason for our in-
sistence that this *berakha* and the
Amida are juxtaposed without
interruption – In halakhic termi-
nology סְמִיכַת גְּאֻלָּה לִתְפִלָּה – is because the *berakha* represents the
link between the *tefillot* that speak
about the previous redemption
from Egypt (in the third paragraph
of the *Shema*) and the future redemption (Mashiaḥ) in the *Amida*.
This is a declaration of faith that
just as Hashem redeemed us previously, He will redeem us again
and bring the Mashiaḥ.

THE AMIDA

*The Amida until "in former years" on page 198, is said standing with feet together.
The Amida is said silently, following the precedent of Hannah when she
prayed for a child (1 Sam. 1:13). If there is a minyan, it is repeated
aloud by the Leader. Take three steps forward, as if formally
entering the place of the Divine Presence.*

O LORD, open my lips,   *Ps. 51*
so that my mouth may declare Your praise.

For many of us, instead of opening our hearts to prayer, something silences our natural instinct to pray. It's like the story of a simple shepherd, who every day would offer his personal prayer to God: "God, I love You so much, that if You were here, I would give You half of my sheep. If it was raining and You were cold, I would share my blanket with You."

One day a man was walking by the field, and he heard the shepherd praying. He said "Do you call that praying? Are you kidding? What would God do with your sheep? Of what use would a blanket be to God? Here, let me show you to pray properly before you further desecrate God's holy name!" The man then took out a siddur, and proceeded to lecture the poor illiterate shepherd on the structure and meaning of the various prayers.

As soon as the man left, the shepherd sat there dumbfounded. He didn't understand a word of it. But he knew the man was quite upset that his prayers were not proper. So he stopped praying.

For too many of us, that's where the story ends. Fortunately for the shepherd, there is more to his story.

Up in heaven, God noticed the silence, and said, "What happened to the beautiful prayers of My humble shepherd?" He sent down an angel to find out what was wrong.

The angel found the shepherd, and the shepherd told him the whole story of his meeting with the man. The angel said, "What does that man know? Would you like to see how we pray in heaven?" The shepherd instantly agreed and the angel whisked him off to heaven, where he saw an angel standing and proclaiming: "God, I love You so much, that if You were here, I would give You half of my sheep. If it was raining and You were cold, I would share my blanket with You." The shepherd happily went back to his prayers, and God happily listened.

עמידה

The עמידה until קְדֻמְנִיּוֹת on page 199, is said standing with feet together.
The עמידה is said silently, following the precedent of Hannah when she
prayed for a child (שמואל א' א, יג). If there is a מנין, it is repeated
aloud by the שליח ציבור. Take three steps forward, as if
formally entering the place of the Divine Presence.

תהלים נא

אֲדֹנָי, שְׂפָתַי תִּפְתָּח, וּפִי יַגִּיד תְּהִלָּתֶךָ:

A prayer to be able to pray...

Have you ever struggled
to start a conversation?
How did you overcome it?

Do you need help starting
a conversation with God?
What are you scared
to say?

What do you want
to praise God for?

On his own, it is impossible for a person to fully understand his own needs and formulate them into a clear prayer. His mouth is inarticulate, his tongue fails. A person requires divine assistance not only for his basic needs but also to recognize his limitations and to arrange his words. Not only are we dependent on God to fulfill our needs, but also to recognize and express them. So the *Amida* opens with the introductory phrase, אֲדֹנָי שְׂפָתַי תִּפְתָּח, "O Lord, open my lips." We cannot contemplate prayer unless we seek God's assistance in formulating our pleas. (Based on the commentary of the Rav's Siddur, 120–121.)

PATRIARCHS

בָּרוּךְ 🔊 Blessed 🔊 are You,
🔊 Lᴏʀᴅ our God and God of our fathers,
God of Abraham, God of Isaac and God of Jacob;
the great, mighty and awesome God, God Most High,
who acts with loving-kindness and creates all,
who remembers the loving-kindness of the fathers
and will bring a Redeemer to their children's children
for the sake of His name, in love.

Between Rosh   Remember us for life, O King who desires life,
HaShana &   and write us in the book of life –
Yom Kippur: for Your sake, O God of life.

King, Helper, Savior, Shield:
🔊 Blessed 🔊 are You, 🔊 Lᴏʀᴅ, Shield of Abraham.

REFLECTION

What merits of our ancestors would you like to "borrow"?

What message would you like our fore-fathers to give God on your behalf?

How are you going to be kind today?

... A THOUSAND WORDS

LEARNING

The *berakha* says God of Avraham, God of Yitzhak, and God of Yaakov indi-vidually instead of God of all three to teach us a profound lesson. A person is required to find his indi-vidual connection to God and not simply rely on the belief taught to him by his forefathers. Each of us have an opportunity to forge our own and individual relation-ships with God, learning from but not merely copy-ing our ancestors.

(Rabbi Meir Eisenstadt,
Panim Me'irot)

אבות

בָּרוּךְ 🔹 אַתָּה 🔹 יהוה, אֱלֹהֵינוּ וֵאלֹהֵי אֲבוֹתֵינוּ
אֱלֹהֵי אַבְרָהָם, אֱלֹהֵי יִצְחָק, וֵאלֹהֵי יַעֲקֹב
הָאֵל הַגָּדוֹל הַגִּבּוֹר וְהַנּוֹרָא, אֵל עֶלְיוֹן
גּוֹמֵל חֲסָדִים טוֹבִים, וְקֹנֵה הַכֹּל
וְזוֹכֵר חַסְדֵי אָבוֹת
וּמֵבִיא גוֹאֵל לִבְנֵי בְנֵיהֶם לְמַעַן שְׁמוֹ בְּאַהֲבָה.

בעשרת ימי תשובה: זָכְרֵנוּ לְחַיִּים, מֶלֶךְ חָפֵץ בַּחַיִּים
וְכָתְבֵנוּ בְּסֵפֶר הַחַיִּים
לְמַעַנְךָ אֱלֹהִים חַיִּים.

מֶלֶךְ עוֹזֵר וּמוֹשִׁיעַ וּמָגֵן.
בָּרוּךְ 🔹 אַתָּה 🔹 יהוה, מָגֵן אַבְרָהָם.

CONNECTION

While in the Janowska Road Concentration Camp, Nazi SS officers forced the Bluzhever Rebbe and fellow prisoners on a death march. The Rebbe walked with a maskil (free thinker) whom he befriended, a man who did not believe in God. As they approached several huge ditches, the prisoners were ordered to jump across, an almost impossible feat. If they landed in the ditch, they would be summarily shot.

"Well Spira," said the maskil to the Rebbe, "it looks like we've reached our end." "Just hold onto my coat and we'll jump across together," replied the Rebbe. They closed their eyes and jumped. They opened their eyes alive on the other side. Shocked, the maskil turned to the Rebbe and asked, "Rebbe, we're alive, we're alive because of you! There must be a God! How did you do it Rebbe?" The Rebbe replied, "I had zekhut avot (ancestral merit). I held on to the bekeshe of my father and his father and all of my ancestors. But tell me," the Rebbe asked the maskil, "how did you reach the other side?" The maskil answered, "I was holding on to you!"

(Hasidic Tales of the Holocaust)

DIVINE MIGHT

אַתָּה גִבּוֹר You are eternally mighty, Lord.
You give life to the dead and have great power to save.

The phrase "He makes the wind blow and the rain fall" is said from
Simḥat Torah until Pesaḥ. In Israel the phrase "He causes the dew to fall"
is said from Pesaḥ until Shemini Atzeret.

In fall & winter: He makes the wind blow and the rain fall.
In Israel, in spring He causes the dew to fall.
& summer:

He sustains the living with loving-kindness,
and with great compassion revives the dead.
He supports the fallen, heals the sick, sets captives free,
and keeps His faith with those who sleep in the dust.
Who is like You, Master of might,
and who can compare to You,
O King who brings death and gives life, and makes salvation grow?

Between Rosh HaShana Who is like You, compassionate Father,
& Yom Kippur: who remembers His creatures in compassion, for life?

Faithful are You to revive the dead.
Blessed are You, Lord, who revives the dead.

When saying the Amida silently, continue with "You are holy" on page 158.

CONNECTION

According to early scientific thought, the bumble-bee's body was too heavy and its wingspan too small. Aerodynamically, it was thought, the bumblebee should not be able to fly. But the bumblebee has no idea of this and it keeps flying. When you don't know your limitations, you go out and surprise yourself. In hindsight, you wonder if you had any limitations. Often, the only limitations a person has are those that are self-imposed. How can you find your own inner strength?

LEARNING

We mention the resurrection of the dead three times in this blessing. The first is to reflect on God's kindness in returning our souls to us each day. The second refers to rainfall which revives the ground and the third refers to the final actual resurrection of the dead in the times of Mashiaḥ. (Abudraham)

גבורות

אַתָּה גִבּוֹר לְעוֹלָם, אֲדֹנָי,
מְחַיֵּה מֵתִים אַתָּה, רַב לְהוֹשִׁיעַ

The phrase מַשִּׁיב הָרְוּחַ *is said from* שמחת תורה *until* פסח.
In ארץ ישראל *the phrase* מוֹרִיד הַטַּל *is said from* פסח *until* שמיני עצרת.

בחורף: מַשִּׁיב הָרְוּחַ וּמוֹרִיד הַגֶּשֶׁם / בארץ ישראל בקיץ: מוֹרִיד הַטָּל

מְכַלְכֵּל חַיִּים בְּחֶסֶד, מְחַיֵּה מֵתִים בְּרַחֲמִים רַבִּים
סוֹמֵךְ נוֹפְלִים, וְרוֹפֵא חוֹלִים, וּמַתִּיר אֲסוּרִים
וּמְקַיֵּם אֱמוּנָתוֹ לִישֵׁנֵי עָפָר.
מִי כָמְוֹךָ, בַּעַל גְּבוּרוֹת, וּמִי דְוֹמֶה לָּךְ
מֶלֶךְ, מֵמִית וּמְחַיֶּה וּמַצְמִיחַ יְשׁוּעָה.

בעשרת ימי תשובה: מִי כָמְוֹךָ אַב הָרַחֲמִים, זוֹכֵר יְצוּרָיו לְחַיִּים בְּרַחֲמִים.

וְנֶאֱמָן אַתָּה לְהַחֲיוֹת מֵתִים.
בָּרוּךְ אַתָּה יהוה, מְחַיֵּה הַמֵּתִים.

When saying the עמידה *silently, continue with* אַתָּה קָדוֹשׁ *on page 159.*

REFLECTION

Are you trying to find
the inner strength to
help yourself?

What area of your life
would you like to turn
around?

Where do you feel like
you need help picking
yourself up, healing,
and freeing yourself?

... A THOUSAND WORDS

KEDUSHA

*During the Leader's Repetition, the following is said standing
with feet together, rising on the toes at the words indicated by ▲.*

Cong. then
Leader:
נְקַדֵּשׁ We will sanctify Your name on earth,
as they sanctify it in the highest heavens,
as is written by Your prophet,
"And they [the angels] call to one another saying: *Is. 6*

Cong. then
Leader:
▲Holy, ▲holy, ▲holy is the LORD of multitudes
the whole world is filled with His glory."
Those facing them say "Blessed – "

Cong. then
Leader:
▲"Blessed is the LORD's glory from His place."   *Ezek. 3*
And in Your holy Writings it is written thus:

Cong. then
Leader:
▲"The LORD shall reign for ever. He is your God, Zion,   *Ps. 146*
from generation to generation, Halleluya!"

Leader:
From generation to generation we will speak of Your greatness,
and we will declare Your holiness for evermore.
Your praise, our God, shall not leave our mouth forever,
for You, God, are a great and holy King. Blessed are You, LORD,
the holy God. / *Between Rosh HaShana & Yom Kippur:* the holy King./

The Leader continues with "You grace humanity" on page 160.

CONNECTION	... A THOUSAND WORDS

The Kotzker Rebbe once asked his students where God was to be found; they answered that "He fills all the world with His glory." He shook his head and said, "No, I asked where is He to be found, not where He is." The students looked at the rabbi with confusion and exasperation. "Did we not already

say that He is everywhere?" "No, no," the Kotzker smiled at them. "You must understand that God is to be found in the place that you open up your hearts and let Him in!"

קדושה

During חזרת הש״ץ, the following is said standing
with feet together, rising on the toes at the words indicated by ▲.

קהל then
ש״ץ: נְקַדֵּשׁ אֶת שִׁמְךָ בָּעוֹלָם

ישעיהו ו

כְּשֵׁם שֶׁמַּקְדִּישִׁים אוֹתוֹ בִּשְׁמֵי מָרוֹם
כַּכָּתוּב עַל יַד נְבִיאֶךָ, וְקָרָא זֶה אֶל־זֶה וְאָמַר

קהל then
ש״ץ: ▲קָדוֹשׁ, ▲קָדוֹשׁ, ▲קָדוֹשׁ, יהוה צְבָאוֹת
מְלֹא כָל־הָאָרֶץ כְּבוֹדוֹ:
לְעֻמָּתָם בָּרוּךְ יֹאמֵרוּ

יחזקאל ג

קהל then
ש״ץ: ▲בָּרוּךְ כְּבוֹד־יהוה מִמְּקוֹמוֹ:
וּבְדִבְרֵי קָדְשְׁךָ כָּתוּב לֵאמֹר

תהלים קמו

קהל then
ש״ץ: ▲יִמְלֹךְ יהוה לְעוֹלָם, אֱלֹהַיִךְ צִיּוֹן לְדֹר וָדֹר, הַלְלוּיָהּ:

ש״ץ: לְדוֹר וָדוֹר נַגִּיד גָּדְלֶךָ, וּלְנֵצַח נְצָחִים קְדֻשָּׁתְךָ נַקְדִּישׁ
וְשִׁבְחֲךָ אֱלֹהֵינוּ מִפִּינוּ לֹא יָמוּשׁ לְעוֹלָם וָעֶד
כִּי אֵל מֶלֶךְ גָּדוֹל וְקָדוֹשׁ אָתָּה.
בָּרוּךְ אַתָּה יהוה, הָאֵל הַקָּדוֹשׁ./בעשרת ימי תשובה: הַמֶּלֶךְ הַקָּדוֹשׁ./

The שליח ציבור continues with אַתָּה חוֹנֵן on page 161.

LEARNING

The first verse we recite in the Kedusha prayer is what the prophet Isaiah heard the angels singing before God every morning. According to Jewish tradition, the angels cannot recite Kedusha in their heavenly realm until the Jewish People recite Kedusha on earth (Ḥullin 91b).

REFLECTION

"The virtue of angels is that they cannot deteriorate; their flaw is that they cannot improve. Humanity's flaw is that we can deteriorate; but our virtue is that we can improve."
(Hasidic proverb)

What does holiness mean to you?

Can you think of a way you can act like an angel today?

Think about how you act on Yom Kippur – how can you act like that for one moment today?

HOLINESS

אַתָּה קָדוֹשׁ You are holy and Your name is holy,
and holy ones praise You daily, Selah!
Blessed are You, LORD,
the holy God. / *Between Rosh HaShana & Yom Kippur:* the holy King./
(If forgotten, repeat the Amida.)

Imagine a city in the middle of a war. The dirt flying in the air. Missiles overhead. Everything in chaos. The smell of chemicals permeating the thick fog that has become the sky and civilians running through the streets in confusion, in panic – a living nightmare. A doctor runs across the blood-stained streets looking for people he can help, wounds he can heal just enough to get people back on their feet so they can keep running, keep living. He tends to a man bleeding from a piece of shrapnel, when he suddenly hears someone call out, "Doctor."

A short distance away he sees the woman calling out. She is hurt and in need of immediate attention. But as soon as he runs toward her, he hears another voice: "David!" He looks over to see his neighbor on the ground with a serious injury. No sooner than two steps to the neighbor's direction, a small voice pierces through the sweaty air and whispers, "Dad." The doctor is paralyzed for a moment before looking for his son amidst the rubble.

"Hashem" is the Jewish People's way of saying Dad.

To most people, the man in the story *was an anonymous person running around the streets – until someone saw him performing a medical act. Then he became "Doctor." To his neighbor, however, he was "David," a name that suggests an attachment that forced him to care just a little bit more. And when he heard "Dad" come through the thick fog, he was paralyzed.*

This is the power of a name. It defines the relationship we have with the person and forces us to treat him in a particular way.

"Hashem" is the Jewish People's way of saying Dad. Dad is not the person's legal name, it's not their Hebrew name, it's not their business title. It's shorthand. It's a way to say that we, as Jews, have a nickname for You, God. It's a nickname that suggests both intimacy and respect, like the appellation "Dad." It's a way to tell your father that you love him, but that you still understand he's the father, he's in charge.

Likewise with Hashem: we love You and feel close to You. And at the same time we recognize our distance and who is really in charge.

(Jon Dabach)

קדושת השם

אַתָּה קָדוֹשׁ וְשִׁמְךָ קָדוֹשׁ
וּקְדוֹשִׁים בְּכָל יוֹם יְהַלְלוּךְ סֶּלָה.
בָּרוּךְ אַתָּה יהוה, הָאֵל הַקָּדוֹשׁ./בעשרת ימי תשובה: הַמֶּלֶךְ הַקָּדוֹשׁ./
(If forgotten, repeat the עמידה.)

REFLECTION	LEARNING
How can I behave today in a way that reflects my inner holiness?	"A person will have to answer for everything that his eye beheld and he did not consume." (Yerushalmi, *Kiddushin* 4:12)
Am I behaving in a way that makes a *kiddush Hashem*?	In Judaism, holiness does not mean denying the physical, rather enjoying that which is permitted to us and uplifting it to make it spiritual. *Kedusha*
What will you do today to bring holiness into the world?	is the transformation and the elevation of the mundane to the holy and spiritual.

... A THOUSAND WORDS

KNOWLEDGE

אַתָּה חוֹנֵן You grace humanity with knowledge
and teach mortals understanding.
Grace us with the knowledge, understanding
and insight that come from You.
Blessed are You, LORD,
who generously gives knowledge.

...A THOUSAND WORDS

we grow wise and are able to say all that
we say, but not because we are greater
than they."
(Rabbi Isaiah di Trani)

"When I went to the moon I was a prag-
matic test pilot. But when I saw the planet

Earth floating in the vastness of space,
the presence of divinity became almost
palpable and I knew that life in the universe was not just an accident."
(Edgar Mitchell,
Apollo 14 Astronaut)

דַּעַת

אַתָּה חוֹנֵן לְאָדָם דַּעַת
וּמְלַמֵּד לֶאֱנוֹשׁ בִּינָה.
חָנֵּנוּ מֵאִתְּךָ דֵּעָה בִּינָה וְהַשְׂכֵּל.
בָּרוּךְ אַתָּה יהוה
חוֹנֵן הַדָּעַת.

LEARNING

On Saturday night we insert Havdala into this *berakha*. Havdala is when we make distinctions and separations, between holy and unholy, between light and dark, between Shabbat and the rest of the week. Being able to distinguish between one thing and another is a type of wisdom, therefore Havdala is included in the *berakha* about wisdom. The word בִּינָה also hints to בְּשָׂמִים ,יַיִן ,נֵר ,הַבְדָּלָה, the four blessings of the Havdala service. (*Mishna Berura* 115:1)

REFLECTION

*"You can't help respecting anybody
who can spell TUESDAY,
even if he doesn't spell it right."*
(A.A. Milne)

What do you wish you could know?

Which is more impressive to you, someone who already has knowledge or someone who continuously tries to gain more knowledge?

Have you ever wished to understand something more? What do you most want to understand?

CONNECTION

"The wisest of the philosophers asked: 'We admit that our predecessors were wiser than we. At the same time we criticize their comments, often rejecting them and claiming that the truth rests with us. How is this possible?' The wise philosopher responded: 'Who sees further, a dwarf or a giant? Surely a giant for his eyes are situated at a higher level than those of the dwarf. But if the dwarf is placed on the shoulders of the giant who sees further?... So too we are dwarfs astride the shoulders of giants. We master their wisdom and move beyond it. Due to their wisdom

REPENTANCE

הֲשִׁיבֵנוּ Bring us back, our Father, to Your Torah.

Draw us near, our King, to Your service.

Lead us back to You in perfect repentance.

Blessed are You, LORD,

who desires repentance.

CONNECTION

Rabbi Yisrael Salanter was returning home very late one night. As he walked through the dark alleyways, he suddenly noticed that a light was still burning in the home of the shoemaker. He knocked on the door and entered his home.

"Why are you still sitting and working at such a late hour?" asked Rabbi Salanter.

"As long as the candle burns," replied the shoemaker, "it is still possible to repair."

Those words made a great impression upon Rabbi Salanter and, from then on, he repeated them on many occasions.

"Do you hear?" Rabbi Salanter would ask. "As long as the candle burns, it is still possible to repair! As long as a person is alive and his soul is within him, he can still rectify his deeds."

REFLECTION

In what respect do you want God to treat you as His child?

Have you moved away from God? How are you trying to return?

Have you asked Him to help you to rekindle your connection?

CONNECTION

"For a righteous person may fall seven times and rise up..."
(Mishlei 24:16)

"God gave Adam a secret – and that secret was not how to begin, but how to begin again."
(Elie Wiesel)

"In a place where one who has achieved teshuva stands even the perfectly righteous cannot stand."
(Berakhot 34b)

תשובה

הֲשִׁיבֵנוּ אָבִינוּ לְתוֹרָתֶךָ
וְקָרְבֵנוּ מַלְכֵּנוּ לַעֲבוֹדָתֶךָ
וְהַחֲזִירֵנוּ בִּתְשׁוּבָה שְׁלֵמָה לְפָנֶיךָ.
בָּרוּךְ אַתָּה יהוה
הָרוֹצֶה בִּתְשׁוּבָה.

...A THOUSAND WORDS

FORGIVENESS

Strike the left side of the chest at °.

סְלַח לָנוּ Forgive us, our Father,
for we have °sinned.
Pardon us, our King,
for we have °transgressed;
for You pardon and forgive.
Blessed are You, LORD,
the generous One who repeatedly forgives.

סליחה

Strike the left side of the chest at °.

סְלַח לָנוּ אָבִינוּ כִּי °חָטָאנוּ
מְחַל לָנוּ מַלְכֵּנוּ כִּי °פָשָׁעְנוּ
כִּי מוֹחֵל וְסוֹלֵחַ אָתָּה.
בָּרוּךְ אַתָּה יהוה
חַנּוּן הַמַּרְבֶּה לִסְלֹחַ.

REFLECTION	LEARNING

REFLECTION

Are all sins forgivable?

What would you like
to erase?

In what area would you
like a second chance?

What do you need
to apologize for?

LEARNING

"Such is the power of *teshuva* that you
can even turn purposeful sins into merits."
(*Yoma* 86b)

Complete *teshuva* can even turn an
evil act into a merit. This is even more
powerful than conquering your inclination and never doing the act. Such is the
power of *teshuva*. (Rav Tzaddok of Lublin)

CONNECTION

*There once was a rabbi on a train who
was meditating peacefully, when a salesman shoved him to the next car because
of his aloofness, not knowing that he
was the rabbi of Brisk. Upon arrival at
the station, a large entourage greeted
the rabbi. The salesman, embarrassed
at having insulted the great rabbi asked
for forgiveness but the rabbi said no.*

*The salesman came to the rabbi's house
and asked for forgiveness, but again,
the rabbi refused. The rabbi's son heard
that his father refused to forgive a man
who visited, and asked him why. He answered, "I cannot forgive him. He did not
know who I was. He offended a common
man. Let the salesman go to him and ask
for forgiveness."*

REDEMPTION

רְאֵה Look on our suffering, plead our cause,
and redeem us soon for Your name's sake,
for You are a powerful Redeemer.
Blessed are You, LORD, the Redeemer of Israel.

On Fast Days the Leader adds:

עֲנֵנוּ Answer us, LORD, answer us on our Fast Day, for we are in great
distress. Look not at our wickedness. Do not hide Your face from us and
do not ignore our plea. Be near to our cry; please let Your loving-kindness
comfort us. Even before we call to You, answer us, as is said, "Before   *Is. 65*
they call, I will answer. While they are still speaking, I will hear." For You,
LORD, are the One who answers in time of distress, redeems and rescues
in all times of trouble and anguish. Blessed are You, LORD, who answers
in time of distress.

LEARNING

The beginning of this *berakha* asks
God to "*see our suffering*." In this
blessing about personal redemption
the first stage of deliverance is a rec-
ognition of suffering. This marks the
beginning of our redemption. We
ask God to see us, to look upon what
is causing us pain, and to rescue us.

"And God saw the Children of
Israel and God knew" (*Shemot* 2:25).

The Jews in Egypt were enslaved
with backbreaking labor and afflic-
tions. The Egyptians would find ways
to abuse them sometimes openly
and sometimes discreetly. Therefore
the text tells us, "And God saw." He
saw and He knew about everything.

REFLECTION

"*The salvation of God is like the blink of an eye.*"
(*Pesikta Zutrata, Ester* 4:17)

What affliction or emotional pain
do you want God to see in your life?

How do you show others that you
see their pain and struggles?

What is your biggest challenge
each day?
What do you need personal help
overcoming?

CONNECTION

"*Challenges make life interesting; however, overcoming them is what makes life meaningful.*"
(Mark Twain)

גאולה

רְאֵה בְעָנְיֵנוּ, וְרִיבָה רִיבֵנוּ
וּגְאָלֵנוּ מְהֵרָה לְמַעַן שְׁמֶךָ
כִּי גּוֹאֵל חָזָק אָתָּה.
בָּרוּךְ אַתָּה יהוה, גּוֹאֵל יִשְׂרָאֵל.

On Fast Days the שליח ציבור *adds:*

עֲנֵנוּ יהוה עֲנֵנוּ בְּיוֹם צוֹם תַּעֲנִיתֵנוּ, כִּי בְצָרָה גְדוֹלָה אֲנָחְנוּ. אַל תֵּפֶן אֶל
רִשְׁעֵנוּ, וְאַל תַּסְתֵּר פָּנֶיךָ מִמֶּנּוּ, וְאַל תִּתְעַלַּם מִתְּחִנָּתֵנוּ. הֱיֵה נָא קָרוֹב
לְשַׁוְעָתֵנוּ, יְהִי נָא חַסְדְּךָ לְנַחֲמֵנוּ, טֶרֶם נִקְרָא אֵלֶיךָ עֲנֵנוּ, כַּדָּבָר שֶׁנֶּאֱמַר:
וְהָיָה טֶרֶם יִקְרָאוּ וַאֲנִי אֶעֱנֶה, עוֹד הֵם מְדַבְּרִים וַאֲנִי אֶשְׁמָע: כִּי אַתָּה   ישעיה סה
יהוה הָעוֹנֶה בְּעֵת צָרָה, פּוֹדֶה וּמַצִּיל בְּכָל עֵת צָרָה וְצוּקָה. בָּרוּךְ אַתָּה
יהוה, הָעוֹנֶה בְּעֵת צָרָה.

... A THOUSAND WORDS

HEALING

רְפָאֵנוּ Heal us, LORD, and we shall be healed.
Save us and we shall be saved,
for You are our praise.
Bring complete recovery for all our illnesses,

The following prayer for a sick person may be said here:
May it be Your will, O LORD my God and God of my ancestors, that You
speedily send a complete recovery from heaven, a healing of both soul
and body, to the patient (*name*), son/daughter of (*mother's name*) among
the other sick of Israel.

---

for You, God, King,
are a faithful and compassionate Healer.
Blessed are You, LORD,
Healer of the sick of His people Israel.

CONNECTION	LEARNING

A 24-year-old man staring out from the train's window shouted, "Dad, look the trees are falling behind us!"

Dad smiled while a young couple sitting nearby looked at the 24-year-old's childish behavior with pity. Suddenly the boy again exclaimed, "Dad, look the clouds are running with us!"

The couple couldn't resist and said to the old man, Why don't you take your son to a good doctor?"

The old man smiled and said, "I did, and we are just coming from the hospital. My son was blind from birth; he just got his eyes today."

In *Bereshit* 21:1, we find the story of our matriarch Sara finally becoming pregnant directly after the incident of Avraham praying on behalf of King Avimelekh to be healed. Avimelekh and his household were stricken by a plague as a punishment for Sara's abduction. This plague caused Sara and Avraham to be unable to have children. Upon Sara's release, Avraham promised to pray for Avimelekh's recovery. Rashi explains that if one prays on behalf of someone else for something that he himself needs, his own prayer will be answered first.

רפואה

רְפָאֵנוּ יהוה וְנֵרָפֵא
הוֹשִׁיעֵנוּ וְנִוָּשֵׁעָה
כִּי תְהִלָּתֵנוּ אָתָּה
וְהַעֲלֵה רְפוּאָה שְׁלֵמָה לְכָל מַכּוֹתֵינוּ

The following prayer for a sick person may be said here:

יְהִי רָצוֹן מִלְּפָנֶיךָ יהוה אֱלֹהַי וֵאלֹהֵי אֲבוֹתַי, שֶׁתִּשְׁלַח מְהֵרָה רְפוּאָה שְׁלֵמָה
מִן הַשָּׁמַיִם רְפוּאַת הַנֶּפֶשׁ וּרְפוּאַת הַגּוּף לַחוֹלֶה/לַחוֹלָה *name of patient*
בֶּן/בַּת *mother's name* בְּתוֹךְ שְׁאָר חוֹלֵי יִשְׂרָאֵל.

כִּי אֵל מֶלֶךְ רוֹפֵא נֶאֱמָן וְרַחֲמָן אָתָּה.
בָּרוּךְ אַתָּה יהוה, רוֹפֵא חוֹלֵי עַמּוֹ יִשְׂרָאֵל.

REFLECTION

...A THOUSAND WORDS

Do you know
someone
who is sick?

Are you
suffering
physically,
emotionally,
or spiritually?

From what
would you
like God
to heal you?

PROSPERITY

> *The phrase "Give dew and rain as a blessing" is said from December 5th*
> *(in the year before a civil leap year, December 6th) until Pesaḥ. In Israel, it*
> *is said from the 7th of Marḥeshvan. The phrase "Give blessing" is said from*
> *Ḥol HaMo'ed Pesaḥ until December 4th (in the year before a civil leap*
> *year, December 5th). In Israel it is said through the 6th of Marḥeshvan.*

בָּרֵךְ Bless this year for us, Lᴏʀᴅ our God,
and all its types of produce for good.

In winter: Give dew and rain as a blessing
In other seasons: Give blessing

on the face of the earth,
and from its goodness satisfy us,
blessing our year as the best of years.
Blessed are You, Lᴏʀᴅ,
who blesses the years.

REFLECTION   ...A THOUSAND WORDS

What are
your needs?
What are
your wants?
Are they
different?
Can you
differentiate
when you
make
requests
of God?

What would
make you
satisfied?

ברכת השנים

The phrase וְתֵן טַל וּמָטָר לִבְרָכָה is said from December 5th (in the year before a civil leap year, December 6th) until פסח. In ארץ ישראל, it is said from מרחשון ז׳. The phrase וְתֵן בְּרָכָה is said from חול המועד פסח until December 4th (in the year before a civil leap year, December 5th). In ארץ ישראל it is said through מרחשון ז׳.

בָּרֵךְ עָלֵינוּ יהוה אֱלֹהֵינוּ אֶת הַשָּׁנָה הַזֹּאת

וְאֶת כָּל מִינֵי תְבוּאָתָהּ, לְטוֹבָה

בחורף: וְתֵן טַל וּמָטָר לִבְרָכָה / בקיץ: וְתֵן בְּרָכָה

עַל פְּנֵי הָאֲדָמָה, וְשַׂבְּעֵנוּ מִטּוּבָהּ

וּבָרֵךְ שְׁנָתֵנוּ כַּשָּׁנִים הַטּוֹבוֹת.

בָּרוּךְ אַתָּה יהוה, מְבָרֵךְ הַשָּׁנִים.

CONNECTION

The naḥash, snake, was punished for inciting Adam and Eve to eat from the Tree of Knowledge by having to eat the dust of the earth (Bereshit 3:14). Rabbi Menachem Mendel of Kotzk is bothered by this choice of punishment; after all, it resulted in the fact that the snake is never lacking sustenance. While other creatures must struggle to find food, the snake never experiences that problem. This appears to be a great blessing; how is this a punishment?

He suggested that the very fact that the snake is never lacking is itself the punishment because there is, therefore, no need for the snake to be dependent on Hashem. And when there is no dependence there is also no relationship. The absence of a relationship with God is the ultimate curse that any creature can receive.

LEARNING

The Talmud (Yoma 74b) teaches, "The blind eat but are not satisfied." The commentators explain that a blind person cannot be truly satisfied by his food because he cannot see his food. What does it mean to be "blind" when it comes to eating? What does it mean to be unable to "see" one's food? Perhaps this statement is not to be taken literally; it has a spiritual meaning as well. If we cannot see the blessings and the bounty that we are being given, if we cannot recognize it, it will never bring us satisfaction.

INGATHERING OF EXILES

תְּקַע Sound the great shofar for our freedom,
raise high the banner to gather our exiles,
and gather us together from the four quarters of the earth.
Blessed are You, LORD,
who gathers the dispersed of His people Israel.

REFLECTION

לִבִּי בְמִזְרָח וְאָנֹכִי בְּסוֹף מַעֲרָב

*"My heart is in the east,
and I in the uttermost west."*
(Rabbi Yehuda HaLevi)

How did the Jewish People come to be scattered all over the world?

How and when will we be gathered together again?

Has this process already started?

... A THOUSAND WORDS

קבוץ גלויות
תְּקַע בְּשׁוֹפָר גָּדוֹל לְחֵרוּתֵנוּ
וְשָׂא נֵס לְקַבֵּץ גָּלֻיּוֹתֵינוּ
וְקַבְּצֵנוּ יַחַד מֵאַרְבַּע כַּנְפוֹת הָאָרֶץ.
בָּרוּךְ אַתָּה יהוה, מְקַבֵּץ נִדְחֵי עַמּוֹ יִשְׂרָאֵל.

CONNECTION

The national flag of the State of Israel was formally adopted on October 28, 1948, five months after the establishment of the State. But its history dates much further back than that. Based on a design that was adopted at the First Zionist Congress in Basel, Switzerland, in 1897, the blue stripes and Star of David design first appeared in 1885 in Rishon LeTziyon, one of the earliest modern Zionist settlements in Eretz Yisrael, as a banner to lead an agricultural procession in the village. The two blue stripes on the flag were inspired by the stripes on the tallit, often black, but light blue/turquoise was chosen for the color of the flag to represent the color of tekhelet, the color of the dyed longer string in the tzitzit that takes its color from the sea snail, the ḥilazon. This color has much spiritual significance in Judaism, representing the color of the heavens, Aharon's staff, and some say the Luḥot HaBrit on which the Ten Commandments were written. The color was also found on the Kohen Gadol's clothes, and considered to be the color of purity and holiness. In time, blue and white became the national colors of the Jewish People, and then in 1948, together with the Magen David, these colors became the national flag of the Jewish People.

Fun Fact: The Guinness Book of Records records that the largest flag in the world was a giant Israeli flag unfurled at the ancient Jewish desert fortress of Masada in 2007.

LEARNING

The language of this berakha is based on the verse from Yeshayahu (27:13):

וְהָיָה בַּיּוֹם הַהוּא,
יִתָּקַע בְּשׁוֹפָר גָּדוֹל,
וּבָאוּ הָאֹבְדִים בְּאֶרֶץ אַשּׁוּר,
וְהַנִּדָּחִים בְּאֶרֶץ מִצְרָיִם;
וְהִשְׁתַּחֲווּ לַיהוה
בְּהַר הַקֹּדֶשׁ, בִּירוּשָׁלָ͏ִם.

"It shall be on that day that a great shofar will be blown and the lost in the land of Assyria and the dispersed in the land of Egypt will come; and they will prostrate themselves before the LORD on the holy mountain, in Jerusalem."

This berakha signals the transition from individual requests and hopes to collective and national ones.

JUSTICE

הָשִׁיבָה Restore our judges as at first,
and our advisors as at the beginning,
and remove from us sorrow and sighing.
May You alone, LORD, reign over us
with loving-kindness and compassion,
and vindicate us in justice.
Blessed are You, LORD,
the King who loves righteousness and justice.

/ *Between Rosh HaShana & Yom Kippur, end the blessing:* the King of justice. /

REFLECTION

"Rabban Shimon ben Gamliel used to say:
On three things does the world stand –
on truth, justice, and peace."
(*Avot* 1:18)

What is justice? Who decides what is just?

How do you live your life by the value of justice?

How will you practice justice today?

LEARNING

This *berakha* follows the last thematically – asking for our exiles to be ingathered and the establishment of a Jewish State is not enough. That State must also be based on the Torah values of justice and compassion.

CONNECTION

"The State of Israel will be open for Jewish immigration and for the Ingathering of the Exiles; it will foster the development of the country for the benefit of all its inhabitants; it will be based on freedom, justice and peace as envisaged by the prophets of Israel; it will ensure complete equality of social and political rights to all its inhabitants irrespective of religion, race or sex; it will guarantee freedom of religion, conscience, language, education and culture; it will safeguard the Holy Places of all religions; and it will be faithful to the principles of the Charter of the United Nations."

(The Declaration of the Establishment of the State of Israel, May 14, 1948)

השבת המשפט

הָשִׁיבָה שׁוֹפְטֵינוּ כְּבָרִאשׁוֹנָה

וְיוֹעֲצֵינוּ כְּבַתְּחִלָּה

וְהָסֵר מִמֶּנּוּ יָגוֹן וַאֲנָחָה

וּמְלֹךְ עָלֵינוּ אַתָּה יהוה לְבַדְּךָ בְּחֶסֶד וּבְרַחֲמִים

וְצַדְּקֵנוּ בַּמִּשְׁפָּט.

בָּרוּךְ אַתָּה יהוה

מֶלֶךְ אוֹהֵב צְדָקָה וּמִשְׁפָּט. / בעשרת ימי תשובה: הַמֶּלֶךְ הַמִּשְׁפָּט./

AGAINST INFORMERS

וְלַמַּלְשִׁינִים For the slanderers let there be no hope,
and may all wickedness perish in an instant.
May all Your people's enemies swiftly be cut down.
May You swiftly uproot, crush, cast down
and humble the arrogant
swiftly in our days.
Blessed are You, LORD,
who destroys enemies and humbles the arrogant.

... A THOUSAND WORDS

ברכת המינים

וְלַמַּלְשִׁינִים אַל תְּהִי תִקְוָה
וְכָל הָרִשְׁעָה כְּרֶגַע תֹּאבֵד
וְכָל אוֹיְבֵי עַמְּךָ מְהֵרָה יִכָּרֵתוּ
וְהַזֵּדִים מְהֵרָה תְעַקֵּר וּתְשַׁבֵּר וּתְמַגֵּר וְתַכְנִיעַ
בִּמְהֵרָה בְיָמֵינוּ.
בָּרוּךְ אַתָּה יהוה, שׁוֹבֵר אוֹיְבִים וּמַכְנִיעַ זֵדִים.

REFLECTION

*"Each maḥloket that is in the name
of heaven will have enduring value;
but one that is not in the name of heaven
will not have enduring value."*
(*Avot* 5:21)

Why do you think Jews fight?

How do we stop Jews from fighting?

**How can you respect someone you
disagree with? When and how
will you do that today?**

LEARNING

The *Shemoneh Esreh* is known by
this name because it originally
contained eighteen *berakhot*.
But this *berakha* was added as
the nineteenth blessing at a later
time to address those (Jews) who
worked against the Jewish community in Roman times. Since
those times it has come to be
considered a *tefilla* against all enemies of the Jewish People.

CONNECTION

*There were thugs in Rabbi Meir's neighbor-
hood who distressed him greatly. Rabbi
Meir prayed to Hashem that they should
die. His wife Beruria asked him, "What
are you thinking? Is this the verse that
inspired you to do this? 'Let sins cease
from the land' (*Tehillim 104:35*)? But
does it say sins or sinners? It says "sins"*

*not "sinners"! You should pray to Hashem
that He should help them do teshuva and
repent!" Rabbi Meir admitted that Beruria
was in fact correct, and he changed his
prayer that Hashem should have mercy
on them and they should repent. And
they did!*

(*Berakhot* 10a)

THE RIGHTEOUS

עַל הַצַּדִּיקִים To the righteous, the pious,
the elders of Your people the house of Israel,
the surviving scholars,
the righteous converts, and to us,
may Your compassion be aroused, LORD our God.
Give a good reward to all who sincerely trust in Your name.
Set our lot with them,
so that we may never be ashamed,
for in You we trust.
Blessed are You, LORD,
who is the support and trust of the righteous.

If you can make one heap of all your winnings
   And risk it on one turn of pitch-and-toss,
And lose, and start again at your beginnings
   And never breathe a word about your loss;
If you can force your heart and nerve and
     sinew
   To serve your turn long after they are gone,
And so hold on when there is nothing in you
   Except the Will which says to them: "Hold on!"

If you can talk with crowds and keep your
     virtue,
   Or walk with Kings – nor lose the common
     touch,
If neither foes nor loving friends can hurt you,
   If all men count with you, but none too
     much;
If you can fill the unforgiving minute
   With sixty seconds' worth of distance run,
Yours is the Earth and everything that's in it,
   And – which is more – you'll be a Man,
     my son.
          (Rudyard Kipling, 1895)

REFLECTION

"We are all called on to be leaders.
But we are also called on to be
followers. In Judaism the two
concepts are not opposites as
they are in many cultures. They
are part of the same process….
A leader is one who challenges
a follower. A follower is one
who challenges a leader."

(Rabbi Jonathan Sacks,
Lessons in Leadership)

What does it take
to be a good leader?

Are you a
good leader?
Are you a
good follower?

How will you
lead today?

על הצדיקים

עַל הַצַּדִּיקִים וְעַל הַחֲסִידִים
וְעַל זִקְנֵי עַמְּךָ בֵּית יִשְׂרָאֵל
וְעַל פְּלֵיטַת סוֹפְרֵיהֶם, וְעַל גֵּרֵי הַצֶּדֶק, וְעָלֵינוּ
יֶהֱמוּ רַחֲמֶיךָ יהוה אֱלֹהֵינוּ
וְתֵן שָׂכָר טוֹב לְכָל הַבּוֹטְחִים בְּשִׁמְךָ בֶּאֱמֶת
וְשִׂים חֶלְקֵנוּ עִמָּהֶם, וּלְעוֹלָם לֹא נֵבוֹשׁ כִּי בְךָ בָּטֶחְנוּ.
בָּרוּךְ אַתָּה יהוה, מִשְׁעָן וּמִבְטָח לַצַּדִּיקִים.

LEARNING	CONNECTION

Glossary:

צַדִּיקִים – The truly righteous who serve Hashem in every possible way.

חֲסִידִים – The pious, who push themselves to do more than is expected.

זִקְנֵי יִשְׂרָאֵל – The elders of Israel, not necessarily just in age, but in wisdom born of life experience.

סוֹפְרֵיהֶם – The scholars who teach.

גֵּרֵי הַצֶּדֶק – The converts to Judaism who join the Jewish People because they believe in the truth of the Torah.

עָלֵינוּ – We, the everyday ordinary Jew. Everyone has a contribution to make.

If

If you can keep your head when all about you
  Are losing theirs and blaming it on you,
If you can trust yourself when all men doubt you,
  But make allowance for their doubting too;
If you can wait and not be tired by waiting,
  Or being lied about, don't deal in lies,
Or being hated, don't give way to hating,
  And yet don't look too good, nor talk too wise:

If you can dream – and not make dreams your master;
  If you can think – and not make thoughts your aim;
If you can meet with Triumph and Disaster
  And treat those two impostors just the same;
If you can bear to hear the truth you've spoken
  Twisted by knaves to make a trap for fools,
Or watch the things you gave your life to, broken,
  And stoop and build 'em up with worn-out tools:

REBUILDING JERUSALEM

וְלִירוּשָׁלַיִם To Jerusalem, Your city, may You return in compassion,
and may You rest Your presence in it as You promised.
May You rebuild it rapidly in our days
as an everlasting structure,
and install within it soon the throne of David.
Blessed are You, LORD, who builds Jerusalem.

לְשָׁנָה הַבָּאָה בִּירוּשָׁלַיִם הַבְּנוּיָה

Should we still say this *berakha* if Jerusalem has been rebuilt?

Have you ever been to Jerusalem? Go there now in your mind.

When will Jerusalem be fully rebuilt? How can we help make that happen?

A very brief Jerusalem timeline:

1000 BCE:	King David conquers Jerusalem, makes it Jewish capital.
960 BCE:	King Solomon builds First Temple.
586 BCE:	First Temple destroyed by Babylonian army.
516 BCE:	Second Temple built and Jews return with permission from Cyrus.
332 BCE:	Alexander the Great conquers Jerusalem.
70 CE:	Second Temple destroyed by Roman army.
135:	Jerusalem rebuilt as a Roman city.
638–1099:	First Muslim Period.
1099–1187:	Crusader Period.
1187–1516:	Second Muslim Period.
1516–1917:	Ottoman Period.
1860:	Mishkenot Sha'ananim built – first Jewish neighborhood outside the walls of the old city.
1917:	British capture Jerusalem – the beginning of the British Mandate Period.
1948:	The Old City of Jerusalem falls to the Jordanian Legion. West Jerusalem declared the capital of the State of Israel.
1967:	Jerusalem reunited as East Jerusalem and the Old City are conquered in the Six-Day War.

בניין ירושלים

וְלִירוּשָׁלַיִם עִירְךָ בְּרַחֲמִים תָּשׁוּב, וְתִשְׁכֹּן בְּתוֹכָהּ כַּאֲשֶׁר דִּבַּרְתָּ
וּבְנֵה אוֹתָהּ בְּקָרוֹב בְּיָמֵינוּ בִּנְיַן עוֹלָם
וְכִסֵּא דָוִד מְהֵרָה לְתוֹכָהּ תָּכִין.
בָּרוּךְ אַתָּה יהוה, בּוֹנֵה יְרוּשָׁלָיִם.

CONNECTION

THE PARATROOPERS CRY

This Kotel *has heard many prayers*
This Kotel *has seen many walls fall*
This Kotel *has felt wailing women's hands and notes pressed*
  between its stones
This Kotel *has seen Rabbi Yehuda HaLevi trampled in front of it*
This Kotel *has seen Caesars rising and falling*
But this Kotel *has never before seen paratroopers cry.*
This Kotel *has seen them tired and exhausted*
This Kotel *has seen them wounded and scratched-up*
Running toward it with beating hearts, with cries and with silence
Pouncing out like predators from the alleyways of the Old City
And they're dust-covered and dry-lipped
And they're whispering: if I forget you, if I forget you, O Jerusalem
And they are lighter than eagles and more tenacious then lions
And their tanks are the fiery chariot of Elijah the Prophet
And they pass like lightning
And they pass in fury
And they remember the thousands of terrible years in which
  we didn't even have a Kotel *in front of which we could cry.*
And here they are standing in front of it and breathing deeply
And here they are looking at it with the sweet pain
And the tears fall and they look awkwardly at each other
How is it that paratroopers cry?
How is it that they touch the wall with feeling?
How is it that from crying they move to singing?
Maybe it's because these 19-year-olds were born with the birth of Israel
Carrying on their backs – 2,000 years.

           (Haim Hefer)

KINGDOM OF DAVID

אֶת צֶמַח May the offshoot
of Your servant David soon flower,
and may his pride be raised high by Your salvation,
for we wait for Your salvation all day.
Blessed are You, LORD,
who makes the glory of salvation flourish.

REFLECTION

"אֲנִי מַאֲמִין בֶּאֱמוּנָה שְׁלֵמָה, בְּבִיאַת הַמָּשִׁיחַ,
וְאַף עַל פִּי שֶׁיִּתְמַהְמֵהַּ,
עִם כָּל זֶה אֲחַכֶּה לוֹ בְּכָל יוֹם שֶׁיָּבוֹא"

*"I believe with perfect faith in the coming
of the Messiah, and though he may delay,
I wait daily for him to come."*

What can you do today to bring the
Mashiaḥ one step closer?

Can you see any signs in the world
that we are closer to the coming
of the Mashiaḥ than previous
generations?

… A THOUSAND WORDS

מלכות בית דוד

אֶת צֶמַח דָּוִד עַבְדְּךָ מְהֵרָה תַצְמִיחַ
וְקַרְנוֹ תָּרוּם בִּישׁוּעָתֶךָ
כִּי לִישׁוּעָתְךָ קִוִּינוּ כָּל הַיּוֹם.
בָּרוּךְ אַתָּה יהוה, מַצְמִיחַ קֶרֶן יְשׁוּעָה.

CONNECTION

Once upon a time, Hashem called for the Melekh HaMashiaḥ to tell Him that the time had come for the final redemption. So the Mashiaḥ got dressed in his very best clothes, and entered the first beit knesset he came to, to announce the good news. Everyone there immediately stopped their learning and stared at him in disbelief. One person called out, "That cannot be the Mashiaḥ. Just look at his hat... it has pinches and the brim is down!" So the Mashiaḥ changed his hat, and put the brim up, and traveled to the next shul on the way. But there he was also received with surprise. "What a strange thought, Mashiaḥ wearing a hat!" they said. "If you were really the Mashiaḥ you would have a knitted kippa!" So the Mashiaḥ took off his hat and placed a knitted kippa *on his head, for he didn't mind what he wore on his head. At the next shul they said to him, "Whoever heard of a Mashiaḥ without a black hat?" "But I have a black hat," he replied. And as he placed it on his head they all laughed and said, "The Mashiaḥ wearing a hat with pinches and the brim down!" With sadness in his eyes the Mashiaḥ realized that his time had not yet come, and he began his journey back to heaven. As he was leaving, Jews of every type ran after him crying, "Wait! Don't leave. It was their fault!" But the Mashiaḥ just continued slowly and sadly walking, saying, "Don't you see? Hashem loves each and every one of you. But my time will only come when you do too!"*

LEARNING

The word **צֶמַח** means offshoot or growth, and in this context refers to the descendant of King David who Jewish tradition tells us will be the Mashiaḥ – the redeemer who will herald the Messianic period. This term could be used because this process will be a slow and incremental one just like the flowering and growth of a plant. This may also be the reason why this term was used to describe the Messianic dimension of the establishment of the State of Israel in the prayer for the State of Israel (page 239).

RESPONSE TO PRAYER

שְׁמַע קוֹלֵנוּ Listen to our voice, LORD our God.
Spare us and have compassion on us,
and in compassion and favor accept our prayer,
for You, God, listen to prayers and pleas.
Do not turn us away, O our King,
empty-handed from Your presence,*

*In times of drought in Israel, some add "And answer us" on page 662.

for You listen with compassion to the prayer of Your people Israel.
Blessed are You, LORD, who listens to prayer.

REFLECTION

"The man who persists in knocking
will succeed in entering."
(Ibn Ezra)

Is there something you want
to ask God for that you cannot
put into words?

How well do you listen to others?

What do you want God to
listen to you about?

LEARNING

The Shulhan Arukh (Orah Hayyim 101:2)
teaches us that a person must hear his
own voice when he prays, though he
must not disturb those around him. So
important is the voice of our prayer, that
the Siftei Hayyim says that we ask God to
hear our prayer based on the sound of our
voice alone even if we lack the proper and
complete intention or wording that would
render our prayers worthy of His attention.

CONNECTION

"We are often taught that if we just pray hard
enough and well enough, God will grant
us our wishes, but it is not like that. Our
relationship with God is more complicated.

How do we educate our children to
pray with all their hearts and souls, but in
parallel to also know that the response to
all those prayers might be 'No'? This is one of
the most difficult challenges of faith – and
yet we just have to accept that we have no

right to make demands. All we can do is be
confident that our prayers are heard. Faith
is stronger than us. What is incredible is that
we continue to believe, despite everything."
(Rachelle Fraenkel,
mother of Naftali Fraenkel HY"D,
who was one of the three boys
kidnapped from a bus stop on their
way home from school in the summer
of 2014, and murdered by Hamas)

שׁוֹמֵעַ תְּפִלָּה

שְׁמַע קוֹלֵנוּ יהוה אֱלֹהֵינוּ

חוּס וְרַחֵם עָלֵינוּ

וְקַבֵּל בְּרַחֲמִים וּבְרָצוֹן אֶת תְּפִלָּתֵנוּ

כִּי אֵל שׁוֹמֵעַ תְּפִלּוֹת וְתַחֲנוּנִים אֶתָּה

וּמִלְּפָנֶיךָ מַלְכֵּנוּ רֵיקָם אַל תְּשִׁיבֵנוּ*

*In times of drought in אֶרֶץ יִשְׂרָאֵל, some add וַעֲנֵנוּ on page 663.

כִּי אַתָּה שׁוֹמֵעַ תְּפִלַּת עַמְּךָ יִשְׂרָאֵל בְּרַחֲמִים.

בָּרוּךְ אַתָּה יהוה, שׁוֹמֵעַ תְּפִלָּה.

... A THOUSAND WORDS

TEMPLE SERVICE

רְצֵה Find favor, LORD our God,
in Your people Israel and their prayer.
Restore the service to Your most holy House,
and accept in love and favor
the fire-offerings of Israel and their prayer.
May the service of Your people Israel always find favor with You.

On Rosh Ḥodesh and Ḥol HaMo'ed, say:

אֱלֹהֵינוּ Our God and God of our ancestors, may there rise, come, reach,
appear, be favored, heard, regarded and remembered before You, our
recollection and remembrance, as well as the remembrance of our
ancestors, and of the Messiah son of David Your servant, and of Jerusalem Your holy city, and of all Your people the house of Israel – for
deliverance and well-being, grace, loving-kindness and compassion,
life and peace, on this day of:

> *On Rosh Ḥodesh:* Rosh Ḥodesh.
> *On Pesaḥ:* the Festival of Matzot.
> *On Sukkot:* the Festival of Sukkot.

On it remember us, LORD our God, for good; recollect us for blessing, and save us for life. In accord with Your promise of salvation and
compassion, spare us and be generous to us; have compassion on us
and save us, for our eyes are turned to You because You, God, are a
generous and compassionate King.

וְתֶחֱזֶינָה And may our eyes witness
Your return to Zion in compassion.
Blessed are You, LORD, who restores His Presence to Zion.

LEARNING

In the Gemara (*Berakhot* 26b) there is a disagreement as to the source for our *tefillot* in their current form. Rabbi Yossi ben Ḥanina says that our *tefillot* were instituted by our forefathers, whereas Rabbi Yehoshua ben Levi says our *tefillot* correspond to the daily sacrifices in the Temple. The conclusion of the Gemara is that both are true, and the theme of the *korbanot* runs all the way through our *tefillot*. This *berakha* is a further ex-ample of this.

‫עבודה‬

רְצֵה יהוה אֱלֹהֵינוּ בְּעַמְּךָ יִשְׂרָאֵל וּבִתְפִלָּתָם
וְהָשֵׁב אֶת הָעֲבוֹדָה לִדְבִיר בֵּיתֶךָ
וְאִשֵּׁי יִשְׂרָאֵל וּתְפִלָּתָם בְּאַהֲבָה תְקַבֵּל בְּרָצוֹן
וּתְהִי לְרָצוֹן תָּמִיד עֲבוֹדַת יִשְׂרָאֵל עַמֶּךָ.

On ‫ראש חודש‬ and ‫חול המועד‬, say:

אֱלֹהֵינוּ וֵאלֹהֵי אֲבוֹתֵינוּ, יַעֲלֶה וְיָבוֹא וְיַגִּיעַ וְיֵרָאֶה וְיֵרָצֶה וְיִשָּׁמַע,
וְיִפָּקֵד וְיִזָּכֵר זִכְרוֹנֵנוּ וּפִקְדוֹנֵנוּ וְזִכְרוֹן אֲבוֹתֵינוּ, וְזִכְרוֹן מָשִׁיחַ בֶּן דָּוִד
עַבְדֶּךָ, וְזִכְרוֹן יְרוּשָׁלַיִם עִיר קָדְשֶׁךָ, וְזִכְרוֹן כָּל עַמְּךָ בֵּית יִשְׂרָאֵל,
לְפָנֶיךָ, לִפְלֵיטָה לְטוֹבָה, לְחֵן וּלְחֶסֶד וּלְרַחֲמִים, לְחַיִּים וּלְשָׁלוֹם בְּיוֹם
בראש חודש: רֹאשׁ הַחֹדֶשׁ / בפסח: חַג הַמַּצּוֹת / בסוכות: חַג הַסֻּכּוֹת
הַזֶּה. זָכְרֵנוּ יהוה אֱלֹהֵינוּ בּוֹ לְטוֹבָה, וּפָקְדֵנוּ בוֹ לִבְרָכָה, וְהוֹשִׁיעֵנוּ
בוֹ לְחַיִּים. וּבִדְבַר יְשׁוּעָה וְרַחֲמִים, חוּס וְחָנֵּנוּ וְרַחֵם עָלֵינוּ וְהוֹשִׁיעֵנוּ,
כִּי אֵלֶיךָ עֵינֵינוּ, כִּי אֵל מֶלֶךְ חַנּוּן וְרַחוּם אָתָּה.

וְתֶחֱזֶינָה עֵינֵינוּ בְּשׁוּבְךָ לְצִיּוֹן בְּרַחֲמִים.
בָּרוּךְ אַתָּה יהוה, הַמַּחֲזִיר שְׁכִינָתוֹ לְצִיּוֹן.

REFLECTION

...A THOUSAND WORDS

What can you
do in your life
instead of
bringing
sacrifices?

Have you
ever been
in Israel for *Ḥag*?
Was it special?
How?

THANKSGIVING

מוֹדִים  We give thanks to You,
for You are ☒ the Lord our God
and God of our ancestors
for ever and all time.
You are the Rock of our lives,
Shield of our salvation
from generation to generation.
We will thank You and
declare Your praise for our lives,
which are entrusted into Your hand;
for our souls,
which are placed in Your charge;
for Your miracles
which are with us every day;
and for Your wonders and favors
at all times, evening,
morning and midday.
You are good –
for Your compassion never fails.
You are compassionate –
for Your loving-kindnesses never cease.
We have always placed our hope in You.

*During the Leader's Repetition,
the congregation says quietly:*

מוֹדִים ☒ We give thanks
to You, for You are
☒ the Lord our God
and God of our ancestors,
God of all flesh,
who formed us
and formed the universe.
Blessings and thanks are due
to Your great and holy name
for giving us life
and sustaining us.
May You continue
to give us life and sustain us;
and may You gather
our exiles to Your holy courts,
to keep Your decrees,
do Your will and serve You
with a perfect heart,
for it is for us
to give You thanks.
Blessed be God to whom
thanksgiving is due.

REFLECTION

*"God gave you a gift of 86,400 seconds today.
Have you used one to say thank you?"*
(William Arthur Ward)

What do you want to thank God for
in your life?
What little miracles in your life can
you recognize?
What can you thank God for today that
you did not thank Him for yesterday?

... A THOUSAND WORDS

הודאה

מוֹדִים אֲנַחְנוּ לָךְ 🔼

שָׁאַתָּה הוּא 🔼 יהוה אֱלֹהֵינוּ
וֵאלֹהֵי אֲבוֹתֵינוּ לְעוֹלָם וָעֶד.
צוּר חַיֵּינוּ, מָגֵן יִשְׁעֵנוּ
אַתָּה הוּא לְדוֹר וָדוֹר.
נוֹדֶה לְּךָ וּנְסַפֵּר תְּהִלָּתֶךָ
עַל חַיֵּינוּ הַמְּסוּרִים בְּיָדֶךָ
וְעַל נִשְׁמוֹתֵינוּ הַפְּקוּדוֹת לָךְ
וְעַל נִסֶּיךָ שֶׁבְּכָל יוֹם עִמָּנוּ
וְעַל נִפְלְאוֹתֶיךָ וְטוֹבוֹתֶיךָ
שֶׁבְּכָל עֵת, עֶרֶב וָבֹקֶר וְצָהֳרָיִם.
הַטּוֹב, כִּי לֹא כָלוּ רַחֲמֶיךָ
וְהַמְרַחֵם, כִּי לֹא תַמּוּ חֲסָדֶיךָ
מֵעוֹלָם קִוִּינוּ לָךְ.

During חזרת הש״ץ,
the קהל says quietly:

🔼 מוֹדִים אֲנַחְנוּ לָךְ
שָׁאַתָּה הוּא 🔼 יהוה אֱלֹהֵינוּ
וֵאלֹהֵי אֲבוֹתֵינוּ
אֱלֹהֵי כָל בָּשָׂר
יוֹצְרֵנוּ, יוֹצֵר בְּרֵאשִׁית.
בְּרָכוֹת וְהוֹדָאוֹת
לְשִׁמְךָ הַגָּדוֹל וְהַקָּדוֹשׁ
עַל שֶׁהֶחֱיִיתָנוּ וְקִיַּמְתָּנוּ.
כֵּן תְּחַיֵּנוּ וּתְקַיְּמֵנוּ
וְתֶאֱסוֹף גָּלֻיּוֹתֵינוּ
לְחַצְרוֹת קָדְשֶׁךָ, לִשְׁמֹר חֻקֶּיךָ
וְלַעֲשׂוֹת רְצוֹנֶךָ וּלְעָבְדְּךָ
בְּלֵבָב שָׁלֵם
עַל שֶׁאֲנַחְנוּ מוֹדִים לָךְ.
בָּרוּךְ אֵל הַהוֹדָאוֹת.

LEARNING

The Gemara (*Berakhot* 7b) says: "From the day that God created the world there was no person who offered thanks to Him until Leah came and thanked Him." Leah our matriarch thanked God by naming her fourth child Yehuda. She saw through prophecy that her husband Yaakov would have twelve sons through his four wives. Upon giving birth to her fourth child, Leah realized that she would have more than the other wives and immediately thanked God for her extra bounty. Leah teaches that real gratitude comes from seeing something as a gift, undeserved and a blessing. When Leah thanked God for her fourth child, her gratitude was so genuine because she never expected to receive him. The name Yehuda is the source of our national name. As Jews, *Yehudim*, gratitude and thanksgiving are an integral part of our national DNA.

On Ḥanukka:

עַל הַנִּסִּים [We thank You also] for the miracles, the redemption, the mighty deeds, the salvations, and the victories in battle which You performed for our ancestors in those days, at this time.

בִּימֵי מַתִּתְיָהוּ In the days of Mattityahu, son of Yoḥanan, the High Priest, the Hasmonean, and his sons, the wicked Greek kingdom rose up against Your people Israel to make them forget Your Torah and to force them to transgress the laws of Your will. It was then that You in Your great compassion stood by them in the time of their distress. You championed their cause, judged their claim, and avenged their wrong. You delivered the strong into the hands of the weak, the many into the hands of the few, the impure into the hands of the pure, the wicked into the hands of the righteous, and the arrogant into the hands of those who were engaged in the study of Your Torah. You made for Yourself a great and holy reputation in Your world, and for Your people Israel You performed a great salvation and redemption as of this very day. Your children then entered the holiest part of Your House, cleansed Your Temple, purified Your Sanctuary, kindled lights in Your holy courts, and designated these eight days of Ḥanukka for giving thanks and praise to Your great name.

Continue with "For all these things."

LEARNING

Each of the *Al HaNisim* prayers thanks God for the salvation of the Jewish People. The threats of each story were very different. In the times of Mattityahu the threat was spiritual, the enemy wanted to force us to abandon our Torah. In the times of Mordekhai and Ester, there was a genocidal threat, to kill every man, woman, and child. Enemies sometimes want to destroy who we are, sometimes they want to destroy what we do. God intervened in both stories saving the Jewish People both from physical and spiritual annihilation.

CONNECTION

"The Egyptian, the Babylonian, and the Persian rose, filled the planet with sound and splendor, then faded to dream-stuff and passed away; the Greek and the Roman followed, and made a vast noise, and they are gone; other peoples have sprung up and held their torch high for a time, but it burned out, and they sit in twilight now, or have vanished. The Jew saw them all, beat them all, and is now what he always was.... All things are mortal but the Jew; all other forces pass, but he remains. What is the secret of his immortality?"

(Mark Twain)

בחנוכה:

עַל הַנִּסִּים וְעַל הַפֻּרְקָן וְעַל הַגְּבוּרוֹת וְעַל הַתְּשׁוּעוֹת וְעַל הַמִּלְחָמוֹת
שֶׁעָשִׂיתָ לַאֲבוֹתֵינוּ בַּיָּמִים הָהֵם בַּזְּמַן הַזֶּה.

בִּימֵי מַתִּתְיָהוּ בֶּן יוֹחָנָן כֹּהֵן גָּדוֹל חַשְׁמוֹנַאי וּבָנָיו, כְּשֶׁעָמְדָה מַלְכוּת יָוָן
הָרְשָׁעָה עַל עַמְּךָ יִשְׂרָאֵל לְהַשְׁכִּיחָם תּוֹרָתֶךָ וּלְהַעֲבִירָם מֵחֻקֵּי רְצוֹנֶךָ,
וְאַתָּה בְּרַחֲמֶיךָ הָרַבִּים עָמַדְתָּ לָהֶם בְּעֵת צָרָתָם, רַבְתָּ אֶת רִיבָם, דַּנְתָּ
אֶת דִּינָם, נָקַמְתָּ אֶת נִקְמָתָם, מָסַרְתָּ גִּבּוֹרִים בְּיַד חַלָּשִׁים, וְרַבִּים
בְּיַד מְעַטִּים, וּטְמֵאִים בְּיַד טְהוֹרִים, וּרְשָׁעִים בְּיַד צַדִּיקִים, וְזֵדִים בְּיַד
עוֹסְקֵי תוֹרָתֶךָ, וּלְךָ עָשִׂיתָ שֵׁם גָּדוֹל וְקָדוֹשׁ בְּעוֹלָמֶךָ, וּלְעַמְּךָ יִשְׂרָאֵל
עָשִׂיתָ תְּשׁוּעָה גְדוֹלָה וּפֻרְקָן כְּהַיּוֹם הַזֶּה. וְאַחַר כֵּן בָּאוּ בָנֶיךָ לִדְבִיר
בֵּיתֶךָ, וּפִנּוּ אֶת הֵיכָלֶךָ, וְטִהֲרוּ אֶת מִקְדָּשֶׁךָ, וְהִדְלִיקוּ נֵרוֹת בְּחַצְרוֹת
קָדְשֶׁךָ, וְקָבְעוּ שְׁמוֹנַת יְמֵי חֲנֻכָּה אֵלּוּ, לְהוֹדוֹת וּלְהַלֵּל לְשִׁמְךָ הַגָּדוֹל.
Continue with וְעַל כֻּלָּם.

... A THOUSAND WORDS

REFLECTION

"There are only two ways to
live your life. One is as though
nothing is a miracle. The other is
as though everything is a miracle."
(Albert Einstein)

Think about the miracle
of Jewish survival
through the millennia.
How are you helping to
maintain its survival?

How can holiness
triumph over impurity?

How are you bringing
light into the world?

On Purim:

עַל הַנִּסִּים [We thank You also] for the miracles, the redemption, the mighty deeds, the salvations, and the victories in battle which You performed for our ancestors in those days, at this time.

בִּימֵי מָרְדְּכַי In the days of Mordekhai and Esther, in Shushan the capital, the wicked Haman rose up against them and sought to destroy, slay *Esther 3* and exterminate all the Jews, young and old, children and women, on one day, the thirteenth day of the twelfth month, which is the month of Adar, and to plunder their possessions. Then You in Your great compassion defeated his counsel, frustrated his plans, and caused his scheme to recoil on his own head, so that they hanged him and his sons on the gallows.

Continue with "For all these things."

REFLECTION

How do you find God hidden in your life?

Have you experienced a miracle?

How do you protest against genocides of other peoples?

CONNECTION

The book of Ester *is the only book in the whole of Tanakh which does not mention God's name. If one chooses to do so, he could read the book as series of unconnected events culminating in an extraordinary turn of events. The Jewish survival could be looked at as a fortuitous coincidence if one chooses to ignore the hidden hand of God. The omission of God's name is not a sign that God was uninvolved in the events of Purim; rather He orchestrated everything from behind the scenes. The book of* Ester *means the book of concealment. The hidden nature of God's role in this story is a challenge to us, to look beneath the surface and to search for God even when we cannot see Him clearly. The miracles of the Purim story teach us to look for God in our natural lives. Every baby born, every sick person recovering, every terror attack survivor, the very existence of the Jewish People are all modern-day Purim miracles, miracles that require us to look closer and not just see.*

בפורים:

עַל הַנִּסִּים וְעַל הַפֻּרְקָן וְעַל הַגְּבוּרוֹת וְעַל הַתְּשׁוּעוֹת וְעַל הַמִּלְחָמוֹת שֶׁעָשִׂיתָ לַאֲבוֹתֵינוּ בַּיָּמִים הָהֵם בַּזְּמַן הַזֶּה.

בִּימֵי מָרְדְּכַי וְאֶסְתֵּר בְּשׁוּשַׁן הַבִּירָה, כְּשֶׁעָמַד עֲלֵיהֶם הָמָן הָרָשָׁע, בִּקֵּשׁ לְהַשְׁמִיד לַהֲרֹג וּלְאַבֵּד אֶת־כָּל־הַיְּהוּדִים מִנַּעַר וְעַד־זָקֵן טַף וְנָשִׁים בְּיוֹם אֶחָד, בִּשְׁלוֹשָׁה עָשָׂר לְחֹדֶשׁ שְׁנֵים־עָשָׂר, הוּא־חֹדֶשׁ אֲדָר, וּשְׁלָלָם לָבוֹז: וְאַתָּה בְּרַחֲמֶיךָ הָרַבִּים הֵפַרְתָּ אֶת עֲצָתוֹ, וְקִלְקַלְתָּ אֶת מַחֲשַׁבְתּוֹ, וַהֲשֵׁבוֹתָ לּוֹ גְּמוּלוֹ בְּרֹאשׁוֹ, וְתָלוּ אוֹתוֹ וְאֶת בָּנָיו עַל הָעֵץ.

Continue with וְעַל כֻּלָּם.

... A THOUSAND WORDS

וְעַל כֻּלָּם For all these things may Your name be blessed and great, our King, continually, for ever and all time.

Between Rosh HaShana And write, for a good life,
& Yom Kippur: all the children of Your covenant.

Let all that lives thank You, Selah! and praise Your name in truth, God, our Savior and Help, Selah!
🔊 Blessed 🔊 are You, 🔊 LORD,
whose name is "the Good" and to whom thanks are due.

The following is said by the Leader during the Repetition of the Amida,
except in a house of mourning and on Tisha B'Av. In Israel, if
Kohanim bless the congregation, turn to page 662.

Our God and God of our fathers, bless us with the threefold blessing in the Torah, written by the hand of Moses Your servant and pronounced by Aaron and his sons the priests, Your holy people, as it is said:

May the LORD bless you and protect you.   *Num. 6*
Cong: May it be Your will.
May the LORD make His face shine on you and be generous to you.
Cong: May it be Your will.
May the LORD turn His face toward you, and give you peace.
Cong: May it be Your will.

REFLECTION

"Gratitude is not only
the greatest of virtues,
but the parent of all others."
(Cicero)

Why thank?

Why bow? How does it feel
to bow?

Who are you going to thank
today and for what?

LEARNING

It is a positive mitzva from the Torah for the Kohen to bless the congregation with the famous words given by Hashem to Aharon in *Bemidbar* 6:24–26 every day when there is a *minyan* of ten men present during Shaḥarit, and also during Musaf on those days when it is said. However, it has become the custom outside of Israel in Ashkenazi communities for the *Ḥazan* to say אֱלֹהֵינוּ וֵאלֹהֵי אֲבוֹתֵינוּ instead.

וְעַל כֻּלָּם יִתְבָּרַךְ וְיִתְרוֹמַם שִׁמְךָ מַלְכֵּנוּ תָּמִיד לְעוֹלָם וָעֶד.

בעשרת ימי תשובה: וּכְתֹב לְחַיִּים טוֹבִים כָּל בְּנֵי בְרִיתֶךָ.

וְכֹל הַחַיִּים יוֹדוּךָ סֶּלָה, וִיהַלְלוּ אֶת שִׁמְךָ בֶּאֱמֶת
הָאֵל יְשׁוּעָתֵנוּ וְעֶזְרָתֵנוּ סֶלָה.

🔲 בָּרוּךְ 🔲 אַתָּה 🔲 יהוה, הַטּוֹב שִׁמְךָ וּלְךָ נָאֶה לְהוֹדוֹת.

The following is said by the שליח ציבור during חזרת הש״ץ, except in a house of mourning and on תשעה באב. In ארץ ישראל if כוהנים say ברכת כוהנים turn to page 663.

אֱלֹהֵינוּ וֵאלֹהֵי אֲבוֹתֵינוּ, בָּרְכֵנוּ בַּבְּרָכָה הַמְשֻׁלֶּשֶׁת בַּתּוֹרָה, הַכְּתוּבָה עַל
יְדֵי מֹשֶׁה עַבְדֶּךָ, הָאֲמוּרָה מִפִּי אַהֲרֹן וּבָנָיו כֹּהֲנִים עַם קְדוֹשֶׁיךָ, כָּאָמוּר

במדבר ו

יְבָרֶכְךָ יהוה וְיִשְׁמְרֶךָ: קהל: כֵּן יְהִי רָצוֹן

יָאֵר יהוה פָּנָיו אֵלֶיךָ וִיחֻנֶּךָּ: קהל: כֵּן יְהִי רָצוֹן

יִשָּׂא יהוה פָּנָיו אֵלֶיךָ וְיָשֵׂם לְךָ שָׁלוֹם: קהל: כֵּן יְהִי רָצוֹן

CONNECTION

We had recently arrived in Atlanta, our new home for two years. This was our first journey on the Georgia State Route 400, when we saw the signs warning that the toll plaza was approaching. So I prepared 50 cents to pay to the toll collector, only to be shocked to find out that the car in front of us had already paid our toll for us. Rather than accept the 50 cents change for their dollar bill they asked the toll collector to use it for our toll. Dumbfounded, I looked up at the toll collector and couldn't even think of what to ask so she could help me understand what had just happened. "She paid it forward. Georgians have been doing that for twenty years on this road. That's just the way we roll down here in the south!" she said with a smile. And so, in a small anonymous act of kindness two sets of strangers became connected. "But I want to thank them," I said to the toll lady. "Well you can't... but you can pay it forward too. That's the best way to thank them!" And she was so right of course. So I did, and smiled to myself as I looked in the rear view mirror at the strangers in the car behind us as I drove away.

PEACE

שִׂים שָׁלוֹם Give peace, goodness and blessing,
grace, loving-kindness and compassion
to us and all Israel Your people.
Bless us, our Father, all as one,
with the light of Your face,
for by the light of Your face
You have given us, LORD our God,
the Torah of life and love of kindness,
righteousness, blessing, compassion, life and peace.
May it be good in Your eyes to bless Your people Israel
at every time, in every hour, with Your peace.

> *Between* In the book of life, blessing, peace and prosperity,
> *Rosh HaShana* may we and all Your people the house of Israel
> *& Yom Kippur:* be remembered and written before You
> for a good life, and for peace.*

Blessed are You, LORD, who blesses His people Israel with peace.

> **Between Rosh HaShana and Yom Kippur
> outside Israel, many end the blessing:*
> Blessed are You, LORD, who makes peace.

*The following verse concludes the Leader's Repetition of the Amida.
Some also say it here as part of the silent Amida.*

May the words of my mouth and the inner thoughts of my heart   *Ps. 19*
find favor before You, LORD, my Rock and Redeemer.

REFLECTION	...A THOUSAND WORDS

*"Her ways are ways of pleasantness,
and all her paths are peace."*
(Mishlei 3:17)

Is peace the most important
value?

How can we achieve peace?

How will you bring some peace
to your world today?

שלום

שִׂים שָׁלוֹם טוֹבָה וּבְרָכָה

חֵן וָחֶסֶד וְרַחֲמִים עָלֵינוּ וְעַל כָּל יִשְׂרָאֵל עַמֶּךָ.

בָּרְכֵנוּ אָבִינוּ כֻּלָּנוּ כְּאֶחָד בְּאוֹר פָּנֶיךָ

כִּי בְאוֹר פָּנֶיךָ נָתַתָּ לָּנוּ יהוה אֱלֹהֵינוּ

תּוֹרַת חַיִּים וְאַהֲבַת חֶסֶד

וּצְדָקָה וּבְרָכָה וְרַחֲמִים וְחַיִּים וְשָׁלוֹם.

וְטוֹב בְּעֵינֶיךָ לְבָרֵךְ אֶת עַמְּךָ יִשְׂרָאֵל

בְּכָל עֵת וּבְכָל שָׁעָה בִּשְׁלוֹמֶךָ.

בעשרת ימי תשובה: בְּסֵפֶר חַיִּים, בְּרָכָה וְשָׁלוֹם, וּפַרְנָסָה טוֹבָה נִזָּכֵר וְנִכָּתֵב לְפָנֶיךָ, אֲנַחְנוּ וְכָל עַמְּךָ בֵּית יִשְׂרָאֵל לְחַיִּים טוֹבִים וּלְשָׁלוֹם.*

בָּרוּךְ אַתָּה יהוה, הַמְבָרֵךְ אֶת עַמּוֹ יִשְׂרָאֵל בַּשָּׁלוֹם.

*During the עשרת ימי תשובה in חוץ לארץ, many end the blessing:

בָּרוּךְ אַתָּה יהוה, עוֹשֶׂה הַשָּׁלוֹם.

The following verse concludes the חזרת הש״ץ.
Some also say it here as part of the silent עמידה.

תהלים יט · יִהְיוּ לְרָצוֹן אִמְרֵי־פִי וְהֶגְיוֹן לִבִּי לְפָנֶיךָ, יהוה צוּרִי וְגֹאֲלִי:

CONNECTION

When Hashem was about to create man, the angels in heaven arranged themselves into two groups, one shouting, "Don't do it!" and the other shouting, "Do it!" Some used kindness as their argument, and said, "Let man be created because he will do acts of kindness." Others used truth and said, "Don't create man because he will bring lies into the world." Others used righteousness and argued, "Let him be created because he will do righteous acts." And others used peace and said, "Don't create him because he will only fight!" When Hashem heard the angels arguing these points He took truth and threw it to the ground, showing them that loving-kindness, righteousness, and peace were more important.

(Bereshit Raba 8:5)

אֱלֹהַי My God, Berakhot 17a
guard my tongue from evil and my lips from dishonest speech.
To those who curse me, let my soul be silent;
may my soul be to all like the dust.
Open my heart to Your Torah
and let my soul pursue Your commandments.
As for all who plan evil against me,
swiftly defeat their counsel and frustrate their plans.

    Act for the sake of Your name; act for the sake of Your right hand;
    act for the sake of Your holiness; act for the sake of Your Torah.
That Your beloved ones may be rescued, Ps. 60
save with Your right hand and answer me.

May the words of my mouth and the inner thoughts of my heart Ps. 19
find favor before You, LORD, my Rock and Redeemer.

Bow, take three steps back, then bow, first left, then right, then center, while saying:
🔹 May He who makes peace in His high places,
🔹 make peace for us 🔹 and all Israel – and say: Amen.

יְהִי רָצוֹן May it be Your will, LORD our God and God of our ancestors, that the
Temple be rebuilt speedily in our days, and give us a share in Your Torah. And
there we will serve You with fear, as in the days of old and as in former years. Then Mal. 3
the offering of Judah and Jerusalem will be pleasing to the LORD as in the days
of old and as in former years.

When praying with a minyan, the Amida is repeated aloud by the Leader.

*On days when Taḥanun is said (see page 206), start Taḥanun on page 214.
On Mondays and Thursdays start Taḥanun on page 206.*

*On fast days (except Tisha B'Av) most congregations say Seliḥot
on page 566 before Avinu Malkenu on the next page.*

*Between Rosh HaShana and Yom Kippur (but not on Erev Yom Kippur,
unless it falls on Friday), say Avinu Malkenu on the next page.*

*On Rosh Ḥodesh, Ḥanukka, Ḥol HaMo'ed, Yom HaAtzma'ut and
Yom Yerushalayim, say Hallel on page 418.*

*On other days when Taḥanun is not said (see page 206),
the Leader says Half Kaddish on page 218.*

LEARNING

The verse beginning יִהְיוּ לְרָצוֹן signifies the
end of the *Amida*. Once you have reached this point, you may answer responsive
prayers such as Kaddish and *Kedusha*.

ברכות יז.

אֱלֹהַי

נְצֹר לְשׁוֹנִי מֵרָע וּשְׂפָתַי מִדַּבֵּר מִרְמָה

וְלִמְקַלְלַי נַפְשִׁי תִדֹּם, וְנַפְשִׁי כֶּעָפָר לַכֹּל תִּהְיֶה.

פְּתַח לִבִּי בְּתוֹרָתֶךָ, וּבְמִצְוֹתֶיךָ תִּרְדּוֹף נַפְשִׁי.

וְכָל הַחוֹשְׁבִים עָלַי רָעָה, מְהֵרָה הָפֵר עֲצָתָם וְקַלְקֵל מַחֲשַׁבְתָּם.

עֲשֵׂה לְמַעַן שְׁמֶךָ, עֲשֵׂה לְמַעַן יְמִינֶךָ

עֲשֵׂה לְמַעַן קְדֻשָּׁתֶךָ, עֲשֵׂה לְמַעַן תּוֹרָתֶךָ.

תהלים ס

לְמַעַן יֵחָלְצוּן יְדִידֶיךָ, הוֹשִׁיעָה יְמִינְךָ וַעֲנֵנִי:

תהלים יט

יִהְיוּ לְרָצוֹן אִמְרֵי־פִי וְהֶגְיוֹן לִבִּי לְפָנֶיךָ, יהוה צוּרִי וְגֹאֲלִי:

Bow, take three steps back, then bow, first left, then right, then center, while saying:

◆ עֹשֶׂה שָׁלוֹם/ בעשרת ימי תשובה: הַשָּׁלוֹם/ בִּמְרוֹמָיו

◆ הוּא יַעֲשֶׂה שָׁלוֹם ◆ עָלֵינוּ וְעַל כָּל יִשְׂרָאֵל, וְאִמְרוּ אָמֵן.

יְהִי רָצוֹן מִלְּפָנֶיךָ יהוה אֱלֹהֵינוּ וֵאלֹהֵי אֲבוֹתֵינוּ, שֶׁיִּבָּנֶה בֵּית הַמִּקְדָּשׁ בִּמְהֵרָה בְיָמֵינוּ, וְתֵן חֶלְקֵנוּ בְּתוֹרָתֶךָ, וְשָׁם נַעֲבָדְךָ בְּיִרְאָה כִּימֵי עוֹלָם וּכְשָׁנִים קַדְמֹנִיּוֹת.

מלאכי ג

וְעָרְבָה לַיהוה מִנְחַת יְהוּדָה וִירוּשָׁלָ͏ִם כִּימֵי עוֹלָם וּכְשָׁנִים קַדְמֹנִיּוֹת:

When praying with a מנין, *the* עמידה *is repeated aloud by the* שליח ציבור.

On days when תחנון *is said (see page 207), start* תחנון *on page 215.*
On Mondays and Thursdays start תחנון *on page 207.*

On fast days (except תשעה באב) *most congregations say* סליחות
on page 567 before אבינו מלכנו *on the next page.*

During the עשרת ימי תשובה (*but not on* ערב יום כיפור,
unless it falls on Friday), say אבינו מלכנו *on the next page.*

On יום ירושלים *and* יום העצמאות, חול המועד, חנוכה, ראש חודש, *say* הלל *on page 419.*

On other days when תחנון *is not said (see page 207), the* שליח ציבור *says* חצי קדיש *on page 219.*

REFLECTION

What might the connection be between peace and *lashon hara*?

What good will you accomplish with your words today?

What damage might you do with your words today? How can you avoid that?

How will you build with your words today and not destroy?

How can you achieve peace today with your words?

AVINU MALKENU

On fast days (except Tisha B'Av) most congregations say Seliḥot
on page 566 before Avinu Malkenu.
Between Rosh HaShana and Yom Kippur (but not on Erev Yom
Kippur, unless it falls on Friday), say Avinu Malkenu below.

The Ark is opened.

אָבִינוּ מַלְכֵּנוּ Our Father, our King, we have sinned before You.

Our Father, our King, we have no king but You.

Our Father, our King, deal kindly with us for the sake of Your name.

Our Father our King, /*bless us with / a good year.

/ *Between Rosh HaShana & Yom Kippur:* renew for us/

Our Father, our King, nullify all harsh decrees against us.

Our Father, our King, nullify the plans of those who hate us.

Our Father, our King, defeat the counsel of our enemies.

Our Father, our King, rid us of every oppressor and enemy.

Our Father, our King, close the mouths of our enemies and accusers.

Our Father, our King, eradicate disease, sword, famine, captivity and
destruction, wrongdoing and eradication
from the people of Your covenant.

Our Father, our King, withhold the plague from Your heritage.

Our Father, our King, forgive and pardon all our wrongdoing.

Our Father, our King, wipe away and remove our crimes and sins
from Your sight.

Our Father, our King, erase in Your great mercy all records of our sins.

The Gemara in *Ta'anit* 25b relates that there was a terrible drought in the Land of Israel. Rabbi Eliezer stepped before the ark to lead the congregation in prayer and recited the *Amida* and six extra *berakhot* for times of drought and his prayer was not answered. Rabbi Akiva stepped before the ark after him and exclaimed:

Our Father, our King! We have no king but You!

Our Father, our King! For Your sake, have compassion for us!

Finally rain fell.

אבינו מלכנו

On fast days (except תשעה באב) most congregations say סליחות
on page 567 before אבינו מלכנו.
During the עשרת ימי תשובה (but not on ערב יום כיפור,
unless it falls on Friday), say אבינו מלכנו below.

The ארון קודש is opened.

אָבִֽינוּ מַלְכֵּֽנוּ, חָטָֽאנוּ לְפָנֶֽיךָ.

אָבִֽינוּ מַלְכֵּֽנוּ, אֵין לָֽנוּ מֶֽלֶךְ אֶלָּא אָֽתָּה.

אָבִֽינוּ מַלְכֵּֽנוּ, עֲשֵׂה עִמָּֽנוּ לְמַֽעַן שְׁמֶֽךָ.

אָבִֽינוּ מַלְכֵּֽנוּ, בָּרֵךְ/ בעשרת ימי תשובה: חַדֵּשׁ/ עָלֵֽינוּ שָׁנָה טוֹבָה.

אָבִֽינוּ מַלְכֵּֽנוּ, בַּטֵּל מֵעָלֵֽינוּ כָּל גְּזֵרוֹת קָשׁוֹת.

אָבִֽינוּ מַלְכֵּֽנוּ, בַּטֵּל מַחְשְׁבוֹת שׂוֹנְאֵֽינוּ. ִ

אָבִֽינוּ מַלְכֵּֽנוּ, הָפֵר עֲצַת אוֹיְבֵֽינוּ.

אָבִֽינוּ מַלְכֵּֽנוּ, כַּלֵּה כָּל צַר וּמַשְׂטִין מֵעָלֵֽינוּ.

אָבִֽינוּ מַלְכֵּֽנוּ, סְתֹם פִּיּוֹת מַשְׂטִינֵֽינוּ וּמְקַטְרִיגֵֽינוּ.

אָבִֽינוּ מַלְכֵּֽנוּ, כַּלֵּה דֶּֽבֶר וְחֶֽרֶב וְרָעָב וּשְׁבִי וּמַשְׁחִית וְעָוֹן וּשְׁמַד
מִבְּנֵי בְרִיתֶֽךָ.

אָבִֽינוּ מַלְכֵּֽנוּ, מְנַע מַגֵּפָה מִנַּחֲלָתֶֽךָ.

אָבִֽינוּ מַלְכֵּֽנוּ, סְלַח וּמְחַל לְכָל עֲוֹנוֹתֵֽינוּ.

אָבִֽינוּ מַלְכֵּֽנוּ, מְחֵה וְהַעֲבֵר פְּשָׁעֵֽינוּ וְחַטֹּאתֵֽינוּ מִנֶּֽגֶד עֵינֶֽיךָ.

אָבִֽינוּ מַלְכֵּֽנוּ, מְחֹק בְּרַחֲמֶֽיךָ הָרַבִּים כָּל שִׁטְרֵי חוֹבוֹתֵֽינוּ.

LEARNING

This special prayer is recited on Rosh
HaShana, the *Aseret Yemei Teshuva*, and
Yom Kippur, as well as fast days. This

tefilla uses language of intense pleading
and supplication, uniquely suitable for
these days.

The following nine sentences are said responsively, first by the Leader, then by the congregation:

Our Father, our King, bring us back to You in perfect repentance.

Our Father, our King, send a complete healing to the sick of Your people.

Our Father, our King, tear up the evil decree against us.

Our Father, our King, remember us with a memory of favorable deeds before You.

Between Rosh HaShana and Yom Kippur:

Our Father, our King, write us in the book of good life.

Our Father, our King, write us in the book of redemption and salvation.

Our Father, our King, write us in the book of livelihood and sustenance.

Our Father, our King, write us in the book of merit.

Our Father, our King, write us in the book of pardon and forgiveness.

On Fast Days:

Our Father, our King, remember us for a good life.

Our Father, our King, remember us for redemption and salvation.

Our Father, our King, remember us for livelihood and sustenance.

Our Father, our King, remember us for merit.

Our Father, our King, remember us for pardon and forgiveness.

End of responsive reading.

REFLECTION

What would you like to ask your father for?

What would you like to ask your king?

What would you like to ask Hashem for?

What is the most important thing you are asking for?

What does a "good life" look like?

The following nine sentences are said responsively, first by the שליח ציבור, *then by the* קהל:

אָבִינוּ מַלְכֵּנוּ, הַחֲזִירֵנוּ בִּתְשׁוּבָה שְׁלֵמָה לְפָנֶיךָ.

אָבִינוּ מַלְכֵּנוּ, שְׁלַח רְפוּאָה שְׁלֵמָה לְחוֹלֵי עַמֶּךָ.

אָבִינוּ מַלְכֵּנוּ, קְרַע רֹעַ גְּזַר דִּינֵנוּ.

אָבִינוּ מַלְכֵּנוּ, זָכְרֵנוּ בְּזִכָּרוֹן טוֹב לְפָנֶיךָ.

During the עשרת ימי תשובה:

אָבִינוּ מַלְכֵּנוּ, כָּתְבֵנוּ בְּסֵפֶר חַיִּים טוֹבִים.

אָבִינוּ מַלְכֵּנוּ, כָּתְבֵנוּ בְּסֵפֶר גְּאֻלָּה וִישׁוּעָה.

אָבִינוּ מַלְכֵּנוּ, כָּתְבֵנוּ בְּסֵפֶר פַּרְנָסָה וְכַלְכָּלָה.

אָבִינוּ מַלְכֵּנוּ, כָּתְבֵנוּ בְּסֵפֶר זְכֻיּוֹת.

אָבִינוּ מַלְכֵּנוּ, כָּתְבֵנוּ בְּסֵפֶר סְלִיחָה וּמְחִילָה.

On Fast Days:

אָבִינוּ מַלְכֵּנוּ, זָכְרֵנוּ לְחַיִּים טוֹבִים.

אָבִינוּ מַלְכֵּנוּ, זָכְרֵנוּ לִגְאֻלָּה וִישׁוּעָה.

אָבִינוּ מַלְכֵּנוּ, זָכְרֵנוּ לְפַרְנָסָה וְכַלְכָּלָה.

אָבִינוּ מַלְכֵּנוּ, זָכְרֵנוּ לִזְכֻיּוֹת.

אָבִינוּ מַלְכֵּנוּ, זָכְרֵנוּ לִסְלִיחָה וּמְחִילָה.

End of responsive reading.

...A THOUSAND WORDS

Our Father, our King, let salvation soon flourish for us.

Our Father, our King, raise the honor of Your people Israel.

Our Father, our King, raise the honor of Your anointed.

Our Father, our King, fill our hands with Your blessings.

Our Father, our King, fill our storehouses with abundance.

Our Father, our King, hear our voice, pity and be compassionate to us.

Our Father, our King, accept, with compassion and favor, our prayer.

Our Father, our King, open the gates of heaven to our prayer.

Our Father, our King, remember that we are dust.

Our Father, our King, please do not turn us away from You empty-handed.

Our Father, our King, may this moment be a moment of compassion
and a time of favor before You.

Our Father, our King, have pity on us, our children and our infants.

Our Father, our King, act for the sake of those who were killed
for Your holy name.

Our Father, our King, act for the sake of those who were slaughtered
for declaring Your Unity.

Our Father, our King, act for the sake of those who went through fire and
water to sanctify Your name.

Our Father, our King, avenge before our eyes
the spilt blood of Your servants.

Our Father, our King, act for Your sake, if not for ours.

Our Father, our King, act for Your sake, and save us.

Our Father, our King, act for the sake of Your great compassion.

Our Father, our King, act for the sake of Your great, mighty and awesome
name by which we are called.

‣ Our Father, our King, be generous to us and answer us, though we
have no worthy deeds; act with us in charity and
loving-kindness and save us.

The Ark is closed.

---

boat pass so I can wave my flag to the captain and he will wave his flag back to me."

The older fellow chuckled, "Young man, any boat that passes on this ocean is likely to be a huge ship and the busy captain won't be able to see you, a small child sitting on the beach."

"Oh no, the captain of the ship will see me," the boy replied.

"How can you be so sure?" asked the man.

"Because the captain is my father," answered the boy.

אָבִינוּ מַלְכֵּנוּ, הַצְמַח לָנוּ יְשׁוּעָה בְּקָרוֹב.

אָבִינוּ מַלְכֵּנוּ, הָרֵם קֶרֶן יִשְׂרָאֵל עַמֶּךָ.

אָבִינוּ מַלְכֵּנוּ, הָרֵם קֶרֶן מְשִׁיחֶךָ.

אָבִינוּ מַלְכֵּנוּ, מַלֵּא יָדֵינוּ מִבִּרְכוֹתֶיךָ.

אָבִינוּ מַלְכֵּנוּ, מַלֵּא אֲסָמֵינוּ שָׂבָע.

אָבִינוּ מַלְכֵּנוּ, שְׁמַע קוֹלֵנוּ, חוּס וְרַחֵם עָלֵינוּ.

אָבִינוּ מַלְכֵּנוּ, קַבֵּל בְּרַחֲמִים וּבְרָצוֹן אֶת תְּפִלָּתֵנוּ.

אָבִינוּ מַלְכֵּנוּ, פְּתַח שַׁעֲרֵי שָׁמַיִם לִתְפִלָּתֵנוּ.

אָבִינוּ מַלְכֵּנוּ, זְכֹר כִּי עָפָר אֲנַחְנוּ.

אָבִינוּ מַלְכֵּנוּ, נָא אַל תְּשִׁיבֵנוּ רֵיקָם מִלְּפָנֶיךָ.

אָבִינוּ מַלְכֵּנוּ, תְּהֵא הַשָּׁעָה הַזֹּאת שְׁעַת רַחֲמִים
וְעֵת רָצוֹן מִלְּפָנֶיךָ.

אָבִינוּ מַלְכֵּנוּ, חֲמֹל עָלֵינוּ וְעַל עוֹלָלֵינוּ וְטַפֵּנוּ.

אָבִינוּ מַלְכֵּנוּ, עֲשֵׂה לְמַעַן הֲרוּגִים עַל שֵׁם קָדְשֶׁךָ.

אָבִינוּ מַלְכֵּנוּ, עֲשֵׂה לְמַעַן טְבוּחִים עַל יִחוּדֶךָ.

אָבִינוּ מַלְכֵּנוּ, עֲשֵׂה לְמַעַן בָּאֵי בָאֵשׁ וּבַמַּיִם עַל קִדּוּשׁ שְׁמֶךָ.

אָבִינוּ מַלְכֵּנוּ, נְקֹם לְעֵינֵינוּ נִקְמַת דַּם עֲבָדֶיךָ הַשָּׁפוּךְ.

אָבִינוּ מַלְכֵּנוּ, עֲשֵׂה לְמַעַנְךָ אִם לֹא לְמַעֲנֵנוּ.

אָבִינוּ מַלְכֵּנוּ, עֲשֵׂה לְמַעַנְךָ וְהוֹשִׁיעֵנוּ.

אָבִינוּ מַלְכֵּנוּ, עֲשֵׂה לְמַעַן רַחֲמֶיךָ הָרַבִּים.

אָבִינוּ מַלְכֵּנוּ, עֲשֵׂה לְמַעַן שִׁמְךָ הַגָּדוֹל הַגִּבּוֹר וְהַנּוֹרָא, שֶׁנִּקְרָא עָלֵינוּ.

‹ אָבִינוּ מַלְכֵּנוּ, חָנֵּנוּ וַעֲנֵנוּ, כִּי אֵין בָּנוּ מַעֲשִׂים
עֲשֵׂה עִמָּנוּ צְדָקָה וָחֶסֶד וְהוֹשִׁיעֵנוּ.

The ארון קודש is closed.

A little boy was playing on an open beach. A man approached the boy and asked him, "Young man, why are you playing here all

alone? Why don't you join the other children?" The boy looked up and responded innocently, "Because I want to see the big

TAḤANUN

On Mondays and Thursdays, when Taḥanun is said, begin with "He is compassionate"
below. On other days when Taḥanun is said, begin with "David said" on page 214.

Taḥanun is not said on: Rosh Ḥodesh, Ḥanukka, Tu BiShvat, the 14th and 15th of Adar I, Purim
and Shushan Purim, in the month of Nisan, Yom HaAtzma'ut, the 14th of Iyar (Pesaḥ Sheni),
Lag BaOmer, Yom Yerushalayim, from Rosh Ḥodesh Sivan through the day after Shavuot (in
Israel through 12th of Sivan), Tisha B'Av, Tu B'Av, Erev Rosh HaShana, and from Erev Yom
Kippur through the day after Simḥat Torah (in Israel through Rosh Ḥodesh Marḥeshvan).

Taḥanun is also not said: on the morning of a Brit Mila, either where the brit will take place
or where the father, Sandek or Mohel are present; if a groom is present (and some say a bride)
on the day of his wedding or during the week of Sheva Berakhot; in a house of mourning.

The following until "David said" on page 214 is said standing.

וְהוּא רַחוּם He is compassionate. He forgives wrongdoing and does not de- *Ps. 78*
stroy. Repeatedly He suppresses His anger, not rousing His full fury. Lᴏʀᴅ,
do not withhold Your compassion from us. May Your loving-kindness and
truth always protect us. Save us, Lᴏʀᴅ our God, and gather us from among *Ps. 106*
the nations, that we may give thanks to Your holy name and glory in Your
praise. If You, Lᴏʀᴅ, should keep account of sins, O Lᴏʀᴅ, who could *Ps. 130*
stand? But with You is forgiveness, that You may be feared. Do not deal *Jer. 14*
with us according to our sins; do not repay us according to our wrongdoing.
Though our wrongdoings testify against us, Lᴏʀᴅ, act for Your name's
sake. Remember, Lᴏʀᴅ, Your compassion and loving-kindness, for they *Ps. 25*

---

loves with a diamond ring outstretched
before her? What is a toddler telling his
parents as he lies face down on the
floor screaming because he dropped
his ice cream? Sometimes words are
not enough.

This helps us to understand the
act of *nefilat apayim* – "falling down
on one's face" – that we do here during *Taḥanun*. We just spent a serious
amount of time pouring our hearts
out before Hashem. And yet there is
still a feeling that we just haven't done
enough. Haven't said enough. So we

throw ourselves down in front of the Creator of the Universe who knows and understands everything, and have faith that
He understands.

Mondays and Thursdays – long Taḥanun
On Mondays and Thursdays an extended
version of *Taḥanun* is said. Tradition has it
that Mondays and Thursdays are days that
are favorable for prayers being answered.
Moshe ascended to receive the second
Luḥot HaBrit on a Thursday and descended
with them on a Monday. Since then, many
have the custom to fast and to add additional requests for forgiveness.

סדר תחנון

On Mondays and Thursdays, when תחנון is said, begin with וְהוּא רַחוּם below.
On other days when תחנון is said, begin with וַיֹּאמֶר דָּוִד on page 215.

תחנון *is not said on:* אֲדָר א׳, פורים, ט״ו בשבט, חנוכה, ראש חודש, *the 14th and 15th of* א׳ אֲדָר, and
ל״ג בעומר, (פסח שני) אייר, *in the month of* נִיסָן, יום העצמאות, *the 14th of* (שושן פורים),
יום ירושלים, *through the day after* שבועות (*in* אֶרֶץ יִשְׂרָאֵל) *through* רֹאשׁ חוֹדֶשׁ סִיוָן *from*,
through (י״ב סיון), תשעה באב, ט״ו באב, עֶרֶב רֹאשׁ הַשָּׁנָה, *and from* עֶרֶב יוֹם כִּיפּוּר
the day after שמחת תורה (*in* אֶרֶץ יִשְׂרָאֵל) *through* רֹאשׁ חוֹדֶשׁ מֵרְחֶשְׁוָן).

תחנון *is also not said: on the morning of a* בְּרִית מִילָה, *either where the* בְּרִית *will take place*
or where the father, מוֹהֵל *or* סַנְדָּק, *are present; if a* חָתָן *is present (and some say a* כַּלָּה)
on the day of his wedding or during the week of שֶׁבַע בְּרָכוֹת; *in a house of mourning.*

The following until וַיֹּאמֶר דָּוִד *on page 215 is said standing.*

תהלים עח
וְהוּא רַחוּם, יְכַפֵּר עָוֹן וְלֹא־יַשְׁחִית, וְהִרְבָּה לְהָשִׁיב אַפּוֹ וְלֹא־יָעִיר
כָּל־חֲמָתוֹ: אַתָּה יהוה לֹא־תִכְלָא רַחֲמֶיךָ מִמֶּנִּי, חַסְדְּךָ וַאֲמִתְּךָ תָּמִיד

תהלים קו
יִצְּרְוּנִי. הוֹשִׁיעֵנוּ יהוה אֱלֹהֵינוּ וְקַבְּצֵנוּ מִן־הַגּוֹיִם, לְהוֹדוֹת לְשֵׁם קָדְשֶׁךָ,

תהלים קל
לְהִשְׁתַּבֵּחַ בִּתְהִלָּתֶךָ: אִם־עֲוֹנוֹת תִּשְׁמָר־יָהּ, אֲדֹנָי מִי יַעֲמֹד: כִּי־עִמְּךָ

הַסְּלִיחָה לְמַעַן תִּוָּרֵא: לֹא כַחֲטָאֵינוּ תַּעֲשֶׂה לָנוּ, וְלֹא כַעֲוֹנֹתֵינוּ תִּגְמֹל

ירמיה יד
תהלים כה
עָלֵינוּ. אִם־עֲוֹנֵינוּ עָנוּ בָנוּ, יהוה עֲשֵׂה לְמַעַן שְׁמֶךָ: זְכֹר־רַחֲמֶיךָ יהוה

LEARNING

Taḥanun signifies a return to private prayer following a break to pray as a community with the repetition of the *Amida*. As the *tefilla* service draws to a close, *Taḥanun*, which means "plea," is one last chance for an intimate audience with Hashem, where we can bare our soul one last time.

The meaning of the word Tahanun
The word *Taḥanun* comes from the root ח-נ-נ which means "to show favor, to be generous, to forgive." But what is unique about *Taḥanun* is how honest we are about our failings. We make no attempt

to hide them or sugar-coat them. We just ask for Hashem's understanding and mercy.

Nefilat Apayim – body language
You can say so much without words – just with your body. What statement is a serviceman making when he stands with his chest puffed out, hand on heart, during the national anthem? What emotion does a mother express as she envelops her child with a protective hug? What powerful message is a man making when he kneels at the feet of the woman he

are everlasting. May the LORD answer us when we are in distress; may the *Ps. 20*
name of Jacob's God protect us. LORD, save! May the King answer us when
we call. Our Father, our King, be generous to us and answer us, though we
have no worthy deeds; act charitably with us for Your name's sake. LORD
our God, hear the sound of our pleas. Remember for us the covenant of
our ancestors, and save us for Your name's sake.

וְעַתָּה And now, My LORD, our God, who took Your people out of the *Dan. 9*
land of Egypt with a mighty hand, creating for Yourself reputation to
this day: we have sinned and acted wrongly. LORD, in keeping with all
Your righteousness, please turn Your rage and anger away from Jerusalem, Your holy mountain. Because of our sins and the wrongdoing of
our ancestors, Jerusalem and Your people have become the scorn of all
those around us. And now, our God, listen to Your servant's prayer and
pleas, and let Your face shine on Your desolate Sanctuary, for Your sake,
O LORD. Incline Your ear, my God, and hear. Open Your eyes and see our
desolation and that of the city called by Your name. Not because of our
righteousness do we lay our pleas before You, but because of Your great
compassion. LORD, hear! LORD, forgive! LORD, listen and act! Do not
delay – for Your sake, my God, because Your city and Your people are called
by Your name.

אָבִינוּ Our Father, compassionate Father, show us a sign for good, and
gather our scattered ones from the four quarters of the earth. Let all the
nations recognize and know that You are the LORD our God. And now, *Is. 64*
LORD, You are our Father. We are the clay and You are our Potter; we are
all the work of Your hand. Save us for the sake of Your name, our Rock, our
King and our Redeemer. Pity Your people, LORD. Let not Your heritage *Joel 2*
become an object of scorn, a byword among nations. Why should they say
among the peoples, "Where is their God?" We know we have sinned and
that there is no one to stand up for us. Let Your great name stand up for us
in time of trouble. We know we have no merits of our own: therefore deal
with us charitably for Your name's sake. As a father has compassion on his
children, so, LORD, have compassion on us, and save us for the sake of Your
name. Have mercy on Your people; have compassion for Your heritage;
take pity in Your great compassion. Be generous to us and answer us, for
righteousness is Yours, LORD. Always You do miracles.

וַחֲסָדֶיךָ, כִּי מֵעוֹלָם הֵמָּה: יַעַנְךָ יהוה בְּיוֹם צָרָה, יְשַׂגֶּבְךָ שֵׁם אֱלֹהֵי יַעֲקֹב. יהוה הוֹשִׁיעָה, הַמֶּלֶךְ יַעֲנֵנוּ בְיוֹם־קָרְאֵנוּ: אָבִינוּ מַלְכֵּנוּ, חָנֵּנוּ וַעֲנֵנוּ, כִּי אֵין בָּנוּ מַעֲשִׂים, צְדָקָה עֲשֵׂה עִמָּנוּ לְמַעַן שְׁמֶךָ. אֲדוֹנֵינוּ אֱלֹהֵינוּ, שְׁמַע קוֹל תַּחֲנוּנֵינוּ, וּזְכָר לָנוּ אֶת בְּרִית אֲבוֹתֵינוּ וְהוֹשִׁיעֵנוּ לְמַעַן שְׁמֶךָ.

תהלים כ

וְעַתָּה אֲדֹנָי אֱלֹהֵינוּ, אֲשֶׁר הוֹצֵאתָ אֶת־עַמְּךָ מֵאֶרֶץ מִצְרַיִם בְּיָד חֲזָקָה וַתַּעַשׂ־לְךָ שֵׁם כַּיּוֹם הַזֶּה, חָטָאנוּ רָשָׁעְנוּ: אֲדֹנָי, כְּכָל־צִדְקֹתֶךָ יָשָׁב־ נָא אַפְּךָ וַחֲמָתְךָ, מֵעִירְךָ יְרוּשָׁלַיִם הַר־קָדְשֶׁךָ, כִּי בַחֲטָאֵינוּ וּבַעֲוֺנוֹת אֲבֹתֵינוּ, יְרוּשָׁלַיִם וְעַמְּךָ לְחֶרְפָּה לְכָל־סְבִיבֹתֵינוּ: וְעַתָּה שְׁמַע אֱלֹהֵינוּ אֶל־תְּפִלַּת עַבְדְּךָ וְאֶל־תַּחֲנוּנָיו, וְהָאֵר פָּנֶיךָ עַל־מִקְדָּשְׁךָ הַשָּׁמֵם, לְמַעַן אֲדֹנָי: הַטֵּה אֱלֹהַי אָזְנְךָ וּשֲׁמָע, פְּקַח עֵינֶיךָ וּרְאֵה שֹׁמְמֹתֵינוּ וְהָעִיר אֲשֶׁר־נִקְרָא שִׁמְךָ עָלֶיהָ, כִּי לֹא עַל־צִדְקֹתֵינוּ אֲנַחְנוּ מַפִּילִים תַּחֲנוּנֵינוּ לְפָנֶיךָ, כִּי עַל־רַחֲמֶיךָ הָרַבִּים: אֲדֹנָי שְׁמָעָה, אֲדֹנָי סְלָחָה, אֲדֹנָי הַקְשִׁיבָה וַעֲשֵׂה אַל־תְּאַחַר, לְמַעַנְךָ אֱלֹהַי, כִּי־שִׁמְךָ נִקְרָא עַל־עִירְךָ וְעַל־עַמֶּךָ:

דניאל ט

אָבִינוּ הָאָב הָרַחֲמָן, הַרְאֵנוּ אוֹת לְטוֹבָה וְקַבֵּץ נְפוּצוֹתֵינוּ מֵאַרְבַּע כַּנְפוֹת הָאָרֶץ. יַכִּירוּ וְיֵדְעוּ כָּל הַגּוֹיִם כִּי אַתָּה יהוה אֱלֹהֵינוּ: וְעַתָּה יהוה אָבִינוּ אָתָּה, אֲנַחְנוּ הַחֹמֶר וְאַתָּה יֹצְרֵנוּ וּמַעֲשֵׂה יָדְךָ כֻּלָּנוּ. הוֹשִׁיעֵנוּ לְמַעַן שְׁמֶךָ, צוּרֵנוּ מַלְכֵּנוּ וְגוֹאֲלֵנוּ. חוּסָה יהוה עַל־עַמֶּךָ, וְאַל־תִּתֵּן נַחֲלָתְךָ לְחֶרְפָּה לִמְשָׁל־בָּם גּוֹיִם, לָמָּה יֹאמְרוּ בָעַמִּים אַיֵּה אֱלֹהֵיהֶם: יָדַעְנוּ כִּי חָטָאנוּ וְאֵין מִי יַעֲמֹד בַּעֲדֵנוּ, שִׁמְךָ הַגָּדוֹל יַעֲמֹד לָנוּ בְּעֵת צָרָה. יָדַעְנוּ כִּי אֵין בָּנוּ מַעֲשִׂים, צְדָקָה עֲשֵׂה עִמָּנוּ לְמַעַן שְׁמֶךָ. כְּרַחֵם אָב עַל בָּנִים כֵּן תְּרַחֵם יהוה עָלֵינוּ, וְהוֹשִׁיעֵנוּ לְמַעַן שְׁמֶךָ. חֲמֹל עַל עַמֶּךָ, רַחֵם עַל נַחֲלָתֶךָ, חוּסָה נָא כְּרֹב רַחֲמֶיךָ, חָנֵּנוּ וַעֲנֵנוּ. כִּי לְךָ יהוה הַצְּדָקָה, עֹשֵׂה נִפְלָאוֹת בְּכָל עֵת.

ישעיה סד

יואל ב

הַבֶּט נָא Please look, please swiftly have compassion for Your people for Your name's sake. In Your great compassion, LORD our God, have pity and compassion, and rescue the flock You tend. Let us not be ruled by fury, for our eyes are turned toward You. Save us for Your name's sake. Have compassion on us for the sake of Your covenant. Look and answer us in time of trouble, for Yours, LORD, is the power to save. Our hope is in You, God of forgiveness. Please forgive, good and forgiving God, for You are a generous, compassionate God and King.

אָנָּא מֶלֶךְ Please, generous and compassionate King, remember and call to mind the Covenant between the Pieces [with Abraham] and let the binding of his only son [Isaac] appear before You for Israel's sake. Our Father, our King, be generous to us and answer us, for we are called by Your great name. You who work miracles at all times, deal with us according to Your loving-kindness. Generous and compassionate One, look and answer us in time of trouble, for salvation is Yours, LORD. Our Father, our King, our Refuge, do not act with us according to our evil deeds. Remember, LORD, Your tender mercies and Your love. Save us in Your great goodness, and have mercy on us, for we have no other god but You, our Rock. Do not abandon us, LORD our God, do not be distant from us, for we are worn out by the sword and captivity, disease and plague, and by every trouble and sorrow. Rescue us, for in You lies our hope. Put us not to shame, LORD our God. Let Your face shine upon us. Remember for us the covenant of our ancestors and save us for Your name's sake. See our troubles and listen to the voice of our prayer, for You listen to the prayer of every mouth.

אֵל רַחוּם וְחַנּוּן O Compassionate and generous God, have compassion on us and on all Your works, for there is none like You, LORD our God. Please, we beg You, forgive our sins, our Father, our King, our Rock, our Redeemer, living and eternal God, mighty in strength, loving and good to all Your works, for You are the LORD our God. O God, slow to anger and full of compassion, act with us according to Your great compassion and save us for Your name's sake. Hear our prayer, our King, and save us from our enemies' hands. Listen to our prayer, our King, and save us from all distress and sorrow. You are our Father, our King. We are called by Your name. Do not desert us. Do not abandon us, our Father. Do not cast us away, our Creator. Do not forget us, our Maker – for You are a generous and compassionate God and King.

הַבֶּט נָא, רַחֶם נָא עַל עַמְּךָ מְהֵרָה לְמַעַן שְׁמֶךָ בְּרַחֲמֶיךָ הָרַבִּים יהוה אֱלֹהֵינוּ. חוּס וְרַחֵם וְהוֹשִׁיעָה צֹאן מַרְעִיתֶךָ, וְאַל יִמְשָׁל בָּנוּ קֶצֶף, כִּי לְךָ עֵינֵינוּ תְלוּיוֹת. הוֹשִׁיעֵנוּ לְמַעַן שְׁמֶךָ. רַחֵם עָלֵינוּ לְמַעַן בְּרִיתֶךָ. הַבִּיטָה וַעֲנֵנוּ בְּעֵת צָרָה, כִּי לְךָ יהוה הַיְשׁוּעָה. בְּךָ תוֹחַלְתֵּנוּ אֱלוֹהַּ סְלִיחוֹת, אָנָּא סְלַח נָא אֵל טוֹב וְסַלָּח, כִּי אֵל מֶלֶךְ חַנּוּן וְרַחוּם אָתָּה.

אָנָּא מֶלֶךְ חַנּוּן וְרַחוּם, זְכֹר וְהַבֵּט לִבְרִית בֵּין הַבְּתָרִים, וְתֵרָאֶה לְפָנֶיךָ עֲקֵדַת יָחִיד לְמַעַן יִשְׂרָאֵל. אָבִינוּ מַלְכֵּנוּ, חָנֵּנוּ וַעֲנֵנוּ, כִּי שִׁמְךָ הַגָּדוֹל נִקְרָא עָלֵינוּ. עֹשֵׂה נִפְלָאוֹת בְּכָל עֵת, עֲשֵׂה עִמָּנוּ כְּחַסְדֶּךָ. חַנּוּן וְרַחוּם, הַבִּיטָה וַעֲנֵנוּ בְּעֵת צָרָה, כִּי לְךָ יהוה הַיְשׁוּעָה. אָבִינוּ מַלְכֵּנוּ מַחֲסֵנוּ, אַל תַּעַשׂ עִמָּנוּ כְּרֹעַ מַעֲלָלֵינוּ. זְכֹר רַחֲמֶיךָ יהוה וַחֲסָדֶיךָ, וּכְרֹב טוּבְךָ הוֹשִׁיעֵנוּ, וַחֲמָל נָא עָלֵינוּ, כִּי אֵין לָנוּ אֱלוֹהַּ אַחֵר מִבַּלְעָדֶיךָ צוּרֵנוּ. אַל תַּעַזְבֵנוּ יהוה אֱלֹהֵינוּ אַל תִּרְחַק מִמֶּנּוּ. כִּי נַפְשֵׁנוּ קָצְרָה, מֵחֶרֶב וּמִשֶּׁבִי וּמִדֶּבֶר וּמִמַּגֵּפָה. וּמִכָּל צָרָה וְיָגוֹן הַצִּילֵנוּ, כִּי לְךָ קִוִּינוּ. וְאַל תַּכְלִימֵנוּ יהוה אֱלֹהֵינוּ, וְהָאֵר פָּנֶיךָ בָּנוּ, וּזְכֹר לָנוּ אֶת בְּרִית אֲבוֹתֵינוּ וְהוֹשִׁיעֵנוּ לְמַעַן שְׁמֶךָ. רְאֵה בְצָרוֹתֵינוּ, וּשְׁמַע קוֹל תְּפִלָּתֵנוּ, כִּי אַתָּה שׁוֹמֵעַ תְּפִלַּת כָּל פֶּה.

אֵל רַחוּם וְחַנּוּן, רַחֶם עָלֵינוּ וְעַל כָּל מַעֲשֶׂיךָ, כִּי אֵין כָּמוֹךָ יהוה אֱלֹהֵינוּ. אָנָּא שָׂא נָא פְשָׁעֵינוּ, אָבִינוּ מַלְכֵּנוּ צוּרֵנוּ וְגוֹאֲלֵנוּ, אֵל חַי וְקַיָּם הֶחָסִין בַּכֹּחַ, חָסִיד וְטוֹב עַל כָּל מַעֲשֶׂיךָ, כִּי אַתָּה הוּא יהוה אֱלֹהֵינוּ. אֵל אֶרֶךְ אַפַּיִם וּמָלֵא רַחֲמִים, עֲשֵׂה עִמָּנוּ כְּרֹב רַחֲמֶיךָ, וְהוֹשִׁיעֵנוּ לְמַעַן שְׁמֶךָ. שְׁמַע מַלְכֵּנוּ תְּפִלָּתֵנוּ, וּמִיַּד אוֹיְבֵינוּ הַצִּילֵנוּ. שְׁמַע מַלְכֵּנוּ תְּפִלָּתֵנוּ, וּמִכָּל צָרָה וְיָגוֹן הַצִּילֵנוּ. אָבִינוּ מַלְכֵּנוּ אַתָּה, וְשִׁמְךָ עָלֵינוּ נִקְרָא. אַל תַּנִּחֵנוּ, אַל תַּעַזְבֵנוּ אָבִינוּ וְאַל תִּטְּשֵׁנוּ בּוֹרְאֵנוּ וְאַל תִּשְׁכָּחֵנוּ יוֹצְרֵנוּ, כִּי אֵל מֶלֶךְ חַנּוּן וְרַחוּם אָתָּה.

אֵין כָּמוֹךָ There is none like You in grace and compassion, LORD our God.
There is none like You, God, slow to anger and abounding in loving-kindness and truth. Save us in Your great compassion; rescue us from storm
and turmoil. Remember Your servants Abraham, Isaac and Jacob; do not
attend to our stubbornness, wickedness and sinfulness. Turn from Your *Ex. 32*
fierce anger, and relent from the evil meant for Your people. Remove from
us the curse of death, for You are compassionate. This is Your way, to show
unearned loving-kindness to every generation. Have pity on Your people,
LORD, and save us from Your fury. Remove from us the curse of plague
and the harsh decree, for You are the Guardian of Israel. You are right, my *Dan. 9*
LORD, and we are shamefaced. How can we complain? What can we say?
What can we plead? How can we justify ourselves? Let us search our ways
and examine them and return to You, for Your right hand is outstretched to
receive those who return. Please, LORD, please save. Please, LORD, please *Ps. 118*
send success. Please, LORD, answer us when we call. For You, LORD, we
wait. For You, LORD, we hope. For You, LORD, we long. Do not be silent
while we suffer, for the nations are saying, "Their hope is lost." To You alone
every knee must bend, and those who hold themselves high bow down.

הַפּוֹתֵחַ יָד You who hold out an open hand of repentance to receive trans-
gressors and sinners – our soul is overwhelmed by our great sorrow. Do not
forget us for ever. Arise and save us, for we seek refuge in You. Our Father,
our King, though we lack righteousness and good deeds, remember for us
the covenant of our fathers, and our testimonies daily that "The LORD is
One." Look on our suffering, for many are our sufferings and heartaches.
Have pity on us, LORD, in the land of our captivity. Do not pour out Your
fury on us, for we are Your people, the children of Your covenant. God, see
how low our glory has sunk among the nations. They hate us as if we were
impure. How long will Your strength be captive, and Your glory in the hand
of the enemy? Arouse Your strength and zeal against Your enemies. Let
them be shamed and deprived of power. Let not our hardships seem small
to You. Swiftly may Your compassion reach us in the day of our distress. If
not for our sake, act for Yours, so that the memory of our survivors be not
destroyed. Be generous to the nation who, in constant love, declare twice
daily the unity of Your name, saying, "Listen, Israel, the LORD is our God, *Deut. 6*
the LORD is One."

אֵין כָּמוֹךָ חַנּוּן וְרַחוּם יהוה אֱלֹהֵינוּ, אֵין כָּמוֹךָ אֵל אֶרֶךְ אַפַּיִם וְרַב
חֶסֶד וֶאֱמֶת. הוֹשִׁיעֵנוּ בְּרַחֲמֶיךָ הָרַבִּים, מֵרַעַשׁ וּמֵרֹגֶז הַצִּילֵנוּ. זְכֹר
לַעֲבָדֶיךָ לְאַבְרָהָם לְיִצְחָק וּלְיַעֲקֹב, אַל תֵּפֶן אֶל קָשְׁיֵנוּ וְאֶל רִשְׁעֵנוּ
וְאֶל חַטָּאתֵנוּ. שׁוּב מֵחֲרוֹן אַפֶּךָ, וְהִנָּחֵם עַל־הָרָעָה לְעַמֶּךָ: וְהָסֵר
שמות לב
מִמֶּנּוּ מַכַּת הַמָּוֶת כִּי רַחוּם אָתָּה, כִּי כֵן דַּרְכֶּךָ, עֹשֶׂה חֶסֶד חִנָּם בְּכָל
דּוֹר וָדוֹר. חוּסָה יהוה עַל עַמֶּךָ וְהַצִּילֵנוּ מִזַּעְמֶךָ, וְהָסֵר מִמֶּנּוּ מַכַּת
הַמַּגֵּפָה וּגְזֵרָה קָשָׁה, כִּי אַתָּה שׁוֹמֵר יִשְׂרָאֵל. לְךָ אֲדֹנָי הַצְּדָקָה וְלָנוּ
דניאל ט
בֹּשֶׁת הַפָּנִים: מַה נִּתְאוֹנֵן, מַה נֹּאמַר, מַה נְּדַבֵּר וּמַה נִּצְטַדָּק. נַחְפְּשָׂה
דְרָכֵינוּ וְנַחְקֹרָה וְנָשׁוּבָה אֵלֶיךָ, כִּי יְמִינְךָ פְּשׁוּטָה לְקַבֵּל שָׁבִים. אָנָּא
תהלים קיח
יהוה הוֹשִׁיעָה נָּא, אָנָּא יהוה הַצְלִיחָה נָּא: אָנָּא יהוה עֲנֵנוּ בְיוֹם
קָרְאֵנוּ. לְךָ יהוה חִכִּינוּ, לְךָ יהוה קִוִּינוּ, לְךָ יהוה נְיַחֵל. אַל תֶּחֱשֶׁה
וּתְעַנֵּנוּ, כִּי נָאֲמוּ גוֹיִם, אָבְדָה תִקְוָתָם. כָּל בֶּרֶךְ וְכָל קוֹמָה, לְךָ לְבַד
תִּשְׁתַּחֲוֶה.

הַפּוֹתֵחַ יָד בִּתְשׁוּבָה לְקַבֵּל פּוֹשְׁעִים וְחַטָּאִים, נִבְהֲלָה נַפְשֵׁנוּ מֵרֹב
עַצְבוֹנֵנוּ. אַל תִּשְׁכָּחֵנוּ נֶצַח, קוּמָה וְהוֹשִׁיעֵנוּ כִּי חָסִינוּ בָךְ. אָבִינוּ
מַלְכֵּנוּ, אִם אֵין בָּנוּ צְדָקָה וּמַעֲשִׂים טוֹבִים, זְכָר לָנוּ אֶת בְּרִית אֲבוֹתֵינוּ
וְעֵדוֹתֵנוּ בְּכָל יוֹם יהוה אֶחָד. הַבִּיטָה בְעָנְיֵנוּ, כִּי רַבּוּ מַכְאוֹבֵינוּ וְצָרוֹת
לְבָבֵנוּ. חוּסָה יהוה עָלֵינוּ בְּאֶרֶץ שִׁבְיֵנוּ, וְאַל תִּשְׁפֹּךְ חֲרוֹנְךָ עָלֵינוּ,
כִּי אֲנַחְנוּ עַמְּךָ בְּנֵי בְרִיתֶךָ. אֵל, הַבִּיטָה, דַּל כְּבוֹדֵנוּ בַּגּוֹיִם וְשִׁקְּצוּנוּ
כְּטֻמְאַת הַנִּדָּה. עַד מָתַי עֻזְּךָ בַּשֶּׁבִי, וְתִפְאַרְתְּךָ בְּיַד צָר. עוֹרְרָה גְבוּרָתְךָ
וְקִנְאָתְךָ עַל אוֹיְבֶיךָ. הֵם יֵבוֹשׁוּ וְיֵחַתּוּ מִגְּבוּרָתָם. וְאַל יִמְעֲטוּ לְפָנֶיךָ
תְלָאוֹתֵינוּ, מַהֵר יְקַדְּמוּנוּ רַחֲמֶיךָ בְּיוֹם צָרָתֵנוּ. וְאִם לֹא לְמַעֲנֵנוּ, לְמַעַנְךָ
פְּעַל, וְאַל תַּשְׁחִית זֵכֶר שְׁאֵרִיתֵנוּ, וְחַן אִם הַמְיַחֲדִים שִׁמְךָ פַּעֲמַיִם
בְּכָל יוֹם תָּמִיד בְּאַהֲבָה, וְאוֹמְרִים, שְׁמַע יִשְׂרָאֵל, יהוה אֱלֹהֵינוּ,
דברים ו
יהוה אֶחָד:

LOWERING THE HEAD

> *On Sundays, Tuesdays, Wednesdays and Fridays, begin Tahanun here.*
> *The following, until "We do not know" on page 218, is said sitting. When praying*
> *in a place where there is a Torah scroll, one should lean forward, resting one's*
> *head on the left arm (unless you are wearing tefillin on the left arm, in which case*
> *rest on the right arm out of respect for the tefillin), until in "sudden shame."*

וַיֹּאמֶר דָּוִד David said to Gad, "I am in great distress.
Let us fall into God's hand, for His mercy is great;
but do not let me fall into the hand of man."

II Sam. 24

Compassionate and generous One,
I have sinned before You.
LORD, full of compassion,
have compassion on me and accept my pleas.

LORD, do not rebuke me in Your anger or chastise me in Your fury. Be *Ps. 6* generous to me, LORD, for I am weak. Heal me, LORD, for my bones are in agony. My soul is in anguish, and You, O LORD – how long? Turn, LORD, set my soul free; save me for the sake of Your love. For no one remembers You when he is dead. Who can praise You from the grave? I am tired with my sighing. Every night I drench my bed, I soak my couch with my tears. My eye grows dim from grief, worn out because of all my enemies. Leave me, all you evildoers, for the LORD has heard the sound of my weeping. The LORD has heard my pleas. The LORD will accept my prayer. All my enemies will be shamed and utterly dismayed. They will turn back in sudden shame.

Sit upright.

"Fie, fie upon her!
There's language
in her eye, her cheek, her lip,
Nay, her foot speaks;
her wanton spirits look out
At every joint and motive
of her body."
(William Shakespeare)

When are words not enough?

What can you say
with your body
that you can't say
with your words?

What are you saying
with your body right now?

נפילת אפיים

On Sundays, Tuesdays, Wednesdays and Fridays, begin תחנון *here.*
The following, until וַאֲנַחְנוּ לֹא נֵדַע *on page 219, is said sitting. When praying*
in a place where there is a ספר תורה, *one should lean forward, resting one's*
head on the left arm (unless you are wearing תפילין *on the left arm, in which*
case rest on the right arm out of respect for the תפילין), *until* יֵבֹשׁוּ רָגַע.

שמואל ב, כד

וַיֹּאמֶר דָּוִד אֶל־גָּד, צַר־לִי מְאֹד
נִפְּלָה־נָּא בְיַד־יהוה, כִּי־רַבִּים רַחֲמָו, וּבְיַד־אָדָם אַל־אֶפְּלָה:

רַחוּם וְחַנּוּן, חָטָאתִי לְפָנֶיךָ.
יהוה מָלֵא רַחֲמִים, רַחֵם עָלַי וְקַבֵּל תַּחֲנוּנָי.

תהלים ו

יהוה, אַל־בְּאַפְּךָ תוֹכִיחֵנִי, וְאַל־בַּחֲמָתְךָ תְיַסְּרֵנִי: חָנֵּנִי יהוה, כִּי אֻמְלַל אָנִי,
רְפָאֵנִי יהוה, כִּי נִבְהֲלוּ עֲצָמָי: וְנַפְשִׁי נִבְהֲלָה מְאֹד, וְאַתְּ יהוה, עַד־מָתָי:
שׁוּבָה יהוה, חַלְּצָה נַפְשִׁי, הוֹשִׁיעֵנִי לְמַעַן חַסְדֶּךָ: כִּי אֵין בַּמָּוֶת זִכְרֶךָ,
בִּשְׁאוֹל מִי יוֹדֶה־לָּךְ: יָגַעְתִּי בְּאַנְחָתִי, אַשְׂחֶה בְכָל־לַיְלָה מִטָּתִי, בְּדִמְעָתִי
עַרְשִׂי אַמְסֶה: עָשְׁשָׁה מִכַּעַס עֵינִי, עָתְקָה בְּכָל־צוֹרְרָי: סוּרוּ מִמֶּנִּי כָּל־פֹּעֲלֵי
אָוֶן, כִּי שָׁמַע יהוה קוֹל בִּכְיִי: שָׁמַע יהוה תְּחִנָּתִי, יהוה תְּפִלָּתִי יִקָּח: יֵבֹשׁוּ
וְיִבָּהֲלוּ מְאֹד כָּל־אֹיְבָי, יָשֻׁבוּ יֵבֹשׁוּ רָגַע:

Sit upright.

LEARNING

This part of *Tahanun*, called נְפִילַת אַפַּיִם, literally, lowering of the head, should be said sitting down, with your head lowered against your weaker arm. If you are wearing tefillin you should rest your head on your other arm. Only lower your head onto your arm when you are in the presence of a *Sefer Torah*. However, in Yerushalayim the custom is to always lower the head, as it is considered as if you are in the presence of the *Aron* of Hashem.

...A THOUSAND WORDS

On Mondays and Thursdays, say the following.
On other days, continue with "Guardian of Israel" below.

Lord, God of Israel, turn away from Your fierce anger,
and relent from the evil against Your people.

Look down from heaven and see how we have become an object of scorn and
derision among the nations. We are regarded as sheep led to the slaughter, to be
killed, destroyed, beaten and humiliated. Yet, despite all this, we have not forgotten Your name. Please do not forget us.

Lord, God of Israel, turn away from Your fierce anger,
and relent from the evil against Your people.

Strangers say, "You have no hope or expectation." Be generous to the nation
whose hope is in Your name. O Pure One, bring our deliverance close. We are
exhausted. We are given no rest. May Your compassion suppress Your anger
against us. Please turn away from Your fierce anger, and have compassion on the
people You chose as Your own.

Lord, God of Israel, turn away from Your fierce anger,
and relent from the evil against Your people.

Have pity on us, Lord, in Your compassion, and do not hand us over to cruel
oppressors. Why should the nations say, "Where is their God now?" For Your
own sake, deal kindly with us, and do not delay. Please turn away from Your fierce
anger, and have compassion on the people You chose as Your own.

Lord, God of Israel, turn away from Your fierce anger,
and relent from the evil against Your people.

Listen to our voice and be generous. Do not abandon us into the hand of our
enemies to blot out our name. Remember what You promised our fathers: "I will
make your descendants as many as the stars of heaven" – yet now we are only a
few left from many. Yet, despite all this, we have not forgotten Your name. Please
do not forget us.

Lord, God of Israel, turn away from Your fierce anger,
and relent from the evil against Your people.

Help us, God of our salvation, for the sake of the glory of Your name. Save us and *Ps. 79*
pardon our sins for Your name's sake.

Lord, God of Israel, turn away from Your fierce anger,
and relent from the evil against Your people.

On all days continue here:

שׁוֹמֵר יִשְׂרָאֵל Guardian of Israel, guard the survivors of Israel,
and let not Israel perish, who declare, "Listen, Israel."

Guardian of a unique nation, guard the survivors of a unique people,
and let not that unique nation perish, who declare the unity
of Your name [saying], "The Lord is our God, the Lord is One."

On Mondays and Thursdays, say the following.
On other days, continue with שׁוֹמֵר יִשְׂרָאֵל below.

יהוה אֱלֹהֵי יִשְׂרָאֵל, שׁוּב מֵחֲרוֹן אַפֶּךָ וְהִנָּחֵם עַל הָרָעָה לְעַמֶּךָ.

הַבֵּט מִשָּׁמַיִם וּרְאֵה כִּי הָיִינוּ לַעַג וָקֶלֶס בַּגּוֹיִם, נֶחְשַׁבְנוּ כַּצֹּאן לַטֶּבַח יוּבָל, לַהֲרֹג וּלְאַבֵּד וּלְמַכָּה וּלְחֶרְפָּה. וּבְכָל זֹאת שִׁמְךָ לֹא שָׁכָחְנוּ, נָא אַל תִּשְׁכָּחֵנוּ.

יהוה אֱלֹהֵי יִשְׂרָאֵל, שׁוּב מֵחֲרוֹן אַפֶּךָ וְהִנָּחֵם עַל הָרָעָה לְעַמֶּךָ.

זָרִים אוֹמְרִים אֵין תּוֹחֶלֶת וְתִקְוָה, חֹן אֹם לְשִׁמְךָ מְקַוֶּה, טָהוֹר יְשׁוּעָתֵנוּ קָרְבָה, יָגַעְנוּ וְלֹא הוּנַח לָנוּ, רַחֲמֶיךָ יִכְבְּשׁוּ אֶת כַּעַסְךָ מֵעָלֵינוּ. אָנָּא שׁוּב מֵחֲרוֹנְךָ וְרַחֵם סְגֻלָּה אֲשֶׁר בָּחָרְתָּ.

יהוה אֱלֹהֵי יִשְׂרָאֵל, שׁוּב מֵחֲרוֹן אַפֶּךָ וְהִנָּחֵם עַל הָרָעָה לְעַמֶּךָ.

חוּסָה יהוה עָלֵינוּ בְּרַחֲמֶיךָ, וְאַל תִּתְּנֵנוּ בִּידֵי אַכְזָרִים. לָמָּה יֹאמְרוּ הַגּוֹיִם אַיֵּה נָא אֱלֹהֵיהֶם, לְמַעַנְךָ עֲשֵׂה עִמָּנוּ חֶסֶד וְאַל תְּאַחַר. אָנָּא שׁוּב מֵחֲרוֹנְךָ וְרַחֵם סְגֻלָּה אֲשֶׁר בָּחָרְתָּ.

יהוה אֱלֹהֵי יִשְׂרָאֵל, שׁוּב מֵחֲרוֹן אַפֶּךָ וְהִנָּחֵם עַל הָרָעָה לְעַמֶּךָ.

קוֹלֵנוּ תִשְׁמַע וְתָחֹן, וְאַל תִּטְּשֵׁנוּ בְּיַד אֹיְבֵינוּ לִמְחוֹת אֶת שְׁמֵנוּ. זְכֹר אֲשֶׁר נִשְׁבַּעְתָּ לַאֲבוֹתֵינוּ כְּכוֹכְבֵי הַשָּׁמַיִם אַרְבֶּה אֶת זַרְעֲכֶם, וְעַתָּה נִשְׁאַרְנוּ מְעַט מֵהַרְבֵּה. וּבְכָל זֹאת שִׁמְךָ לֹא שָׁכָחְנוּ, נָא אַל תִּשְׁכָּחֵנוּ.

יהוה אֱלֹהֵי יִשְׂרָאֵל, שׁוּב מֵחֲרוֹן אַפֶּךָ וְהִנָּחֵם עַל הָרָעָה לְעַמֶּךָ.

עָזְרֵנוּ אֱלֹהֵי יִשְׁעֵנוּ עַל־דְּבַר כְּבוֹד־שְׁמֶךָ, וְהַצִּילֵנוּ וְכַפֵּר עַל־חַטֹּאתֵינוּ לְמַעַן שְׁמֶךָ: תהלים עט

יהוה אֱלֹהֵי יִשְׂרָאֵל, שׁוּב מֵחֲרוֹן אַפֶּךָ וְהִנָּחֵם עַל הָרָעָה לְעַמֶּךָ.

On all days continue here:

שׁוֹמֵר יִשְׂרָאֵל, שְׁמֹר שְׁאֵרִית יִשְׂרָאֵל, וְאַל יֹאבַד יִשְׂרָאֵל הָאוֹמְרִים שְׁמַע יִשְׂרָאֵל.

שׁוֹמֵר גּוֹי אֶחָד, שְׁמֹר שְׁאֵרִית עַם אֶחָד, וְאַל יֹאבַד גּוֹי אֶחָד הַמְיַחֲדִים שִׁמְךָ, יהוה אֱלֹהֵינוּ יהוה אֶחָד.

Guardian of a holy nation, guard the survivors of that holy people,
      and let not the holy nation perish, who three times repeat
      the threefold declaration of holiness to the Holy One.

You who are conciliated by calls for compassion and placated by pleas,
      be conciliated and placated toward an afflicted generation,
      for there is no other help.

Our Father, our King, be generous to us and answer us,
      though we have no worthy deeds;
      act with us in charity and loving-kindness and save us.

Stand at ⸰.

וַאֲנַחְנוּ We do not know ⸰what to do, but our eyes are turned to You. Remember, LORD, Your compassion and loving-kindness, for they are everlasting. May Your loving-kindness, LORD, be with us, for we have put our hope in You. Do not hold against us the sins of those who came before us. May Your mercies meet us swiftly, for we have been brought very low. Be generous to us, LORD, be generous to us, for we are full with contempt. In fury, remember mercy. He knows our nature; He remembers that we are dust. ⸰ Help us, God of our salvation, for the sake of the glory of Your name. Save us and give atonement for our sins for Your name's sake.

II Chr. 12
Ps. 25
Ps. 33
Ps. 79
Ps. 123
Hab. 3
Ps. 103
Ps. 79

HALF KADDISH

Leader: יִתְגַּדַּל Magnified and sanctified may His great name be,
      in the world He created by His will.
      May He establish His kingdom
      in your lifetime and in your days,
      and in the lifetime of all the house of Israel,
      swiftly and soon –
      and say: Amen.

All: May His great name be blessed for ever and all time.

Leader: Blessed and praised, glorified and great,
      raised and honored, uplifted and praised
      be the name of the Holy One,
      blessed be He,
      beyond any blessing, song, praise and consolation
      uttered in the world –
      and say: Amen.

שׁוֹמֵר גּוֹי קָדוֹשׁ, שְׁמֹר שְׁאֵרִית עַם קָדוֹשׁ, וְאַל יֹאבַד גּוֹי קָדוֹשׁ הַמְשַׁלְּשִׁים בְּשָׁלֹשׁ קְדֻשּׁוֹת לְקָדוֹשׁ.

מִתְרַצֶּה בְּרַחֲמִים וּמִתְפַּיֵּס בְּתַחֲנוּנִים, הִתְרַצֵּה וְהִתְפַּיֵּס לְדוֹר עָנִי כִּי אֵין עוֹזֵר.

אָבִינוּ מַלְכֵּנוּ, חָנֵּנוּ וַעֲנֵנוּ, כִּי אֵין בָּנוּ מַעֲשִׂים עֲשֵׂה עִמָּנוּ צְדָקָה וָחֶסֶד וְהוֹשִׁיעֵנוּ.

Stand at ˄.

וַאֲנַחְנוּ לֹא נֵדַע מַה נַּעֲשֶׂה, כִּי עָלֶיךָ עֵינֵינוּ: זְכֹר רַחֲמֶיךָ יהוה וַחֲסָדֶיךָ, כִּי מֵעוֹלָם הֵמָּה: יְהִי חַסְדְּךָ יהוה עָלֵינוּ, כַּאֲשֶׁר יִחַלְנוּ לָךְ: אַל תִּזְכָּר לָנוּ עֲוֹנֹת רִאשׁוֹנִים, מַהֵר יְקַדְּמוּנוּ רַחֲמֶיךָ, כִּי דַלּוֹנוּ מְאֹד: חָנֵּנוּ יהוה חָנֵּנוּ, כִּי רַב שָׂבַעְנוּ בוּז: בְּרֹגֶז רַחֵם תִּזְכּוֹר: כִּי הוּא יָדַע יִצְרֵנוּ, זָכוּר כִּי עָפָר אֲנָחְנוּ: ˄ עָזְרֵנוּ אֱלֹהֵי יִשְׁעֵנוּ עַל דְּבַר כְּבוֹד שְׁמֶךָ, וְהַצִּילֵנוּ וְכַפֵּר עַל חַטֹּאתֵינוּ לְמַעַן שְׁמֶךָ:

דברי
הימים ב׳ י״ב
תהלים כה
תהלים ל״ג
תהלים עט
תהלים קכג
חבקוק ג
תהלים קג
תהלים עט

חצי קדיש

ש״ץ: יִתְגַּדַּל וְיִתְקַדַּשׁ שְׁמֵהּ רַבָּא (קהל: אָמֵן)

בְּעָלְמָא דִּי בְרָא כִרְעוּתֵהּ

וְיַמְלִיךְ מַלְכוּתֵהּ

בְּחַיֵּיכוֹן וּבְיוֹמֵיכוֹן וּבְחַיֵּי דְּכָל בֵּית יִשְׂרָאֵל

בַּעֲגָלָא וּבִזְמַן קָרִיב, וְאִמְרוּ אָמֵן. (קהל: אָמֵן)

קהל
 וש״ץ: יְהֵא שְׁמֵהּ רַבָּא מְבָרַךְ לְעָלַם וּלְעָלְמֵי עָלְמַיָּא.

ש״ץ: יִתְבָּרַךְ וְיִשְׁתַּבַּח וְיִתְפָּאַר וְיִתְרוֹמַם וְיִתְנַשֵּׂא וְיִתְהַדָּר וְיִתְעַלֶּה וְיִתְהַלָּל

שְׁמֵהּ דְּקֻדְשָׁא בְּרִיךְ הוּא (קהל: בְּרִיךְ הוּא)

לְעֵלָּא מִן כָּל בִּרְכָתָא / בעשרת ימי תשובה: לְעֵלָּא לְעֵלָּא מִכָּל בִּרְכָתָא/

וְשִׁירָתָא, תֻּשְׁבְּחָתָא וְנֶחֱמָתָא

דַּאֲמִירָן בְּעָלְמָא, וְאִמְרוּ אָמֵן. (קהל: אָמֵן)

REMOVING THE TORAH FROM THE ARK

On Mondays and Thursdays, Rosh Ḥodesh, Ḥol HaMo'ed, Ḥanukka,
Purim and Fast Days, the Torah is read when a minyan is present. On
Yom HaAtzma'ut that is not Thursday, the Haftara on page 560 is read.
On all other days, continue with "Happy are those" on page 244.

Before taking the Torah out of the Ark, on Mondays and Thursdays, stand
while reciting "God, slow to anger." It is not said on Rosh Ḥodesh, Ḥol HaMo'ed,
Erev Pesaḥ, Ḥanukka, the 14th and 15th of Adar I, Purim and Shushan Purim,
Yom HaAtzma'ut, Yom Yerushalayim, Tisha B'Av or in a house of mourning, and
in Israel on Isru Ḥag. Most people say both paragraphs; some say only the first.

God, slow to anger, abounding in loving-kindness and truth, do not rebuke us in Your anger. Have pity on Your people, LORD, and save us from all evil. We have sinned against You, LORD. Please forgive in accordance with Your great compassion, God.	God, slow to anger, full of compassion, do not hide Your face from us. Have pity on the survivors of Israel Your people, LORD, and deliver us from all evil. We have sinned against You, LORD. Please forgive in accordance with Your great compassion, God.

The Ark is opened and the congregation stands. All say:

וַיְהִי בִּנְסֹעַ Whenever the Ark set out, Moses would say, *Num. 10*
"Arise, LORD, and may Your enemies be scattered.
May those who hate You flee before You."
For the Torah shall come forth from Zion, *Is. 2*
and the word of the LORD from Jerusalem.
Blessed is He who in His holiness
gave the Torah to His people Israel.

REFLECTION

"So says the LORD of Hosts: "In those days it
will be that ten men of all the languages
of the nations will grasp; they will grasp
the hem of a Judean man, saying:
'We will go with you, for we have
heard that God is with you."'

(Zekharia 8:23)

Does the Torah
and the word of Hashem
emanate from Yerushalayim
to all over the world today?

How is your religious life
influenced by Israel
and Israelis?

הוצאת ספר תורה

On Mondays and Thursdays, פורים, חנוכה, חול המועד, ראש חודש and Fast Days,
the תורה is read when a מנין is present. On יום העצמאות that is not Thursday, the
הפטרה on page 561 is read. On all other days, continue with אשרי on page 245.

Before taking the תורה out of the ארון קודש, on Mondays and Thursdays, stand while reciting
אֵל אֶרֶךְ אַפַּיִם. It is not said on: ראש חודש, חול המועד, ערב פסח, חנוכה, the 14th and 15th of
תשעה באב, יום ירושלים, יום העצמאות, שושן פורים, פורים and אדר א׳ or in a house of mourning,
and in אסרו on חג אדר א׳ ישראל. Most people say both paragraphs, some say only the first.

אֵל אֶרֶךְ אַפַּיִם וּמָלֵא רַחֲמִים	אֵל אֶרֶךְ אַפַּיִם וְרַב חֶסֶד וֶאֱמֶת
אַל תַּסְתֵּר פָּנֶיךָ מִמֶּנּוּ.	אַל בְּאַפְּךָ תוֹכִיחֵנוּ.
חוּסָה יהוה עַל שְׁאֵרִית יִשְׂרָאֵל עַמֶּךָ	חוּסָה יהוה עַל עַמֶּךָ
וְהַצִּילֵנוּ מִכָּל רָע.	וְהוֹשִׁיעֵנוּ מִכָּל רָע.
חָטָאנוּ לְךָ אָדוֹן	חָטָאנוּ לְךָ אָדוֹן
סְלַח נָא כְּרֹב רַחֲמֶיךָ אֵל.	סְלַח נָא כְּרֹב רַחֲמֶיךָ אֵל.

The ארון קודש is opened and the קהל stands. All say:

במדברי

וַיְהִי בִּנְסֹעַ הָאָרֹן וַיֹּאמֶר מֹשֶׁה
קוּמָה יהוה וְיָפֻצוּ אֹיְבֶיךָ וְיָנֻסוּ מְשַׂנְאֶיךָ מִפָּנֶיךָ:
ישעיה ב
כִּי מִצִּיּוֹן תֵּצֵא תוֹרָה וּדְבַר־יהוה מִירוּשָׁלָם:
בָּרוּךְ שֶׁנָּתַן תּוֹרָה לְעַמּוֹ יִשְׂרָאֵל בִּקְדֻשָּׁתוֹ.

LEARNING

On Mondays and Thursdays, Rosh Ḥodesh,
Ḥol HaMo'ed, Ḥanukka, Purim, and Fast Days,
the Torah is read if there is a *minyan* present.
Together with Shabbat and *Ḥagim*, these are
the times when the community comes together to experience, hear, and learn from
the Torah. Even if you are not able to read or
understand the words of the Torah, this public
reading allows you to experience it, and as a
microcosm experience the original giving of
the Torah. In this act, the *beit knesset* becomes
a *beit midrash*, and we focus not on our words
to God, but on His words to us.

CONNECTION

"[The] people of Israel must have their
own social and political state and
a national kingdom with its own
culture… In order that this nation
can teach the world that living in the
way of God is available not just to
the very wise and holy people who
live according to this divine notion
privately, but that it is accessible to
entire peoples…[who] are able to
live in the way of God and become
upright and moral."

(Rav Kook, *Orot*)

Blessed is the name of the Master of the Universe. Blessed is Your crown *Zohar,*
and Your place. May Your favor always be with Your people Israel. Show *Vayak-hel*
Your people the salvation of Your right hand in Your Temple. Give us
the gift of Your good light, and accept our prayers in mercy. May it be
Your will to prolong our life in goodness. May I be counted among the
righteous, so that You will have compassion on me and protect me and
all that is mine and all that is Your people Israel's. You feed all; You sustain
all; You rule over all; You rule over kings, for sovereignty is Yours. I am a
servant of the Holy One, blessed be He, before whom and before whose
glorious Torah I bow at all times. Not in man do I trust, nor on any angel
do I rely, but on the God of heaven who is the God of truth, whose Torah
is truth, whose prophets speak truth, and who abounds in acts of love
and truth. ‣ In Him I trust, and to His holy and glorious name I offer
praises. May it be Your will to open my heart to the Torah, and to fulfill
the wishes of my heart and of the hearts of all Your people Israel for good,
for life, and for peace.

CONNECTION

כִּי־אֵשֵׁב בַּחֹשֶׁךְ יהוה אוֹר לִי

*"When I sat in the darkness
the Lᴏʀᴅ was a light for me."*
(Mikha 7:8)

*The Ba'al Shem Tov explains that this
does not mean that Hashem was a
light to me in darkness but rather because of the time I spent in darkness I
was able to appreciate and understand
the light of God. Both darkness and
light serve a purpose in spiritual development. Sometimes when things seem
dark and hopeless, there is an opportunity to learn and to grow; this is the
light that can be found in the darkness.*

LEARNING

According to Rabbi Aharon Lichtenstein,
talmud Torah can be seen on three different religious levels. First and foremost it is
the halakhic fulfillment of a mitzva obligation. Secondly, *talmud Torah* is a value,
encouraging the gaining of knowledge
and broadening of religious horizons, as
well as having a moral educational impact, encouraging ethical behavior. Finally
talmud Torah has cosmic and spiritual impact on the individual, the collective, and
the universe as a whole.

That the siddur makes the mitzva of
talmud Torah a recurring theme in the siddur, makes a profound statement on its
importance and value to our everyday life.

זוהר ויקהל

בְּרִיךְ שְׁמֵהּ דְּמָרֵא עָלְמָא, בְּרִיךְ כִּתְרָךְ וְאַתְרָךְ. יְהֵא רְעוּתָךְ עִם עַמָּךְ
יִשְׂרָאֵל לְעָלַם, וּפֻרְקַן יְמִינָךְ אַחֲזִי לְעַמָּךְ בְּבֵית מַקְדְּשָׁךְ, וּלְאַמְטוּיֵי לָנָא
מִטּוּב נְהוֹרָךְ, וּלְקַבֵּל צְלוֹתָנָא בְּרַחֲמִין. יְהֵא רַעֲוָא קֳדָמָךְ דְּתוֹרִיךְ לַן חַיִּין
בְּטִיבוּ, וְלֶהֱוֵי אֲנָא פְּקִידָא בְּגוֹ צַדִּיקַיָּא, לְמִרְחַם עֲלַי וּלְמִנְטַר יָתִי וְיָת כָּל
דִּי לִי וְדִי לְעַמָּךְ יִשְׂרָאֵל. אַנְתְּ הוּא זָן לְכֹלָּא וּמְפַרְנֵס לְכֹלָּא, אַנְתְּ הוּא
שַׁלִּיט עַל כֹּלָּא, אַנְתְּ הוּא דְּשַׁלִּיט עַל מַלְכַיָּא, וּמַלְכוּתָא דִּילָךְ הִיא. אֲנָא
עַבְדָּא דְקֻדְשָׁא בְּרִיךְ הוּא, דְּסָגִדְנָא קַמֵּהּ וּמִקַּמֵּי דִּיקַר אוֹרַיְתֵהּ בְּכָל עִדָּן
וְעִדָּן. לָא עַל אֱנָשׁ רְחִיצְנָא וְלָא עַל בַּר אֱלָהִין סָמִיכְנָא, אֶלָּא בֵּאלָהָא
דִשְׁמַיָּא, דְּהוּא אֱלָהָא קְשׁוֹט, וְאוֹרַיְתֵהּ קְשׁוֹט, וּנְבִיאוֹהִי קְשׁוֹט, וּמַסְגֵּא
לְמֶעְבַּד טָבְוָן וּקְשׁוֹט. ‹ בֵּהּ אֲנָא רְחִיץ, וְלִשְׁמֵהּ קַדִּישָׁא יַקִּירָא אֲנָא אֵמַר
תֻּשְׁבְּחָן. יְהֵא רַעֲוָא קֳדָמָךְ דְּתִפְתַּח לִבַּאי בְּאוֹרַיְתָא, וְתַשְׁלִים מִשְׁאֲלִין
דְּלִבַּאי וְלִבָּא דְכָל עַמָּךְ יִשְׂרָאֵל לְטַב וּלְחַיִּין וְלִשְׁלָם.

REFLECTION

... A THOUSAND WORDS

What language
is this *tefilla*
written in?

Why do
you think
it is written
in a language
that is
not Hebrew?

Do you prefer
to pray
in Hebrew
or English?
What are the
benefits of each?

The Leader takes the Torah scroll in his right arm, bows toward the Ark and says:
Magnify the LORD with me, and let us elevate His name together. *Ps. 34*

The Ark is closed. The Leader carries the Torah scroll to the bima and the congregation says:
לְךָ Yours, LORD, are the greatness and the power, the glory and the *1 Chr. 29* majesty and splendor, for everything in heaven and earth is Yours. Yours, LORD, is the kingdom; You are elevated as Head over all.

רוֹמְמוּ Elevate the LORD our God and bow to His footstool; He is holy. *Ps. 99* Elevate thE Lord our God, and bow at His holy mountain, for holy is the LORD our God.

אַב הָרַחֲמִים May the Father of compassion have compassion on the people borne by Him. May He remember the covenant with the mighty [patriarchs], and deliver us from evil times. May He reproach the evil instinct in the people carried by Him, and generously grant that we be an everlasting remnant. May He fulfill in good measure our requests for salvation and compassion.

The Torah scroll is placed on the bima and the Gabbai calls a Kohen to the Torah.
May His kingship over us be soon revealed and made seen. May He be generous to our surviving remnant, the survivors of His people the house of Israel in grace, loving-kindness, compassion and favor, and let us say: Amen. Let us all give greatness to our God and give honor to the Torah. *Let the Kohen come forward. Arise (*name* son of *father's name*), the Kohen.

*If no Kohen is present, a Levi or Yisrael is called up as follows:
/As there is no Kohen, arise (*name* son of *father's name*) in place of a Kohen./

Blessed is He who, in His holiness, gave the Torah to His people Israel.

Congregation followed by the Gabbai:
You who cling to the LORD your God are all alive today. *Deut. 4*

The appropriate Torah portions are to be found from page 668.

CONNECTION

"The public reading of the Torah is as ancient an institution as prayer itself. The synagogue thus became not only a house of prayer but also a house of study. The result is a dynamic tension between speaking and listening. In prayer, we speak to God. In study we listen to God speaking to us, His word unchanged and undiminished across the centuries."

(Rabbi Jonathan Sacks)

The שליח ציבור *takes the* ספר תורה *in his right arm, bows toward the* ארון קודש *and says:*

תהלים לד

גַּדְּלוּ לַיהוה אִתִּי וּנְרוֹמְמָה שְׁמוֹ יַחְדָּו:

The ארון קודש *is closed. The* שליח ציבור *carries the* ספר תורה *to the* בימה *and the* קהל *says:*

דברי
הימים א,
כט

לְךָ יהוה הַגְּדֻלָּה וְהַגְּבוּרָה וְהַתִּפְאֶרֶת וְהַנֵּצַח וְהַהוֹד, כִּי־כֹל
בַּשָּׁמַיִם וּבָאָרֶץ, לְךָ יהוה הַמַּמְלָכָה וְהַמִּתְנַשֵּׂא לְכֹל לְרֹאשׁ:

תהלים צט

רוֹמְמוּ יהוה אֱלֹהֵינוּ וְהִשְׁתַּחֲווּ לַהֲדֹם רַגְלָיו, קָדוֹשׁ הוּא: רוֹמְמוּ
יהוה אֱלֹהֵינוּ וְהִשְׁתַּחֲווּ לְהַר קָדְשׁוֹ, כִּי־קָדוֹשׁ יהוה אֱלֹהֵינוּ:

אַב הָרַחֲמִים הוּא יְרַחֵם עַם עֲמוּסִים, וְיִזְכֹּר בְּרִית אֵיתָנִים, וְיַצִּיל
נַפְשׁוֹתֵינוּ מִן הַשָּׁעוֹת הָרָעוֹת, וְיִגְעַר בְּיֵצֶר הָרָע מִן הַנְּשׂוּאִים,
וְיָחֹן אוֹתָנוּ לִפְלֵיטַת עוֹלָמִים, וִימַלֵּא מִשְׁאֲלוֹתֵינוּ בְּמִדָּה טוֹבָה
יְשׁוּעָה וְרַחֲמִים.

The ספר תורה *is placed on the* שולחן *and the* גבאי *calls a* כהן *to the* תורה.

וְתִגָּלֶה וְתֵרָאֶה מַלְכוּתוֹ עָלֵינוּ בִּזְמַן קָרוֹב, וְיָחֹן פְּלֵיטָתֵנוּ וּפְלֵיטַת עַמּוֹ בֵּית יִשְׂרָאֵל
לְחֵן וּלְחֶסֶד וּלְרַחֲמִים וּלְרָצוֹן וְנֹאמַר אָמֵן. הַכֹּל הָבוּ גֹדֶל לֵאלֹהֵינוּ וּתְנוּ כָבוֹד לַתּוֹרָה.
*כֹּהֵן קְרַב, יַעֲמֹד (פלוני בֶּן פלוני) הַכֹּהֵן.

**If no* כהן *is present, a* לוי *or* ישראל *is called up as follows:*
/אֵין כָּאן כֹּהֵן, יַעֲמֹד (פלוני בֶּן פלוני) בִּמְקוֹם כֹּהֵן./

בָּרוּךְ שֶׁנָּתַן תּוֹרָה לְעַמּוֹ יִשְׂרָאֵל בִּקְדֻשָּׁתוֹ.

קהל *followed by the* גבאי:

דברים ד

וְאַתֶּם הַדְּבֵקִים בַּיהוה אֱלֹהֵיכֶם חַיִּים כֻּלְּכֶם הַיּוֹם:

The appropriate תורה *portions are to be found from page 668.*

REFLECTION

"Keriat HaTorah is a reenactment of the original experience of Matan Torah.*"*
(Rabbi J.B. Soloveitchik)

Is there a significant difference
between reading the Torah
at the following times?

- Together in public in the *beit knesset.*
- On our own at home.
- With a *ḥavruta* in the *beit midrash.*

The Reader shows the oleh the section to be read. The oleh touches the scroll at that place with the tzitzit of his tallit, which he then kisses. Holding the handles of the scroll, he says:

Oleh: Bless the LORD, the blessed One.

Cong: Bless the LORD, the blessed One, for ever and all time.

Oleh: Bless the LORD, the blessed One, for ever and all time.
Blessed are You, LORD our God, King of the Universe,
who has chosen us from all peoples
and has given us His Torah.
Blessed are You, LORD, Giver of the Torah.

After the reading, the oleh says:

Oleh: Blessed are You, LORD our God, King of the Universe,
who has given us the Torah of truth,
planting everlasting life in our midst.
Blessed are You, LORD, Giver of the Torah.

One who has survived a situation of danger says:
Blessed are You, LORD our God, King of the Universe,
who bestows good on the unworthy, who has bestowed on me much good.

The congregation responds:
Amen. May He who bestowed much good on you
continue to bestow on you much good, Selah.

After a Bar Mitzva boy has finished the Torah blessing, his father says aloud:
Blessed is He who has released me from the responsibility for this child.

---

should hold the handles of the *Sefer Torah*, and take care to look away from the *Sefer Torah* so it doesn't look like he is reading the *berakha* from the *Sefer Torah*.

4. Originally the custom was that each *oleh* would read the section that he was called up for. But so as not to embarrass those who cannot, generally one person (the *ba'al koreh*) reads all the sections. However, the *oleh* should

read along in a whisper the verses that are being read from the *Sefer Torah*.

5. After saying the *berakha* after the reading, the *oleh* should remain at the *bima*, either alongside the next *oleh* or on the other side of the reader (depending on the community's custom), for the following *aliya*, so as to show honor to the Torah and not appear as if he is trying to escape as quickly as possible.

The קורא *shows the* עולה *the section to be read. The* עולה *touches the* ספר תורה *at that place*
with the ציצית *of his* טלית, *which he then kisses. Holding the handles of the* ספר תורה, *he says:*

עולה: בָּרְכוּ אֶת יהוה הַמְבֹרָךְ.

קהל: בָּרוּךְ יהוה הַמְבֹרָךְ לְעוֹלָם וָעֶד.

עולה: בָּרוּךְ יהוה הַמְבֹרָךְ לְעוֹלָם וָעֶד.
בָּרוּךְ אַתָּה יהוה, אֱלֹהֵינוּ מֶלֶךְ הָעוֹלָם
אֲשֶׁר בָּחַר בָּנוּ מִכָּל הָעַמִּים, וְנָתַן לָנוּ אֶת תּוֹרָתוֹ.
בָּרוּךְ אַתָּה יהוה, נוֹתֵן הַתּוֹרָה.

After the קריאת התורה, *the* עולה *says:*

עולה: בָּרוּךְ אַתָּה יהוה אֱלֹהֵינוּ מֶלֶךְ הָעוֹלָם
אֲשֶׁר נָתַן לָנוּ תּוֹרַת אֱמֶת, וְחַיֵּי עוֹלָם נָטַע בְּתוֹכֵנוּ.
בָּרוּךְ אַתָּה יהוה, נוֹתֵן הַתּוֹרָה.

One who has survived a situation of danger says:

בָּרוּךְ אַתָּה יהוה אֱלֹהֵינוּ מֶלֶךְ הָעוֹלָם
הַגּוֹמֵל לְחַיָּבִים טוֹבוֹת, שֶׁגְּמָלַנִי כָּל טוֹב.

The קהל *responds:*

אָמֵן. מִי שֶׁגְּמָלְךָ כָּל טוֹב הוּא, יִגְמָלְךָ כָּל טוֹב, סֶלָה.

After a בר מצווה *has finished the* תורה *blessing, his father says aloud:*

בָּרוּךְ שֶׁפְּטָרַנִי מֵעָנְשׁוֹ שֶׁלָּזֶה.

LEARNING

A guide to getting an *aliya*:

Since it is a mitzva to read from the Torah publicly, each section of the reading is
preceded and followed by *berakhot* said by the one who is called up (the "*oleh*").

1. To show his love of this mitzva and
not to delay the community the *oleh*
should take the shortest, most direct
route to the *bima*.

2. The *oleh* should be shown by the

reader where the section to be read
starts. Some have the custom to kiss
the first words with the *tzitzit* of their
tallit before making the *berakha*.

3. While making the *berakha*, the *oleh*

Special blessings and memorial prayers may be said at this point (below).

FOR A SICK MAN

May He who blessed our fathers, Abraham, Isaac and Jacob, Moses and Aaron, David and Solomon, bless and heal one who is ill, (*sick person's name, son of mother's name*), on whose behalf (*name of the one making the offering*) is making a contribution to charity. As a reward for this, may the Holy One, blessed be He, be filled with compassion for him, to restore his health, cure him, strengthen and revive him, sending him a swift and full recovery from heaven to all his 248 organs and 365 sinews, amongst the other sick ones in Israel, a healing of the spirit and a healing of the body, now, swiftly and soon, and let us say: Amen.

FOR A SICK WOMAN

May He who blessed our fathers, Abraham, Isaac and Jacob, Moses and Aaron, David and Solomon, bless and heal one who is ill, (*sick person's name*, daughter of *mother's name*), on whose behalf (*name of the one making the offering*) is making a contribution to charity. As a reward for this, may the Holy One, blessed be He, be filled with compassion for her, to restore her health, cure her, strengthen and revive her, sending her a swift and full recovery from heaven to all her organs and sinews, amongst the other sick ones in Israel, a healing of the spirit and a healing of the body, now, swiftly and soon, and let us say: Amen.

For a male close relative:

אֵל מָלֵא רַחֲמִים God, full of mercy, who is on high, give fitting rest on the wings of the Divine Presence, in the heights of the holy and the pure who shine like the radiance of heaven, to the soul of (*name* son of *father's name*) who has gone to his eternal home, and to this I pledge (without formal vow) to give charity in his memory, may his resting place be in the Garden of Eden. Therefore, Master of compassion, shelter him in the shadow of Your wings forever and bind his soul in the bond of everlasting life. The LORD is his heritage; may he rest in peace, and let us say: Amen.

For a female close relative:

אֵל מָלֵא רַחֲמִים God, full of mercy, who is on high, give fitting rest on the wings of the Divine Presence, in the heights of the holy and the pure who shine like the radiance of heaven, to the soul of (*name* daughter of *father's name*) who has gone to her eternal home, and to this I pledge (without formal vow) to give charity in her memory, may her resting place be in the Garden of Eden. Therefore, Master of compassion, shelter her in the shadow of Your wings forever and bind her soul in the bond of everlasting life. The LORD is her heritage; may she rest in peace, and let us say: Amen.

Special מי שבירך *and memorial prayers may be said at this point (below).*

מי שבירך לחולה

מִי שֶׁבֵּרַךְ אֲבוֹתֵינוּ אַבְרָהָם יִצְחָק וְיַעֲקֹב, מֹשֶׁה וְאַהֲרֹן דָּוִד וּשְׁלֹמֹה הוּא יְבָרֵךְ וִירַפֵּא אֶת הַחוֹלֶה (פלוני בן פלונית) בַּעֲבוּר שֶׁ(פלוני בֶּן פלוני) נוֹדֵר צְדָקָה בַּעֲבוּרוֹ. בִּשְׂכַר זֶה הַקָּדוֹשׁ בָּרוּךְ הוּא יִמָּלֵא רַחֲמִים עָלָיו לְהַחֲלִימוֹ וּלְרַפֹּאתוֹ וּלְהַחֲזִיקוֹ וּלְהַחֲיוֹתוֹ וְיִשְׁלַח לוֹ מְהֵרָה רְפוּאָה שְׁלֵמָה מִן הַשָּׁמַיִם לִרְמַ"ח אֵבָרָיו וּשְׁסָ"ה גִּידָיו בְּתוֹךְ שְׁאָר חוֹלֵי יִשְׂרָאֵל, רְפוּאַת הַנֶּפֶשׁ וּרְפוּאַת הַגּוּף, הַשְׁתָּא בַּעֲגָלָא וּבִזְמַן קָרִיב, וְנֹאמַר אָמֵן.

מי שבירך לחולה

מִי שֶׁבֵּרַךְ אֲבוֹתֵינוּ אַבְרָהָם יִצְחָק וְיַעֲקֹב, מֹשֶׁה וְאַהֲרֹן דָּוִד וּשְׁלֹמֹה הוּא יְבָרֵךְ וִירַפֵּא אֶת הַחוֹלָה (פלונית בת פלונית) בַּעֲבוּר שֶׁ(פלוני בֶּן פלוני) נוֹדֵר צְדָקָה בַּעֲבוּרָהּ. בִּשְׂכַר זֶה הַקָּדוֹשׁ בָּרוּךְ הוּא יִמָּלֵא רַחֲמִים עָלֶיהָ לְהַחֲלִימָהּ וּלְרַפֹּאתָהּ וּלְהַחֲזִיקָהּ וּלְהַחֲיוֹתָהּ וְיִשְׁלַח לָהּ מְהֵרָה רְפוּאָה שְׁלֵמָה מִן הַשָּׁמַיִם לְכָל אֵבָרֶיהָ וּלְכָל גִּידֶיהָ בְּתוֹךְ שְׁאָר חוֹלֵי יִשְׂרָאֵל, רְפוּאַת הַנֶּפֶשׁ וּרְפוּאַת הַגּוּף, הַשְׁתָּא בַּעֲגָלָא וּבִזְמַן קָרִיב, וְנֹאמַר אָמֵן.

For a male close relative:

אֵל מָלֵא רַחֲמִים, שׁוֹכֵן בַּמְּרוֹמִים, הַמְצֵא מְנוּחָה נְכוֹנָה עַל כַּנְפֵי הַשְּׁכִינָה, בְּמַעֲלוֹת קְדוֹשִׁים וּטְהוֹרִים, כְּזֹהַר הָרָקִיעַ מַזְהִירִים, לְנִשְׁמַת (פלוני בֶּן פלוני) שֶׁהָלַךְ לְעוֹלָמוֹ, בַּעֲבוּר שֶׁבְּלִי נֶדֶר אֶתֵּן צְדָקָה בְּעַד הַזְכָּרַת נִשְׁמָתוֹ, בְּגַן עֵדֶן תְּהֵא מְנוּחָתוֹ. לָכֵן, בַּעַל הָרַחֲמִים יַסְתִּירֵהוּ בְּסֵתֶר כְּנָפָיו לְעוֹלָמִים, וְיִצְרֹר בִּצְרוֹר הַחַיִּים אֶת נִשְׁמָתוֹ, יהוה הוּא נַחֲלָתוֹ, וְיָנוּחַ בְּשָׁלוֹם עַל מִשְׁכָּבוֹ, וְנֹאמַר אָמֵן.

For a female close relative:

אֵל מָלֵא רַחֲמִים, שׁוֹכֵן בַּמְּרוֹמִים, הַמְצֵא מְנוּחָה נְכוֹנָה עַל כַּנְפֵי הַשְּׁכִינָה, בְּמַעֲלוֹת קְדוֹשִׁים וּטְהוֹרִים, כְּזֹהַר הָרָקִיעַ מַזְהִירִים, לְנִשְׁמַת (פלונית בַּת פלוני) שֶׁהָלְכָה לְעוֹלָמָהּ, בַּעֲבוּר שֶׁבְּלִי נֶדֶר אֶתֵּן צְדָקָה בְּעַד הַזְכָּרַת נִשְׁמָתָהּ, בְּגַן עֵדֶן תְּהֵא מְנוּחָתָהּ. לָכֵן, בַּעַל הָרַחֲמִים יַסְתִּירָה בְּסֵתֶר כְּנָפָיו לְעוֹלָמִים, וְיִצְרֹר בִּצְרוֹר הַחַיִּים אֶת נִשְׁמָתָהּ, יהוה הוּא נַחֲלָתָהּ, וְתָנוּחַ בְּשָׁלוֹם עַל מִשְׁכָּבָהּ, וְנֹאמַר אָמֵן.

HALF KADDISH

> *After the Reading of the Torah, the Reader says Half Kaddish:*

Reader: יִתְגַּדַּל Magnified and sanctified may His great name be,
in the world He created by His will.
May He establish His kingdom in your lifetime and in your days,
and in the lifetime of all the house of Israel,
swiftly and soon – and say: Amen.

All: May His great name be blessed for ever and all time.

Reader: Blessed and praised, glorified and great,
raised and honored, uplifted and praised
be the name of the Holy One, blessed be He,
beyond any blessing, song, praise and consolation
uttered in the world – and say: Amen.

> *The Torah scroll is lifted and the congregation says:*

וְזֹאת הַתּוֹרָה This is the Torah   *Deut. 4*
that Moses placed before the children of Israel,
at the LORD's commandment, by the hand of Moses.   *Num. 9*

> *Some add:* It is a tree of life to those who grasp it, and those who uphold *Prov. 3*
> it are happy. Its ways are ways of pleasantness, and all its
> paths are peace. Long life is at its right hand; at its left, riches
> and honor. It pleased the LORD for the sake of [Israel's] *Is. 42*
> righteousness, to make the Torah great and glorious.

... A THOUSAND WORDS

חצי קדיש

:חצי קדיש says קורא the ,קריאת התורה After the

קורא: יִתְגַּדַּל וְיִתְקַדַּשׁ שְׁמֵהּ רַבָּא (קהל: אָמֵן)

בְּעָלְמָא דִּי בְרָא כִרְעוּתֵהּ

וְיַמְלִיךְ מַלְכוּתֵהּ

בְּחַיֵּיכוֹן וּבְיוֹמֵיכוֹן

וּבְחַיֵּי דְכָל בֵּית יִשְׂרָאֵל

בַּעֲגָלָא וּבִזְמַן קָרִיב

וְאִמְרוּ אָמֵן. (קהל: אָמֵן)

קורא
וקהל: יְהֵא שְׁמֵהּ רַבָּא מְבָרַךְ לְעָלַם וּלְעָלְמֵי עָלְמַיָּא.

קורא: יִתְבָּרַךְ וְיִשְׁתַּבַּח וְיִתְפָּאַר וְיִתְרוֹמַם וְיִתְנַשֵּׂא

וְיִתְהַדָּר וְיִתְעַלֶּה וְיִתְהַלָּל

שְׁמֵהּ דְּקֻדְשָׁא בְּרִיךְ הוּא (קהל: בְּרִיךְ הוּא)

לְעֵלָּא מִן כָּל בִּרְכָתָא

/ בעשרת ימי תשובה: לְעֵלָּא לְעֵלָּא מִכָּל בִּרְכָתָא/

וְשִׁירָתָא, תֻּשְׁבְּחָתָא וְנֶחָמָתָא

דַּאֲמִירָן בְּעָלְמָא

וְאִמְרוּ אָמֵן. (קהל: אָמֵן)

The ספר תורה is lifted and the קהל says:

דברים ד
וְזֹאת הַתּוֹרָה אֲשֶׁר־שָׂם מֹשֶׁה לִפְנֵי בְּנֵי יִשְׂרָאֵל:

במדבר ט
עַל־פִּי יהוה בְּיַד־מֹשֶׁה:

משלי ג
Some add עֵץ־חַיִּים הִיא לַמַּחֲזִיקִים בָּהּ וְתֹמְכֶיהָ מְאֻשָּׁר:

דְּרָכֶיהָ דַרְכֵי־נֹעַם וְכָל־נְתִיבוֹתֶיהָ שָׁלוֹם:

אֹרֶךְ יָמִים בִּימִינָהּ, בִּשְׂמֹאולָהּ עֹשֶׁר וְכָבוֹד:

ישעיה מב
יהוה חָפֵץ לְמַעַן צִדְקוֹ יַגְדִּיל תּוֹרָה וְיַאְדִּיר:

On those Mondays and Thursdays when Taḥanun is said,
the Leader says the following while the Torah scroll is being bound:

יְהִי רָצוֹן May it be the will of our Father in heaven
to establish (the Temple), home of our life,
and to restore His Presence to our midst,
swiftly in our days –
and let us say: Amen.

יְהִי רָצוֹן May it be the will of our Father in heaven
to have compassion on us and our remnant,
and to keep destruction and plague away from us
and from all His people the house of Israel –
and let us say: Amen.

יְהִי רָצוֹן May it be the will of our Father in heaven
to preserve among us the sages of Israel:
them, their wives, their sons and daughters,
their disciples and their disciples' disciples,
in all their dwelling places –
and let us say: Amen.

יְהִי רָצוֹן May it be the will of our Father in heaven
that we may hear and be given good tidings
of salvation and consolation,
and that our dispersed be gathered
from the four quarters of the earth –
and let us say: Amen.

All:

אַחֵינוּ As for our brothers of the whole house of Israel
who are in distress or captivity, on sea or land,
may the All-Present have compassion on them
and lead them from distress to relief,
from darkness to light, and from oppression to freedom,
now, swiftly and soon –
and let us say: Amen.

On those Mondays and Thursdays when תחנון *is said,*
the שליח ציבור *says the following while the* ספר תורה *is being bound:*

יְהִי רָצוֹן מִלְּפָנֶי אָבִינוּ שֶׁבַּשָּׁמַיִם
לְכוֹנֵן אֶת בֵּית חַיֵּינוּ
וּלְהָשִׁיב אֶת שְׁכִינָתוֹ בְּתוֹכֵנוּ
בִּמְהֵרָה בְּיָמֵינוּ, וְנֹאמַר אָמֵן.

יְהִי רָצוֹן מִלְּפָנֶי אָבִינוּ שֶׁבַּשָּׁמַיִם
לְרַחֵם עָלֵינוּ וְעַל פְּלֵיטָתֵנוּ
וְלִמְנֹעַ מַשְׁחִית וּמַגֵּפָה מֵעָלֵינוּ
וּמֵעַל כָּל עַמּוֹ בֵּית יִשְׂרָאֵל, וְנֹאמַר אָמֵן.

יְהִי רָצוֹן מִלְּפָנֶי אָבִינוּ שֶׁבַּשָּׁמַיִם
לְקַיֵּם בָּנוּ חַכְמֵי יִשְׂרָאֵל
הֵם וּנְשֵׁיהֶם וּבְנֵיהֶם וּבְנוֹתֵיהֶם
וְתַלְמִידֵיהֶם וְתַלְמִידֵי תַלְמִידֵיהֶם
בְּכָל מְקוֹמוֹת מוֹשְׁבוֹתֵיהֶם, וְנֹאמַר אָמֵן.

יְהִי רָצוֹן מִלְּפָנֶי אָבִינוּ שֶׁבַּשָּׁמַיִם
שֶׁנִּשְׁמַע וְנִתְבַּשֵּׂר בְּשׂוֹרוֹת טוֹבוֹת, יְשׁוּעוֹת וְנֶחָמוֹת
וִיקַבֵּץ נִדָּחֵינוּ מֵאַרְבַּע כַּנְפוֹת הָאָרֶץ, וְנֹאמַר אָמֵן.

All:

אַחֵינוּ כָּל בֵּית יִשְׂרָאֵל
הַנְּתוּנִים בְּצָרָה וּבְשִׁבְיָה
הָעוֹמְדִים בֵּין בַּיָּם וּבֵין בַּיַּבָּשָׁה
הַמָּקוֹם יְרַחֵם עֲלֵיהֶם וְיוֹצִיאֵם מִצָּרָה לִרְוָחָה
וּמֵאֲפֵלָה לְאוֹרָה, וּמִשִּׁעְבּוּד לִגְאֻלָּה
הַשְׁתָּא בַּעֲגָלָא וּבִזְמַן קָרִיב
וְנֹאמַר אָמֵן.

The prayer for the Welfare of the Canadian Government is on the next page.

PRAYER FOR THE WELFARE OF THE AMERICAN GOVERNMENT

The Leader says the following:

הַנּוֹתֵן תְּשׁוּעָה May He who gives salvation to kings and dominion to princes, whose kingdom is an everlasting kingdom, who delivers His servant David from the evil sword, who makes a way in the sea and a path through the mighty waters, bless and protect, guard and help, exalt, magnify and uplift the President, Vice President and all officials of this land. May the Supreme King of kings in His mercy put into their hearts and the hearts of all their advisors and officials, to deal kindly with us and all Israel. In their days and in ours, may Judah be saved and Israel live in safety, and may the Redeemer come to Zion. May this be His will, and let us say: Amen.

PRAYER FOR THE SAFETY OF THE AMERICAN MILITARY

The Leader says the following:

אַדִּיר בַּמָּרוֹם God on high who exists in might, the King to whom peace belongs, look down from Your holy habitation and bless the soldiers of the American military forces who risk their lives for the sake of peace on earth. Be their shelter and stronghold, and let them not falter. Give them the strength and courage to defeat the plans of the enemy and end the rule of evil. May their enemies be scattered and their foes flee before them, and may they rejoice in Your salvation. Bring them back safely to their homes, as is written: "The LORD will guard you from all harm, He will guard your life. *Ps. 121* The LORD will guard your going and coming, now and for evermore." And may there be fulfilled for us the verse: "Nation shall not *Is. 2* lift up sword against nation, nor shall they learn war any more." Let all the inhabitants on earth know that sovereignty is Yours and Your name inspires awe over all You have created – and let us say: Amen.

The prayer for the Welfare of the Canadian Government is on the next page.

תפילה לשלום המלכות

The שליח ציבור says the following:

הַנּוֹתֵן תְּשׁוּעָה לַמְּלָכִים וּמֶמְשָׁלָה לַנְּסִיכִים, מַלְכוּתוֹ מַלְכוּת כָּל
עוֹלָמִים, הַפּוֹצֶה אֶת דָּוִד עַבְדּוֹ מֵחֶרֶב רָעָה, הַנּוֹתֵן בַּיָּם דֶּרֶךְ
וּבְמַיִם עַזִּים נְתִיבָה, הוּא יְבָרֵךְ וְיִשְׁמֹר וְיִנְצֹר וְיַעֲזֹר וִירוֹמֵם וִיגַדֵּל
וִינַשֵּׂא לְמַעְלָה אֶת הַנָּשִׂיא וְאֶת מִשְׁנֵהוּ וְאֶת כָּל שָׂרֵי הָאָרֶץ
הַזֹּאת. מֶלֶךְ מַלְכֵי הַמְּלָכִים, בְּרַחֲמָיו יִתֵּן בְּלִבָּם וּבְלֵב כָּל יוֹעֲצֵיהֶם
וְשָׂרֵיהֶם לַעֲשׂוֹת טוֹבָה עִמָּנוּ וְעִם כָּל יִשְׂרָאֵל. בִּימֵיהֶם וּבְיָמֵינוּ
תִּוָּשַׁע יְהוּדָה, וְיִשְׂרָאֵל יִשְׁכֹּן לָבֶטַח, וּבָא לְצִיּוֹן גּוֹאֵל. וְכֵן יְהִי
רָצוֹן, וְנֹאמַר אָמֵן.

תפילה לשלום חיילי צבא ארצות הברית

The שליח ציבור says the following:

אַדִּיר בַּמָּרוֹם שׁוֹכֵן בִּגְבוּרָה, מֶלֶךְ שֶׁהַשָּׁלוֹם שֶׁלּוֹ, הַשְׁקִיפָה מִמְּעוֹן
קָדְשְׁךָ, וּבָרֵךְ אֶת חַיָּלֵי צְבָא אַרְצוֹת הַבְּרִית, הַמְחָרְפִים נַפְשָׁם
בְּלֶכְתָּם לָשִׂים שָׁלוֹם בָּאָרֶץ. הֱיֵה נָא לָהֶם מַחֲסֶה וּמָעוֹז, וְאַל תִּתֵּן
לַמּוֹט רַגְלָם, חַזֵּק יְדֵיהֶם וְאַמֵּץ רוּחָם לְהָפֵר עֲצַת אוֹיֵב וּלְהַעֲבִיר
מֶמְשֶׁלֶת זָדוֹן, יָפֻצוּ אוֹיְבֵיהֶם וְיָנוּסוּ מְשַׂנְאֵיהֶם מִפְּנֵיהֶם, וְיִשְׂמְחוּ
בִּישׁוּעָתֶךָ. הֲשִׁיבֵם בְּשָׁלוֹם אֶל בֵּיתָם, כַּכָּתוּב בְּדִבְרֵי קָדְשֶׁךָ: יהוה
יִשְׁמָרְךָ מִכָּל־רָע, יִשְׁמֹר אֶת־נַפְשֶׁךָ: יהוה יִשְׁמָר־צֵאתְךָ וּבוֹאֶךָ,
מֵעַתָּה וְעַד־עוֹלָם: וְקַיֵּם בָּנוּ מִקְרָא שֶׁכָּתוּב: לֹא־יִשָּׂא גוֹי אֶל־גּוֹי
חֶרֶב, וְלֹא־יִלְמְדוּ עוֹד מִלְחָמָה: וְיֵדְעוּ כָּל יוֹשְׁבֵי תֵבֵל כִּי לְךָ מְלוּכָה
יָאָתָה, וְשִׁמְךָ נוֹרָא עַל כָּל מַה שֶּׁבָּרָאתָ. וְנֹאמַר אָמֵן.

תהלים קכא

ישעיה ב

PRAYER FOR THE WELFARE OF THE CANADIAN GOVERNMENT

The Leader says the following:

הַנּוֹתֵן תְּשׁוּעָה May He who gives salvation to kings and dominion to princes, whose kingdom is an everlasting kingdom, who delivers His servant David from the evil sword, who makes a way in the sea and a path through the mighty waters, bless and protect, guard and help, exalt, magnify and uplift the Prime Minister and all the elected and appointed officials of Canada. May the Supreme King of kings in His mercy put into their hearts and the hearts of all their advisors and officials, to deal kindly with us and all Israel. In their days and in ours, may Judah be saved and Israel live in safety, and may the Redeemer come to Zion. May this be His will, and let us say: Amen.

PRAYER FOR THE SAFETY OF THE CANADIAN MILITARY FORCES

The Leader says the following:

אַדִּיר בַּמָּרוֹם God on high who exists in might, the King to whom peace belongs, look down from Your holy habitation and bless the soldiers of the Canadian Forces who risk their lives for the sake of peace on earth. Be their shelter and stronghold, and let them not falter. Give them the strength and courage to defeat the plans of the enemy and end the rule of evil. May their enemies be scattered and their foes flee before them, and may they rejoice in Your salvation. Bring them back safely to their homes, as is written: "The Lord will guard you from all harm, He will guard your life. *Ps. 121* The Lord will guard your going and coming, now and for evermore." And may there be fulfilled for us the verse: "Nation shall *Is. 2* not lift up sword against nation, nor shall they learn war any more." Let all the inhabitants on earth know that sovereignty is Yours and Your name inspires awe over all You have created – and let us say: Amen.

תפילה לשלום המלכות

The שליח ציבור says the following:

הַנּוֹתֵן תְּשׁוּעָה לַמְּלָכִים וּמֶמְשָׁלָה לַנְּסִיכִים, מַלְכוּתוֹ מַלְכוּת כָּל
עוֹלָמִים, הַפּוֹצֶה אֶת דָּוִד עַבְדּוֹ מֵחֶרֶב רָעָה, הַנּוֹתֵן בַּיָּם דֶּרֶךְ וּבְמַיִם
עַזִּים נְתִיבָה, הוּא יְבָרֵךְ וְיִשְׁמֹר וְיִנְצֹר וְיַעֲזֹר וִירוֹמֵם וִיגַדֵּל וִינַשֵּׂא
לְמַעְלָה אֶת רֹאשׁ הַמֶּמְשָׁלָה וְאֶת כָּל שָׂרֵי הָאָרֶץ הַזֹּאת. מֶלֶךְ
מַלְכֵי הַמְּלָכִים, בְּרַחֲמָיו יִתֵּן בְּלִבָּם וּבְלֵב כָּל יוֹעֲצֵיהֶם וְשָׂרֵיהֶם
לַעֲשׂוֹת טוֹבָה עִמָּנוּ וְעִם כָּל יִשְׂרָאֵל. בִּימֵיהֶם וּבְיָמֵינוּ תִּוָּשַׁע
יְהוּדָה, וְיִשְׂרָאֵל יִשְׁכֹּן לָבֶטַח, וּבָא לְצִיּוֹן גּוֹאֵל. וְכֵן יְהִי רָצוֹן,
וְנֹאמַר אָמֵן.

תפילה לשלום חיילי צבא קנדה

The שליח ציבור says the following:

אַדִּיר בַּמָּרוֹם שׁוֹכֵן בִּגְבוּרָה, מֶלֶךְ שֶׁהַשָּׁלוֹם שֶׁלּוֹ, הַשְׁקִיפָה
מִמְּעוֹן קָדְשֶׁךָ, וּבָרֵךְ אֶת חַיָּלֵי צְבָא קָנָדָה, הַמְחָרְפִים נַפְשָׁם
בְּלֶכְתָּם לָשִׂים שָׁלוֹם בָּאָרֶץ. הֱיֵה נָא לָהֶם מַחֲסֶה וּמָעוֹז, וְאַל
תִּתֵּן לַמּוֹט רַגְלָם, חַזֵּק יְדֵיהֶם וְאַמֵּץ רוּחָם לְהָפֵר עֲצַת אוֹיֵב
וּלְהַעֲבִיר מֶמְשֶׁלֶת זָדוֹן, יָפוּצוּ אוֹיְבֵיהֶם וְיָנוּסוּ מְשַׂנְאֵיהֶם מִפְּנֵיהֶם,
וְיִשְׂמְחוּ בִישׁוּעָתֶךָ. הֲשִׁיבֵם בְּשָׁלוֹם אֶל בֵּיתָם, כַּכָּתוּב בְּדִבְרֵי
קָדְשֶׁךָ: יהוה יִשְׁמָרְךָ מִכָּל־רָע, יִשְׁמֹר אֶת־נַפְשֶׁךָ: יהוה יִשְׁמָר־
צֵאתְךָ וּבוֹאֶךָ, מֵעַתָּה וְעַד־עוֹלָם: וְקַיֵּם בָּנוּ מִקְרָא שֶׁכָּתוּב: לֹא־
יִשָּׂא גוֹי אֶל־גּוֹי חֶרֶב, וְלֹא־יִלְמְדוּ עוֹד מִלְחָמָה: וְיֵדְעוּ כָּל יוֹשְׁבֵי
תֵבֵל כִּי לְךָ מְלוּכָה יָאָתָה, וְשִׁמְךָ נוֹרָא עַל כָּל מַה שֶׁבָּרָאתָ.
וְנֹאמַר אָמֵן.

תהלים קכא

ישעיה ב

PRAYER FOR THE STATE OF ISRAEL

The Leader says the following prayer:

אָבִינוּ שֶׁבַּשָּׁמַיִם Heavenly Father, Israel's Rock and Redeemer, bless the State of Israel, the first flowering of our redemption. Shield it under the wings of Your loving-kindness and spread over it the Tabernacle of Your peace. Send Your light and truth to its leaders, ministers and advisors, and direct them with good counsel before You.

Strengthen the hands of the defenders of our Holy Land; give them deliverance, our God, and crown them with the crown of victory. Give peace in the land and everlasting joy to its inhabitants.

As for our brothers, the whole house of Israel, remember them in all the lands of our (*In Israel say:* their) dispersion, and swiftly lead us (*In Israel say:* them) upright to Zion Your city, and Jerusalem Your dwelling place, as is written in the Torah of Moses Your servant: "Even if you are scattered to the furthermost lands under the heav- *Deut. 30* ens, from there the LORD your God will gather you and take you back. The LORD your God will bring you to the land your ancestors possessed and you will possess it; and He will make you more prosperous and numerous than your ancestors. Then the LORD your God will open up your heart and the heart of your descendants, to love the LORD your God with all your heart and with all your soul, that you may live."

Unite our hearts to love and fear Your name and observe all the words of Your Torah, and swiftly send us Your righteous anointed one of the house of David, to redeem those who long for Your salvation.

Appear in Your glorious majesty over all who live on earth, and let all who breathe declare: The LORD God of Israel is King and His kingship has dominion over all. Amen, Selah.

תפילה לשלום מדינת ישראל

The שליח ציבור *says the following prayer:*

אָבִינוּ שֶׁבַּשָּׁמַיִם, צוּר יִשְׂרָאֵל וְגוֹאֲלוֹ, בָּרֵךְ אֶת מְדִינַת
יִשְׂרָאֵל, רֵאשִׁית צְמִיחַת גְּאֻלָּתֵנוּ. הָגֵן עָלֶיהָ בְּאֶבְרַת חַסְדֶּךָ
וּפְרֹשׂ עָלֶיהָ סֻכַּת שְׁלוֹמֶךָ, וּשְׁלַח אוֹרְךָ וַאֲמִתְּךָ לְרָאשֶׁיהָ, שָׂרֶיהָ
וְיוֹעֲצֶיהָ, וְתַקְּנֵם בְּעֵצָה טוֹבָה מִלְּפָנֶיךָ.

חַזֵּק אֶת יְדֵי מְגִנֵּי אֶרֶץ קָדְשֵׁנוּ, וְהַנְחִילֵם אֱלֹהֵינוּ יְשׁוּעָה וַעֲטֶרֶת
נִצָּחוֹן תְּעַטְּרֵם, וְנָתַתָּ שָׁלוֹם בָּאָרֶץ וְשִׂמְחַת עוֹלָם לְיוֹשְׁבֶיהָ.

וְאֶת אַחֵינוּ כָּל בֵּית יִשְׂרָאֵל, פְּקָד נָא בְּכָל אַרְצוֹת פְּזוּרֵינוּ,
וְתוֹלִיכֵנוּ /בארץ ישראל: פְּזוּרֵיהֶם, וְתוֹלִיכֵם/ מְהֵרָה קוֹמְמִיּוּת לְצִיּוֹן
עִירֶךָ וְלִירוּשָׁלַיִם מִשְׁכַּן שְׁמֶךָ, כַּכָּתוּב בְּתוֹרַת מֹשֶׁה עַבְדֶּךָ:
אִם־יִהְיֶה נִדַּחֲךָ בִּקְצֵה הַשָּׁמָיִם, מִשָּׁם יְקַבֶּצְךָ יהוה אֱלֹהֶיךָ
וּמִשָּׁם יִקָּחֶךָ: וֶהֱבִיאֲךָ יהוה אֱלֹהֶיךָ אֶל־הָאָרֶץ אֲשֶׁר־יָרְשׁוּ
אֲבֹתֶיךָ וִירִשְׁתָּהּ, וְהֵיטִבְךָ וְהִרְבְּךָ מֵאֲבֹתֶיךָ: וּמָל יהוה אֱלֹהֶיךָ
אֶת־לְבָבְךָ וְאֶת־לְבַב זַרְעֶךָ, לְאַהֲבָה אֶת־יהוה אֱלֹהֶיךָ בְּכָל־
לְבָבְךָ וּבְכָל־נַפְשְׁךָ, לְמַעַן חַיֶּיךָ:

דברים ל

וְיַחֵד לְבָבֵנוּ לְאַהֲבָה וּלְיִרְאָה אֶת שְׁמֶךָ, וְלִשְׁמֹר אֶת כָּל דִּבְרֵי
תוֹרָתֶךָ, וּשְׁלַח לָנוּ מְהֵרָה בֶּן דָּוִד מְשִׁיחַ צִדְקֶךָ, לִפְדּוֹת מְחַכֵּי
קֵץ יְשׁוּעָתֶךָ.

וְהוֹפַע בַּהֲדַר גְּאוֹן עֻזֶּךָ עַל כָּל יוֹשְׁבֵי תֵבֵל אַרְצֶךָ וְיֹאמַר כֹּל
אֲשֶׁר נְשָׁמָה בְאַפּוֹ, יהוה אֱלֹהֵי יִשְׂרָאֵל מֶלֶךְ וּמַלְכוּתוֹ בַּכֹּל
מָשָׁלָה, אָמֵן סֶלָה.

PRAYER FOR ISRAEL'S DEFENSE FORCES

The Leader says the following prayer:

מִי שֶׁבֵּרַךְ May He who blessed our ancestors, Abraham, Isaac and Jacob, bless the members of Israel's Defense Forces and its security services who stand guard over our land and the cities of our God from the Lebanese border to the Egyptian desert, from the Mediterranean sea to the approach of the Aravah, and wherever else they are, on land, in air and at sea. May the LORD make the enemies who rise against us be struck down before them. May the Holy One, blessed be He, protect and deliver them from all trouble and distress, suffering and illness, and send blessing and success to all the work of their hands. May He subdue our enemies under them and crown them with deliverance and victory. And may there be fulfilled in them the verse, "It is the LORD your God who goes *Deut. 20* with you to fight for you against your enemies, to deliver you." And let us say: Amen.

RETURNING THE TORAH TO THE ARK

The Ark is opened. The Leader takes the Torah scroll and says:
יְהַלְלוּ Let them praise the name of the LORD,   *Ps. 148*
    for His name alone is sublime.

The congregation responds:
הוֹדוֹ His majesty is above earth and heaven.
    He has raised the horn of His people,
    for the glory of all His devoted ones,
    the children of Israel, the people close to Him.
    Halleluya!

מי שבירך לחיילי צה״ל

מי שבירך לחיילי צה״ל

The שליח ציבור *says the following prayer:*

מִי שֶׁבֵּרַךְ אֲבוֹתֵינוּ אַבְרָהָם יִצְחָק וְיַעֲקֹב הוּא יְבָרֵךְ אֶת חַיָּלֵי
צְבָא הַהֲגָנָה לְיִשְׂרָאֵל וְאַנְשֵׁי כֹּחוֹת הַבִּטָּחוֹן, הָעוֹמְדִים עַל
מִשְׁמַר אַרְצֵנוּ וְעָרֵי אֱלֹהֵינוּ, מִגְּבוּל הַלְּבָנוֹן וְעַד מִדְבַּר מִצְרַיִם
וּמִן הַיָּם הַגָּדוֹל עַד לְבוֹא הָעֲרָבָה וּבְכָל מָקוֹם שֶׁהֵם, בַּיַּבָּשָׁה,
בָּאֲוִיר וּבַיָּם. יִתֵּן יהוה אֶת אוֹיְבֵינוּ הַקָּמִים עָלֵינוּ נִגָּפִים לִפְנֵיהֶם.
הַקָּדוֹשׁ בָּרוּךְ הוּא יִשְׁמֹר וְיַצִּיל אֶת חַיָּלֵינוּ מִכָּל צָרָה וְצוּקָה
וּמִכָּל נֶגַע וּמַחֲלָה, וְיִשְׁלַח בְּרָכָה וְהַצְלָחָה בְּכָל מַעֲשֵׂי יְדֵיהֶם.
יַדְבֵּר שׂוֹנְאֵינוּ תַּחְתֵּיהֶם וִיעַטְּרֵם בְּכֶתֶר יְשׁוּעָה וּבַעֲטֶרֶת נִצָּחוֹן.
וִיקֻיַּם בָּהֶם הַכָּתוּב: כִּי יהוה אֱלֹהֵיכֶם הַהֹלֵךְ עִמָּכֶם לְהִלָּחֵם
לָכֶם עִם־אֹיְבֵיכֶם לְהוֹשִׁיעַ אֶתְכֶם: וְנֹאמַר אָמֵן.

דברים כ

הכנסת ספר תורה

The ארון קודש *is opened. The* שליח ציבור *takes the* ספר תורה *and says:*

תהלים קמח

יְהַלְלוּ אֶת־שֵׁם יהוה, כִּי נִשְׂגָּב־שְׁמוֹ, לְבַדּוֹ

The קהל *responds:*

הוֹדוֹ עַל־אֶרֶץ וְשָׁמָיִם:
וַיָּרֶם קֶרֶן לְעַמּוֹ
תְּהִלָּה לְכָל־חֲסִידָיו
לִבְנֵי יִשְׂרָאֵל עַם קְרֹבוֹ
הַלְלוּיָהּ:

As the Torah scroll is returned to the Ark, say:

לְדָוִד מִזְמוֹר A psalm of David. The earth is the Lord's and all it *Ps. 24* contains, the world and all who live in it. For He founded it on the seas and established it on the streams. Who may climb the mountain of the Lord? Who may stand in His holy place? He who has clean hands and a pure heart, who has not taken My name in vain, or sworn falsely. He shall receive blessing from the Lord, and just reward from God, his salvation. This is a generation of those who seek Him, the descendants of Jacob who seek Your presence, Selah! Lift up your heads, O gates; be uplifted, eternal doors, so that the King of glory may enter. Who is the King of glory? It is the Lord, strong and mighty, the Lord mighty in battle. Lift up your heads, O gates; lift them up, eternal doors, so that the King of glory may enter. Who is He, the King of glory? The Lord of multitudes, He is the King of glory, Selah!

As the Torah scroll is placed into the Ark, say:

וּבְנֻחֹה יֹאמַר When the Ark came to rest, Moses would say:
"Return, O Lord, to the countless thousands of Israel."   *Num. 10*
Advance, Lord, to Your resting place,   *Ps. 132*
  You and Your mighty Ark.
Your priests are clothed in righteousness,
  and Your devoted ones sing in joy.
For the sake of Your servant David,
  do not reject Your anointed one.
For I give you good instruction;   *Prov. 4*
  do not abandon My Torah.
It is a tree of life to those who grasp it,   *Prov. 3*
  and those who uphold it are happy.
Its ways are ways of pleasantness,
  and all its paths are peace.
▸ Turn us back, O Lord, to You, and we will return.   *Lam. 5*
  Renew our days as of old.

The Ark is closed.

As the ספר תורה is returned to the ארון קודש, say:

תהלים כד

לְדָוִד מִזְמוֹר, לַיהוה הָאָרֶץ וּמְלוֹאָהּ, תֵּבֵל וְיֹשְׁבֵי בָהּ: כִּי־הוּא עַל־
יַמִּים יְסָדָהּ, וְעַל־נְהָרוֹת יְכוֹנְנֶהָ: מִי־יַעֲלֶה בְהַר־יהוה, וּמִי־יָקוּם
בִּמְקוֹם קָדְשׁוֹ: נְקִי כַפַּיִם וּבַר־לֵבָב, אֲשֶׁר לֹא־נָשָׂא לַשָּׁוְא נַפְשִׁי
וְלֹא נִשְׁבַּע לְמִרְמָה: יִשָּׂא בְרָכָה מֵאֵת יהוה, וּצְדָקָה מֵאֱלֹהֵי יִשְׁעוֹ:
זֶה דּוֹר דֹּרְשָׁו, מְבַקְשֵׁי פָנֶיךָ, יַעֲקֹב, סֶלָה: שְׂאוּ שְׁעָרִים רָאשֵׁיכֶם,
וְהִנָּשְׂאוּ פִּתְחֵי עוֹלָם, וְיָבוֹא מֶלֶךְ הַכָּבוֹד: מִי זֶה מֶלֶךְ הַכָּבוֹד, יהוה
עִזּוּז וְגִבּוֹר, יהוה גִּבּוֹר מִלְחָמָה: שְׂאוּ שְׁעָרִים רָאשֵׁיכֶם, וּשְׂאוּ פִּתְחֵי
עוֹלָם, וְיָבֹא מֶלֶךְ הַכָּבוֹד: מִי הוּא זֶה מֶלֶךְ הַכָּבוֹד, יהוה צְבָאוֹת
הוּא מֶלֶךְ הַכָּבוֹד, סֶלָה:

As the ספר תורה is placed into the ארון קודש, say:

במדבר י

וּבְנֻחֹה יֹאמַר, שׁוּבָה יהוה רִבְבוֹת אַלְפֵי יִשְׂרָאֵל:

תהלים קלב

קוּמָה יהוה לִמְנוּחָתֶךָ, אַתָּה וַאֲרוֹן עֻזֶּךָ:

כֹּהֲנֶיךָ יִלְבְּשׁוּ־צֶדֶק, וַחֲסִידֶיךָ יְרַנֵּנוּ:

בַּעֲבוּר דָּוִד עַבְדֶּךָ אַל־תָּשֵׁב פְּנֵי מְשִׁיחֶךָ:

משלי ד

כִּי לֶקַח טוֹב נָתַתִּי לָכֶם, תּוֹרָתִי אַל־תַּעֲזֹבוּ:

משלי ג

עֵץ־חַיִּים הִיא לַמַּחֲזִיקִים בָּהּ, וְתֹמְכֶיהָ מְאֻשָּׁר:

דְּרָכֶיהָ דַרְכֵי־נֹעַם וְכָל־נְתִיבוֹתֶיהָ שָׁלוֹם:

איכה ה

◂ הֲשִׁיבֵנוּ יהוה אֵלֶיךָ וְנָשׁוּבָה, חַדֵּשׁ יָמֵינוּ כְּקֶדֶם:

The ארון קודש is closed.

... A THOUSAND WORDS

CONCLUSION OF THE SERVICE

Some have the custom to touch the hand-tefillin at °, and the head-tefillin at °°.

אַשְׁרֵי Happy are those who live in Your House;   *Ps. 84*
they shall continue to praise You, Selah!
Happy are the people for whom this is so;   *Ps. 144*
happy are the people whose God is the Lord.

A song of praise by David.   *Ps. 145*

I will elevate You, my God, the King, and bless Your name for
ever and all time. Every day I will bless You, and praise Your
name for ever and all time. Great is the Lord and greatly to
be praised; His greatness is unfathomable. One generation
will praise Your works to the next, and tell of Your mighty
deeds. On the glorious splendor of Your majesty I will meditate, and on the acts of Your wonders. They shall talk of the
power of Your awesome deeds, and I will tell of Your greatness. They shall recite the record of Your great goodness, and
sing with joy of Your righteousness. The Lord is generous
and compassionate, slow to anger and great in loving-kindness. The Lord is good to all, and His compassion extends
to all His works. All Your works shall thank You, Lord, and
Your devoted ones shall bless You. They shall talk of the glory
of Your kingship, and speak of Your might. To make known
to mankind His mighty deeds and the glorious majesty of
His kingship. Your kingdom is an everlasting kingdom, and
Your reign is for all generations. The Lord supports all who
fall, and raises all who are bowed down. All raise their eyes
to You in hope, and You give them their food in due season.
°You open Your hand, °°and satisfy every living thing with
favor. The Lord is righteous in all His ways, and kind in
all He does. The Lord is close to all who call on Him, to
all who call on Him in truth. He fulfills the will of those
who fear Him; He hears their cry and saves them. The Lord

סיום התפילה

Some have the custom to touch the תפילין של יד *at* °, *and the* תפילין של ראש *at* °°.

תהלים פד

תהלים קמד

תהלים קמה

אַשְׁרֵי יוֹשְׁבֵי בֵיתֶךָ, עוֹד יְהַלְלוּךָ סֶּלָה:

אַשְׁרֵי הָעָם שֶׁכָּכָה לּוֹ, אַשְׁרֵי הָעָם שֶׁיהוה אֱלֹהָיו:

תְּהִלָּה לְדָוִד

אֲרוֹמִמְךָ אֱלוֹהַי הַמֶּלֶךְ, וַאֲבָרְכָה שִׁמְךָ לְעוֹלָם וָעֶד:

בְּכָל־יוֹם אֲבָרְכֶךָּ, וַאֲהַלְלָה שִׁמְךָ לְעוֹלָם וָעֶד:

גָּדוֹל יהוה וּמְהֻלָּל מְאֹד, וְלִגְדֻלָּתוֹ אֵין חֵקֶר:

דּוֹר לְדוֹר יְשַׁבַּח מַעֲשֶׂיךָ, וּגְבוּרֹתֶיךָ יַגִּידוּ:

הֲדַר כְּבוֹד הוֹדֶךָ, וְדִבְרֵי נִפְלְאֹתֶיךָ אָשִׂיחָה:

וֶעֱזוּז נוֹרְאֹתֶיךָ יֹאמֵרוּ, וּגְדוּלָּתְךָ אֲסַפְּרֶנָּה:

זֵכֶר רַב־טוּבְךָ יַבִּיעוּ, וְצִדְקָתְךָ יְרַנֵּנוּ:

חַנּוּן וְרַחוּם יהוה, אֶרֶךְ אַפַּיִם וּגְדָל־חָסֶד:

טוֹב־יהוה לַכֹּל, וְרַחֲמָיו עַל־כָּל־מַעֲשָׂיו:

יוֹדוּךָ יהוה כָּל־מַעֲשֶׂיךָ, וַחֲסִידֶיךָ יְבָרְכוּכָה:

כְּבוֹד מַלְכוּתְךָ יֹאמֵרוּ, וּגְבוּרָתְךָ יְדַבֵּרוּ:

לְהוֹדִיעַ לִבְנֵי הָאָדָם גְּבוּרֹתָיו, וּכְבוֹד הֲדַר מַלְכוּתוֹ:

מַלְכוּתְךָ מַלְכוּת כָּל־עֹלָמִים, וּמֶמְשַׁלְתְּךָ בְּכָל־דּוֹר וָדֹר:

סוֹמֵךְ יהוה לְכָל־הַנֹּפְלִים, וְזוֹקֵף לְכָל־הַכְּפוּפִים:

עֵינֵי־כֹל אֵלֶיךָ יְשַׂבֵּרוּ, וְאַתָּה נוֹתֵן־לָהֶם אֶת־אָכְלָם בְּעִתּוֹ:

°פּוֹתֵחַ אֶת־יָדֶךָ, °°וּמַשְׂבִּיעַ לְכָל־חַי רָצוֹן:

צַדִּיק יהוה בְּכָל־דְּרָכָיו, וְחָסִיד בְּכָל־מַעֲשָׂיו:

קָרוֹב יהוה לְכָל־קֹרְאָיו, לְכֹל אֲשֶׁר יִקְרָאֻהוּ בֶאֱמֶת:

רְצוֹן־יְרֵאָיו יַעֲשֶׂה, וְאֶת־שַׁוְעָתָם יִשְׁמַע, וְיוֹשִׁיעֵם:

guards all who love Him, but all the wicked He will destroy.
‣ My mouth shall speak the praise of the LORD, and all creatures shall bless His holy name for ever and all time.
We will bless the LORD now and for ever. Halleluya! *Ps. 115*

*Omit on Rosh Ḥodesh, Ḥol HaMo'ed, Erev Pesaḥ, Erev Yom Kippur, Ḥanukka,
the 14th and 15th of Adar I, Purim and Shushan Purim, Yom HaAtzma'ut,
Yom Yerushalayim, Tisha B'Av, or in a house of mourning, and in Israel on Isru Ḥag.*

לַמְנַצֵּחַ For the conductor of music. A psalm of David. May the *Ps. 20*
LORD answer you when you are in distress; may the name of Jacob's
God protect you. May He send you help from the Sanctuary and
support from Zion. May He remember all your meal-offerings and
accept your burnt-offerings, Selah! May He give you your heart's
desire and make all your plans succeed. We will shout for joy at
Your salvation and lift a banner in the name of our God. May the
LORD fulfill all your requests. Now I know that the LORD saves His
anointed; He answers him from His holy heaven with the saving
power of His right hand. Some trust in chariots, others in horses,
but we call on the name of the LORD our God. They were brought
to their knees and fell, but we rose up and stood firm. ‣ LORD, save!
May the King answer us on the day we call.

CONNECTION

There was once a man sitting in his house when a hurricane struck. As the house and neighborhood flooded, he ran upstairs to the roof. Suddenly a helicopter flew by and the people inside it threw down a ladder. They shouted down to him, "Grab on."

"No. Go away. I trust that God will save me," he refused.

A boat came and threw him a life saver. The sailor said, "Grab on."

"No. Go away. I trust that God will save me," he shouted as the water kept rising.

The man drowned. When he entered heaven, he turned to God and said, "Hashem, I trusted in You that You would save me. Why didn't You save me?"

God turned to him and said, "Who do you think sent you the helicopter and the boat?"

שׁוֹמֵר יהוה אֶת־כָּל־אֹהֲבָיו, וְאֵת כָּל־הָרְשָׁעִים יַשְׁמִיד:

‹ תְּהִלַּת יהוה יְדַבֶּר פִּי, וִיבָרֵךְ כָּל־בָּשָׂר שֵׁם קָדְשׁוֹ לְעוֹלָם וָעֶד:

וַאֲנַחְנוּ נְבָרֵךְ יָהּ מֵעַתָּה וְעַד־עוֹלָם, הַלְלוּיָהּ: תהלים קטו

Omit on ראש חודש, חול המועד, ערב פסח, ערב יום כיפור, חנוכה,
the 14th and 15th of אדר א' *and* פורים, שושן פורים, יום העצמאות,
.אסרו חג *on* ארץ ישראל, תשעה באב, יום ירושלים *or in a house of mourning, and in*

לַמְנַצֵּחַ מִזְמוֹר לְדָוִד: יַעַנְךָ יהוה בְּיוֹם צָרָה, יְשַׂגֶּבְךָ שֵׁם אֱלֹהֵי תהלים כ
יַעֲקֹב: יִשְׁלַח־עֶזְרְךָ מִקֹּדֶשׁ, וּמִצִּיּוֹן יִסְעָדֶךָּ: יִזְכֹּר כָּל־מִנְחֹתֶךָ,
וְעוֹלָתְךָ יְדַשְּׁנֶה סֶלָה: יִתֶּן־לְךָ כִלְבָבֶךָ וְכָל־עֲצָתְךָ יְמַלֵּא: נְרַנְּנָה
בִּישׁוּעָתֶךָ, וּבְשֵׁם־אֱלֹהֵינוּ נִדְגֹּל, יְמַלֵּא יהוה כָּל־מִשְׁאֲלוֹתֶיךָ:
עַתָּה יָדַעְתִּי כִּי הוֹשִׁיעַ יהוה מְשִׁיחוֹ, יַעֲנֵהוּ מִשְּׁמֵי קָדְשׁוֹ,
בִּגְבוּרוֹת יֵשַׁע יְמִינוֹ: אֵלֶּה בָרֶכֶב וְאֵלֶּה בַסּוּסִים, וַאֲנַחְנוּ בְּשֵׁם־
יהוה אֱלֹהֵינוּ נַזְכִּיר: הֵמָּה כָּרְעוּ וְנָפָלוּ, וַאֲנַחְנוּ קַמְנוּ וַנִּתְעוֹדָד:
‹ יהוה הוֹשִׁיעָה, הַמֶּלֶךְ יַעֲנֵנוּ בְיוֹם־קָרְאֵנוּ:

This *mizmor* was originally composed when David
sent his captain Yoav with the army to confront the
massive forces that Avshalom had assembled against
David's kingdom (*Shmuel Beit* 18). On this occasion
David chose not to accompany his army. He felt that
he would be more effective if he stayed in Jerusalem
and prayed for the success of his army.

This *mizmor* is a prayer, although he presented
it in the form of a blessing to the men who were
about to face the danger of fighting and who would
desperately need God's help. In the *mizmor* David
emphasizes our belief that God will respond to our
supplications.

*"Sometimes one
must look into ashes
to find a solitary spark."*
(Rabbi Dov Ber
of Mezeritch)

**How has God
supported you
in difficult times?**

**What difficulties
in your life
have made you
turn to God?**

In a house of mourning and on Tisha B'Av omit the verse beginning
"As for Me" and continue with "You are the Holy One."

וּבָא לְצִיּוֹן גּוֹאֵל "A redeemer will come to Zion, to those in Jacob who *Is. 59* repent of their sins," declares the Lord.

"As for Me, this is My covenant with them," says the Lord. "My spirit, that is on you, and My words I have placed in your mouth will not depart from your mouth, or from the mouth of your children, or from the mouth of their descendants from this time on and for ever," says the Lord.

▸ You are the Holy One, enthroned on the praises of Israel. And (the *Ps. 22* angels) call to one another, saying, "Holy, holy, holy is the Lord of *Is. 6* multitudes; the whole world is filled with His glory."

And they receive permission from one another, saying: "Holy in the highest heavens, *Targum* home of His Presence; holy on earth, the work of His strength; holy for ever and *Yonatan* all time is the Lord of multitudes; the whole earth is full of His radiant glory." *Is. 6*

▸ Then a wind lifted me up and I heard behind me the sound of a great *Ezek. 3* noise, saying, "Blessed is the Lord's glory from His place."

Then a wind lifted me up and I heard behind me the sound of a great tempest of *Targum* those who uttered praise, saying, "Blessed is the Lord's glory from the place of *Yonatan* the home of His Presence." *Ezek. 3*

The Lord shall reign for ever and all time. *Ex. 15*

The Lord's kingdom is established for ever and all time. *Targum Onkelos Ex. 15*

---

to *ḥol*, from the presence of God to the mundane world outside. The answer of the sages in constructing the morning prayer is to "learn a little bit of Torah." After prayer, one must engage in learning. When you have finished praying, it is truly over. But when you finish learning, the Torah accompanies you because it is part of you. In other words, even though the Torah is the word of the living God and an intimate encounter with Him, it can accompany us in the everyday world.

CONNECTION

The Maggid of Kosznitz once turned to a little boy and said to him, "I'll give you a ruble if you can tell me where God is."

The little boy paused thoughtfully and with a smile replied to the Maggid, "I'll give you two if you can tell me where He isn't."

The little boy became the first Hasidic Gerer Rebbe.

In a house of mourning and on תשעה באב *omit the verse*
beginning וַאֲנִי זֹאת בְּרִיתִי, *and continue with* וְאַתָּה קָדוֹשׁ.

ישעיה נט

וּבָא לְצִיּוֹן גּוֹאֵל, וּלְשָׁבֵי פֶשַׁע בְּיַעֲקֹב, נְאֻם יהוה:
וַאֲנִי זֹאת בְּרִיתִי אוֹתָם, אָמַר יהוה, רוּחִי אֲשֶׁר עָלֶיךָ וּדְבָרַי
אֲשֶׁר־שַׂמְתִּי בְּפִיךָ, לֹא־יָמוּשׁוּ מִפִּיךָ וּמִפִּי זַרְעֲךָ וּמִפִּי זֶרַע זַרְעֲךָ,
אָמַר יהוה, מֵעַתָּה וְעַד־עוֹלָם:

תהלים כב
ישעיה ו

‹ וְאַתָּה קָדוֹשׁ יוֹשֵׁב תְּהִלּוֹת יִשְׂרָאֵל: וְקָרָא זֶה אֶל־זֶה וְאָמַר
קָדוֹשׁ, קָדוֹשׁ, קָדוֹשׁ, יהוה צְבָאוֹת, מְלֹא כָל־הָאָרֶץ כְּבוֹדוֹ:

תרגום
יונתן
ישעיה ו

וּמְקַבְּלִין דֵּין מִן דֵּין וְאָמְרִין, קַדִּישׁ בִּשְׁמֵי מְרוֹמָא עִלָּאָה בֵּית שְׁכִינְתֵּהּ,
קַדִּישׁ עַל אַרְעָא עוֹבַד גְּבוּרְתֵּהּ, קַדִּישׁ לְעָלַם וּלְעָלְמֵי עָלְמַיָּא, יהוה צְבָאוֹת,
מַלְיָא כָל אַרְעָא זִיו יְקָרֵהּ.

יחזקאל ג

‹ וַתִּשָּׂאֵנִי רוּחַ, וָאֶשְׁמַע אַחֲרַי קוֹל רַעַשׁ גָּדוֹל, בָּרוּךְ כְּבוֹד־יהוה
מִמְּקוֹמוֹ:

תרגום
יונתן
יחזקאל ג

וּנְטָלַתְנִי רוּחָא, וּשְׁמָעִית בַּתְרַי קָל זִיעַ סַגִּיא, דִּמְשַׁבְּחִין וְאָמְרִין, בְּרִיךְ יְקָרָא
דַּיהוה מֵאֲתַר בֵּית שְׁכִינְתֵּהּ.

שמות טו
תרגום
אונקלוס
שמות טו

יהוה יִמְלֹךְ לְעֹלָם וָעֶד:
יהוה מַלְכוּתֵהּ קָאֵם לְעָלַם וּלְעָלְמֵי עָלְמַיָּא.

─────────────────────────────

LEARNING

The *Kedusha* in the beginning of *Uva LeTziyon* is known as *Kedusha deSidra*. The Gemara (*Sota* 49a) asks: "On what does the world endure? On the *Kedusha deSidra* and on the *Yeheh shemeh raba* of *aggadeta*."

Rashi explains that *Kedusha deSidra* contains two elements, the sanctification of the name and the study of Torah.

These two points interrelate and combine to create something unique.

The morning prayer is now basically complete. *Tefilla* ends with *Taḥanun*. What we are doing now is answering an important question: What do we do, how do we live, when we depart from *tefilla*, from the presence of God? This is a very difficult transition, from *kodesh*

יהוה LORD, God of Abraham, Isaac and Yisrael, our ancestors, may You keep ⟨1 Chr. 29⟩ this for ever so that it forms the thoughts in Your people's heart, and directs their heart toward You. He is compassionate. He forgives wrongdoing and ⟨Ps. 78⟩ does not destroy. Repeatedly He suppresses His anger, not rousing His full fury. For You, my LORD, are good and forgiving, generously kind to all who ⟨Ps. 86⟩ call on You. Your righteousness is eternally righteous, and Your Torah is truth. ⟨Ps. 119⟩ Give truth to Jacob, loving-kindness to Abraham, as You promised our ances- ⟨Mic. 7⟩ tors in ancient times. Blessed is my LORD for day after day He burdens us [with His blessings]; God is our salvation, Selah! The LORD of multitudes is with ⟨Ps. 46⟩ us; the God of Jacob is our refuge, Selah! LORD of multitudes, happy is the ⟨Ps. 84⟩ one who trusts in You. LORD, save! May the King answer us on the day we call. ⟨Ps. 20⟩

בָּרוּךְ Blessed is He, our God, who created us for His glory, separating us from those who go astray; who gave us the Torah of truth, planting within us eternal life. May He open our heart to His Torah, imbuing our heart with the love and awe of Him, that we may do His will and serve Him with a perfect heart, so that we neither toil in vain nor give birth to confusion.

יְהִי רָצוֹן May it be Your will, O LORD our God and God of our ancestors, that we keep Your laws in this world, and thus be worthy to live, see and inherit goodness and blessing in the Messianic Age and in the life of the World to Come. So that my soul may sing to You and not be silent. LORD, my God, for ⟨Ps. 30⟩ ever I will thank You. Blessed is the man who trusts in the LORD, whose trust ⟨Jer. 17⟩ is in the LORD alone. Trust in the LORD for evermore, for God, the LORD, is ⟨Is. 26⟩ an everlasting Rock. ▸ Those who know Your name trust in You, for You, LORD, ⟨Ps. 9⟩ do not abandon those who seek You. The LORD desired, for the sake of Israel's ⟨Is. 42⟩ merit, to make the Torah great and glorious.

On Rosh Ḥodesh and Ḥol HaMo'ed, the Leader says Half Kaddish, page 230. The service then continues with Musaf for Rosh Ḥodesh on page 432. for Ḥol HaMo'ed on page 478.

On other days, the Leader continues with Full Kaddish on the next page.

---

that he would like to buy a sizable amount of furs. However, it was the set learning time of Rav Kotler. His wife knocked on the door of his room, once, twice, and three times, and urged her husband to utilize this opportunity for his business.

Rav Kotler answered from behind the door, "Go tell him that if he's willing to wait until I finish my learning, good!

If not – he should go in peace. A person's livelihood is determined on Rosh HaShana until Rosh HaShana. If it was decreed that I will sell the merchandise, I'll find a buyer!"

Rav Aharon concluded his story, "My father's wondrous *mesirat nefesh* for Torah instilled in us the basic belief, 'When you learn Torah, you never lose out!' All of my *mesirat nefesh* for Torah – I acquired from him!"

דברי הימים
א' כט
תהלים עח
תהלים פו
תהלים קיט
מיכה ז
תהלים סח
תהלים פד
תהלים כ

יהוה אֱלֹהֵי אַבְרָהָם יִצְחָק וְיִשְׂרָאֵל אֲבֹתֵינוּ, שָׁמְרָה־זֹּאת לְעוֹלָם לְיֵצֶר מַחְשְׁבוֹת לְבַב עַמֶּךָ, וְהָכֵן לְבָבָם אֵלֶיךָ: וְהוּא רַחוּם יְכַפֵּר עָוֹן וְלֹא־יַשְׁחִית, וְהִרְבָּה לְהָשִׁיב אַפּוֹ, וְלֹא־יָעִיר כָּל־חֲמָתוֹ: כִּי־אַתָּה אֲדֹנָי טוֹב וְסַלָּח, וְרַב־חֶסֶד לְכָל־קֹרְאֶיךָ: צִדְקָתְךָ צֶדֶק לְעוֹלָם וְתוֹרָתְךָ אֱמֶת: תִּתֵּן אֱמֶת לְיַעֲקֹב, חֶסֶד לְאַבְרָהָם, אֲשֶׁר־נִשְׁבַּעְתָּ לַאֲבֹתֵינוּ מִימֵי קֶדֶם: בָּרוּךְ אֲדֹנָי יוֹם יוֹם יַעֲמָס־לָנוּ, הָאֵל יְשׁוּעָתֵנוּ סֶלָה: יהוה צְבָאוֹת עִמָּנוּ, מִשְׂגָּב לָנוּ אֱלֹהֵי יַעֲקֹב סֶלָה: יהוה צְבָאוֹת, אַשְׁרֵי אָדָם בֹּטֵחַ בָּךְ: יהוה הוֹשִׁיעָה, הַמֶּלֶךְ יַעֲנֵנוּ בְיוֹם־קָרְאֵנוּ:

בָּרוּךְ הוּא אֱלֹהֵינוּ שֶׁבְּרָאָנוּ לִכְבוֹדוֹ, וְהִבְדִּילָנוּ מִן הַתּוֹעִים, וְנָתַן לָנוּ תּוֹרַת אֱמֶת, וְחַיֵּי עוֹלָם נָטַע בְּתוֹכֵנוּ. הוּא יִפְתַּח לִבֵּנוּ בְּתוֹרָתוֹ, וְיָשֵׂם בְּלִבֵּנוּ אַהֲבָתוֹ וְיִרְאָתוֹ וְלַעֲשׂוֹת רְצוֹנוֹ וּלְעָבְדוֹ בְּלֵבָב שָׁלֵם, לְמַעַן לֹא נִיגַע לָרִיק וְלֹא נֵלֵד לַבֶּהָלָה.

יְהִי רָצוֹן מִלְּפָנֶיךָ יהוה אֱלֹהֵינוּ וֵאלֹהֵי אֲבוֹתֵינוּ, שֶׁנִּשְׁמֹר חֻקֶּיךָ בָּעוֹלָם הַזֶּה, וְנִזְכֶּה וְנִחְיֶה וְנִרְאֶה וְנִירַשׁ טוֹבָה וּבְרָכָה, לִשְׁנֵי יְמוֹת הַמָּשִׁיחַ וּלְחַיֵּי הָעוֹלָם הַבָּא. לְמַעַן יְזַמֶּרְךָ כָבוֹד וְלֹא יִדֹּם, יהוה אֱלֹהַי, לְעוֹלָם אוֹדֶךָ: בָּרוּךְ הַגֶּבֶר אֲשֶׁר יִבְטַח בַּיהוה, וְהָיָה יהוה מִבְטַחוֹ: בִּטְחוּ בַיהוה עֲדֵי־עַד, כִּי בְּיָהּ יהוה צוּר עוֹלָמִים: ‹ וְיִבְטְחוּ בְךָ יוֹדְעֵי שְׁמֶךָ, כִּי לֹא־עָזַבְתָּ דֹרְשֶׁיךָ, יהוה: יהוה חָפֵץ לְמַעַן צִדְקוֹ, יַגְדִּיל תּוֹרָה וְיַאְדִּיר:

On חצי קדיש says שליח ציבור the, חול המועד and ראש חודש, page 231.
The service then continues with מוסף for ראש חודש on page 433. for חול המועד on page 479.
On other days the שליח ציבור continues with קדיש שלם on the next page.

CONNECTION

Rav Aharon Kotler told a story about his father's mesirat nefesh *(self sacrifice) for Torah. His father was a fur merchant in Lithuania. At a certain period, his business dwindled, and it reached a point where his family was lacking food to sustain themselves.*

Every day after Shaḥarit, his father would learn Torah for two hours, and was very particular to maintain this learning schedule his entire life. One day, a wealthy merchant knocked on the door of the Kotler family home, and informed them

FULL KADDISH

Leader: יִתְגַּדַּל Magnified and sanctified may His great name be,
in the world He created by His will.
May He establish His kingdom in your lifetime
and in your days, and in the lifetime
of all the house of Israel,
swiftly and soon –
and say: Amen.

All: May His great name be blessed
for ever and all time.

Leader: Blessed and praised,
glorified and great,
raised and honored,
uplifted and praised
be the name of the Holy One,
blessed be He,
beyond any blessing,
song, praise and consolation
uttered in the world –
and say: Amen.

*On Tisha B'Av, omit the next verse and continue
with "May there be great peace."*
May the prayers and pleas of all Israel
be accepted by their Father in heaven –
and say: Amen.

May there be great peace from heaven,
and life for us and all Israel –
and say: Amen.

*Bow, take three steps back, as if taking leave of the Divine Presence,
then bow, first left, then right, then center, while saying:*
May He who makes peace in His high places,
make peace for us and all Israel –
and say: Amen.

קדיש שלם

ש"ץ: יִתְגַּדַּל וְיִתְקַדַּשׁ שְׁמֵהּ רַבָּא (קהל: אָמֵן)

בְּעָלְמָא דִּי בְרָא כִרְעוּתֵהּ

וְיַמְלִיךְ מַלְכוּתֵהּ

בְּחַיֵּיכוֹן וּבְיוֹמֵיכוֹן וּבְחַיֵּי דְכָל בֵּית יִשְׂרָאֵל

בַּעֲגָלָא וּבִזְמַן קָרִיב, וְאִמְרוּ אָמֵן. (קהל: אָמֵן)

קהל
ושׁ"ץ: יְהֵא שְׁמֵהּ רַבָּא מְבָרַךְ לְעָלַם וּלְעָלְמֵי עָלְמַיָּא.

ש"ץ: יִתְבָּרַךְ וְיִשְׁתַּבַּח וְיִתְפָּאַר

וְיִתְרוֹמַם וְיִתְנַשֵּׂא וְיִתְהַדָּר וְיִתְעַלֶּה וְיִתְהַלָּל

שְׁמֵהּ דְּקֻדְשָׁא בְּרִיךְ הוּא (קהל: בְּרִיךְ הוּא)

לְעֵלָּא מִן כָּל בִּרְכָתָא

/ בעשרת ימי תשובה: לְעֵלָּא לְעֵלָּא מִכָּל בִּרְכָתָא/

וְשִׁירָתָא, תֻּשְׁבְּחָתָא וְנֶחֱמָתָא

דַּאֲמִירָן בְּעָלְמָא, וְאִמְרוּ אָמֵן. (קהל: אָמֵן)

On תשעה באב, omit the next verse and continue with יְהֵא שְׁלָמָא.

תִּתְקַבֵּל צְלוֹתְהוֹן וּבָעוּתְהוֹן דְּכָל יִשְׂרָאֵל

קֳדָם אֲבוּהוֹן דִּי בִשְׁמַיָּא, וְאִמְרוּ אָמֵן. (קהל: אָמֵן)

יְהֵא שְׁלָמָא רַבָּא מִן שְׁמַיָּא

וְחַיִּים, עָלֵינוּ וְעַל כָּל יִשְׂרָאֵל, וְאִמְרוּ אָמֵן. (קהל: אָמֵן)

*Bow, take three steps back, as if taking leave of the Divine Presence,
then bow, first left, then right, then center, while saying:*

עֹשֶׂה שָׁלוֹם/בעשרת ימי תשובה: הַשָּׁלוֹם/ בִּמְרוֹמָיו

הוּא יַעֲשֶׂה שָׁלוֹם

עָלֵינוּ וְעַל כָּל יִשְׂרָאֵל, וְאִמְרוּ אָמֵן. (קהל: אָמֵן)

Stand while saying Aleinu.

עָלֵינוּ It is our duty to praise the Master of all,
and ascribe greatness to the Author of creation,
who has not made us like the nations of the lands
nor placed us like the families of the earth;
who has not made our portion like theirs,
nor our destiny like all their multitudes.
(For they worship vanity and emptiness,
and pray to a god who cannot save.)
🚩 But we bow in worship and thank the Supreme King of kings,
the Holy One, blessed be He,
who extends the heavens and establishes the earth,
whose throne of glory is in the heavens above,
and whose power's Presence is in the highest of heights.
He is our God; there is no other.
Truly He is our King, there is none else, as it is written in His Torah:
"You shall know and take to heart this day   *Deut. 4*
that the LORD is God, in heaven above and on earth below.
There is no other."

| CONNECTION | ... A THOUSAND WORDS |

"Yes I do accept the Chosen People concept as affirmed by Judaism in its holy writ, its prayers and its millennial tradition. In fact, I believe every people – and indeed in a more limited way, every individual – is 'chosen' or destined for some distinct purpose in advanc-

ing the designs of Providence. Only, some fulfill their assignment and others do not.

Maybe the Greeks were chosen for their unique contributions to art and philosophy, the Romans for their pioneering services in law and government, the British for bringing parliamentary rule into the world, and the Americans for piloting democracy in a pluralistic society.

The Jews were chosen by God to be 'special unto Me' as the pioneers of religion and morality: that was and is their national purpose."

(Rabbi Immanuel Jakobovits)

Stand while saying עָלֵינוּ.

עָלֵינוּ לְשַׁבֵּחַ לַאֲדוֹן הַכֹּל, לָתֵת גְּדֻלָּה לְיוֹצֵר בְּרֵאשִׁית
שֶׁלֹּא עָשָׂנוּ כְּגוֹיֵי הָאֲרָצוֹת, וְלֹא שָׂמָנוּ כְּמִשְׁפְּחוֹת הָאֲדָמָה
שֶׁלֹּא שָׂם חֶלְקֵנוּ כָּהֶם וְגוֹרָלֵנוּ כְּכָל הֲמוֹנָם.
(שֶׁהֵם מִשְׁתַּחֲוִים לְהֶבֶל וָרִיק וּמִתְפַּלְלִים אֶל אֵל לֹא יוֹשִׁיעַ.)
🖐 וַאֲנַחְנוּ כּוֹרְעִים וּמִשְׁתַּחֲוִים וּמוֹדִים
לִפְנֵי מֶלֶךְ מַלְכֵי הַמְּלָכִים, הַקָּדוֹשׁ בָּרוּךְ הוּא
שֶׁהוּא נוֹטֶה שָׁמַיִם וְיוֹסֵד אָרֶץ
וּמוֹשַׁב יְקָרוֹ בַּשָּׁמַיִם מִמַּעַל, וּשְׁכִינַת עֻזּוֹ בְּגָבְהֵי מְרוֹמִים.
הוּא אֱלֹהֵינוּ, אֵין עוֹד.
אֱמֶת מַלְכֵּנוּ, אֶפֶס זוּלָתוֹ
כַּכָּתוּב בְּתוֹרָתוֹ, וְיָדַעְתָּ הַיּוֹם וַהֲשֵׁבֹתָ אֶל־לְבָבֶךָ
כִּי יהוה הוּא הָאֱלֹהִים בַּשָּׁמַיִם מִמַּעַל וְעַל־הָאָרֶץ מִתָּחַת
אֵין עוֹד:

דברים ד

| LEARNING | REFLECTION |

The *Aleinu* prayer is from the Rosh HaShana liturgy where it is used as an introduction to the *berakha* of *Malkhiyot* (Kingship) in Musaf. The text of the *tefilla* declares Hashem's sovereignty in the world, and this was considered so central to what it means to see the world through Jewish eyes that it was later chosen as the conclusion to all *tefilla* services in the siddur as the closing message.

"And now, if you will heed My voice and observe My covenant, and you shall be a distinction for Me from among all the peoples; as all the earth is Mine. And you shall be for Me a kingdom of priests and a holy nation. These are the words that you shall speak to the Children of Israel." (Shemot 19:5–6)

What does being a chosen nation mean to you?

What do you think you personally have been chosen for?

What does it mean to you to be a Jew?

What does it mean to you to be part of the Jewish People?

Therefore, we place our hope in You, LORD our God,
that we may soon see the glory of Your power,
when You will remove abominations from the earth,
and idols will be utterly destroyed,
when the world will be perfected
under the sovereignty of the Almighty,
when all humanity will call on Your name,
to turn all the earth's wicked toward You.
All the world's inhabitants will realize and know
that to You every knee must bow and every tongue swear loyalty.
Before You, LORD our God, they will kneel and bow down
and give honor to Your glorious name.
They will all accept the yoke of Your kingdom,
and You will reign over them soon and for ever.
For the kingdom is Yours, and to all eternity You will reign in glory,
as it is written in Your Torah: "The LORD will reign for ever and ever." *Ex. 15*
▸ And it is said: "Then the LORD shall be King over all the earth; *Zech. 14*
on that day the LORD shall be One and His name One."

Some add:

Have no fear of sudden terror or of the ruin when it overtakes the wicked. *Prov. 3*
Devise your strategy, but it will be defeated, propose your plan, *Is. 8*
but it will not stand, for God is with us.
When you grow old, I will still be the same. *Is. 46*
When your hair turns gray, I will still carry you.
I made you, I will bear you, I will carry you, and I will rescue you.

LEARNING

The two paragraphs of the prayer *Aleinu* represent two distinct but related themes. The first paragraph explores our chosenness in the eyes of Hashem, while the second speaks of our mission in the world – to improve it (*tikkun olam*), which is the reason why we have been chosen. In the words of Rabbi Jonathan Sacks: "No prayer more eloquently expresses the dual nature of the Jewish People: its singular history as the nation chosen to be God's witness on earth, and its universal aspiration for the time when all the inhabitants of earth will recognize the God in whose image we are formed."

עַל כֵּן נְקַוֶּה לְךָ יהוה אֱלֹהֵינוּ, לִרְאוֹת מְהֵרָה בְּתִפְאֶרֶת עֻזֶּךָ
לְהַעֲבִיר גִּלּוּלִים מִן הָאָרֶץ, וְהָאֱלִילִים כָּרוֹת יִכָּרֵתוּן
לְתַקֵּן עוֹלָם בְּמַלְכוּת שַׁדַּי.

וְכָל בְּנֵי בָשָׂר יִקְרְאוּ בִשְׁמֶךָ לְהַפְנוֹת אֵלֶיךָ כָּל רִשְׁעֵי אָרֶץ.
יַכִּירוּ וְיֵדְעוּ כָּל יוֹשְׁבֵי תֵבֵל
כִּי לְךָ תִּכְרַע כָּל בֶּרֶךְ, תִּשָּׁבַע כָּל לָשׁוֹן.
לְפָנֶיךָ יהוה אֱלֹהֵינוּ יִכְרְעוּ וְיִפֹּלוּ
וְלִכְבוֹד שִׁמְךָ יְקָר יִתֵּנוּ
וִיקַבְּלוּ כֻלָּם אֶת עֹל מַלְכוּתֶךָ
וְתִמְלֹךְ עֲלֵיהֶם מְהֵרָה לְעוֹלָם וָעֶד.
כִּי הַמַּלְכוּת שֶׁלְּךָ הִיא וּלְעוֹלְמֵי עַד תִּמְלֹךְ בְּכָבוֹד

שמות טו   כַּכָּתוּב בְּתוֹרָתֶךָ, יהוה יִמְלֹךְ לְעֹלָם וָעֶד:
זכריה יד   ◀ וְנֶאֱמַר, וְהָיָה יהוה לְמֶלֶךְ עַל־כָּל־הָאָרֶץ
בַּיּוֹם הַהוּא יִהְיֶה יהוה אֶחָד וּשְׁמוֹ אֶחָד:

Some add:

משלי ג   אַל־תִּירָא מִפַּחַד פִּתְאֹם וּמִשֹּׁאַת רְשָׁעִים כִּי תָבֹא:
ישעיה ח   עֻצוּ עֵצָה וְתֻפָר, דַּבְּרוּ דָבָר וְלֹא יָקוּם, כִּי עִמָּנוּ אֵל:
ישעיה מו   וְעַד־זִקְנָה אֲנִי הוּא, וְעַד־שֵׂיבָה אֲנִי אֶסְבֹּל, אֲנִי עָשִׂיתִי וַאֲנִי אֶשָּׂא וַאֲנִי אֶסְבֹּל וַאֲמַלֵּט:

REFLECTION

"[Hillel says]: That which is hateful to you, do not do to your friend. That is the entire Torah. The rest is just explanation. Go and study it!"
(Shabbat 31a)

How would you sum up Judaism in one sentence?

...A THOUSAND WORDS

MOURNER'S KADDISH

The following prayer, said by mourners, requires the presence of a minyan.
A transliteration can be found on page 749.

Mourner: יִתְגַּדַּל Magnified and sanctified
may His great name be,
in the world He created by His will.
May He establish His kingdom
in your lifetime and in your days,
and in the lifetime of all the house of Israel,
swiftly and soon –
and say: Amen.

All: May His great name be blessed
for ever and all time.

Mourner: Blessed and praised,
glorified and great,
raised and honored,
uplifted and praised
be the name of the Holy One,
blessed be He,
beyond any blessing, song,
praise and consolation
uttered in the world –
and say: Amen.

May there be great peace from heaven,
and life for us and all Israel –
and say: Amen.

Bow, take three steps back, as if taking leave of the Divine Presence,
then bow, first left, then right, then center, while saying:

May He who makes peace in His high places,
make peace for us and all Israel –
and say: Amen.

קדיש יתום

The following prayer, said by mourners, requires the presence of a מנין.
A transliteration can be found on page 749.

אבל: יִתְגַּדַּל וְיִתְקַדַּשׁ שְׁמֵהּ רַבָּא (קהל: אָמֵן)

בְּעָלְמָא דִּי בְרָא כִרְעוּתֵהּ

וְיַמְלִיךְ מַלְכוּתֵהּ

בְּחַיֵּיכוֹן וּבְיוֹמֵיכוֹן וּבְחַיֵּי דְּכָל בֵּית יִשְׂרָאֵל

בַּעֲגָלָא וּבִזְמַן קָרִיב

וְאִמְרוּ אָמֵן. (קהל: אָמֵן)

קהל
ואבל: יְהֵא שְׁמֵהּ רַבָּא מְבָרַךְ לְעָלַם וּלְעָלְמֵי עָלְמַיָּא.

אבל: יִתְבָּרַךְ וְיִשְׁתַּבַּח וְיִתְפָּאַר

וְיִתְרוֹמַם וְיִתְנַשֵּׂא וְיִתְהַדָּר וְיִתְעַלֶּה וְיִתְהַלָּל

שְׁמֵהּ דְּקֻדְשָׁא בְּרִיךְ הוּא (קהל: בְּרִיךְ הוּא)

לְעֵלָּא מִן כָּל בִּרְכָתָא

/ בעשרת ימי תשובה: לְעֵלָּא לְעֵלָּא מִכָּל בִּרְכָתָא/

וְשִׁירָתָא, תֻּשְׁבְּחָתָא וְנֶחֱמָתָא

דַּאֲמִירָן בְּעָלְמָא

וְאִמְרוּ אָמֵן. (קהל: אָמֵן)

יְהֵא שְׁלָמָא רַבָּא מִן שְׁמַיָּא

וְחַיִּים, עָלֵינוּ וְעַל כָּל יִשְׂרָאֵל

וְאִמְרוּ אָמֵן. (קהל: אָמֵן)

Bow, take three steps back, as if taking leave of the Divine Presence,
then bow, first left, then right, then center, while saying:

עֹשֶׂה שָׁלוֹם/בעשרת ימי תשובה: הַשָּׁלוֹם/ בִּמְרוֹמָיו

הוּא יַעֲשֶׂה שָׁלוֹם עָלֵינוּ וְעַל כָּל יִשְׂרָאֵל

וְאִמְרוּ אָמֵן. (קהל: אָמֵן)

THE DAILY PSALM

One of the following psalms is said on the appropriate day of the week as indicated.
After the psalm, the Mourner's Kaddish on page 258 is said.

After the Daily Psalm, on Rosh Ḥodesh, add Barekhi Nafshi, page 272
(in Israel, some only say Barekhi Nafshi). On Ḥanukka, add Psalm 30, page 72
followed by Mourner's Kaddish. From the second day of Rosh Ḥodesh Elul
through Shemini Atzeret (in Israel, through Hoshana Raba), add Psalm 27
on page 276. In a house of mourning the service concludes on page 278.

Sunday: Today is the first day of the week,
on which the Levites used to say this psalm in the Temple:

לְדָוִד מִזְמוֹר A psalm of David. The earth is the Lᴏʀᴅ's and all it contains, the   *Ps. 24*
world and all who live in it. For He founded it on the seas and established
it on the streams. Who may climb the mountain of the Lᴏʀᴅ? Who may
stand in His holy place? He who has clean hands and a pure heart, who
has not taken My name in vain or sworn falsely. He shall receive a blessing
from the Lᴏʀᴅ, and just reward from the God of his salvation. This is a
generation of those who seek Him, the descendants of Jacob who seek Your
presence, Selah! Lift up your heads, O gates; be uplifted, eternal doors, so
that the King of glory may enter. Who is the King of glory? It is the Lᴏʀᴅ,
strong and mighty, the Lᴏʀᴅ mighty in battle. Lift up your heads, O gates;
lift them up, eternal doors, that the King of glory may enter. ‣ Who is He,
the King of glory? The Lᴏʀᴅ of multitudes, He is the King of glory, Selah!

Mourner's Kaddish (page 258)

REFLECTION	LEARNING
Have you ever wondered why God created the world?	During the times of the *Beit HaMikdash*, the *Levi'im* would sing a psalm each day which related to the significance of that particular day of the week (*Tamid* 7:4). Furthermore, mentioning each day, *Yom Rishon, Sheni, Shelishi… beShabbat*, helps us build up anticipation for Shabbat. By mentioning the day of the week in relation to Shabbat, we fulfill the commandment to remember Shabbat every day and eagerly anticipate it.
What did you come up with?	
How are you going to aspire to come close to God this week?	
What do you think God wants you to do with your time in the world?	

שיר של יום

One of the following psalms is said on the appropriate day of the week as indicated.
After the psalm, קדיש יתום on page 259 is said.

After שיר של יום, on ראש חודש, add בָּרְכִי נַפְשִׁי, page 273 (in ארץ ישראל, some only say בָּרְכִי נַפְשִׁי). On חנוכה, add מִזְמוֹר שִׁיר־חֲנֻכַּת הַבַּיִת, page 73 followed by קדיש יתום. From the second day of אלול through שמיני עצרת (in ארץ ישראל, through הושענא רבה), add לְדָוִד, יהוה אוֹרִי on page 277. In a house of mourning the service concludes on page 279.

Sunday הַיּוֹם יוֹם רִאשׁוֹן בְּשַׁבָּת, שֶׁבּוֹ הָיוּ הַלְוִיִּם אוֹמְרִים בְּבֵית הַמִּקְדָּשׁ:

תהלים כד לְדָוִד מִזְמוֹר, לַיהוה הָאָרֶץ וּמְלוֹאָהּ, תֵּבֵל וְיֹשְׁבֵי בָהּ: כִּי־הוּא עַל־יַמִּים יְסָדָהּ, וְעַל־נְהָרוֹת יְכוֹנְנֶהָ: מִי־יַעֲלֶה בְהַר־יהוה, וּמִי־יָקוּם בִּמְקוֹם קָדְשׁוֹ: נְקִי כַפַּיִם וּבַר־לֵבָב, אֲשֶׁר לֹא־נָשָׂא לַשָּׁוְא נַפְשִׁי, וְלֹא נִשְׁבַּע לְמִרְמָה: יִשָּׂא בְרָכָה מֵאֵת יהוה, וּצְדָקָה מֵאֱלֹהֵי יִשְׁעוֹ: זֶה דּוֹר דֹּרְשָׁו, מְבַקְשֵׁי פָנֶיךָ יַעֲקֹב סֶלָה: שְׂאוּ שְׁעָרִים רָאשֵׁיכֶם, וְהִנָּשְׂאוּ פִּתְחֵי עוֹלָם, וְיָבוֹא מֶלֶךְ הַכָּבוֹד: מִי זֶה מֶלֶךְ הַכָּבוֹד, יהוה עִזּוּז וְגִבּוֹר, יהוה גִּבּוֹר מִלְחָמָה: שְׂאוּ שְׁעָרִים רָאשֵׁיכֶם, וּשְׂאוּ פִּתְחֵי עוֹלָם, וְיָבֹא מֶלֶךְ הַכָּבוֹד: ‹ מִי הוּא זֶה מֶלֶךְ הַכָּבוֹד, יהוה צְבָאוֹת הוּא מֶלֶךְ הַכָּבוֹד סֶלָה:

קדיש יתום *(page 259)*

...A THOUSAND WORDS

CONNECTION

"He looks for the image of God not in the mathematical formula or the natural relational law but in every beam of light, in every bud and blossom, in the morning breeze and the stillness of a star-lit evening. In a word, Adam [the Second] explores not the scientific abstract universe but the irresistibly fascinating qualitative world where he establishes an intimate relation with God."

(Rabbi J.B. Soloveitchik, *Lonely Man of Faith*)

Monday: Today is the second day of the week,
on which the Levites used to say this psalm in the Temple:

שִׁיר מִזְמוֹר A song. A psalm of the sons of Korah. **Great is the** LORD **and** *Ps. 48*
greatly to be praised in the city of God, on His holy mountain – beautiful in its heights, joy of all the earth, **Mount Zion on its northern side,**
city of the great King. In its castles God is known as a stronghold. See
how the kings joined forces, advancing together. They saw, they were astounded, they panicked, they fled. There fear seized them, like the pains
of a woman giving birth, like ships of Tarshish wrecked by an eastern
wind. What we had heard, now we have seen, in the city of the LORD of
multitudes, in the city of our God. May God preserve it for ever, Selah!
In the midst of Your Temple, God, we meditate on Your love. As is Your
name, God, so is Your praise: it reaches to the ends of the earth. Your
right hand is filled with righteousness. Let Mount Zion rejoice, let the
towns of Judah be glad, because of Your judgments. Walk around Zion
and encircle it. Count its towers, note its strong walls, view its castles,
so that you may tell a future generation ▸ that this is God, our God, for
ever and ever. He will guide us for evermore.

Mourner's Kaddish (page 258)

Where
in your life
do you feel
conflicted?

How
do you
make choices
in those areas?

Can
conflict
ever be good?

Monday הַיּוֹם יוֹם שֵׁנִי בְּשַׁבָּת, שֶׁבּוֹ הָיוּ הַלְוִיִּם אוֹמְרִים בְּבֵית הַמִּקְדָּשׁ:

תהלים מח

שִׁיר מִזְמוֹר לִבְנֵי־קֹרַח: גָּדוֹל יהוה וּמְהֻלָּל מְאֹד, בְּעִיר אֱלֹהֵינוּ, הַר־
קָדְשׁוֹ: יְפֵה נוֹף מְשׂוֹשׂ כָּל־הָאָרֶץ, הַר־צִיּוֹן יַרְכְּתֵי צָפוֹן, קִרְיַת מֶלֶךְ
רָב: אֱלֹהִים בְּאַרְמְנוֹתֶיהָ נוֹדַע לְמִשְׂגָּב: כִּי־הִנֵּה הַמְּלָכִים נוֹעֲדוּ, עָבְרוּ
יַחְדָּו: הֵמָּה רָאוּ כֵּן תָּמָהוּ, נִבְהֲלוּ נֶחְפָּזוּ: רְעָדָה אֲחָזָתַם שָׁם, חִיל
כַּיּוֹלֵדָה: בְּרוּחַ קָדִים תְּשַׁבֵּר אֳנִיּוֹת תַּרְשִׁישׁ: כַּאֲשֶׁר שָׁמַעְנוּ כֵּן רָאִינוּ,
בְּעִיר־יהוה צְבָאוֹת, בְּעִיר אֱלֹהֵינוּ, אֱלֹהִים יְכוֹנְנֶהָ עַד־עוֹלָם סֶלָה:
דִּמִּינוּ אֱלֹהִים חַסְדֶּךָ, בְּקֶרֶב הֵיכָלֶךָ: כְּשִׁמְךָ אֱלֹהִים כֵּן תְּהִלָּתְךָ עַל־
קַצְוֵי־אֶרֶץ, צֶדֶק מָלְאָה יְמִינֶךָ: יִשְׂמַח הַר־צִיּוֹן, תָּגֵלְנָה בְּנוֹת יְהוּדָה,
לְמַעַן מִשְׁפָּטֶיךָ: סֹבּוּ צִיּוֹן וְהַקִּיפוּהָ, סִפְרוּ מִגְדָּלֶיהָ: שִׁיתוּ לִבְּכֶם לְחֵילָה,
פַּסְּגוּ אַרְמְנוֹתֶיהָ, לְמַעַן תְּסַפְּרוּ לְדוֹר אַחֲרוֹן: ‹ כִּי זֶה אֱלֹהִים אֱלֹהֵינוּ
עוֹלָם וָעֶד, הוּא יְנַהֲגֵנוּ עַל־מוּת:

קדיש יתום (page 259)

LEARNING

The Gemara in *Rosh HaShana* 31a teaches us the reason why each day's psalm was chosen for that specific day. On the second day of Creation, God separated between the waters above and below, and distinguished heaven. *Resisei Laila* comments that by separating the physical and spiritual realms, God set off the continual strife that would exist between the two; Rabbeinu Baḥya actually cites this as the source of all subsequent conflict. That is why the *Levi'im* chose a psalm composed by the *Benei Koraḥ*, since Koraḥ initiated a rebellion against Moshe's authority as the medium between the nation and God's word, part of the perpetuation of this strife. By singing this psalm we can remind ourselves of the consequences of strife and conflict.

CONNECTION

There was once a wise man whom people visited from far and wide to seek his counsel. One day a cynical boy visited the man hoping to catch him out and prove him no wiser than anyone else. He approached the wise man with cupped hands in front of him. "I hold a butterfly in my hand; tell me, wise master, is it alive or dead?" He smirked to himself, if the man says dead, I will release the butterfly, if he says alive, I will squash it that moment. The man would be wrong no matter what he said. The wise man sighed and looked at the young boy and said, "hakol beyadekha – it's all in your hands."

The smirk vanished from the boy's face as he realized the man's wisdom and the greater lesson behind his words. Indeed, the butterfly's life rested in his own very hands, but on a deeper level, so much more rests in our hands. We can make choices and decide which path to take.

Tuesday: Today is the third day of the week,
on which the Levites used to say this psalm in the Temple:

מִזְמוֹר לְאָסָף A psalm of Asaph. God stands in the divine assembly. Among   *Ps. 82*
the judges He delivers judgment. How long will you judge unjustly, showing favor to the wicked? Selah. Do justice to the weak and the orphaned.
Vindicate the poor and destitute. Rescue the weak and needy. Save them
from the hand of the wicked. They do not know nor do they understand.
They walk about in darkness while all the earth's foundations shake. I once
said, "You are like gods, all of you are sons of the Most High." But you shall
die like mere men, you will fall like any prince. ‣ Arise, O Lord, judge the
earth, for all the nations are Your possession.

Mourner's Kaddish (page 258)

... A THOUSAND WORDS

Tuesday הַיּוֹם יוֹם שְׁלִישִׁי בְּשַׁבָּת, שֶׁבּוֹ הָיוּ הַלְוִיִּם אוֹמְרִים בְּבֵית הַמִּקְדָּשׁ:

תהלים פב מִזְמוֹר לְאָסָף, אֱלֹהִים נִצָּב בַּעֲדַת־אֵל, בְּקֶרֶב אֱלֹהִים יִשְׁפֹּט: עַד־מָתַי
תִּשְׁפְּטוּ־עָוֶל, וּפְנֵי רְשָׁעִים תִּשְׂאוּ־סֶלָה: שִׁפְטוּ־דָל וְיָתוֹם, עָנִי וָרָשׁ
הַצְדִּיקוּ: פַּלְּטוּ־דַל וְאֶבְיוֹן, מִיַּד רְשָׁעִים הַצִּילוּ: לֹא יָדְעוּ וְלֹא יָבִינוּ,
בַּחֲשֵׁכָה יִתְהַלָּכוּ, יִמּוֹטוּ כָּל־מוֹסְדֵי אָרֶץ: אֲנִי־אָמַרְתִּי אֱלֹהִים אַתֶּם,
וּבְנֵי עֶלְיוֹן כֻּלְּכֶם: אָכֵן כְּאָדָם תְּמוּתוּן, וּכְאַחַד הַשָּׂרִים תִּפֹּלוּ: ‹ קוּמָה
אֱלֹהִים שָׁפְטָה הָאָרֶץ, כִּי־אַתָּה תִנְחַל בְּכָל־הַגּוֹיִם:
קדיש יתום (page 259)

REFLECTION

"There may be times when we are power-
less to prevent injustice, but there must
never be a time when we fail to protest."
(Elie Wiesel)

**Why do you think justice
is so important?**

**Do you act fairly
and judge people fairly?**

**How do you stand up for people
who cannot stand up for themselves?**

LEARNING

On the third day of Creation the waters that covered the earth were with-
drawn and dry land appeared. Thus,
the world became habitable. Just like
the careful balance of dry land and
water borders needs to constantly be
maintained and monitored, so, too,
the continued existence of our world
depends on the maintenance of justice which must always be exact and
monitored.

CONNECTION

We have a positive mitzva to judge our
fellow man with righteousness. Rabbi
Shlomo Wolbe in Alei Shur explains: Someone who judges others favorably really
hopes that his fellow man is guiltless. He
seeks ways of understanding the other's
actions as good.

This is the extent to which one must

regard another person with a positive at-
titude, and wish to see his actions as issuing
from a good source. We should search out
another's positive qualities. This is the opposite of what most people usually do, which
is to immediately notice another person's
shortcomings and ignore his strong points.
(Alei Shur, vol. II)

Wednesday: Today is the fourth day of the week,
on which the Levites used to say this psalm in the Temple:

אֵל־נְקָמוֹת God of retribution, LORD, God of retribution, appear! Rise up, *Ps. 94*
Judge of the earth. Repay to the arrogant what they deserve. How long shall
the wicked, LORD, how long shall the wicked triumph? They pour out in-
solent words. All the evildoers are full of boasting. They crush Your people,
LORD, and oppress Your inheritance. They kill the widow and the stranger.
They murder the orphaned. They say, "The LORD does not see. The God of
Jacob pays no heed." Take heed, you most brutish people. You fools, when
will you grow wise? Will He who implants the ear not hear? Will He who
formed the eye not see? Will He who disciplines nations – He who teaches
man knowledge – not punish? The LORD knows that the thoughts of man
are a mere fleeting breath. Happy is the man whom You discipline, LORD, the
one You instruct in Your Torah, giving him tranquility in days of trouble, until
a pit is dug for the wicked. For the LORD will not abandon His people, nor
abandon His heritage. Judgment shall again accord with justice, and all the
upright in heart will follow it. Who will rise up for me against the wicked?
Who will stand up for me against wrongdoers? Had the LORD not been my
help, I would soon have dwelt in death's silence. When I thought my foot was
slipping, Your loving-kindness, LORD, gave me support. When I was filled
with anxiety, Your consolations soothed my soul. Can a corrupt throne be
allied with You? Can injustice be framed into law? They join forces against
the life of the righteous, and condemn the innocent to death. But the LORD
is my stronghold, my God is the Rock of my refuge. He will bring back on
them their wickedness, and destroy them for their evil deeds. The LORD our
God will destroy them.

▸ Come, let us sing for joy to the LORD; let us shout aloud to the Rock of our *Ps. 95*
salvation. Let us greet Him with thanksgiving, shout aloud to Him with songs
of praise. For the LORD is the great God, the King great above all powers.

Mourner's Kaddish (page 258)

On the fourth day we say, "God, He is a God of retribution," because on this day God created the sun, moon, and stars to benefit mankind with their light and radiance. Though they were intended for this purpose, mankind took to worshiping them as gods. God is not pleased with those who foolishly believe that any of His creations are to be worshiped and God will not tolerate this evil. Eventually He will vengefully remove all idolatry from the world.

הַיּוֹם יוֹם רְבִיעִי בְּשַׁבָּת, שֶׁבּוֹ הָיוּ הַלְוִיִּם אוֹמְרִים בְּבֵית הַמִּקְדָּשׁ: *Wednesday*

תהלים צד אֵל־נְקָמוֹת יהוה, אֵל נְקָמוֹת הוֹפִיעַ: הִנָּשֵׂא שֹׁפֵט הָאָרֶץ, הָשֵׁב גְּמוּל עַל־גֵּאִים: עַד־מָתַי רְשָׁעִים, יהוה, עַד־מָתַי רְשָׁעִים יַעֲלֹזוּ: יַבִּיעוּ יְדַבְּרוּ עָתָק, יִתְאַמְּרוּ כָּל־פֹּעֲלֵי אָוֶן: עַמְּךָ יהוה יְדַכְּאוּ, וְנַחֲלָתְךָ יְעַנּוּ: אַלְמָנָה וְגֵר יַהֲרֹגוּ, וִיתוֹמִים יְרַצֵּחוּ: וַיֹּאמְרוּ לֹא יִרְאֶה־יָּהּ, וְלֹא־יָבִין אֱלֹהֵי יַעֲקֹב: בִּינוּ בֹּעֲרִים בָּעָם, וּכְסִילִים מָתַי תַּשְׂכִּילוּ: הֲנֹטַע אֹזֶן הֲלֹא יִשְׁמָע, אִם־יֹצֵר עַיִן הֲלֹא יַבִּיט: הֲיֹסֵר גּוֹיִם הֲלֹא יוֹכִיחַ, הַמְלַמֵּד אָדָם דָּעַת: יהוה יֹדֵעַ מַחְשְׁבוֹת אָדָם, כִּי־הֵמָּה הָבֶל: אַשְׁרֵי הַגֶּבֶר אֲשֶׁר־תְּיַסְּרֶנּוּ יָּהּ, וּמִתּוֹרָתְךָ תְלַמְּדֶנּוּ: לְהַשְׁקִיט לוֹ מִימֵי רָע, עַד יִכָּרֶה לָרָשָׁע שָׁחַת: כִּי לֹא־יִטֹּשׁ יהוה עַמּוֹ, וְנַחֲלָתוֹ לֹא יַעֲזֹב: כִּי־עַד־צֶדֶק יָשׁוּב מִשְׁפָּט, וְאַחֲרָיו כָּל־יִשְׁרֵי־לֵב: מִי־יָקוּם לִי עִם־מְרֵעִים, מִי־יִתְיַצֵּב לִי עִם־פֹּעֲלֵי אָוֶן: לוּלֵי יהוה עֶזְרָתָה לִּי, כִּמְעַט שָׁכְנָה דוּמָה נַפְשִׁי: אִם־אָמַרְתִּי מָטָה רַגְלִי, חַסְדְּךָ יהוה יִסְעָדֵנִי: בְּרֹב שַׂרְעַפַּי בְּקִרְבִּי, תַּנְחוּמֶיךָ יְשַׁעַשְׁעוּ נַפְשִׁי: הַיְחָבְרְךָ כִּסֵּא הַוּוֹת, יֹצֵר עָמָל עֲלֵי־חֹק: יָגוֹדּוּ עַל־נֶפֶשׁ צַדִּיק, וְדָם נָקִי יַרְשִׁיעוּ: וַיְהִי יהוה לִי לְמִשְׂגָּב, וֵאלֹהַי לְצוּר מַחְסִי: וַיָּשֶׁב עֲלֵיהֶם אֶת־אוֹנָם, וּבְרָעָתָם יַצְמִיתֵם, יַצְמִיתֵם יהוה אֱלֹהֵינוּ:

תהלים צה ‏◂‏ לְכוּ נְרַנְּנָה לַיהוה, נָרִיעָה לְצוּר יִשְׁעֵנוּ: נְקַדְּמָה פָנָיו בְּתוֹדָה, בִּזְמִרוֹת נָרִיעַ לוֹ: כִּי אֵל גָּדוֹל יהוה, וּמֶלֶךְ גָּדוֹל עַל־כָּל־אֱלֹהִים:

קדיש יתום (*page 259*)

(*page 259*)

REFLECTION	**... A THOUSAND WORDS**

"Right is right, even if everyone is against it, and wrong is wrong, even if everyone is for it."
(William Penn)

Have you ever seen injustice that you want God to avenge?

Why do you think God sometimes seems to fail to stop wrongdoing?

Have you ever stood up to injustice? What did you do?

Thursday: Today is the fifth day of the week,
on which the Levites used to say this psalm in the Temple:

לַמְנַצֵּחַ For the conductor of music. On the Gittit. By Asaph. Sing for joy to *Ps. 81* God, our strength. Shout aloud to the God of Jacob. Raise a song, beat the drum, play the sweet harp and lyre. Sound the shofar on the new moon, on our feast day when the moon is hidden. For it is a law for Israel, an ordinance of the God of Jacob. He established it as a testimony for Joseph when He went forth against the land of Egypt, where I heard a language that I did not know. I relieved his shoulder of the burden. His hands were freed from the builder's basket. In distress you called and I rescued you. I answered you from the secret place of thunder; I tested you at the waters of Meribah, Selah! Hear, My people, and I will warn you. Israel, if you would only listen to Me! Let there be no strange god among you. Do not bow down to an alien god. I am the Lord your God who brought you out of the land of Egypt. Open your mouth wide and I will fill it. But My people would not listen to Me. Israel would have none of Me. So I left them to their stubborn hearts, letting them follow their own devices. If only My people would listen to Me, if Israel would walk in My ways, I would soon subdue their enemies, and turn My hand against their foes. Those who hate the Lord would cower before Him and their doom would last for ever. ‣ He would feed Israel with the finest wheat – with honey from the rock I would satisfy you.

Mourner's Kaddish (page 258)

REFLECTION

How do you serve God with joy?

How do you share joy with others?

... A THOUSAND WORDS

LEARNING

The Gemara in *Shabbat* 156a states that a person born on the fifth day of the week will be a person who shares joy with others. Rashi explains this is because the fish and birds, also "born" on the fifth day, were blessed with abundant food supplies enabling them to shift their focus away from the extreme effort usually required to obtain food. So, too, people born on the fifth day of the week will have excess energy to expend with and for others.

תהלים פא

Thursday הַיּוֹם יוֹם חֲמִישִׁי בְּשַׁבָּת, שֶׁבּוֹ הָיוּ הַלְוִיִּם אוֹמְרִים בְּבֵית הַמִּקְדָּשׁ:

לַמְנַצֵּחַ עַל־הַגִּתִּית לְאָסָף: הַרְנִינוּ לֵאלֹהִים עוּזֵּנוּ, הָרִיעוּ לֵאלֹהֵי
יַעֲקֹב: שְׂאוּ־זִמְרָה וּתְנוּ־תֹף, כִּנּוֹר נָעִים עִם־נָבֶל: תִּקְעוּ בַחֹדֶשׁ שׁוֹפָר,
בַּכֵּסֶה לְיוֹם חַגֵּנוּ: כִּי חֹק לְיִשְׂרָאֵל הוּא, מִשְׁפָּט לֵאלֹהֵי יַעֲקֹב: עֵדוּת
בִּיהוֹסֵף שָׂמוֹ, בְּצֵאתוֹ עַל־אֶרֶץ מִצְרָיִם, שְׂפַת לֹא־יָדַעְתִּי אֶשְׁמָע:
הֲסִירוֹתִי מִסֵּבֶל שִׁכְמוֹ, כַּפָּיו מִדּוּד תַּעֲבֹרְנָה: בַּצָּרָה קָרָאתָ וָאֲחַלְּצֶךָּ,
אֶעֶנְךָ בְּסֵתֶר רַעַם, אֶבְחָנְךָ עַל־מֵי מְרִיבָה סֶלָה: שְׁמַע עַמִּי וְאָעִידָה
בָּךְ, יִשְׂרָאֵל אִם־תִּשְׁמַע־לִי: לֹא־יִהְיֶה בְךָ אֵל זָר, וְלֹא תִשְׁתַּחֲוֶה לְאֵל
נֵכָר: אָנֹכִי יהוה אֱלֹהֶיךָ, הַמַּעַלְךָ מֵאֶרֶץ מִצְרָיִם, הַרְחֶב־פִּיךָ וַאֲמַלְאֵהוּ:
וְלֹא־שָׁמַע עַמִּי לְקוֹלִי, וְיִשְׂרָאֵל לֹא־אָבָה לִי: וָאֲשַׁלְּחֵהוּ בִּשְׁרִירוּת
לִבָּם, יֵלְכוּ בְּמוֹעֲצוֹתֵיהֶם: לוּ עַמִּי שֹׁמֵעַ לִי, יִשְׂרָאֵל בִּדְרָכַי יְהַלֵּכוּ:
כִּמְעַט אוֹיְבֵיהֶם אַכְנִיעַ, וְעַל־צָרֵיהֶם אָשִׁיב יָדִי: מְשַׂנְאֵי יהוה יְכַחֲשׁוּ־
לוֹ, וִיהִי עִתָּם לְעוֹלָם: ‹ וַיַּאֲכִילֵהוּ מֵחֵלֶב חִטָּה, וּמִצּוּר, דְּבַשׁ אַשְׂבִּיעֶךָ:

קדיש יתום (page 259)

CONNECTION

A SMILE COSTS NOTHING, BUT GIVES MUCH

It enriches those who receive, without making poorer those who give.
It takes but a moment, but the memory of it sometimes lasts forever.

None is so rich or mighty that he can get along without it,
and none is so poor but that he can be made rich by it.

A smile creates happiness in the home, fosters good will in business,
and is the countersign of friendship.

It brings rest to the weary, cheer to the discouraged,
sunshine to the sad, and is nature's best antidote for trouble.

Yet it cannot be bought, begged, borrowed, or stolen,
for it is something that is of no value to anyone until it is given away.

Some people are too tired to give you a smile.
Give them one of yours,
as none needs a smile so much as he who has no more to give.

Friday: Today is the sixth day of the week,
on which the Levites used to say this psalm in the Temple:

יהוה מָלָךְ The LORD reigns. He is robed in majesty. The LORD is robed, Ps. 93
clothed with strength. The world is firmly established; it cannot be moved.
Your throne stands firm as of old; You are eternal. Rivers lift up, LORD,
rivers lift up their voice, rivers lift up their crashing waves. Mightier than
the noise of many waters, than the mighty waves of the sea is the LORD
on high. ‣ Your testimonies are very sure; holiness adorns Your House,
LORD, for evermore.

Mourner's Kaddish (page 258)

LEARNING

On the sixth day of the week, Erev Shabbat, we prepare ourselves and don our
finest clothing in honor of Shabbat. God
"robed in majesty" is like the preparation we do for Shabbat by donning our
finest clothing. We read about God in
this psalm with very human descrip-
tions and imagery to connect God
and humanity, just as Friday connects
the holy day of Shabbat to the rest of
the week.

REFLECTION

How do you imagine God?
What imagery of God
does this psalm paint for you?

How do you experience
the transition of Friday
into Shabbat?

What do you do
to prepare for Shabbat?
How do you help your family
prepare for Shabbat?

CONNECTION

*The Midrash (Mekhilta Shemot 20:7) de-
scribes Shammai's method of shopping
for Shabbat. Whenever he would see a
fine food, he would buy it and set it aside
for Shabbat. If he would subsequently find*
*something better, he would buy that for
Shabbat and eat the earlier, lesser food.
In this way, he turned his weekdays into
a search for the best items with which to
sanctify Shabbat.*

הַיּוֹם יוֹם שִׁשִּׁי בְּשַׁבָּת, שֶׁבּוֹ הָיוּ הַלְוִיִּם אוֹמְרִים בְּבֵית הַמִּקְדָּשׁ *Friday*

יהוה מָלָךְ, גֵּאוּת לָבֵשׁ, לָבֵשׁ יהוה עֹז הִתְאַזָּר, אַף־תִּכּוֹן תֵּבֵל בַּל־ תהלים צג
תִּמּוֹט: נָכוֹן כִּסְאֲךָ מֵאָז, מֵעוֹלָם אָתָּה: נָשְׂאוּ נְהָרוֹת יהוה, נָשְׂאוּ נְהָרוֹת
קוֹלָם, יִשְׂאוּ נְהָרוֹת דָּכְיָם: מִקֹּלוֹת מַיִם רַבִּים, אַדִּירִים מִשְׁבְּרֵי־יָם,
אַדִּיר בַּמָּרוֹם יהוה: ‹ עֵדֹתֶיךָ נֶאֶמְנוּ מְאֹד, לְבֵיתְךָ נָאֲוָה־קֹּדֶשׁ, יהוה
לְאֹרֶךְ יָמִים:

קדיש יתום *(page 259)*

... A THOUSAND WORDS

On Rosh Ḥodesh, the following psalm is said:

בָּרְכִי נַפְשִׁי **Bless the Lord, my soul. Lord, my God, You are very great,** *Ps. 104* clothed in majesty and splendor, wrapped in a robe of light. You have spread out the heavens like a tent. He has laid the beams of His lofts in the waters. He makes the clouds His chariot, riding on the wings of the wind. He makes the winds His messengers, flames of fire His ministers. He has fixed the earth on its foundations so that it will never be shaken. You covered it with the deep like a cloak; the waters stood above the mountains. At Your rebuke they fled; at the sound of Your thunder they rushed away, flowing over the hills, pouring down into the valleys to the place You appointed for them. You fixed a boundary they were not to pass, so that they would never cover the earth again. He makes springs flow in the valleys; they make their way between the hills, giving drink to all the beasts of the field; the wild donkeys quench their thirst. The birds of the sky live beside them, singing among the foliage. He waters the mountains from His lofts: the earth is full with the fruit of Your work. He makes grass grow for the cattle, and plants for the use of man, that he may produce bread from the earth, wine to cheer the heart of man, oil to make the face shine, and bread to

---

LEARNING

Barekhi Nafshi is recited on Rosh Ḥodesh. Rabbi Soloveitchik explains that the Jew can identify personally with the moon. Just like our people, the moon is regularly revived from an almost nonexistent state and its illumination always returns from a state of darkness. Rosh Ḥodesh speaks to this eternal faith in redemption yet to come, in the coming light though it is yet dark. Rosh Ḥodesh, when the moon itself teaches us about the concept of renewal and rebirth, reminds the Jewish People to hope and have faith.

The Gemara in *Menaḥot* states in the name of Rabbi Yishmael: God told Moshe, "Observe the moon and recognize that from darkness shall emanate light. The moon will teach you and all future Jewish generations that Israel will be renewed and revitalized, just as the moon is. Just as at certain times of the month it is impossible to contemplate or even imagine a moon, at certain points of history it will be hard to imagine Jews and Judaism. But I promise you, Moshe, *kazeh re'eh vekadesh*, like this, see and sanctify, precisely when the moon is so tiny, hidden, and insignificant, sanctify it and renew your hopes in its capacity to shine." (Rabbi Eliyahu Safran)

On ראש חודש, *the following psalm is said:*

תהלים קד

בָּרְכִי נַפְשִׁי אֶת־יהוה, יהוה אֱלֹהַי גָּדַלְתָּ מְּאֹד, הוֹד וְהָדָר לָבָשְׁתָּ׃ עֹטֶה־אוֹר כַּשַּׂלְמָה, נוֹטֶה שָׁמַיִם כַּיְרִיעָה׃ הַמְקָרֶה בַמַּיִם עֲלִיּוֹתָיו, הַשָּׂם־עָבִים רְכוּבוֹ, הַמְהַלֵּךְ עַל־כַּנְפֵי־רוּחַ׃ עֹשֶׂה מַלְאָכָיו רוּחוֹת, מְשָׁרְתָיו אֵשׁ לֹהֵט׃ יָסַד־אֶרֶץ עַל־מְכוֹנֶיהָ, בַּל־תִּמּוֹט עוֹלָם וָעֶד׃ תְּהוֹם כַּלְּבוּשׁ כִּסִּיתוֹ, עַל־הָרִים יַעַמְדוּ־מָיִם׃ מִן־גַּעֲרָתְךָ יְנוּסוּן, מִן־ קוֹל רַעַמְךָ יֵחָפֵזוּן׃ יַעֲלוּ הָרִים, יֵרְדוּ בְקָעוֹת, אֶל־מְקוֹם זֶה יָסַדְתָּ לָהֶם׃ גְּבוּל־שַׂמְתָּ בַּל־יַעֲבֹרוּן, בַּל־יְשׁוּבוּן לְכַסּוֹת הָאָרֶץ׃ הַמְשַׁלֵּחַ מַעְיָנִים בַּנְּחָלִים, בֵּין הָרִים יְהַלֵּכוּן׃ יַשְׁקוּ כָּל־חַיְתוֹ שָׂדָי, יִשְׁבְּרוּ פְרָאִים צְמָאָם׃ עֲלֵיהֶם עוֹף־הַשָּׁמַיִם יִשְׁכּוֹן, מִבֵּין עֳפָאיִם יִתְּנוּ־קוֹל׃ מַשְׁקֶה הָרִים מֵעֲלִיּוֹתָיו, מִפְּרִי מַעֲשֶׂיךָ תִּשְׂבַּע הָאָרֶץ׃ מַצְמִיחַ חָצִיר לַבְּהֵמָה, וְעֵשֶׂב לַעֲבֹדַת הָאָדָם, לְהוֹצִיא לֶחֶם מִן־הָאָרֶץ׃ וְיַיִן

... A THOUSAND WORDS

sustain man's heart. The trees of the LORD drink their fill, the cedars of Lebanon which He planted. There, birds build their nests; the stork makes its home in the cypresses. High hills are for the wild goats; crags are shelter for the badgers. He made the moon to mark the seasons, and makes the sun know when to set. You bring darkness and it is night; then all the beasts of the forests stir. The young lions roar for prey, seeking their food from God. When the sun rises, they slink away and seek rest in their lairs. Man goes out to his work and his labor until evening. How numerous are Your works, LORD; You made them all in wisdom; the earth is full of Your creations. There is the vast, immeasurable sea with its countless swarming creatures, living things great and small. There ships sail. There is Leviathan You formed to sport there. All of them look to You in hope, to give them their food when it is due. What You give them, they gather up. When You open Your hand, they are filled with good. When You hide Your face, they are dismayed. When You take away their breath, they die and return to dust. When You send back Your breath, they are created, giving new life to the earth. May the glory of the LORD be for ever; may the LORD rejoice in His works. When He looks at the earth, it trembles. When He touches the mountains, they pour forth smoke. I will sing to the LORD as long as I live; I will sing psalms to my God all my life. ▸ May my prayers be pleasing to Him; I shall rejoice in the LORD. May sinners vanish from the earth, and the wicked be no more. Bless the LORD, my soul. Halleluya!

Mourner's Kaddish (page 258)

... A THOUSAND WORDS

יְשַׂמַּח לְבַב־אֱנוֹשׁ, לְהַצְהִיל פָּנִים מִשָּׁמֶן, וְלֶחֶם לְבַב־אֱנוֹשׁ יִסְעָד:
יִשְׂבְּעוּ עֲצֵי יהוה, אַרְזֵי לְבָנוֹן אֲשֶׁר נָטָע: אֲשֶׁר־שָׁם צִפֳּרִים יְקַנֵּנוּ,
חֲסִידָה בְּרוֹשִׁים בֵּיתָהּ: הָרִים הַגְּבֹהִים לַיְּעֵלִים, סְלָעִים מַחְסֶה
לַשְׁפַנִּים: עָשָׂה יָרֵחַ לְמוֹעֲדִים, שֶׁמֶשׁ יָדַע מְבוֹאוֹ: תָּשֶׁת־חֹשֶׁךְ
וִיהִי לָיְלָה, בּוֹ־תִרְמֹשׂ כָּל־חַיְתוֹ־יָעַר: הַכְּפִירִים שֹׁאֲגִים לַטָּרֶף,
וּלְבַקֵּשׁ מֵאֵל אָכְלָם: תִּזְרַח הַשֶּׁמֶשׁ יֵאָסֵפוּן, וְאֶל־מְעוֹנֹתָם יִרְבָּצוּן:
יֵצֵא אָדָם לְפָעֳלוֹ, וְלַעֲבֹדָתוֹ עֲדֵי־עָרֶב: מָה־רַבּוּ מַעֲשֶׂיךָ יהוה,
כֻּלָּם בְּחָכְמָה עָשִׂיתָ, מָלְאָה הָאָרֶץ קִנְיָנֶךָ: זֶה הַיָּם גָּדוֹל וּרְחַב
יָדָיִם, שָׁם־רֶמֶשׂ וְאֵין מִסְפָּר, חַיּוֹת קְטַנּוֹת עִם־גְּדֹלוֹת: שָׁם אֳנִיּוֹת
יְהַלֵּכוּן, לִוְיָתָן זֶה־יָצַרְתָּ לְשַׂחֶק־בּוֹ: כֻּלָּם אֵלֶיךָ יְשַׂבֵּרוּן, לָתֵת
אָכְלָם בְּעִתּוֹ: תִּתֵּן לָהֶם יִלְקֹטוּן, תִּפְתַּח יָדְךָ יִשְׂבְּעוּן טוֹב: תַּסְתִּיר
פָּנֶיךָ יִבָּהֵלוּן, תֹּסֵף רוּחָם יִגְוָעוּן, וְאֶל־עֲפָרָם יְשׁוּבוּן: תְּשַׁלַּח רוּחֲךָ
יִבָּרֵאוּן, וּתְחַדֵּשׁ פְּנֵי אֲדָמָה: יְהִי כְבוֹד יהוה לְעוֹלָם, יִשְׂמַח יהוה
בְּמַעֲשָׂיו: הַמַּבִּיט לָאָרֶץ וַתִּרְעָד, יִגַּע בֶּהָרִים וְיֶעֱשָֽׁנוּ: אָשִֽׁירָה
לַיהוה בְּחַיָּי, אֲזַמְּרָה לֵאלֹהַי בְּעוֹדִי: ‣ יֶעֱרַב עָלָיו שִׂיחִי, אָנֹכִי
אֶשְׂמַח בַּיהוה: יִתַּמּוּ חַטָּאִים מִן־הָאָרֶץ, וּרְשָׁעִים עוֹד אֵינָם,
בָּרְכִי נַפְשִׁי אֶת־יהוה, הַלְלוּיָהּ:

קדיש יתום (page 259)

---

*"The more we understand of the complexity
of life, the more we appreciate
'How numerous are Your works, Lord;
You made them all in wisdom;
the earth is full of Your creations.'"*
(Tehillim 104:24)

(Rabbi Jonathan Sacks,
Koren Sacks Siddur)

How do you see God in nature?

Why do we focus on God's mastery
over nature at the beginning
of each new month?

What would you like to renew
this month?
How would you like to start again?

*During the month of Elul (except Erev Rosh HaShana), the shofar is sounded (some
sound the shofar after the psalm below). From the second day of Rosh Ḥodesh Elul
through Shemini Atzeret (in Israel through Hoshana Raba), the following psalm is said:*

לְדָוִד By David. The Lᴏʀᴅ is my light and my salvation – whom then shall I fear? Ps. 27
The Lᴏʀᴅ is the stronghold of my life – of whom shall I be afraid? When evil men
close in on me to devour my flesh, it is they, my enemies and foes, who stumble
and fall. Should an army besiege me, my heart would not fear. Should war break
out against me, still I would be confident. One thing I ask of the Lᴏʀᴅ, only this
do I seek: to live in the House of the Lᴏʀᴅ all the days of my life, to gaze on the
beauty of the Lᴏʀᴅ and worship in His Temple. For He will keep me safe in His
pavilion on the day of trouble. He will hide me under the cover of His tent. He will
set me high upon a rock. Now my head is high above my enemies who surround
me. I will sacrifice in His tent with shouts of joy. I will sing and chant praises to
the Lᴏʀᴅ. Lᴏʀᴅ, hear my voice when I call. Be generous to me and answer me.
On Your behalf my heart says, "Seek My face." Your face, Lᴏʀᴅ, will I seek. Do not
hide Your face from me. Do not turn Your servant away in anger. You have been
my help. Do not reject or abandon me, God, my Savior. Were my father and my
mother to abandon me, the Lᴏʀᴅ would take me in. Teach me Your way, Lᴏʀᴅ,
and lead me on a level path, because of my oppressors. Do not abandon me to the
will of my enemies, for false witnesses have risen against me, breathing violence.
▸ Were it not for my faith that I shall see the Lᴏʀᴅ's goodness in the land of the
living. Hope in the Lᴏʀᴅ. Be strong and of good courage, and hope in the Lᴏʀᴅ!

Mourner's Kaddish (page 258)

Think *ought*.
Not what *is* a Jew, but what *ought* a Jew to be.
Not what *is* a synagogue, but what *ought* a synagogue to be.
Not what prayer *is*, but what prayer *ought* to be.
Not what ritual *is*, but what ritual *ought* to be.
Focus from *is* to *ought*, and our mindset is affected. *Is* faces me toward the present;
    ought turns me to the future. *Ought* challenges my creative imagination and opens
    me to the realm of possibilities and responsibilities to realize yesterday's dream.
Ought and *is* are complementary. Without an *is*, the genius of our past and present
    collective wisdom is forgotten. Without an *ought*, the great visions of tomorrow fade.
Ought demands not only a knowledge of history but of exciting expectation. *Is* is a
    being, *ought* is a becoming.
Ought emancipates me from status quo thinking.
Ought is the freedom of spirit.
Ought we not *Ought*?   (Harold Schulweis)

During the month of אלול (*except* ערב ראש השנה), *the* שופר *is sounded* (*some sound the* שופר *after the psalm below*). *From the second day of* ראש חודש אלול *through* שמיני עצרת (*in* ארץ ישראל *through* הושענא רבה), *the following psalm is said:*

תהלים כז

לְדָוִד, יהוה אוֹרִי וְיִשְׁעִי, מִמִּי אִירָא, יהוה מָעוֹז־חַיַּי, מִמִּי אֶפְחָד: בִּקְרֹב עָלַי מְרֵעִים לֶאֱכֹל אֶת־בְּשָׂרִי, צָרַי וְאֹיְבַי לִי, הֵמָּה כָשְׁלוּ וְנָפָלוּ: אִם־תַּחֲנֶה עָלַי מַחֲנֶה, לֹא־יִירָא לִבִּי, אִם־תָּקוּם עָלַי מִלְחָמָה, בְּזֹאת אֲנִי בוֹטֵחַ: אַחַת שָׁאַלְתִּי מֵאֵת־יהוה, אוֹתָהּ אֲבַקֵּשׁ, שִׁבְתִּי בְּבֵית־יהוה כָּל־יְמֵי חַיַּי, לַחֲזוֹת בְּנֹעַם־יהוה, וּלְבַקֵּר בְּהֵיכָלוֹ: כִּי יִצְפְּנֵנִי בְּסֻכֹּה בְּיוֹם רָעָה, יַסְתִּרֵנִי בְּסֵתֶר אָהֳלוֹ, בְּצוּר יְרוֹמְמֵנִי: וְעַתָּה יָרוּם רֹאשִׁי עַל אֹיְבַי סְבִיבוֹתַי, וְאֶזְבְּחָה בְאָהֳלוֹ זִבְחֵי תְרוּעָה, אָשִׁירָה וַאֲזַמְּרָה לַיהוה: שְׁמַע־יהוה קוֹלִי אֶקְרָא, וְחָנֵּנִי וַעֲנֵנִי: לְךָ אָמַר לִבִּי בַּקְּשׁוּ פָנָי, אֶת־פָּנֶיךָ יהוה אֲבַקֵּשׁ: אַל־תַּסְתֵּר פָּנֶיךָ מִמֶּנִּי, אַל־תַּט־בְּאַף עַבְדֶּךָ, עֶזְרָתִי הָיִיתָ, אַל־תִּטְּשֵׁנִי וְאַל־תַּעַזְבֵנִי, אֱלֹהֵי יִשְׁעִי: כִּי־אָבִי וְאִמִּי עֲזָבוּנִי, וַיהוה יַאַסְפֵנִי: הוֹרֵנִי יהוה דַּרְכֶּךָ, וּנְחֵנִי בְּאֹרַח מִישׁוֹר, לְמַעַן שׁוֹרְרָי: אַל־תִּתְּנֵנִי בְּנֶפֶשׁ צָרָי, כִּי קָמוּ־בִי עֵדֵי־שֶׁקֶר, וִיפֵחַ חָמָס: ‹ לוּלֵא הֶאֱמַנְתִּי לִרְאוֹת בְּטוּב־יהוה בְּאֶרֶץ חַיִּים: קַוֵּה אֶל־יהוה, חֲזַק וְיַאֲמֵץ לִבֶּךָ, וְקַוֵּה אֶל־יהוה:

קדיש יתום (*page 259*)

REFLECTION	LEARNING
What is David's central request in this psalm? If you could ask God for only one thing, what would it be? What do you pray for most?	This *mizmor* is said every day in the month of Elul and until Shemini Atzeret. The custom is based on a midrash (*Vayikra Raba* 21) that explains that "*Ori* – my light" refers to Rosh HaShana and "*Yishi* – my salvation" refers to Yom Kippur. While there is no mention of repentance in this psalm, the theme of the Days of Awe is clear. David focuses on his main request: to be close to God. This is surely an apt theme for the Days of Awe, returning to God and becoming close with Him.

After the regular service, the following psalm is read in a house of mourning during the shiva week. On those days on which Tahanun is not said, Psalm 16 (below) is substituted.

לַמְנַצֵּחַ For the conductor of music. Of the sons of Korah. A sacred song. Hear *Ps. 49* this, all you peoples. Listen, all inhabitants of the world, low and high, rich and poor alike. My mouth will speak words of wisdom; the utterance of my heart will give understanding. I listen with care to a parable; I expound my mystery to the music of the harp. Why should I fear when evil days come, when the wickedness of my enemies surrounds me, trusting in their wealth, boasting of their great riches? No man can redeem his brother or pay God the price of his release, for the ransom of a life is costly; no payment is ever enough that would let him live for ever, never seeing the grave. For all can see that wise men die, that the foolish and senseless all perish and leave their wealth to others. They think their houses will remain for ever, their dwellings for all generations; they give their names to their estates. But man, despite his splendor, does not endure; he is like the beasts that perish. Such is the fate of the foolish and their followers who approve their words, Selah. Like sheep they are destined for the grave: death will be their shepherd. The upright will rule over them in the morning. Their forms will decay in the grave, far from their mansions. But God will redeem my life from the grave; He will surely take me to Himself, Selah. Do not be overawed when a man grows rich, when the glory of his house increases, for he will take nothing with him when he dies; his wealth will not descend with him. Though while he lived he counted himself blessed – men always praise you when you prosper – he will join the generation of his ancestors who will never again see the light. A man who, despite his splendor, lacks understanding, is like the beasts that perish.

Mourner's Kaddish (page 258)

On those days on which Tahanun is not said, substitute:

מִכְתָּם לְדָוִד A musical composition of David. Protect me, God, for in You I *Ps. 16* have found refuge. I have said to the Lord: You are my Lord: from You alone comes the good I enjoy. All my delight is in the holy ones, the mighty in the land. Those who run after other gods multiply their sorrows. I shall never offer them libations of blood, nor will their names pass my lips. The Lord is my portion and my cup: You direct my fate. The lines have fallen for me in pleasant places; I am well content with my inheritance. I will bless the Lord who has guided me; at night my innermost being rebukes me. I have set the Lord before me at all times. He is at my right hand: I shall not be shaken. Therefore my heart is glad, my spirit rejoices, and my body rests secure. For You will not abandon me to the grave, nor let Your faithful one see the pit. You will teach me the path of life. In Your presence is fullness of joy; at Your right hand, bliss for evermore.

Mourner's Kaddish (page 258)

After the regular service, the following psalm is read in a house of mourning during
the שבעה week. On those days on which תחנון is not said, תהלים טז (below) is substituted.

תהלים מט

לַמְנַצֵּחַ לִבְנֵי־קֹרַח מִזְמוֹר: שִׁמְעוּ־זֹאת כָּל־הָעַמִּים, הַאֲזִינוּ כָּל־יֹשְׁבֵי
חָלֶד: גַּם־בְּנֵי אָדָם, גַּם־בְּנֵי־אִישׁ, יַחַד עָשִׁיר וְאֶבְיוֹן: פִּי יְדַבֵּר חָכְמוֹת,
וְהָגוּת לִבִּי תְבוּנוֹת: אַטֶּה לְמָשָׁל אָזְנִי, אֶפְתַּח בְּכִנּוֹר חִידָתִי: לָמָּה
אִירָא בִּימֵי רָע, עֲוֹן עֲקֵבַי יְסֻבֵּנִי: הַבֹּטְחִים עַל־חֵילָם, וּבְרֹב עָשְׁרָם
יִתְהַלָּלוּ: אָח לֹא־פָדֹה יִפְדֶּה אִישׁ, לֹא־יִתֵּן לֵאלֹהִים כָּפְרוֹ: וְיֵקַר פִּדְיוֹן
נַפְשָׁם, וְחָדַל לְעוֹלָם: וִיחִי־עוֹד לָנֶצַח, לֹא יִרְאֶה הַשָּׁחַת: כִּי יִרְאֶה
חֲכָמִים יָמוּתוּ, יַחַד כְּסִיל וָבַעַר יֹאבֵדוּ, וְעָזְבוּ לַאֲחֵרִים חֵילָם: קִרְבָּם
בָּתֵּימוֹ לְעוֹלָם, מִשְׁכְּנֹתָם לְדֹר וָדֹר, קָרְאוּ בִשְׁמוֹתָם עֲלֵי אֲדָמוֹת: וְאָדָם
בִּיקָר בַּל־יָלִין, נִמְשַׁל כַּבְּהֵמוֹת נִדְמוּ: זֶה דַרְכָּם, כֵּסֶל לָמוֹ, וְאַחֲרֵיהֶם
בְּפִיהֶם יִרְצוּ סֶלָה: כַּצֹּאן לִשְׁאוֹל שַׁתּוּ, מָוֶת יִרְעֵם, וַיִּרְדּוּ בָם יְשָׁרִים
לַבֹּקֶר, וְצוּרָם לְבַלּוֹת שְׁאוֹל מִזְּבֻל לוֹ: אַךְ־אֱלֹהִים יִפְדֶּה נַפְשִׁי מִיַּד
שְׁאוֹל, כִּי יִקָּחֵנִי סֶלָה: אַל־תִּירָא כִּי־יַעֲשִׁר אִישׁ, כִּי־יִרְבֶּה כְּבוֹד בֵּיתוֹ:
כִּי לֹא בְמוֹתוֹ יִקַּח הַכֹּל, לֹא־יֵרֵד אַחֲרָיו כְּבוֹדוֹ: כִּי־נַפְשׁוֹ בְּחַיָּיו יְבָרֵךְ,
וְיוֹדֻךָ כִּי־תֵיטִיב לָךְ: תָּבוֹא עַד־דּוֹר אֲבוֹתָיו, עַד־נֵצַח לֹא יִרְאוּ־אוֹר:
אָדָם בִּיקָר וְלֹא יָבִין, נִמְשַׁל כַּבְּהֵמוֹת נִדְמוּ:

קדיש יתום (page 259)

On those days on which תחנון is not said, substitute:

תהלים טז

מִכְתָּם לְדָוִד, שָׁמְרֵנִי אֵל כִּי־חָסִיתִי בָךְ: אָמַרְתְּ לַיהוה, אֲדֹנָי אָתָּה,
טוֹבָתִי בַּל־עָלֶיךָ: לִקְדוֹשִׁים אֲשֶׁר־בָּאָרֶץ הֵמָּה, וְאַדִּירֵי כָּל־חֶפְצִי־
בָם: יִרְבּוּ עַצְּבוֹתָם אַחֵר מָהָרוּ, בַּל־אַסִּיךְ נִסְכֵּיהֶם מִדָּם, וּבַל־אֶשָּׂא
אֶת־שְׁמוֹתָם עַל־שְׂפָתָי: יהוה, מְנָת־חֶלְקִי וְכוֹסִי, אַתָּה תּוֹמִיךְ גּוֹרָלִי:
חֲבָלִים נָפְלוּ־לִי בַּנְּעִמִים, אַף־נַחֲלָת שָׁפְרָה עָלָי: אֲבָרֵךְ אֶת־יהוה
אֲשֶׁר יְעָצָנִי, אַף־לֵילוֹת יִסְּרוּנִי כִלְיוֹתָי: שִׁוִּיתִי יהוה לְנֶגְדִּי תָמִיד, כִּי
מִימִינִי בַּל־אֶמּוֹט: לָכֵן שָׂמַח לִבִּי וַיָּגֶל כְּבוֹדִי, אַף־בְּשָׂרִי יִשְׁכֹּן לָבֶטַח:
כִּי לֹא־תַעֲזֹב נַפְשִׁי לִשְׁאוֹל, לֹא־תִתֵּן חֲסִידְךָ לִרְאוֹת שָׁחַת: תּוֹדִיעֵנִי
אֹרַח חַיִּים, שֹׂבַע שְׂמָחוֹת אֶת־פָּנֶיךָ, נְעִמוֹת בִּימִינְךָ נֶצַח:

קדיש יתום (page 259)

The Koren Magerman Educational Siddur Series

Age-appropriate Siddurim for
Connection, Reflection, and Learning

≈

The Koren Children's Siddur

with Educators' Companion

(*Nusaḥ Ashkenaz and Sepharadim*)

·

The Koren Youth Siddur

with Educators' Companion

(*Nusaḥ Ashkenaz and Sepharadim*)

·

The Koren Aviv Siddur

Full edition available Spring 2017

·

The Koren Ani Tefilla Siddur Series

(*Nusaḥ Ashkenaz and Sepharadim – coming soon!*)

Available in Weekday and Summer Camp editions

≈

For more information, contact sales@korenpub.com
Special discounts available on bulk orders.

קורן ירושלים   OUPRESS